JUSTICE

ALTERNATIVE
POLITICAL PERSPECTIVES

JUSTICE

ALTERNATIVE POLITICAL PERSPECTIVES

second edition

JAMES P. STERBA
University of Notre Dame

Wadsworth Publishing Company
Belmont, California
A Division of Wadsworth, Inc.

Philosophy Editor: Kenneth King
Editorial Assistant: Cynthia Campbell
Production Editor: Brian Williams, Sawyer & Williams
Print Buyer: Martha Branch
Designers: Donna Davis and Brian Williams
Copy Editor: Elizabeth Judd
Compositor: Kachina Typesetting Inc.
Cover: Albert Burkhardt

This book is printed on acid-free paper that meets Environmental Protection Agency standards for recycled paper.

Printed in the United States of America

2 3 4 5 6 7 8 9 10—96 95 94

Library of Congress Cataloging-in-Publication data

Justice: alternative political perspectives / [edited by] James P.
    Sterba.—2nd ed.
        p.   cm.
    Includes bibliographical references (p.   ).
    ISBN 0-534-16164-2
    1. Justice.   I. Sterba, James P.
JC578.J87   1991
320.5 — dc20   91-3560
                                                         CIP

ISBN 0-534-16164-2

To Janet
As always
A philosopher's philosopher

Contents

Preface

The first edition of *Justice: Alternative Political Perspectives* was published in the fall of 1979. At the time, philosophical discussion was still focused on the debate between contractarians and utilitarians and on the debate between libertarians and welfare liberals. Discussion was just beginning to broaden to address the concerns of socialist justice. The discussion with defenders of socialist justice has now developed over the years, and more recently discussion has broadened still further to address the concerns of defenders of communitarian justice and very recently to address the concerns of defenders of feminist justice. This present edition attempts to capture this broader discussion while retaining the central readings of the earlier edition. It is the only book of its kind. It contains classical and contemporary defenses and critiques of the five major conceptions of justice, and the introduction provides background and critique for each of the selections.

For help in putting this second edition together, I would like to thank Ken King of Wadsworth Publishing Company; Brian Williams of Sawyer & Williams; the copyeditor, Elizabeth Judd; Douglas Rasmussen of St. John's University; and the following reviewers: Kenneth Aman, Montclair State College; Douglas Butler, University of Dayton; Joy Kroeger Mappes, Frostburg State University; A. John Simmons, University of Virginia; Charlottesville; Robert E. Weinberg, St. Ambrose University; and Clark Wolf, University of Arizona. Work on the anthology was made possible by financial assistance from the University of Notre Dame and the MacArthur Foundation.

James P. Sterba

■■■■■□

PART I

Introduction

Introduction

JAMES P. STERBA

Virtually all of us become involved at some time or another in disputes about justice. Sometimes our involvement in such disputes is rooted in the fact that we believe ourselves to be victims of some form of injustice; sometimes our involvement is rooted in the fact that others believe us to be the perpetrators or at least the beneficiaries of some form of injustice affecting them. Sometimes the injustice at issue seems to require for its elimination a drastic reform, or even a revolutionary change in the political system—such as is taking place in Eastern Europe. Sometimes it seems to require for its elimination only some electoral pressure or administrative decision—what might be required, say, in ending a war. But whatever the origin and whatever the practical effect, such disputes about justice are difficult to avoid, especially when dealing with issues (like the distribution of income, the control and use of natural resources, and the distribution of educational and employment opportunities) that have widespread social effects.

But if we can hardly avoid getting involved in disputes about justice, how can we resolve such disputes in a reasonable way? A reasonable resolution of such disputes requires a critical evaluation of the alternative conceptions of justice available to us. We need to carefully consider whatever reasons have been, or might be, advanced in favor of the alternative conceptions of justice that are available to us. Hopefully, through such a process of critical evaluation, one of these conceptions will begin to emerge as the most defensible—maybe it will even be the conception we initially endorsed.

This anthology has been designed to help you carry out this process of critical evaluation. The readings in it defend and critique five contemporary conceptions of justice. These conceptions of justice have certain features in common. Each regards its requirements as belonging to the domain of obligation rather than to the domain of charity; they simply disagree about where to draw the line between these two domains. Each of these conceptions is also concerned to give people what they deserve or should rightfully possess; they simply tend to disagree about what it is that people deserve or rightfully possess.

Turning from common ground to disputed territory, each of these conceptions of justice appeals to a different political ideal. First is a Libertarian Conception of Justice. In recent elections, libertarian party candidates have not done very well. But Ronald Reagan, George Bush, and Margaret Thatcher, whose views on economic issues are close to a Libertarian Conception of Justice, have been successful politically and have refashioned the economies of their respective nations. According to this conception of justice, liberty is the ultimate political ideal. Thus all assignments of rights and duties are ultimately to be justified in terms of an ideal of liberty.

Second is a Socialist Conception of Justice. In the United States there has never been a viable socialist presidential candidate, but elsewhere there have been many successful socialist candidates. For example, the late Olof Palme led the Social Democrats back to power in Sweden and François Mitterrand, a socialist, has been for some time president of France. According to a Socialist Conception of Justice, equality is the ultimate political ideal. Thus all assignments of rights and duties are ultimately to be justified in terms of an ideal of equality.

Third is a Welfare Liberal Conception of Justice. This is the conception of justice endorsed, for example, by the left wing of the Democratic party in the United States, whose leaders have been George McGovern, Ted Kennedy, and Jesse Jackson. According to this conception of justice, the ultimate political ideal is a blend of liberty and equality, and this blend can be characterized as contractual fairness or maximal utility. Thus all assignments of rights and duties are ultimately to be justified in terms of an ideal of contractual fairness or maximal utility.

Fourth is a Communitarian Conception of Justice. This conception is somewhat difficult to associate with any particular political group, but it does seem to be reflected in a wide range of Supreme Court decisions in the United States today, and has its roots in the republicanism of Madison and Jefferson. According to this Communitarian Conception of Justice, the common good is proclaimed to be the ultimate political ideal, and this ideal is said to support a virtue-based conception of human flourishing.

Last is a Feminist Conception of Justice. This is the conception endorsed by the National Organization for Women (NOW) and by numerous other women's organizations in the United States and elsewhere. According to a Feminist Conception of Justice, the ultimate political ideal is androgyny. Thus all assignments of rights and duties are ultimately to be justified in terms of an ideal of androgyny.

What we need to do, therefore, is to examine each of these conceptions of justice along with their historical roots in order to determine which is most defensible. Happily the readings in this anthology have been designed to help you do just that by providing classical and contemporary defenses and critiques of each of the five conceptions of justice. Working through these readings will not always be an easy task. Some articles will be clear on the first reading, whereas others will require closer scrutiny. You should also make sure you give each selection a fair hearing, for while some will accord with your current views, others will not. It is important that you evaluate the latter with an open mind, allowing for the possibility that after sufficient reflection you may come to view them as the most defensible. Indeed, to approach the selections in this anthology in any other way would surely undermine your ability to reasonably resolve those disputes about justice in which you are inescapably involved.

Libertarian Justice

Libertarians frequently cite the work of F. A. Hayek as an intellectual source of their view.[1] In selection 1, F. A. Hayek argues that the libertarian ideal of liberty requires "equality before the law" and "reward according to perceived value" but not "substantial equality" or "reward according to merit." Hayek further argues that the inequalities due to upbringing, inheritance, and education that are permitted by an ideal of liberty actually tend to benefit society as a whole.

In basic sympathy with Hayek, contemporary libertarians such as John Hospers (selection 2) take liberty to be the ultimate moral and political ideal and typically define *liberty* as "the state of being unconstrained by other persons from doing what one wants." This definition limits the scope of liberty in two ways. First, not all constraints, whatever the source, count as a restriction on liberty; the constraints must come from other persons. For example, people who are constrained by natural forces from getting to the top of Mount Everest do not lack liberty in this regard. Second, the constraints must run counter to people's wants. Thus, people who do not want to hear Beethoven's Fifth Symphony do not feel their liberty is restricted when other people forbid its performance, even though the proscription does in fact constrain what they are able to do.

Of course, libertarians may argue that these contraints do restrict a person's liberty because people normally want to be unconstrained by others. But other philosophers have claimed that such constraints point to a serious defect in the libertarian's definition of liberty, which can only be remedied by defining *liberty* more broadly as "the state of being unconstrained by other persons from doing what one is able to do." If we apply this revised definition to the previous example, we find that people's liberty to hear Beethoven's Fifth Symphony would be restricted even if they did not want to hear it (and even if, perchance, they did not want to be unconstrained by others) because other people would still be constraining them from doing what they are able to do.

Confident that problems of defining liberty can be overcome in some satisfactory manner, libertarians go on to characterize their moral and political ideal as requiring that each person should have the greatest amount of liberty commensurate with the same liberty for all. From this ideal, libertarians claim that a number of more specific requirements—in particular a right to life, a right to freedom of speech, press, and assembly, and a right to property—can be derived.

It is important to note that the libertarian's right to life is not a right to receive from others the goods and resources necessary for preserving one's life; it is simply a right not to be killed unjustly. So understood, the right to life is not a right to receive welfare. In fact, there are no welfare rights in the libertarian view. Accordingly, the libertarian's understanding of the right to property is not a right to receive from others the goods and resources necessary for one's welfare, but rather a right to acquire goods and resources either by initial acquisition or by voluntary agreement.

Obviously, by defending rights such as these, libertarians can only support a limited role for government. That role is simply to prevent and punish initial acts of coercion—the only wrongful actions for libertarians.

Libertarians do not deny that it is a good thing for people to have sufficient goods and resources to meet at least their basic nutritional needs, but libertarians do deny that government has a duty to provide for such needs. Some good things, such as the provision of welfare to the needy, are requirements of charity rather than justice, libertarians claim. Accordingly, failure to make such provisions is neither blameworthy nor punishable.

In selection 3, I argue that a libertarian ideal of liberty, which appears to reject the rights of a welfare state, can be seen to support such rights through an application of the "ought" implies "can" principle to conflicts between the rich and the poor. In one interpretation, the principle supports such rights by favoring the liberty of the poor over the liberty of the rich. In another interpretation, the principle supports such rights by favoring a conditional right to property over an unconditional right to property. In either interpretation, what is crucial in the derivation of these rights is the claim that it would be unreasonable to ask the poor to deny their basic needs and accept anything less than these rights as the condition for their willing cooperation.

In selection 4, Tibor Machan attacks my view that a libertarian ideal of liberty leads to what I call "action welfare rights." An action welfare right is the right of the poor, under certain conditions, not to be interfered with when taking from the rich what is required to satisfy their basic needs. An action welfare right differs from what are usually called "welfare rights" because it is a negative right rather than a positive right. However, I further argue that when libertarians are brought to see the legitimacy of action welfare rights they will want to institutionalize positive welfare rights in order to avoid the possibly arbitrary exercise by the poor of their action welfare rights. In this way, I claim, a welfare liberal state would come to have a grounding in a libertarian ideal of (negative) liberty.

In criticizing my argument that a libertarian ideal of liberty leads to action welfare rights and thence to positive welfare rights, Machan accepts the theoretical thrust of my argument but rejects its practical significance. He grants that if the type of conflict cases I describe between the rich and the poor actually obtained, the poor would have action welfare rights. But he then denies that the type of conflict cases I describe—in which the poor have done all that they legitimately can to satisfy their basic needs in a libertarian society—actually does obtain. "Normally," he writes, "persons do not lack the opportunities and resources to satisfy their basic needs."

This response brings our views very close together. Theoretically nothing divides us. Our only difference is a practical one. Machan thinks that virtually all of the poor have sufficient opportunities and resources to satisfy their basic needs and that, therefore, welfare rights are not justified. I think that many of the poor do not have sufficient opportunities and resources to satisfy their basic needs and that, therefore, welfare rights are justified. Obviously, if a convincing case could be made as to what are the actual opportunities of the poor, this practical dispute could be resolved.

Socialist Justice

In contrast with libertarians, socialists take equality to be the ultimate political ideal. In the first part of selection 5, which is taken from the *Communist Manifesto,* Karl Marx and Friedrich Engels maintain that the abolition of bourgeois property and bourgeois family structure is a necessary first requirement for building a society that accords with the political ideal of equality. In the second part of selection 5 Marx provides a much more positive account of what is required to build a society based on the political ideal of equality. In such a society, Marx claims that the distribution of social goods must conform, at least initially, to the principle "from each according to his ability, to each according to his contribution." But when the highest stage of communist society has been reached, Marx adds, distribution will conform to the principle "from each according to his ability, to each according to his need."

This final principle of socialist justice is discussed and defended by Edward Nell and Onora O'Neill in selection 6. They argue that any incentive problems associated with the principle will be resolved when, quoting Marx, "labor is no longer a means of life but has become life's principal need." They further contend that when it is at last appropriate to apply this principle of socialist justice there will exist a system for distributing the burdens of nonfulfilling but socially necessary tasks as well as a system for equitably distributing the benefits of goods not required for anyone's needs. What this means is that because some jobs, such as collecting garbage or changing bedpans, probably cannot be made intrinsically rewarding, socialists propose to divide them up in some equitable manner. Some people might, for example, collect garbage one day a week and then work at intrinsically rewarding jobs for the rest of the week. Others would change bedpans or do some other menial job one day a week and then work at an intrinsically rewarding job the other days of the week. By making jobs intrinsically as rewarding as possible, in part through democratic control of the workplace and an equitable assignment of unrewarding tasks, socialists believe people will contribute according to their ability even when distribution proceeds according to need.

Finally, it is important to note that the socialist ideal of equality does not accord with what exists in such countries as the Soviet Union or Albania. Judging the acceptability of the socialist ideal of equality by what takes place in those countries would be as unfair as judging the acceptability of the libertarian ideal of liberty by what takes place in countries like El Salvador or South Korea, where citizens are arrested and imprisoned without cause. By analogy, it would be like judging the merits of college football by the way Vanderbilt's or Northwestern's teams play rather than by the way Alabama's or Notre Dame's play. Actually, a fairer comparison would be to judge the socialist ideal of equality by what takes place in countries like Sweden and to judge the libertarian ideal of liberty by what takes place in the United States. Even these comparisons, however, are not wholly appropriate because none of these countries fully conforms to those ideals.

To justify the ideal of equality, Kai Nielson (selection 7) argues that it is required by liberty or at least by a fair distribution of liberty. By *liberty* Nielson means both "positive liberty to receive certain goods" and "negative liberty not to be interfered with," and so his argument from liberty will not have much weight with libertarians, who only value negative liberty. Rather, his argument is directed primarily at welfare liberals, who value both positive and negative liberty as well as a fair distribution of liberty.

Another basic difficulty with Nielson's socialist conception of justice concerns the proclaimed necessity of abolishing private property and socializing the means of production. It seems perfectly possible to give workers more control over their workplace while at the same time the means of production remain privately owned. Of course, private ownership would have a somewhat different character in a society with democratic control of the workplace, but it need not cease to be private ownership. After all, private ownership would also have a somewhat different character in a society where private holdings, and hence bargaining power, were distributed more equally than is found in most capitalist societies, yet it would not cease to be private ownership. Accordingly, we could imagine a society where the means of production are privately owned but where—because ownership is so widely dispersed throughout the society (for example, nearly everyone owns 10 shares of major industrial stock and no one more than 20 shares) and because of the degree of democratic control of the workplace—many of the valid criticisms social-ists make of existing capitalist societies would no longer apply.

In selection 8, Robert Nozick illustrates another argument often used against a socialist conception of justice—that it is opposed to liberty. Nozick asks us to imagine that we are in a society that has just distributed income according to some ideal pattern, possibly a pattern of equality. We are to further imagine that in such a society Wilt Chamberlain (or Michael Jordan, if we wish to update the example) offers to play basketball for us provided that he receives a quarter for every home game ticket that is sold. Suppose we agree to these terms and a million people attend the home games to see Wilt Chamberlain (or Michael Jordan) play, thereby securing him an income of $250,000. Since such an income would surely upset the initial pattern of income distribution, whatever that happened to be, Nozick contends that this illustrates how an ideal of liberty upsets the patterns required by other political ideals and hence calls for their rejection.

Nozick's critique, however, seems to apply only to political ideals that require an absolute equality of income. Yet for many political ideals, the inequalities of income generated in Nozick's example would be objectionable only if they deprived people of something to which they had a right, such as equal opportunity. And whether people were so deprived would depend on to what uses the Wilt Chamberlains or Michael Jordans of the world put their greater income. However, there is no necessity for those who have legitimately acquired greater income to use it in ways that violate the rights of others.

Welfare Liberal Justice: The Contractarian Perspective

Finding merit in both the libertarian's ideal of liberty and the socialist's ideal of equality, welfare liberals attempt to combine both liberty and equality into one political ideal that can be characterized as contractual fairness or maximal utility.

A classical example of the contractual approach to welfare liberal justice is found in the work of Immanuel Kant, from which selection 9 is taken. In this selection, Kant claims that a civil state ought to be founded on an original contract satisfying the requirements of freedom (the freedom to seek happiness in whatever way one sees fit as long one does not infringe on the freedom of others to pursue a similar end), equality (the equal right of each person to coerce others to use their freedom in a way that harmonizes with one's own freedom), and independence (that independence of each person that is necessarily presupposed by the free agreement of the original contract).

According to Kant, the original contract, which ought to be the foundation of every civil state, does not have to "actually exist as a fact." It suffices that the laws of a civil state are such that people would agree to them under conditions in which the requirements of freedom, equality, and independence obtain. Laws that accord with this original contract would then, Kant claims, give all members of society the right to reach any degree of rank that they could earn through their labor, industry, and good fortune. Thus, the equality demanded by the original contract would not, in Kant's view, exclude a considerable amount of economic liberty.

The Kantian ideal of a hypothetical contract as the moral foundation for a welfare liberal conception of justice has been further developed by John Rawls in *A Theory of Justice*. In selection 10, taken from the book, Rawls, like Kant, argues that principles of justice are those principles that free and rational persons who are concerned to advance their own interests would accept in an initial position of equality. Yet Rawls goes beyond Kant by interpreting the conditions of his "original position" to explicitly require a "veil of ignorance." This veil of ignorance, Rawls claims, has the effect of depriving persons in the original position of the knowledge they would need to advance their own interests in ways that are morally arbitrary.

The justification Rawls offers for the conditions he imposes on the original position takes two forms. First, Rawls claims that the conditions express weak but widely shared moral presumptions. Second, Rawls, assures us that the choice of principles in the original position will always conform to our considered moral judgments. In cases of conflict, this will be accomplished either by revising our considered moral judgments or by revising the particular conditions on the original position that gave rise to them.

Rawls presents the principles of justice he believes would be derived in the original position in two successive formulations. The first formulation is as follows:

I. Special conception of justice
   1. Each person is to have an equal right to the most extensive basic liberty compatible with a similar liberty for others.
   2. Social and economic inequalities are to be arranged so that they are (a) reasonably expected to be to everyone's advantage and (b) attached to positions and offices open to all.
II. General conception of justice
   All social values—liberty and opportunity, income and wealth, and the bases of self-respect—are to be distributed equally unless an unequal distribution of any or all of these values is to everyone's advantage.

Later these principles are more accurately formulated as:

I. Special conception of justice
   1. Each person is to have an equal right to the most extensive total system of equal basic liberties compatible with a similar system of liberty for all.
   2. Social and economic inequalities are to be arranged so that they are (a) to the greatest benefit of the least advantaged, consistent with the just savings principle and (b) attached to offices and positions open to all under conditions of fair equality of opportunity.
II. General conception of justice
   All social goods—liberty and opportunity, income and wealth, and the bases of self-respect—are to be distributed equally unless an unequal distribution of any or all of these goods is to the advantage of the least favored.

Under both formulations, the general conception of justice differs from the special conception of justice by allowing trade-offs between liberty and other social goods. According to Rawls, persons in the original position would want the special conception of justice to be applied in place of the general conception of justice whenever social conditions allowed all representative persons to exercise their basic liberties.

Rawls holds that these principles of justice would be chosen in the original position because persons so situated would find it reasonable to follow the conservative dictates of a "maximim strategy" and thereby secure for themselves the highest minimum payoff.

Rawls's defense of a welfare liberal conception of justice has been challenged in a variety of ways. Some critics have endorsed Rawls's contractual approach while disagreeing with Rawls over what principles of justice would be derived thereby. These critics usually attempt to undermine the use of a maximin strategy in the original position. Other critics, however, have found fault with the contractual approach itself. The criticism that Ronald Dworkin directs at Rawls's theory of justice in selection 11 is of this sort.

Dworkin argues that hypothetical agreements do not (unlike actual agreements) provide independent arguments for the fairness of those agreements. For example, suppose because I did not know the value of a painting I owned, if you had offered me $100 for it yesterday, I would have accepted your offer. Such hypothetical acceptance, Dworkin argues, in no way shows that it would be fair to force me to sell the painting to you today for $100 now that I have discovered it to be more valuable. Accordingly, Dworkin holds that the fact that a person would agree to do something in the original position does not provide an independent argument for abiding by that agreement in everyday life.

But while it seems correct to argue that hypothetical agreement in the painting case does not support a demand that I presently sell you the painting for $100, it is not clear how this undermines the normal relevance of the hypothetical agreement that emerges from the original position. For surely a defender of the original position is not committed to the view that all hypothetical agreements are morally binding. Nor could Dworkin reasonably argue that his example supports the conclusion that no hypothetical agreements are morally binding. For by parity of reasoning from the fact that some actual agreements are not binding (such as an agreement to commit murder), it would follow that *no* actual agreements are morally binding, which is absurd. Consequently, further argument is required to show that the specific agreement that would result from the original position is not morally binding.

Dworkin goes on to argue that the true warrant for accepting the principles that Rawls derives from his original position is that these principles give expression to an underlying natural right. This underlying right is not a right to liberty, nor even, presumably, a right to fair treatment, but rather a right to equal concern and respect; and the original position, Dworkin maintains, is simply designed to accord with that right. Dworkin thus concludes that the original position is unnecessary and dispensable, for he assumes that it is always possible to argue directly from each person's equal right to concern and respect.

In more recent work, Dworkin has argued that this equal right to concern and respect does not require equality of welfare but rather equality of resources.[2] In attempting to set out more precisely the type of equality of resources that is demanded, Dworkin introduces the idea of a hypothetical insurance market in which people ignorant of the economic rent their talents would attract choose to insure themselves against faring poorly through lack of social and economic opportunities. Payments that would have gone to this hypothetical insurance fund are said to determine the compensation that is due to the less talented members of a society.

Dworkin appeals to a similar hypothetical insurance market to determine the compensation required for the handicapped. In this hypothetical insurance market, the participants are to suppose that they have the same risk of developing physical or mental handicaps in the future (which assumes that no one has developed these yet) but where the total number of handicaps remains whatever it happens to be in the society.

Unfortunately, Dworkin does not work out these two applications of his hypothetical insurance market in parallel fashion. In the talent case, to distinguish his hypothetical choice situation from the original position, Dworkin allows the participants to *know* what the talents happen to be. But with such knowledge the more talented, even when ignorant of their social and economic opportunities, would still have reason to purchase less insurance than those less favored in the natural lottery. Dworkin fails to detect this consequence because he thinks that even with the knowlege provided in his hypothetical choice situation each participant would still suppose that she "has the same chance as anyone else of occupying any particular level of income in the economy." But there is no reason why the more talented should be this pessimistic about their chances of faring well in their society. Of course, this objection could be answered just by removing the knowledge of talents from Dworkin's hypothetical choice situation, but then his choice situation would be virtually equivalent to the original position. So interpreted, Dworkin would be simply disagreeing with Rawls over what principles of justice would be chosen in that choice situation.

In selection 12, Richard Miller also directs his criticism of Rawls's theory to the contractual approach itself. However, he does so from the point of view of Marxist social theory. Miller maintains that if certain elements of Marxist social theory are correct then neither Rawls's principles of justice nor any other candidates for "morally acceptable principles" would emerge from the original position.

The elements of Marxist social theory in question are the following: (1) no social arrangement that is acceptable to the best-off class is acceptable to the worst-off class; (2) the best-off class is a ruling class, that is, a class whose interests are served by the major political and ideological institutions; and (3) the need for wealth and power typical of the best-off class is much more acute than what is typical of the rest of society. What Miller is claiming is that if persons in the original position accepted these elements of Marxist social theory (and persons in the original position are presumed to have access to all available general information) then they would not choose Rawls's principles of justice nor any other "morally acceptable principles" you like.

To understand the force of Miller's critique, it is necessary to understand the various ways in which persons' needs and interests can be related in a society. One possibility is that the needs and interests of different members of a society are in fact perfectly complementary. If that were the case, there would be little difficulty in designing a social arrangement that was acceptable to every member. Nor would the original position be needed to design a fair solution. In such a society, no conflicts would arise as long as each person acted in her overall self-interest.

A second possibility is that the needs and interests of different members of a society are in moderate conflict. In deriving his principles of justice, Rawls actually limits himself to a consideration of social conditions where only moderate conflict obtains. For such conditions it seems clear that the original position could be usefully employed to design a fair social arrangement. In such a society the more talented members would be motivated to contribute sufficiently to support a social minimum, and the less talented would also be motivated to contribute sufficiently to reduce the burden on the more talented members. Consequently, persons in the original position would know that the members of such a society when aided by a minimal enforcement system would be able to abide by the principles that would be chosen.

A third possibility is that the needs and interests of the different members of a society are in extreme conflict, and that the conflict has the form of what Marx calls "class conflict." Let us consider the case in which the opposing classes are the capitalist class and the proletariat class. No doubt persons in the original position would know that in such a society compliance with almost any principles of conflict resolution could be achieved only by means of a stringent enforcement system. But why should that fact keep them from choosing any principles of social cooperation whatsoever? Surely persons in the original position would still have reason to provide for the basic needs of the members of the proletariat class, and thus would be inclined to favor an adequate social minimum. However, would they not also have reason to temper the sacrifice to be imposed on the members of the capitalist class in the transition to a society that accords with the principles they would favor, knowing, as they do, how much less prosperous and satisfied the members of that class would be under such principles? Yet if considerations of this latter sort could serve as reasons for persons in the original position, then it could be argued that any principles of social cooperation that would be derived would not constitute a morally adequate conception of justice, for a morally adequate conception of justice would simply not provide grounds for tempering the sacrifice to be imposed on the members of the capitalist class in the transition to a just society.

Fortunately for an ideal of contractual fairness, this modified version of Miller's critique can be avoided. For it can be shown that considerations favoring tempering the sacrifice to be imposed on the members of the capitalist class in the transition to a just society would not serve as reasons for persons in the original position. This is because persons in the original position, imagining themselves to be ignorant of whether they belong to the capitalist or the proletariat class, would have grounds to discount such considerations in deciding on principles of social cooperation. They would realize that members of the capitalist class would have a status analogous to that of criminals who have taken goods that rightfully belong to others. For the members of the capitalist class are not "compelled" to pursue their interest by depriving the members of the proletariat class of an acceptable minimum of social goods. They act as they do, depriving others of an adequate social minimum, simply to acquire more social goods for themselves. Unlike members of the proletariat class, the members of the capitalist class could be reasonably expected to act otherwise. Persons in the original position, therefore, have no more reason to temper the sacrifice to be imposed on the members of the capitalist class than they would have to temper the sacrifice to be imposed on criminals who have grown accustomed to the benefits provided by their ill-gotten goods.

Someone might object to the analogy between criminals and capitalists on the grounds that while the actions of criminals are usually condemned by the conventional standards of their society, the actions of capitalists usually find approval from those same standards. How can we blame capitalists for acting in accord with the conventional standards of their society?

Despite the fact that capitalist exploitation differs from criminal activity in that it is supported by conventional standards, capitalists who engage in such exploitation still cannot escape blame for acting unjustly for two basic reasons. First, capitalists have alternatives to pursuing their own advantage to the limit allowed by conventional standards. For while some capitalists are pursuing their own advantage, others are attempting to restrict at least some of the rights enjoyed by capitalists under those standards, and still others are trying to effect a drastic reform, even a revolutionary change, of those rights. Second, although supported by conventional standards, capitalist exploitation is contrary to the moral presuppositions of capitalist society, in the same manner that "separate but equal education," although supported by state and local laws, was contrary to the supreme law of the land contained in the equal protection clause of the Fourteenth Amendment. This is because the moral presuppositions of capitalist society as standardly expressed by a libertarian conception of justice or a welfare liberal conception of justice can be shown to be contrary to capitalist exploitation. For these reasons, capitalists cannot escape blame for acting unjustly if they deny people their rights required by these conceptions of justice, despite the existence of supportive conventional standards.

Nevertheless, while the disanalogies between capitalists and criminals would not lead persons in the original position to temper the sacrifice to be imposed on the members of the capitalist class, it would lead them to place some limits on the demands for restitution that can legitimately be made against capitalists. Thus, for example, they would not require of capitalists, as they typically would of criminals, that they not derive any net benefit from their past injustice.[3] Rather, they would simply require that the transition to a just society proceed with all due speed and without any special allowances for the special needs that capitalists have acquired in unjust societies.

Of course, it goes without saying that many capitalists will be reluctant to accept the practical requirements of their own conceptions of justice. Many would be strongly tempted to endorse uncritically the justification for their favored status provided by the conventional standards of their society. But this is exactly what they cannot do if they are to avoid blame for acting unjustly. For all of us when faced with choices that have social impact are required to evaluate critically the alternatives open to us in light of our conceptions of justice; and the greater the social impact our choices will have, the greater is our responsibility for performing this critical evaluation well. Since even a cursory examination of the alternatives open to capitalists in our times gives rise to serious doubts about the justice of the conventional standards supporting capitalist exploitation, capitalists who continue to engage in such exploitation surely will not be able to escape blame. Consequently, persons in the original position would have no reason to temper the sacrifice to be imposed on the members of the capitalist class in the transition to a just society.

Yet it is important to note that even though the assumption of class conflict would not lead persons in the original position to temper the sacrifice to be imposed on the members of the capitalist class, the assumption of moderate conflict would lead to somewhat different results. Under the assumption of class conflict, persons in the original position would tend to justify drastic measures, even violent revolution to bring into existence a just society, together with a stringent enforcement system to preserve such a society by preventing capitalists from lapsing back into exploitative ways. On the other hand, under the assumption of moderate conflict persons in the original position would tend to justify only less drastic means both with regard to bringing into existence and preserving a just society. Accordingly, the question of which type of conflict characterizes a particular society is of considerable practical moral significance. But whichever obtains, persons in the original position would still be able to use the information to arrive at morally acceptable results.

Welfare Liberal Justice: The Utilitarian Perspective

One way to avoid the challenges that have been directed at a contractarian defense of welfare liberal justice is to find some alternative way of defending welfare liberal justice. Historically, utilitarianism has been thought to provide such an alternative defense. What has been claimed is that the requirements of a welfare liberal conception of justice can be derived from considerations of utility in such a way that following these requirements will result in the maximization of total happiness or satisfaction in society. The best known classical defense of this utilitarian approach is certainly that presented by John Stuart Mill in Chapter 5 of *Utilitarianism*, from which selection 13 is drawn.

In this section, Mill surveys various types of actions and situations that are ordinarily described as just or unjust and concludes that justice (by which he understands a welfare liberal conception of justice) simply denotes a certain class of fundamental rules, the adherence to which is essential for maximizing social utility. Thus Mill rejects the ideal that justice and social utility are ultimately distinct ideals, maintaining instead that (welfare liberal) justice is in fact derivable from the moral ideal of social utility.

Nevertheless, various problems remain for the utilitarian defense of welfare liberal justice. Consider, for example, a society in which the members are equally divided between the Privileged Rich and the Alienated Poor, and suppose that the incomes for two alternative social arrangements for this society are the following:

Social Arrangement A	Social Arrangement B
Privileged Rich $100,000	$60,000
Alienated Poor $5,000	$15,000

Given these alternatives, considerations of maximizing utility would appear to favor Social Arrangement A over Social Arrangement B. But suppose that liberal justice required a high minimum for each person in society. Then it would seem that welfare liberal justice would favor Social Arrangement B over Social Arrangement A, in apparent conflict with the requirements of utility. Obviously, the possibility of such a conflict places the utilitarian defense of welfare liberal justice in some doubt. In selection 14, R. M. Hare attempts to remove the grounds for that doubt.

Hare argues that in fashioning a theory of justice we must proceed in accordance with the formal constraints of the concept of justice; that is, our judgments must be universalizable and impartial. But in addition, Hare argues, we must take relevant empirical considerations into account, such as the fact that people experience a declining marginal utility for money and other social goods. For example, considerations of declining marginal utility of money and other social goods, Hare believes, would render a utilitarian approach to a theory of justice moderately egalitarian in its requirements. Applied to our example, considerations of declining marginal utility of money and other social goods would seem to render Social Arrangement B preferable to Social Arrangement A from a utilitarian point of view, thus removing the grounds for thinking that liberal justice and social utility conflict in this case.

Of course, when considerations of declining marginal utility of money and other social goods are taken into account, the utility values for the two alternatives given on the previous page might end up to be something like:

Social Arrangement A	Social Arrangement B
Privileged Rich 55	40
Alienated Poor 10	20

And if they did, then there would still remain a conflict between welfare liberal justice and utility, with welfare liberal justice favoring Social Arrangement B and utility favoring Social Arrangement A . . . unless, of course, additional empirical considerations could be advanced to show that this is not the case.

Still another objection to a utilitarian defense of liberal justice is developed by John Rawls in selection 15. In this selection Rawls criticizes utilitarianism, particularly classical utilitarianism, for applying to society as a whole the principle of rational choice for one person, and thereby treating the desires and satisfactions of separate persons as if they were the desires and satisfactions of just one person. In this way, Rawls claims, utilitarianism fails to preserve the distinction between persons.

What Rawls must be claiming is that even after considerations of declining marginal utility of money and other social goods are taken into account, utilitarianism will still fail to adequately preserve the distinction between persons. But is Rawls right? It may well be that a proper assessment of the relative merits of the contractarian and utilitarian approaches to welfare liberal justice will turn on this very issue.

Communitarian Justice

Another prominent political ideal defended by contemporary philosophers is the communitarian ideal of the common good. As one might expect, many contemporary defenders of a communitarian conception of justice regard their conception as rooted in Aristotelian moral theory. In selection 16, Aristotle distinguishes between different varieties of justice. He first distinguishes between justice as the whole of virtue and justice as a particular part of virtue. In the former sense, justice is understood as what is lawful and the just person is equivalent to the moral person.

In the latter sense, justice is understood as what is fair or equal and the just person is the person who takes only a proper share. Aristotle focuses his discussion on justice in the latter sense, which further divides into distributive justice, corrective justice, and justice in exchange. Each of these varieties of justice can be understood to be concerned with achieving equality. For distributive justice it is equality between equals; for corrective justice it is equality between punishment and the crime; and for justice in exchange it is equality between whatever goods are exchanged. Aristotle also claims that justice has both its natural and conventional aspects: This twofold character of justice seems to be behind Aristotle's discussion of equity, in which equality is described as a corrective to legal or conventional justice.

Note that few of the distinctions Aristotle makes here seem tied to the acceptance of any particular conception of justice. One could, for example, accept the view that justice requires formal equality but then specify the equality that is required in different ways. Even the ideal of justice as giving people what they deserve, which has its roots in Aristotle's account of distributive justice, is also subject to various interpretations. For a correct analysis of the concept of desert would show that there is no conceptual difficulty with claiming, for example, that everyone deserves to have his or her needs satisfied or that everyone deserves an equal share of the goods distributed by his or her society.[4] Consequently, Aristotle's account is primarily helpful for getting clear about the distinctions belonging to the concept of justice that can be made without committing oneself to any particular conceptions of justice.

Yet rather than draw out the particular requirements of their own conception of justice, contemporary communitarians have frequently chosen to defend their conception by attacking other conceptions of justice, and, by and large, they have focused their attacks on the welfare liberal conception of justice.

One of the best-known attacks of this sort has been put forth by Michael J. Sandel (selection 17). Sandel claims that a welfare liberal conception of justice is founded on an inadequate conception of the nature of persons, according to which none of the particular wants, interests, or ends that we happen to have at any given time constitute what we are essentially. According to this conception, we are independent of and prior to all such wants, interests, or ends.

Sandel claims that this conception of the nature of persons is inadequate because:

> . . . we cannot regard ourselves as independent in this way without great cost to those loyalties and convictions whose moral force consists partly in the fact that living by them is inseparable from understanding ourselves as the particular persons we are—as members of this family or community or nation or people, as bearers of this history, as sons and daughters of that revolution, as citizens of this republic. Allegiances such as these are more than values I happen to have or aims I "espouse at any given time." They go beyond the obligations I voluntarily incur and the "natural duties" I owe to human beings as such. They allow that to some I owe more than justice requires or even permits, not by reason of agreements I have made but instead in virtue of those more of less enduring attachments and commitments which taken together partly define the person I am.[5]

Thus, according to Sandel, the conception of the nature of persons required by a welfare liberal conception of justice is inadequate because it fails to take into account the fact that some of our wants, interests, and ends are at least in part constitutive of what we are essentially. Without these desires, interests, and ends, we would not be the same persons we presently happen to be.

Sandel contends that welfare liberals are led to rely on this inadequate conception of persons for reasons that are fundamental to the conception of justice they want to defend. Specifically, welfare liberals want to maintain the priority of justice and more generally the priority of the right over the good. For example, according to Rawls; "The principles of right and so of justice put limits on which satisfactions have value; they impose restrictions on what are reasonable conceptions of one's good. We can express this by saying that in justice as fairness the concept of right is prior to that of the good."[6]

To support these priorities, Sandel argues that welfare liberals endorse this inadequate conception of the nature of persons. For example, Rawls argues:

> It is not our aims that primarily reveal our nature but rather the principles that we would acknowledge to govern the background conditions under which these aims are to be found and the manner in which they are to be pursued. *For the self is prior to the ends which are affirmed by it;* even a dominant end must be chosen from among numerous possibilities. . . . We should therefore reverse the relation between the right and the good proposed by teleological doctrines and view the right as prior.[7]

What this passage shows, according to Sandel, is that welfare liberals like Rawls believe that the priority of justice and the priority of the right are grounded in the priority of the self to its ends.

At first glance, Sandel's case against welfare liberalism looks particularly strong. After all, Rawls actually does say that "the self is prior to the ends which are affirmed by it," and this claim seems to express just the inadequate conception of the nature of persons that Sandel contends underlies a welfare liberal conception of justice. Nor is Rawls's claim made specifically about persons in the original position. So Sandel cannot be dismissed for failing to distinguish between the characterization of persons in the original position and the characterization of persons in ordinary life. Nevertheless, Sandel's case against welfare liberalism presupposes that there is no other plausible interpretation that can be given to Rawls's claim than the metaphysical one that Sandel favors. And unfortunately for Sandel's argument, a more plausible interpretation of Rawls's claim does appear to be available. According to this interpretation, to say that persons are prior to their ends means simply that they are morally responsible for their ends, either because they can or could have changed those ends. Of course, the degree to which people can or could have changed their ends is a matter of considerable debate, but what is clear is that it is the degree to which people can or could have changed their ends that determines the degree to which they are morally responsible for those ends.

Nor does this interpretation deny that certain ends may in fact be constitutive of the persons we are, so that if those ends were to change we would become different persons. We can see, therefore, that nothing in this interpretation of Rawls's claim presupposes a self that is metaphysically prior to its ends. Rather, the picture we are given is that of a self that is responsible for its ends insofar as its ends can or could have been revised. Such a self may well be constituted by at least some of its ends, but it is only responsible for those ends to the degree to which they can or could have been revised. So the sense in which a self is prior to its ends is simply moral: Insofar as its ends can or could have been revised, a self may be called on to change them or compensate others for their effects when they turn out to be morally objectionable. Clearly, this interpretation of Rawls's claim avoids any commitment to the inadequate conception of the nature of persons that Sandel contends underlies a welfare liberal conception of justice. Of course, this does not show that a communitarian conception of justice might not in the end be the most morally defensible. It only shows that this particular communitarian attack on a welfare liberal conception of justice is not successful.

In selection 18, John Finnis specifies the communitarian ideal of the common good as a set of conditions that enables the members of communities to attain for themselves the basic goods for the sake of which they have reason to collaborate with each other in their communities.[8] Finnis characterizes these basic goods as life, knowledge, play, aesthetic experience, friendship, religion, and practical reasonableness. Any other goods we might recognize and pursue, Finnis argues, will turn out to represent or be constituted by some or all of these basic goods.

In pursuing these basic goods, Finnis claims that we must adhere to a number of requirements of practical reasonableness, the most important of which are the following:

1. No arbitrary preferences among these basic goods.
2. Consequences should have limited relevance in moral decision making.
3. Every basic good must be respected in every act.

In large part, Finnis defends these requirements by attacking utilitarianism of the sort defended by R. M. Hare in selection 14. Finnis seems to think that once utilitarianism is seen to be defective as a moral theory, the merits of his own view become apparent.

Finnis also contrasts his own account of basic human goods with Rawls's thin theory of the good. In Rawls's theory, basic human goods are generally useful means for the pursuit of whatever ends one may have. For Finnis, basic human goods are the ends for which we strive. But while this contrast does exist, there seems to be no reason why both Rawls and Finnis could not incorporate each other's account of basic human goods without affecting any substantial change in their conceptions of justice.

Where Finnis and Rawls do seem to disagree, however, is not with respect to the nature of basic human goods themselves but rather with respect to the principles that apply to the pursuit of such goods. In particular, Finnis's requirements of practical reasonableness rule out the sacrifice of any basic good to achieve a greater total of basic goods. Thus, for Finnis, one may never do evil that good may come of it. By contrast, persons in Rawls's original position would reject an absolute prohibition on doing evil that good may come of it because there are cases where the evil or intended harm is either

1. Trivial (for example, as in the case of stepping on someone's foot to get out of a crowded subway),
2. Easily reparable (for instance, as in the case of lying to a temporarily depressed friend to keep her from committing suicide), or
3. Sufficiently outweighed by the consequences of the action (for example, the case of shooting 1 of 200 civilian hostages to prevent in the only way possible the execution of all 200).

Finnis's main justification for maintaining an absolute prohibition at least in the most morally difficult cases is to appeal to divine command theory.[9] Unfortunately, when divine command theory is used to resolve morally difficult cases, it can only do so by embracing an anything-could-be-right-if-God-commanded-it view, with all the absurdities that are traditionally associated with that view.[10] Consequently, there just does not appear to be any reasonable alternative to a nonabsolutist stance that allows moral requirements to bend but not break in difficult cases.

In selection 19, Alasdair MacIntyre argues that virtually all forms of liberalism attempt to separate rules defining right action from conceptions of the human good. Or, as Rawls has put it, in all these forms of liberalism "the right is prior to the good."

Now Macintyre contends that these forms of liberalism not only fail but have to fail because the rules defining right action cannot be adequately grounded apart from a conception of the good. For this reason, Macintyre claims, only some version of an Aristotelian theory that grounds rules supporting right action in a complete conception of the good can ever hope to be adequate.

But why can't we view most forms of liberalism as attempting to ground moral rules on part of a conception of the good—specifically, that part of a conception of the good that is more easily recognized, and needs to be publicly recognized, as good? For Rawls, for example, this partial conception of the good is a conception of fairness, according to which no one deserves his or her native abilities nor his or her initial starting place in society. For Ronald Dworkin, it is a conception of equal concern and respect for each and every person. And similarly for other liberals. If this way of interpreting forms of liberalism is correct, then in order to properly evaluate liberal and Aristotelian political theories we would need to do a comparative analysis of their conceptions of the good and their practical requirements. If Finnis's work provides any indication it may turn out that the practical requirement of both liberal and communitarian conceptions of justice, when correctly understood, are quite similar.

In selection 20, Will Kymlicka attempts to defend liberalism against the communitarian critique by providing an account of the way in which liberalism is neutral among conceptions of the good. Kymlicka argues that liberalism, especially the form of liberalism defended by John Rawls, is committed to neutrality in the justification of governmental policy but not to neutrality with respect to the consequences of governmental policy. This is because although the "marketplace of ideas" endorsed by liberals favors some conceptions of the good over others, the justification for this marketplace is not that it favors these conceptions of the good over others but that it provides a range of choice to individuals. According to Kymlicka, liberals have a certain distrust of the operation of state forums and a certain faith in the operation of nonstate forums and processes for evaluating the good. By contrast, he claims that communitarians have a certain faith in the operation of state forums and procedures, but that neither side has defended its preference.

Now Kymlicka may be right to focus the discussion between liberals and communitarians on the wisdom of state forums for evaluating the good. Nevertheless, it should be pointed out that there is a perfectly straightforward sense in which liberals, like Rawls, are not neutral with respect to the justification of governmental policy. In Rawls's view, conceptions of the good that conflict with the welfare liberal conception of fairness are not to be tolerated. So the neutrality among conceptions of the good only holds for those conceptions that are compatible with the welfare liberal ideal of fairness, which, I would claim, in itself constitutes a partial conception of the good.

Feminist Justice

Defenders of a feminist conception of justice present a distinctive challenging critique to defenders of other conceptions of justice. John Stuart Mill, one of the earliest male defenders of women's liberation, argues in selection 21 that the subjection of women was never justified but was imposed on them because they were physically weaker than men and that later this subjection was confirmed by law. Mill argues that society must remove the legal restrictions that deny women the same opportunities that are enjoyed by men in society. However, Mill does not consider whether because of past discrimination against women it may be necessary to do more than simply removing legal restrictions to provide women with the same opportunities that men now enjoy. He does not consider whether positive assistance may also be required.

But usually it is not enough simply to remove unequal restrictions to make a competition fair among those who have been participating. Positive assistance to those who have been disadvantaged in the past may also be required, as would be the case if one were running a race in which one was unfairly impeded by having to carry a 10-pound weight. Similarly, positive assistance, such as affirmative action programs, may be necessary if women who have been disadvantaged in the past are now for the first time to enjoy equal opportunity with men.

In selection 22, Susan Okin points out that in the face of the radical inequality that exists between women and men in our society there is still a widespread failure of political philosophers to address gender issues in their political theories. Ironically this is true even among those philosophers who have seen the need to adopt gender neutral language. Okin argues that no theory of justice can be adequate until it address these issues.

In selection 23 Alison M. Jaggar defends socialist feminism as the only adequate political theory. Socialist feminism is best understood by distinguishing it from both Marxist feminism and radical feminism. On the one hand, socialist feminism shares with Marxist feminism a commitment to a historical materialist method but then denies that women's liberation can be achieved simply by replacing capitalism with socialism. On the other hand, socialist feminism shares with radical feminism a commitment to changing human biology but then views such a change as only part of what is needed to bring about women's liberation. According to socialist feminists, equality between the sexes can only be achieved by replacing capitalism with socialism *and* changing human biology.

Jaggar also claims that the socialist feminist ideal can be described as an ideal of androgyny, but so understood, she hastens to add, it must involve a transformation of both physical and psychological capacities. Such a transformation might even include the capacities for insemination, lactation, and gestation so that, for instance, one woman could inseminate another, men and non-child-bearing women could lactate, and fertilized ova could be transplanted into men's or women's bodies. Thus, given Jaggar's understanding of the view, socialist feminism would retain most of the commitments of radical feminism and simply integrate them with those of Marxist feminism.

In selection 24, I set out and defend an ideal of androgyny that I identify with feminist justice. This ideal requires that traits that are truly desirable in society be equally available to both women and men, or in the case of virtues, equally inculcated in both women and men. I consider attempts to derive the ideal of androgyny either from a right to equal opportunity that is a central requirement of a welfare liberal conception of justice or from an equal right of self-development that is a central requirement of a socialist conception of justice. I argue that although the ideal of androgyny is compatible with the requirements of these two conceptions of justice, it also transcends them by requiring that all virtues be equally inculcated in both women and men.

I further argue that the ideal of androgyny would require (1) that all children irrespective of their sex must be given the same type of upbringing consistent with their native capabilities and (2) that mothers and fathers must also have the same opportunities for education and employment consistent with their native capabilities. I go on to consider how achieving equal opportunity for women and men requires vastly improved day care facilities and flexible (usually part-time) work schedules for both women and men.

In selection 25, Janet Radcliffe Richards sets out three objections to feminist justice. The first is that there is no reasonable case for feminist justice at all. The second is that the case for feminist justice is exaggerated. The third is that the feminist movement itself is unattractive. While Richards rejects the first objection, she thinks that there is some substance to the second and third. With respect to the second objection, Richards argues that by making the pursuit of feminist justice primary, feminists have exaggerated the case for feminist justice. But while Richards may be right that there are more morally important objectives than the pursuit of feminist justice (for example, the elimination of world hunger and Third World poverty), feminists may also be right that because injustice to women is so deeply rooted in society, we could not rid society of that injustice without remedying many other injustices as well.

There is, however, considerable merit to Richards's objection that feminists have created an unattractive movement. One reason for this is the one that Richard gives—that feminists have failed to distinguish between practices that are bad in themselves and practices that are bad simply because of their consequences— leading to the rejection of too many practices that could be rendered acceptable by simply eliminating their sexist consequences. Another reason is that feminists have tended to stress the radicalness of their proposals rather than the fact that they are grounded in ideals that are commonly accepted. If people could be led to see that feminist justice is compatible or required by the ideals of libertarian justice, welfare liberal justice, socialist justice, and communitarian justice that they hold dear, then the case for feminist justice would be strengthened immeasurably. It could make the practical requirements of feminist justice virtually inescapable.

What this suggests is that our overall task of critically evaluating alternative conceptions of justice in order to reasonably resolve disputes about justice may not be as difficult as it initially appeared. If libertarian justice, welfare liberal justice, socialist justice, communitarian justice, and feminist justice, when correctly interpreted, can all be seen to have virtually the same practical requirements, then there is really no need to choose between them. To reasonably resolve our disputes about justice, all we would have to do is get clear about what the shared practical requirements of these conceptions of justice are and then simply act on them.[11]

Notes

1. Murray Rothbard, *For a New Liberty* (New York: Collier Books, 1973); Robert Nozick, *State, Anarchy and Utopia* (New York: Basic Books, 1974); John Hospers, *Libertarianism* (Los Angeles: Nash, 1971).

2. Ronald Dworkin, "Liberalism," in Stuart Hampshire (ed.), *Public and Private Morality* (Cambridge, England: Cambridge University Press, 1978), pp. 113–143; "What is Equality? Parts I and II," *Philosophy and Public Affairs* 10 (1981) pp. 185–246, 283–345; "Why Liberals Should Believe in Equality," *The New York Review of Books,* February 3, 1983, pp. 32–34.

3. James P. Sterba, "Is There a Rationale for Punishment?", *American Journal of Jurisprudence* 29 (1984), pp. 29–43.

4. For further argument, see my article "Justice and the Concept of Desert," *The Personalist* 57 (1976), pp. 188–197.

5. Michael J. Sandel, *Liberalism and the Limits of Justice* (Cambridge, England: Cambridge University Press, 1982), p. 179.

6. John Rawls, *A Theory of Justice* (Cambridge, Mass: Harvard University Press, 1971), p. 31.

7. Rawls, p. 560.

8. John Finnis, *Natural Law and Natural Right* (Oxford, England: Clarendon Press, 1980), p. 165.

9. Finnis, especially part 3.

10. See John Chandler, "Divine Command Theories and the Appeal of Love," *American Philosophical Quarterly* 22 (1985), pp. 231–239.

11. For further argument for this practical reconciliation thesis, see my book *How to Make People Just* (Totowa, N.J.: Rowman and Littlefield, 1988).

PART II

Libertarian Justice

Liberty, Equality, and Merit

F. A. HAYEK

I have no respect for the passion for equality, which seems to me merely idealizing envy.

—Oliver Wendell Holmes, Jr.

The great aim of the struggle for liberty has been equality before the law. This equality under the rules which the state enforces may be supplemented by a similar equality of the rules that men voluntarily obey in their relations with one another. This extension of the principle of equality to the rules of moral and social conduct is the chief expression of what is commonly called the democratic spirit—and probably that aspect of it that does most to make inoffensive the inequalities that liberty necessarily produces.

Equality of the general rules of law and conduct, however, is the only kind of equality conducive to liberty and the only equality which we can secure without destroying liberty. Not only has liberty nothing to do with any other sort of equality, but it is even bound to produce inequality in many respects. This is the necessary

From *The Constitution of Liberty* (1960), pp. 85–100. Reprinted by permission of the author and The University of Chicago Press.

result and part of the justification of individual liberty: if the result of individual liberty did not demonstrate that some manners of living are more successful than others, much of the case for it would vanish.

It is neither because it assumes that people are in fact equal nor because it attempts to make them equal that the argument for liberty demands that government treat them equally. This argument not only recognizes that individuals are very different but in a great measure rests on that assumption. It insists that these individual differences provide no justification for government to treat them differently. And it objects to the differences in treatment by the state that would be necessary if persons who are in fact very different were to be assured equal positions in life.

Modern advocates of a more far-reaching material equality usually deny that their demands are based on any assumption of the factual equality of all men.[1] It is nevertheless still widely believed that this is the main justification for such demands. Nothing, however, is more damaging to the demand for equal treatment than to base it on so obviously untrue an assumption as that of the factual equality of all men. To rest the case for equal treatment of national or racial minorities on the assertion that they do not differ from other men is implicitly to admit that factual inequality would justify unequal treatment; and the proof that some differences do, in fact, exist would not be long in forthcoming. It is of the essence of the demand for equality before the law that people should be treated alike in spite of the fact that they are different.

The Importance of Individual Differences

The boundless variety of human nature—the wide range of differences in individual capacities and potentialities—is one of the most distinctive facts about the human species. Its evolution has made it probably the most variable among all kinds of creatures. It has been well said that "biology, with variability as its cornerstone, confers on every human individual a unique set of attributes which give him a dignity he could not otherwise possess. Every newborn baby is an unknown quantity so far as potentialities are concerned because there are many thousands of unknown interrelated genes and gene-patterns which contribute to his makeup. As a result of nature and nurture the newborn infant may become one of the greatest of men or women ever to have lived. In every case he or she has the making of a distinctive individual. . . . If the differences are not very important, then freedom is not very important and the idea of individual worth is not very important."[2] The writer justly adds that the widely held uniformity theory of human nature," which on the surface appears to accord with democracy . . . would in time undermine the very basic ideals of freedom and individual worth and render life as we know it meaningless."[3]

It has been the fashion in modern times to minimize the importance of congenital differences between men and to ascribe all the important differences to the influence of environment.[4] However important the latter may be, we must not overlook the fact that individuals are very different from the outset. The importance of individual differences would hardly be less if all people were brought up in very similar environments. As a statement of fact, it just is not true that "all men are born equal." We may continue to use this hallowed phrase to express the ideal that legally and morally all men ought to be treated alike. But if we want to understand what this ideal of equality can or should mean, the first requirement is that we free ourselves from the belief in factual equality.

From the fact that people are very different it follows that, if we treat them equally, the result must be inequality in their actual position,[5] and that the only way to place them in an equal position would be to treat them differently. Equality before the law and material equality are therefore not only different but are in conflict with each other; and we can achieve either the one or the other, but not both at the same time. The equality before the law which freedom requires leads to material inequality. Our argument will be that, though where the state must use coercion for other reasons, it should treat all people alike, the desire of making people more alike in their condition cannot be accepted in a free society as a justification for further and discriminatory coercion.

We do not object to equality as such. It merely happens to be the case that a demand for equality is the professed motive of most of those who desire to impose upon society a preconceived pattern of distribution. Our objection is against all attempts to impress upon society a deliberately chosen pattern of distribution, whether it be an order of equality or of inequality. We shall indeed see that many of those who demand an extension of equality do not really demand equality but a distribution that conforms more closely to human conceptions of individual merit and that their desires are as irreconcilable with freedom as the more strictly egalitarian demands.

If one objects to the use of coercion in order to bring about a more even or a more just distribution, this does not mean that one does not regard these as desirable. But if we wish to preserve a free society, it is essential that we recognize that the desirability of a particular object is not sufficient justification for the use of coercion. One may well feel attracted to a community in which there are no extreme contrasts between rich and poor and may welcome the fact that the general increase in wealth seems gradually to reduce those differences. I fully share these feelings and certainly regard the degree of social equality that the United States has achieved as wholly admirable.

There also seems no reason why these widely felt preferences should not guide policy in some respects. Wherever there is a legitimate need for government action and we have to choose between different methods of satisfying such a need, those that incidentally also reduce inequality may well be preferable. If, for example, in the law of intestate succession one kind of provision will be more conducive to equality than another, this may be a strong argument in its favor. It is a different matter, however, if it is demanded that, in order to produce substantive equality, we should abandon the basic postulate of a free society, namely, the limitation of all coercion by equal law. Against this we shall hold that economic inequality is not one of the evils which justify our resorting to discriminatory coercion or privilege as a remedy.

Nature and Nurture

Our contention rests on two basic propositions which probably need only be stated to win fairly general assent. The first of them is an expression of the belief in a certain similarity of all human beings: it is the proposition that no man or group of men possesses the capacity to determine conclusively the potentialities of other human beings and that we should certainly never trust anyone invariably to exercise such a capacity. However great the differences between men may be, we have no ground for believing that they will ever be so great as to enable one man's mind in a particular instance to comprehend fully all that another responsible man's mind is capable of.

The second basic proposition is that the acquisition by any member of the community of additional capacities to do things which may be valuable must always be regarded as a gain for that community. It is true that particular people may be worse off because of the superior ability of some new competitor in their field; but any such additional ability in the community is likely to benefit the majority. This implies that the desirability of increasing the abilities and opportunities of any individual does not depend on whether the same can also be done for others—provided, of course, that others are not thereby deprived of the opportunity of acquiring the same or other abilities which might have been accessible to them had they not been secured by that individual.

Egalitarians generally regard differently those differences in individual capacities which are inborn and those which are due to the influences of environment, or those which are the result of "nature" and those which are the result of "nurture." Neither, be it said at once, has anything to do with moral merit.[6] Though either may greatly affect the value which an individual has for his fellows, no more credit belongs to him for having been born with desirable qualities than for having grown up under favorable circumstances. The distinction between the two is important only because the former advantages are due to circumstances clearly beyond human control, while the latter are due to factors which we might be able to alter. The important question is whether there is a case for so changing our institutions as to eliminate as much as possible those advantages due to environment. Are we to agree that "all inequalities that rest on birth and inherited property ought to be abolished and none remain unless it is an effect of superior talent and industry"?[7]

The fact that certain advantages rest on human arrangements does not necessarily mean that we could provide the same advantages for all or that, if they are given to some, somebody else is thereby deprived of them. The most important factors to be considered in this connection are the family, inheritance, and education, and it is against the inequality which they produce that criticism is mainly directed. They are, however, not the only important factors of environment. Geographic conditions such as climate and landscape, not to speak of local and sectional differences in cultural and moral traditions, are scarcely less important. We can, however, consider here only the three factors whose effects are most commonly impugned.

So far as the family is concerned, there exists a curious contrast between the esteem most people profess for the institution and their dislike of the fact that being born into a particular family should confer on a person special advantages. It seems to be widely believed that, while useful qualities which a person acquires because of his native gifts under conditions which are the same for all are socially beneficial, the same qualities become somehow undesirable if they are the result of environmental advantages not available to others. Yet it is difficult to see why the same useful quality which is welcomed when it is the result of a person's natural endowment should be less valuable when it is the product of such circumstances as intelligent parents or a good home.

The value which most people attach to the institution of the family rests on the belief that, as a rule, parents can do more to prepare their children for a satisfactory life than anyone else. This means not only that the benefits which particular people derive from their family environment will be different but also that these benefits may operate cumulatively through several generations. What reason can there be for believing that a desirable quality in a person is less valuable to society if it has been the result of family background than if it has not? There is, indeed, good reason to think that there are some socially valuable qualities which will be rarely acquired in a single generation but which will generally be formed only by the continuous efforts of two or three. This means simply that there are parts of the cultural heritage of a society that are more effectively transmitted through the family. Granted this, it would be unreasonable to deny that a society is likely to get a better elite if ascent is not limited to one generation, if individuals are not deliberately made to start from the same level, and if children are not deprived of the chance to benefit from the better education and material environment which their parents may be able to provide. To admit this is merely to recognize that belonging to a particular family is part of the individual personality, that society is made up as much of families as of individuals, and that the transmission of the heritage of civilization within the family is as important a tool in man's striving toward better things as is the heredity of beneficial physical attributes.

Many people who agree that the family is desirable as an instrument for the transmission of morals, tastes, and knowledge still question the desirability of the transmission of material property. Yet there can be little doubt that, in order that the former may be possible, some continuity of standards, of the external forms of life, is essential, and that this will be achieved only if it is possible to transmit not only immaterial but also material advantages. There is, of course, neither greater merit nor any greater injustice involved in some people being born to wealthy parents than there is in others being born to kind or intelligent parents. The fact is that it is no less of an advantage to the community if at least some children can start with the advantages which at any given time only wealthy homes can offer than if some children inherit great intelligence or are taught better morals at home.

We are not concerned here with the chief argument for private inheritance, namely, that it seems essential as a means to preserve the dispersal in the control of capital and as an inducement for its accumulation. Rather, our concern here is whether the fact that it confers unmerited benefits on some is a valid argument against the institution. It is unquestionably one of the institutional causes of inequality. In the present context we need not inquire whether liberty demands unlimited freedom of bequest. Our problem here is merely whether people ought to be free to pass on to children or others such material possessions as will cause substantial inequality.

Once we agree that it is desirable to harness the natural instincts of parents to equip the new generation as well as they can, there seems no sensible ground for limiting this to nonmaterial benefits. The family's function of passing on standards and traditions is closely tied up with the possibility of transmitting material goods. And it is difficult to see how it would serve the true interest of society to limit the gain in material conditions to one generation.

There is also another consideration which, though it may appear somewhat cynical, strongly suggests that if we wish to make the best use of the natural partiality of parents for their children, we ought not to preclude the transmission of property. It seems certain that among the many ways in which those who have gained power and influence might provide for their children, the bequest of a fortune is socially by far the cheapest. Without this outlet, these men would look for other ways of providing for their children, such as placing them in positions which might bring them the income and the prestige that a fortune would have done; and this would cause a waste of resources and an injustice much greater than is caused by the inheritance of property. Such is the case with all societies in which inheritance of property does not exist, including the communist. Those who dislike the inequalities caused by inheritance should therefore recognize that, men being what they are, it is the least of evils, even from their point of view.

Equality of Opportunity

Though inheritance used to be the most widely criticized source of inequality, it is today probably no longer so. Egalitarian agitation now tends to concentrate on the unequal advantages due to differences in education. There is a growing tendency to express the desire to secure equality of conditions in the claim that the best education we have learned to provide for some should be made gratuitously available for all and that, if this is not possible, one should not be allowed to get a better education than the rest merely because one's parents are able to pay for it, but only those and all those who can pass a uniform test of ability should be admitted to the benefits of the limited resources of higher education.

The problem of educational policy raises too many issues to allow of their being discussed incidentally under the general heading of equality. . . . For the present we shall only point out that enforced equality in this field can hardly avoid preventing some from getting the education they otherwise might. Whatever we might do, there is no way of preventing those advantages which only some can have, and which it is desirable that some should have, from going to people who neither individually merit them nor will make as good a use of them as some other person might have done. Such a problem cannot be satisfactorily solved by the exclusive and coercive powers of the state.

It is instructive at this point to glance briefly at the change that the ideal of equality has undergone in this field in modern times. A hundred years ago, at the height of the classical liberal movement, the demand was generally expressed by the phrase *la carrière ouverte aux talents*. It was a demand that all manmade obstacles to the rise of some should be removed, that all privileges of individuals should be abolished, and that what the state contributed to the chance of improving one's conditions should be the same for all. That so long as people were different and grew up in different families this could not assure an equal start was fairly generally accepted. It was understood that the duty of government was not to ensure that everybody had the same prospect of reaching a given position but merely to make available to all on equal terms those facilities which in their nature depended on government action. That the results were bound to be different, not only because the individuals were different, but also because only a small part of the relevant circumstances depended on government action, was taken for granted.

This conception that all should be allowed to try has been largely replaced by the altogether different conception that all must be assured an equal start and the same prospects. This means little less than that the government, instead of providing the same circumstances for all, should aim at controlling all conditions relevant to a particular individual's prospects and so adjust them to his capacities as to assure him of the same prospects as everybody else. Such deliberate adaptation of opportunities to individual aims and capacities would, of course, be the opposite of freedom. Nor could it be justified as a means of making the best use of all available knowledge except on the assumption that government knows best how individual capacities can be used.

When we inquire into the justification of these demands, we find that they rest on the discontent that the success of some people often produces in those that are less successful, or, to put it bluntly, on envy. The modern tendency to gratify this passion and to disguise it in the respectable garment of social justice is developing into a serious threat to freedom. Recently an attempt was made to base these demands on the argument that it ought to be the aim of politics to remove all sources of discontent.[8] This would, of course, necessarily mean that it is the responsibility of government to see that nobody is healthier or possesses a happier temperament, a better-suited spouse or more prospering children, than anybody else. If really all unfulfilled desires have a claim on the community, individual responsibility is at an end. However human, envy is certainly not one of the sources of discontent that a free society can eliminate. It is probably one of the essential conditions for the preservation of such a society that we do not countenance envy, not sanction its demands by camoflaging it as social justice, but treat it, in the words of John Stuart Mill, as "the most antisocial and evil of all passions."[9]

The Conflict Between Merit and Value

While most of the strictly egalitarian demands are based on nothing better than envy, we must recognize that much that on the surface appears as a demand for greater equality is in fact a demand for a juster distribution of the good things of this world and springs therefore from much more creditable motives. Most people will object not to the bare fact of inequality but to the fact that the differences in reward do not correspond to any recognizable differences in the merits of those who receive them. The answer commonly given to this is that a free society on the whole achieves this kind of justice.[10] This, however, is an indefensible contention if by justice is meant proportionality of reward to moral merit. Any attempt to found the case for freedom on this argument is very damaging to it, since it concedes that material rewards ought to be made to correspond to recognizable merit and then opposes the conclusion that most people will draw from this by an assertion which is untrue. The proper answer is that in a free system it is neither desirable nor practicable that material rewards should be made generally to correspond to what men recognize as merit and that it is an essential characteristic of a free society that an individual's position should not necessarily depend on the views that his fellows hold about the merit he has acquired.

This contention may appear at first so strange and even shocking that I will ask the reader to suspend judgment until I have further explained the distinction between value and merit.[11] The difficulty in making the point clear is due to the fact that the term "merit," which is the only one available to describe what I mean, is also used in a wider and vaguer sense. It will be used here exclusively to describe the attributes of conduct that make it deserving of praise, that is, the moral character of the action and not the value of the achievement.[12]

As we have seen throughout our discussion, the value that the performance or capacity of a person has to his fellows has no necessary connection with its ascertainable merit in this sense. The inborn as well as the acquired gifts of a person clearly have a value to his fellows which does not depend on any credit due to him for possessing them. There is little a man can do to alter the fact that his special talents are very common or exceedingly rare. A good mind or a fine voice, a beautiful face or a skillful hand, and a ready wit or an attractive personality are in a large measure as independent of a person's efforts as the opportunities or the experiences he has had. In all these instances the value which a person's capacities or services have for us and for which he is recompensed has little relation to anything that we can call moral merit or deserts. Our problem is whether it is desirable that people should enjoy advantages in proportion to the benefits which their fellows derive from their activities or whether the distribution of these advantages should be based on other men's views of their merits.

Reward according to merit must in practice mean reward according to assessable merit, merit that other people can recognize and agree upon and not merit merely in the sight of some higher power. Assessable merit in this sense presupposes that we can ascertain that a man has done what some accepted rule of conduct demanded of him and that this has cost him some pain and effort. Whether this has been the case cannot be judged by the result: merit is not a matter of the objective outcome but of subjective effort. The attempt to achieve a valuable result may be highly meritorious but a complete failure, and full success may be entirely the result of accident and thus without merit. If we know that a man has done his best, we will often wish to see him rewarded irrespective of the result; and if we know that a most valuable achievement is almost entirely due to luck or favorable circumstances, we will give little credit to the author.

We may wish that we were able to draw this distinction in every instance. In fact, we can do so only rarely with any degree of assurance. It is possible only where we possess all the knowledge which was at the disposal of the acting person, including a knowledge of his skill and confidence, his state of mind and his feelings, his capacity for attention, his energy and persistence, etc. The possibility of a true judgment of merit thus depends on the presence of precisely those conditions whose general absence is the main argument for liberty. It is because we want people to use knowledge which we do not possess that we let them decide for themselves. But insofar as we want them to be free to use capacities and knowledge of facts which we do not have, we are not in a position to judge the merit of their achievements. To decide on merit presupposes that we can judge whether people have made such use of their opportunities as they ought to have made and how much effort of will or self-denial this has cost them; it presupposes also that we can distinguish between that part of their achievement which is due to circumstances within their control and that part which is not.

Principles of Remuneration and Freedom of Choice

The incompatibility of reward according to merit with freedom to choose one's pursuit is most evident in those areas where the uncertainty of the outcome is particularly great and our individual estimates of the chances of various kinds of effort very different.[13] In those speculative efforts which we call "research" or "exploration," or in economic activities which we commonly describe as "speculation," we cannot expect to attract those best qualified for them unless we give the successful ones all the credit or gain, though many others may have striven as meritoriously. For the same reason that nobody can know beforehand who will be the successful ones, nobody can say who has earned greater merit. It would clearly not serve our purpose if we let all who have honestly striven share in the prize. Moreover, to do so would make it necessary that somebody have the right to decide who is to be allowed to strive for it. If in their pursuit of uncertain goals people are to use their own knowledge and capacities, they must be guided, not by what other people think they ought to do, but by the value others attach to the result at which they aim.

What is so obviously true about those undertakings which we commonly regard as risky is scarcely less true of any chosen object we decide to pursue. Any such decision is beset with uncertainty, and if the choice is to be as wise as it is humanly possible to make it, the alternative results anticipated must be labeled according to their value. If the remuneration did not correspond to the value that the product of a man's efforts has for his fellows, he would have no basis for deciding whether the pursuit of a given object is worth the effort and risk. He would necessarily have to be told what to do, and some other person's estimate of what was the best use of his capacities would have to determine both his duties and his remuneration.[14]

The fact is, of course, that we do not wish people to earn a maximum of merit but to achieve a maximum of usefulness at a minimum of pain and sacrifice and therefore a minimum of merit. Not only would it be impossible for us to reward all merit justly, but it would not even be desirable that people should aim chiefly at earning a maximum of merit. Any attempt to induce them to do this would necessarily result in people being rewarded differently for the same service. And it is only the value of the result that we can judge with any degree of confidence, not the different degrees of effort and care that it has cost different people to achieve it.

The prizes that a free society offers for the result serve to tell those who strive for them how much effort they are worth. However, the same prizes will go to all those who produce the same result, regardless of effort. What is true here of the remuneration for the same services rendered by different people is even more true of the relative remuneration for different services requiring different gifts and capacities: they will have little relation to merit. The market will generally offer for services of any kind the value they will have for those who benefit from them; but it will rarely be known whether it was necessary to offer so much in order to obtain these services, and often, no doubt, the community could have had them for much less. The pianist who was reported not long ago to have said that he would perform even if he had to pay for the privilege probably described the position of many who earn large incomes from activities which are also their chief pleasure.

The Consequences of Distribution According to Merit

Though most people regard as very natural the claim that nobody should be rewarded more than he deserves for his pain and effort, it is nevertheless based on a colossal presumption. It presumes that we are able to judge in every individual instance how well people use the different opportunities and talents given to them and how meritorious their achievements are in the light of all the circumstances which have made them possible. It presumes that some human beings are in a position to determine conclusively what a person is worth and are entitled to determine what he may achieve. It presumes, then, what the argument for liberty specifically rejects: that we can and do know all that guides a person's action.

A society in which the position of the individuals was made to correspond to human ideas of moral merit would therefore be the exact opposite of a free society. It would be a society in which people were rewarded for duty performed instead of for success, in which every move of every individual was guided by what other people thought he ought to do, and in which the individual was thus relieved of the responsibility and the risk of decision. But if nobody's knowledge is sufficient to guide all human action, there is also no human being who is competent to reward all efforts according to merit.

In our individual conduct we generally act on the assumption that it is the value of a person's performance and not his merit that determines our obligation to him. Whatever may be true in more intimate relations, in the ordinary business of life we do not feel that, because a man has rendered us a service at a great sacrifice, our debt to him is determined by this, so long as we could have had the same service provided with ease by somebody else. In our dealings with other men we feel that we are doing justice if we recompense value rendered with equal value, without inquiring what it might have cost the particular individual to supply us with these services. What determines our responsibility is the advantage we derive from what others offer us, not their merit in providing it. We also expect in our dealings with others to be remunerated not according to our subjective merit but according to what our services are worth to them. Indeed, so long as we think in terms of our relations to particular people, we are generally quite aware that the mark of the free man is to be dependent for his livelihood not on other people's views of his merit but solely on what he has to offer them. It is only when we think of our position or our income as determined by "society" as a whole that we demand reward according to merit.

Though moral value or merit is a species of value, not all value is moral value, and most of our judgments of value are not moral judgments. That this must be so in a free society is a point of cardinal importance; and the failure to distinguish between value and merit has been the source of serious confusion. We do not necessarily admire all activities whose product we value; and in most instances where we value what we get, we are in no position to assess the merit of those who have provided it for us. If a man's ability in a given field is more valuable after thirty years' work than it was earlier, this is independent of whether these thirty years were most profitable and enjoyable or whether they were a time of unceasing sacrifice and worry. If the pursuit of a hobby produces a special skill or an accidental invention turns out to be extremely useful to others, the fact that there is little merit in it does not make it any less valuable than if the result had been produced by painful effort.

This difference between value and merit is not peculiar to any one type of society—it would exist anywhere. We might, of course, attempt to make rewards correspond to merit instead of value, but we are not likely to succeed in this. In attempting it, we would destroy the incentives which enable people to decide for themselves what they should do. Moreover, it is more than doubtful whether even a fairly successful attempt to make rewards correspond to merit would produce a more attractive or even a tolerable social order. A society in which it was generally presumed that a high income was proof of merit and a low income of the lack of it, in which it was universally believed that position and remuneration corresponded to merit, in which there was no other road to success than the approval of one's conduct by the majority of one's fellows, would probably be much more unbearable to the unsuccessful ones than one in which it was frankly recognized that there was no necessary connection between merit and success.[15]

It would probably contribute more to human happiness if, instead of trying to make remuneration correspond to merit, we made clearer how uncertain is the connection between value and merit. We are probably all much too ready to ascribe personal merit where there is, in fact, only superior value. The possession by an individual or a group of a superior civilization or education certainly represents an important value and constitutes an asset for the community to which they belong; but it usually constitutes little merit. Popularity and esteem do not depend more on merit than does financial success. It is, in fact, largely because we are so used to assuming an often nonexistent merit wherever we find value that we balk when, in particular instances, the discrepancy is too large to be ignored.

There is every reason why we ought to endeavor to honor special merit where it has gone without adequate reward. But the problem of rewarding action of outstanding merit which we wish to be widely known as an example is different from that of the incentives on which the ordinary functioning of society rests. A free society produces institutions in which, for those who prefer it, a man's advancement depends on the judgment of some superior or of the majority of his fellows. Indeed, as organizations grow larger and more complex, the task of ascertaining the individual's contribution will become more difficult; and it will become increasingly necessary that, for many, merit in the eyes of the managers rather than the ascertainable value of the contribution should determine the rewards. So long as this does not produce a situation in which a single comprehensive scale of merit is imposed upon the whole society, so long as a multiplicity of organizations compete with one another in offering different prospects, this is not merely compatible with freedom but extends the range of choice open to the individual.

Freedom and Distributive Justice

Justice, like liberty and coercion, is a concept which, for the sake of clarity, ought to be confined to the deliberate treatment of men by other men. It is an aspect of the intentional determination of those conditions of people's lives that are subject to such control. Insofar as we want the efforts of individuals to be guided by their own views about prospects and chances, the results of the individual's efforts are necessarily unpredictable, and the question as to whether the resulting distribution of incomes is just has no meaning.[16] Justice does require that those conditions of people's lives that are determined by government be provided equally for all. But equality of those conditions must lead to inequality of results. Neither the equal provision of particular public facilities nor the equal treatment of different partners in our voluntary dealings with one another will secure reward that is proportional to merit. Reward for merit is reward for obeying the wishes of others in what we do, not compensation for the benefits we have conferred upon them by doing what we thought best.

It is, in fact, one of the objections against attempts by government to fix income scales that the state must attempt to be just in all it does. Once the principle of reward according to merit is accepted as the just foundation for the distribution of incomes, justice would require that all who desire it should be rewarded according to that principle. Soon it would also be demanded that the same principle be applied to all and that incomes not in proportion to recognizable merit not be tolerated. Even an attempt merely to distinguish between those incomes or gains which are "earned" and those which are not will set up a principle which the state will have to try to apply but cannot in fact apply generally.[17] And every such attempt at deliberate control of some remunerations is bound to create further demands for new controls. The principle of distributive justice, once introduced, would not be fulfilled until the whole of society was organized in accordance with it. This would produce a kind of society which in all essential respects would be the opposite of a free society—a society in which authority decided what the individual was to do and how he was to do it.

Notes

1. See, e.g., R. H. Tawney, *Equality* (London, 1931), p. 47.

2. Roger J. Williams, *Free and Unequal: The Biological Basis of Individual Liberty* (Austin: University of Texas Press, 1953), pp. 23 and 70; cf. also J. B. S. Haldane, *The Inequality of Man* (London, 1932), and P. B. Medawar, *The Uniqueness of the Individual* (London, 1957).

3. Williams, *op. cit.,* p. 152.

4. See the description of this fashionable view in H. M. Kallen's article "Behaviorism," *E. E. S.,* II, 498: "At birth human infants, regardless of their heredity, are as equal as Fords."

5. Cf. Plato, *Laws* vi. 757A: "To unequals equals become unequal."

6. Cf. F. H. Knight, *Freedom and Reform* (New York, 1947), p. 151: "There is no visible reason why anyone is more or less entitled to the earnings of inherited personal capacities than to those of inherited property in any other form"; and the discussion in W. Roepke, *Mass und Mitte* (Erlenbach and Zurich, 1950), pp. 65–75.

7. This is the position of R. H. Tawney as summarized by J. P. Plamenatz, "Equality of Opportunity," in *Aspects of Human Equality,* ed. L. Bryson and others (New York, 1956), p. 100.

8. C. A. R. Crosland, *The Future of Socialism* (London, 1956), p. 205.

9. J. S. Mill, *On Liberty,* ed. R. B. McCallum (Oxford, 1946), p. 70.

10. Cf. W. B. Gallie, "Liberal Morality and Socialist Morality," in *Philosophy, Politics, and Society,* ed. P. Laslett (Oxford, 1956), pp. 123–25. The author represents it as the essence of "liberal morality" that it claims that rewards are equal to merit in a free society. This was the position of some nineteenth-century liberals which often weakened their argument. A characteristic example is W. G. Sumner, who argued (*What Social Classes Owe to Each Other,* reprinted in *Freeman,* VI [Los Angeles, n.d.], 141) that if all "have equal chances so far as chances are provided or limited by society," this will "produce inequal results—that is, results which shall be proportioned to the merits of individuals." This is true only if "merit" is used in the sense in which we have used "value," without any moral connotations, but certainly not if it is meant to suggest proportionality to any endeavor to do the good or right thing, or to any subjective effort to conform to an ideal standard.

    But, as we shall presently see, Mr. Gallie is right that, in the Aristotelian terms he uses, liberalism aims at commutative justice and socialism at distributive justice. But, like most socialists, he does not see that distributive justice is irreconcilable with freedom in the choice of one's activities: it is the justice of a hierarchic organization, not of a free society.

11. Although I believe that this distinction between merit and value is the same as that which Aristotle and Thomas Aquinas had in mind when they distinguished "distributive justice" from "commutative justice," I prefer not to tie up the discussion with all the difficulties and confusions which in the course of time have become associated with these traditional concepts. That what we call here "reward according to merit" corresponds to the Aristotelian distributive justice

seems clear. The difficult concept is that of "commutative justice," and to speak of justice in this sense seems always to cause a little confusion. Cf. M. Solomon, *Der Begriff der Gerechtigkeit bei Aristoteles* (Leiden, 1937); and for a survey of the extensive literature G. del Vecchio, *Die Gerechtigkeit* (2nd ed.; Basel, 1950).

12. The terminological difficulties arise from the fact that we use the word merit also in an objective sense and will speak of the "merit" of an idea, a book, or a picture, irrespective of the merit acquired by the person who has created them. Sometimes the word is also used to describe what we regard as the "true" value of some achievement as distinguished from its market·value. Yet even a human achievement which has the greatest value or merit in this sense is not necessarily proof of moral merit on the part of him to whom it is due. It seems that our use has the sanction of philosophical tradition. Cf., for instance, D. Hume, *Treatise,* II, 252: "The external performance has no merit. We must look within to find the moral quality. . . . The ultimate object of our praise and approbation is the motive, that produc'd them."

13. Cf. the important essay by A. A. Alchian, "Uncertainty, Evolution, and Economic Theory," *J. P. E.,* L VIII (1950), esp. 213–14, Sec. II, headed "Success Is Based on Results, Not Motivation." It probably is also no accident that the American economist who has done most to advance our understanding of a free society, F. H. Knight, began his professional career with a study of *Risk, Uncertainty, and Profit.* Cf. also B. de Jouvenel, *Power* (London, 1948), p. 298.

14. It is often maintained that justice requires that remuneration be proportional to the unpleasant-ness of the job and that for this reason the street cleaner or the sewage worker ought to be paid more than the doctor or office worker. This, indeed, would seem to be the consequence of the principle of remuneration according to merit (or "distributive justice"). In a market such a result would come about only if all people were equally skillful in all jobs so that those who could earn as much as others in the more pleasant occupations would have to be paid more to undertake the distaseful ones. In the actual world those unpleasant jobs provide those whose usefulness in the more attractive jobs is small an opportunity to earn more than they could elsewhere. That persons who have little to offer their fellows should be able to earn an income similar to that of the rest only at a much greater sacrifice is inevitable in any arrangement under which the individual is allowed to choose his own sphere of usefulness.

15. Cf. Crosland, *op. cit.,* p. 235: "Even if all the failures could be convinced that they had an equal chance, their discontent would still not be assuaged; indeed it might actually be intensified. When opportunities are known to be unequal, and the selection clearly biased toward wealth or lineage, people can comfort themselves for failure by saying that they never had a proper chance—the system was unfair, the scales too heavily weighted against them. But if the selection is obviously by merit, this source of comfort disappears, and failure induces a total sense of inferiority, with no excuse or consolation; and this, by a natural quirk of human nature, actually increases the envy and resentment at the success of others." Cf. also chap. xxiv, at n. 8. I have not yet seen Michael Young, *The Rise of the Meritocracy* (London, 1958), which, judging from reviews, appears to bring out these problems very clearly.

16. See the interesting discussion in R. G. Collingwood, "Economics as a Philosophical Science," *Ethics,* Vol. XXXVI (1926), who concludes (p. 174): "A just price, a just wage, a just rate of interest, is a contradiction in terms. The question what a person ought to get in return for his goods and labor is a question absolutely devoid of meaning. The only valid questions are what he *can* get in return for his goods or labor, and whether he ought to sell them at all."

17. It is, of course, possible to give the distinction between "earned" and "unearned" incomes, gains, or increments a fairly precise legal meaning, but it then rapidly ceases to correspond to the moral distinction which provides its justification. Any serious attempt to apply the moral distinction in practice soon meets the same insuperable difficulties as any attempt to assess subjective merit. How little these difficulties are generally understood by philosophers (except in rare instances, as that quoted in the preceding note) is well illustrated by a discussion in L. S. Stebbing, *Thinking to Some Purpose* ("Pelican Books" [London, 1939]), p. 184, in which, as an illustration of a distinction which is clear but not sharp, she chooses that between "legitimate" and "excess" profits and asserts: "The distinction is clear between 'excess profits' (or 'profiteer-ing') and 'legitimate profits,' although it is not a sharp distinction."

2

The Libertarian Manifesto

JOHN HOSPERS

The political philosophy that is called libertarianism (from the Latin *libertas,* liberty) is the doctrine that every person is the owner of his own life, and that no one is the owner of anyone else's life: and that consequently every human being has the right to act in accordance with his own choices, unless those actions infringe on the equal liberty of other human beings to act in accordance with their choices.

There are several other ways of stating the same libertarian thesis:

1. *No one is anyone else's master, and no one is anyone else's slave.* Since I am the one to decide how my life is to be conducted just as you decide about yours, I have no right (even if I had the power) to make you my slave and be your master, nor have you the right to become the master by enslaving me. Slavery is *forced* servitude, and since no one owns the life of anyone else, no one has the right to enslave another. Political theories past and present have traditionally been concerned with who should be the master (usually the king, the dictator, or government bureaucracy) and who should be the slaves, and what the extent of the slavery should be. Libertarianism holds that no one has the right to use force to enslave the life of another, or any portion or aspect of that life.

2. *Other men's lives are not yours to dispose of.* I enjoy seeing operas; but operas are expensive to produce. Opera-lovers often say, "The state (or the city, etc.) should subsidize opera, so that we can all see it. Also it would be for people's betterment,

From "What Libertarianism Is," in *The Libertarian Alternative,* edited by Tibor Machan (1974). Reprinted by permission of Nelson–Hall Inc.

cultural benefit, etc." But what they are advocating is nothing more or less than legalized plunder. They can't pay for the productions themselves, and yet they want to see opera, which involves a large number of people and their labor; so what they are saying in effect is, "Get the money through legalized force. Take a little bit more out of every worker's paycheck every week to pay for the operas we want to see." But I have no right to take by force from the workers' pockets to pay for what I want.

Perhaps it would be better if he *did* go to see opera—then I should try to convince him to go voluntarily. But to take the money from him forcibly, because in my opinion it would be good for *him,* is still seizure of his earnings, which is plunder.

Besides, if I have the right to force him to help pay for my pet projects, hasn't he equally the right to force me to help pay for his? Perhaps he in turn wants the government to subsidize rock-and-roll, or his new car, or a house in the country? If I have the right to milk him, why hasn't he the right to milk me? If I can be a moral cannibal, why can't he too?

We should beware of the inventors of utopias. They would remake the world according to their vision—with the lives and fruits of the labor of *other* human beings. Is it someone's utopian vision that others should build pyramids to beautify the landscape? Very well, then other men should provide the labor; and if he is in a position of political power, and he can't get men to do it voluntarily, then he must *compel* them to "cooperate"—i.e. he must enslave them.

A hundred men might gain great pleasure from beating up or killing just one insignificant human being; but other men's lives are not theirs to dispose of. "In order to achieve the worthy goals of the next five-year-plan, we must forcibly collectivize the peasants . . ."; but other men's lives are not theirs to dispose of. Do you want to occupy, rent-free, the mansion that another man has worked for twenty years to buy? But other men's lives are not yours to dispose of. Do you want operas so badly that everyone is forced to work harder to pay for their subsidization through taxes? But other men's lives are not yours to dispose of. Do you want to have free medical care at the expense of other people, whether they wish to provide it or not? But this would require them to work longer for you whether they want to or not, and other men's lives are not yours to dispose of. . . .

3. *No human being should be a nonvoluntary mortgage on the life of another.* I cannot claim your life, your work, or the products of your effort as mine. The fruit of one man's labor should not be fair game for every freeloader who comes along and demands it as his own. The orchard that has been carefully grown, nurtured, and harvested by its owner should not be ripe for the plucking for any bypasser who has a yen for the ripe fruit. The wealth that some men have produced should not be fair game for looting by government, to be used for whatever purposes its representatives determine, no matter what their motives in so doing may be. The theft of your money by a robber is not justified by the fact that he used it to help his injured mother.

It will already be evident that libertarian doctrine is embedded in a view of the rights of man. Each human being has the right to live his life as he chooses, compatibly with the equal right of all other human beings to live their lives as they choose.

All man's rights are implicit in the above statement. Each man has the right to life: any attempt by others to take it away from him, or even to injure him, violates this right, through the use of coercion against him. Each man has the right to liberty: to conduct his life in accordance with the alternatives open to him without coercive action by others. And every man has the right to property: to work to sustain his life (and the lives of whichever others he chooses to sustain, such as his family) and to retain the fruits of his labor.

People often defend the rights of life and liberty but denigrate property rights, and yet the right to property is as basic as the other two: indeed, without property rights no other rights are possible. Depriving you of property is depriving you of the means by which you live. . . .

I have no right to decide how *you* should spend your time or your money. I can make that decision for myself, but not for you, my neighbor. I may deplore your choice of life-style, and I may talk with you about it provided you are willing to listen to me. But I have no right to use force to change it. Nor have I the right to decide how you should spend the money you have earned. I may appeal to you to give it to the Red Cross, and you may prefer to go to prize-fights. But that is your decision, and however much I may chafe about it I do not have the right to interfere forcibly with it, for example by robbing you in order to use the money in accordance with *my* choices. (If I have the right to rob you, have you also the right to rob me?)

When I claim a right, I carve out a niche, as it were, in my life, saying in effect, "This activity I must be able to perform without interference from others. For you and everyone else, this is off limits." And so I put up a "no trespassing" sign, which marks off the area of my right. Each individual's right is his "no traspassing" sign in relation to me and others. I may not encroach upon his domain any more than he upon mine, without my consent. Every right entails a duty, true—but the duty is only that of *forbearance*—that is, of *refraining* from violating the other person's right. If you have a right to life, I have no right to take your life; if you have a right to the products of your labor (property), I have no right to take it from you without your consent. The nonviolation of these rights will not guarantee you protection against natural catastrophes such as floods and earthquakes, but it will protect you against the aggressive activities *of other men.* And rights, after all, have to do with one's relations to other human beings, not with one's relations to physical nature.

Nor were these rights created by government; governments—some governments, obviously not all—*recognize* and *protect* the rights that individuals already have. Governments regularly forbid homicide and theft; and, at a more advanced stage, protect individuals against such things as libel and breach of contract. . . .

The *right to property* is the most misunderstood and unappreciated of human rights, and it is one most constantly violated by governments. "Property" of course does not mean only real estate; it includes anything you can call your own—your clothing, your car, your jewelry, your books and papers.

The right of property is not the right to just *take* it from others, for this would interfere with *their* property rights. It is rather the right to work for it, to obtain non-coercively, the money or services which you can present in voluntary exchange.

The right to property is consistently underplayed by intellectuals today, sometimes even frowned upon, as if we should feel guilty for upholding such a right in view of all the poverty in the world. But the right to property is abolutely basic. It is your hedge against the future. It is your assurance that what you have worked to earn will still be there and be yours, when you wish or need to use it, especially when you are too old to work any longer.

Government has always been the chief enemy of the right to property. The officials of government, wishing to increase their power, and finding an increase of wealth an effective way to bring this about, seize some or all of what a person has earned—and since government has a monopoly of physical force within the geographical area of the nation, it has the power (but not the right) to do this. When this happens, of course, every citizen of that country is insecure: he knows that no matter how hard he works the government can swoop down on him at any time and confiscate his earnings and possessions. A person sees his life savings wiped out in a moment when the tax-collectors descend to deprive him of the fruits of his work; or, an industry which has been fifty years in the making and cost millions of dollars and millions of hours of time and planning, is nationalized overnight. Or the government, via inflation, cheapens the currency, so that hard-won dollars aren't worth anything any more. The effect of such actions, of course, is that people lose hope and incentive: if no matter how hard they work the government agents can take it all away, why bother to work at all, for more than today's needs? Depriving people of property is *depriving them of the means by which they live*—the freedom of the individual citizen to do what he wishes with his own life and to plan for the future. Indeed only if property rights are respected is there any point to planning for the future and working to achieve one's goals. *Property rights are what makes long-range planning possible*—the kind of planning which is a distinctively human endeavor, as oppposed to the day-by-day activity of the lion who hunts, who depends on the supply of game tomorrow but has no real insurance against starvation in a day or a week. Without the right to property, the right to life itself amounts to little: how can you sustain your life if you cannot plan ahead? and how can you plan ahead if the fruits of your labor can at any moment by confiscated by government? . . .

Indeed, the right to property may well be considered second only to the right to life. Even the freedom of speech is limited by considerations of property. If a person visiting in your home behaves in a way undesired by you, you have every right to evict him; he can scream or agitate elsewhere if he wishes, but not in your home without your consent. Does a person have a right to shout obscenities in a cathedral? No, for the owners of the cathedral (presumably the Church) have not allowed others on their property for that purpose; one may go there to worship or to visit, but not just for any purpose one wishes. Their property right is prior to your or my wish to scream or expectorate or write graffiti on their building. Or, to take the stock example, does a person have a right to shout "Fire!" falsely in a crowded theater? No, for the theater owner has permitted others to enter and use his property only for a specific purpose, that of seeing a film or watching a stage show. If a person heckles or otherwise disturbs other members of the audience, he can be thrown out. (In fact, he can be removed for any reason the owner chooses, provided his admission money is returned.) And if he shouts "Fire!" when there is no fire, he may be endangering other lives by causing a panic or a stampede. The right to free speech doesn't give one the right to say anything anywhere; it is circumscribed by property rights.

Again, some people seem to assume that the right to free speech (including written speech) means that they can go to a newspaper publisher and demand that he print in his newspaper some propaganda or policy statement for their political party (or other group). But of course they have no right to the use of his newspaper. Ownership of the newspaper is the product of his labor, and he has a right to put into his newspaper whatever he wants, for whatever reason. If he excludes material which many readers would like to have in, perhaps they can find it in another newspaper or persuade him to print it himself (if there are enough of them, they will usually do just that). Perhaps they can even cause his newspaper to fail. But as long as he owns it, he has the right to put in it what he wishes; what would a property right be if he could not do this? They have no right to place their material in his newspaper without his consent—not for free, nor even for a fee. Perhaps other newspapers will include it, or perhaps they can start their own newspaper (in which case they have a right to put in it what they like). If not, an option open to them would be to mimeograph and distribute some handbills.

In exactly the same way, no one has a right to "free television time" unless the owner of the television station consents to give it; it is his station, he has the property rights over it, and it is for him to decide how to dispose of his time. He may not decide wisely, but it is his right to decide as he wishes. If he makes enough unwise decisions, and courts enough unpopularity with the viewing public or the sponsors, he may have to go out of business; but as he is free to make his own decisions, so is he free to face their consequences. (If the government owns the television station, then government officials will make the decisions, and there is no guarantee of *their* superior wisdom. The difference is that when "the government" owns the station, you are forced to help pay for its upkeep through your taxes, whether the bureaucrat in charge decides to give you television time or not.)

"But why have *individual* property rights? Why not have lands and houses owned by everybody together?" Yes, this involves no violation of individual rights, as long as everybody consents to this arrangement and no one is forced to join it. The parties to it may enjoy the communal living enough (at least for a time) to overcome certain inevitable problems: that some will work and some not, that some will achieve more in an hour than others can do in a day, and still they will all get the same income. The few who do the most will in the end consider themselves "workhorses" who do the work of two or three or twelve, while the others will be "freeloaders" on the efforts of these few. But as long as they can get out of the arrangement if they no longer like it, no violation of rights is involved. They got in voluntarily, and they can get out voluntarily; no one had used force.

"But why not say that everybody owns everything? That we *all* own everything there is?"

To some this may have a pleasant ring—but let us try to analyze what it means.

If everybody owns everything, then everyone has an equal right to go everywhere, do what he pleases, take what he likes, destroy if he wishes, grow crops or burn them, trample them under, and so on. Consider what it would be like in practice. Suppose you have saved money to buy a house for yourself and your family. Now suppose that the principle, "everybody owns everything," becomes adopted. Well then, why shouldn't every itinerant hippie just come in and take over, sleeping in your beds and eating in your kitchen and not bothering to replace the food supply or clean up the mess? After all, it belongs to all of us, doesn't it? So we have just as much right to it as you, the buyer, have. What happens if we *all* want to sleep in the bedroom and there's not room for all of us? Is it the strongest who wins?

What would be the result? Since no one would be responsible for anything, the property would soon be destroyed, the food used up, the facilities nonfunctional. Beginning as a house that *one* family could use, it would end up as a house that *no one* could use. And if the principle continued to be adopted, no one would build houses any more—or anything else. What for? They would only be occupied and used by others, without remuneration.

Suppose two men are cast ashore on an island, and they agree that each will cultivate half of it. The first man is industrious and grows crops and builds a shelter, making the most of the situation with which he is confronted. The second man, perhaps thinking that the warm days will last forever, lies in the sun, picks coconuts while they last, and does a minimum of work to sustain himself. At the time of harvest, the second man has nothing to harvest, nor does he assist the first man in his labors. But later when there is a dearth of food on the island, the second man comes to the first man and demands half of the harvest as his right. But of course he has no right to the product of the first man's labors. The first man may freely choose to give part of his harvest to the second out of charity rather than see him starve; but that is just what it is—charity, not the second man's right.

How can any of man's rights be violated? Ultimately, only by the use of force. I can make suggestions to you, I can reason with you, entreat you (if you are willing to listen), but I cannot *force* you without violating your rights; only by forcing you do I cut the cord between your free decisions and your actions. Voluntary relations between individuals involve no deprivation of rights, but murder, assault, and rape do, because in doing these things I make you the unwilling victim of my actions. A man's beating his wife involves no violation of rights if she *wanted* to be beaten. *Force is behavior that requires the unwilling involvement of other persons.*

Thus the use of force need not involve the use of physical violence. If I trespass on your property or dump garbage on it, I am violating your property rights, as indeed I am when I steal your watch; although this is not force in the sense of violence, it *is* a case of your being an unwilling victim of my action. Similarly, if you shout at me so that I cannot be heard when I try to speak, or blow a siren in my ear, or start a factory next door which pollutes my land, you are again violating my rights (to free speech, to property); I am, again, an unwilling victim of your actions. Similarly, if you steal a manuscript of mine and publish it as your own, you are confiscating a piece of my property and thus violating my right to keep what is the product of my labor. Of course, if I give you the manuscript with permission to sign your name to it and keep the proceeds, no violation of rights is involved—any more than if I give you permission to dump garbage on my yard.

According to libertarianism, the role of government should be limited to the retaliatory use of force against those who have initiated its use. It should not enter into any other areas, such as religion, social organization, and economics.

Government

Government is the most dangerous institution known to man. Throughout history it has violated the rights of men more than any individual or group of individuals could do: it has killed people, enslaved them, sent them to forced labor and concentration camps, and regularly robbed and pillaged them of the fruits of their expended labor. Unlike individual criminals, government has the power to arrest and try; unlike individual criminals, it can surround and encompass a person totally, dominating every aspect of one's life, so that one has no recourse from it but to leave the country (and in totalitarian nations even that is prohibited). Government throughout history has a much sorrier record than any individual, even that of a ruthless mass murderer. The signs we see on bumper stickers are chillingly accurate: "Beware: the Government Is Armed and Dangerous."

The only proper role of government, according to libertarians, is that of the protector of the citizen against aggression by other individuals. The government, of course, should never initiate aggression; its proper role is as the embodiment of the *retaliatory* use of force against anyone who initiates its use.

If each individual had constantly to defend himself against possible aggressors, he would have to spend a considerable portion of his life in target practice, karate exercises, and other means of self-defense, and even so he would probably be helpless against groups of individuals who might try to kill, maim, or rob him. He would have little time for cultivating those qualities which are essential to civilized life, nor would improvements in science, medicine, and the arts be likely to occur. The function of government is to take this responsibility off his shoulders: the government undertakes to defend him against aggressors and to punish them if they attack him. When the government is effective in doing this, it enables the citizen to go about his business unmolested and without constant fear for his life. To do this, of course, government must have physical power—the police, to protect the citizen from aggression within its borders, and the armed forces, to protect him from aggressors outside. Beyond that, the government should not intrude upon his life, either to run his business, or adjust his daily activities, or prescribe his personal moral code.

Government, then, undertakes to be the individual's protector; but historically governments have gone far beyond this function. Since they already have the physical power, they have not hesitated to use it for purposes far beyond that which was entrusted to them in the first place. Undertaking initially to protect its citizens against aggression, it has often itself become an aggressor—a far greater aggressor, indeed, than the criminals against whom it was supposed to protect its citizens.

Governments have done what no private citizen can do: arrrest and imprison individuals without a trial and send them to slave labor camps. Government must have power in order to be effective—and yet the very means by which alone it can be effective make it vulnerable to the abuse of power, leading to managing the lives of individuals and even inflicting terror upon them.

What then should be the function of government? In a word, the *protection of human rights.*

1. *The right to life:* libertarians support all such legislation as will protect human beings against the use of force by others, for example, laws against killing, attempting killing, maiming, beating, and all kinds of physical violence.
2. *The right to liberty:* there should be no laws compromising in any way freedom of speech, of the press, and peaceable assembly. There should be no censorship of ideas, books, films, or of anything else by government.
3. *The right to property:* libertarians support legislation that protects the property rights of individuals against confiscation, nationalization, eminent domain, robbery, trespass, fraud and misrepresentation, patent and copyright, libel and slander.

Someone has violently assaulted you. Should he be legally liable? Of course. He has violated one of your rights. He has knowingly injured you and since he has initiated aggression against you he should be made to expiate.

Someone has negligently left his bicycle on the sidewalk where you trip over it in the dark and injure yourself. He didn't do it intentionally; he didn't mean you any harm. Should he be legally liable? Of course; he has, however unwittingly, injured you, and since the injury is caused by him and you are the victim, he should pay.

Someone across the street is unemployed. Should you be taxed extra to pay for his expenses? Not at all. You have not injured him, you are not responsible for the fact that he is unemployed (unless you are a senator or bureaucrat who agitated for further curtailing of business, which legislation passed, with the result that your neighbor was laid off by the curtailed business). You may voluntarily wish to help him out, or better still, try to get him a job to put him on his feet again; but since you have initiated no aggressive act against him, and neither purposely nor accidentally injured him in any way, you should not be legally penalized for the fact of his unemployment. (Actually, it is just such penalties that increase unemployment.)

One man, A, works hard for years and finally earns a high salary as a professional man. A second man, B, prefers not to work at all, and to spend wastefully what money he has (through inheritance), so that after a year or two he has nothing left. At the end of this time he has a long siege of illness and lots of medical bills to pay. He demands that the bills be paid by the government—that is, by the taxpayers of the land, including Mr. A.

But of course B has no such right. He chose to lead his life in a certain way—that was his voluntary decision. One consequence of that choice is that he must depend on charity in case of later need. Mr. A chose not to live that way. (And if everyone lived like Mr. B, on whom would he depend in case of later need?) Each has a right to live in the way he pleases, but each must live with the consequences of his own decision (which, as always, fall primarily on himself). He cannot, in time of need, claim A's beneficence as his right.

If a house-guest of yours starts to carve his initials in your walls and break up your furniture, you have a right to evict him, and call the police if he makes trouble. If someone starts to destroy the machinery in a factory, the factory-owner is also entitled to evict him and call the police. In both cases, persons other than the owner are permitted on the property only under certain conditions, at the pleasure of the owner. If those conditions are violated, the owner is entitled to use force to set things straight. The case is exactly the same on a college or university campus: if a campus demonstrator starts breaking windows, occupying the president's office, and setting fire to a dean, the college authorities are certainly within their rights to evict him forcibly; one is permitted on the college grounds only under specific conditions, set by the administration: study, peaceful student activity, even political activity if those in charge choose to permit it. If they do not choose to permit peaceful political activity on campus, they may be unwise, since a campus is after all a place where all sides of every issue should get discussed, and the college that doesn't permit this may soon lose its reputation and its students. All the same, the college official who does not permit it is quite within his rights; the students do not own the campus, nor do the hired troublemakers imported from elsewhere. In the case of a privately owned college, the owners, or whoever they have delegated to administer it, have the right to make the decisions as to who shall be permitted on the campus and under what conditions. In the case of a state university or college, the ownership problem is more complex: one could say that the "government" owns the campus or that "the people" do since they are the taxpayers who support it; but in either case, the university administration has the delegated task of keeeping order, and until they are removed by the state administration or the taxpayers, it is theirs to decide who shall be permitted on campus, and what nonacademic activities will be permitted to their students on the premises.

Property rights can be violated by physical trespass, of course, or by anyone entering on your property for any reason without your consent. (If you *do* consent to having your neighbor dump garbage on your yard, there is no violation of your rights.) But the physical trespass of a person is only a special case of violation of property rights. Property rights can be violated by sound-waves, in the form of a loud noise, or the sounds of your neighbor's hi-fi set while you are trying to sleep. Such violations of property rights are of course the subject of action in the courts.

But there is another violation of property rights that has not thus far been honored by the courts; this has to do with the effects of *pollution* of the atmosphere.

From the beginnings of modern air pollution, the courts made a conscious decision not to protect, for example, the orchards of farmers from the smoke of nearby factories or locomotives. They said, in effect, to the farmers: yes, your private property is being invaded by this smoke, but we hold that "public policy" is more important than private property, and public policy holds factories and locomotives to be good things. These goods were allowed to override the defense of property rights—with our consequent headlong rush into pollution disaster. The remedy is both "radical" and crystal clear, and it has nothing to do with multibillion dollar palliative programs at the expense of the taxpayers which do not even meet the real issue. The remedy is simply to enjoin anyone from injecting pollutants into the air, and thereby invading the rights of persons and property. Period. The argument that such an injunction prohibition would add to the costs of industrial production is as reprehensible as the pre-Civil War argument that the abolition of slavery would add to the costs of growing cotton, and therefore should not take place. For this means that the polluters are able to impose the high costs of pollution upon those whose property rights they are allowed to invade with impunity.[1]

What about automobiles, the chief polluters of the air? One can hardly sue every automobile owner. But one can sue the manufacturers of automobiles who do not install anti-smog devices on the cars which they distribute—and later (though this is more difficult), owners of individual automobiles if they discard the equipment or do not keep it functional.

The violation of rights does not apply only to air-pollution. If someone with a factory upstream on a river pollutes the river, anyone living downstream from him, finding his water polluted, should be able to sue the owner of the factory. In this way the price of adding the anti-pollutant devices will be the owner's responsibility, and will probably be added to the cost of the products which the factory produces and thus spread around among all consumers, rather than the entire cost being borne by the users of the river in the form of polluted water, with the consequent impossibility of fishing, swimming, and so on. In each case, pollution would be stopped at the source rather than having its ill effects spread around to numerous members of the population.

What about property which you do not work to earn, but which you *inherit* from someone else? Do you have a right to that? You have no right to it until someone decides to give it to you. Consider the man who willed it to you; it was his, he had the right to use and dispose of it as *he* saw fit; and if he decided to give it to you, this is a windfall for you, but it was only the exercise of *his* right. Had the property been seized by the government at the man's death, or distributed among numerous other people designated by the government, it *would* have been a violation of his rights: for he, who worked to earn and sustain it, would not have been able to dispose of it according to his own judgment. If he doesn't have the right to determine who shall have it, who does?

What about the property status of your intellectual activity, such as inventions you may devise and books you write? These, of course, are your property also; they are the products of your mind; you worked at them, you created them. Prior to that, they did not exist. If you worked five years to write a book, and someone stole it and published it as his own, receiving royalties from its sales, he would have stolen your property just as surely as if he had robbed your home. The same is true if someone used and sold without your permission an invention which was the product of your labor and ingenuity.

The role of government with respect to this issue, at least most governments of the Western world, is a proper one: government protects the products of your labor from the moment they materialize. Copyright law protects your writings from piracy. In the United States, one's writings are protected for a period of twenty-seven years, and another twenty-seven if one applies for renewal of the copyright. In most other countries, they are protected for a period of fifty years after the author's death, permitting both himself and his surviving heirs to reap the fruits of his labor. After that they enter the "public domain"—that is, anyone may reprint them without your or your heir's permission. Patent law protects your inventions for a limited period, which varies according to the type of invention. In no case are you forced to avail yourself of this protection; you need not apply for patent or copyright coverage if you do not wish to do so. But the protection of your intellectual property is there, in case you wish to use it.

What about the property status of the airwaves? Here the government's position is far more questionable. The government now claims ownership of the airwaves, leasing them to individuals and corporations. The government renews leases or refuses them depending on whether the programs satisfy authorities in the Federal Communications Commission. The official position is that "we all own the airwaves": but since only one party can broadcast on a certain frequency at a certain time without causing chaos, it is simply a fact of reality that "everyone" cannot use it. In fact the government decides who shall use the airwaves and one courts its displeasure only at the price of a revoked license. One can write without government approval, but one cannot use the airwaves without the approval of government.

What policy should have been observed with regard to the airwaves? Much the same as the policy that was followed in the case of the Homestead Act, when the lands of the American West were opening up for settlement. There was a policy of "first come, first served," with the government parcelling out a certain acreage for each individual who wanted to claim the land as his own. There was no charge for the land, but if a man had not used it and built a dwelling during the first two-year period, it was assumed that he was not homesteading and the land was given to the next man in line. The airwaves too could have been given out on a "first come, first served" basis. The first man who used a given frequency would be its owner, and the government would protect him in the use of it against trespassers. If others wanted to use the same frequency, they would have to buy it from the first man, if he was willing to sell, or try to buy another, just as one now does with the land.

Laws may be classified into three types: (1) laws protecting individuals against themselves, such as laws against fornication and other sexual behavior, alcohol, and drugs; (2) laws protecting individuals against aggressions by other individuals, such as laws against murder, robbery, and fraud; (3) laws requiring people to help one another; for example, all laws which rob Peter to pay Paul, such as welfare.

Libertarians reject the first class of laws totally. Behavior which harms no one else is strictly the individual's own affair. Thus, there should be no laws against becoming intoxicated, since whether or not to become intoxicated is the individual's own decision: but there should be laws against driving while intoxicated, since the drunken driver is a threat to every other motorist on the highway (drunken driving falls into type 2). Similarly, there should be no laws against drugs (except the prohitition of sale of drugs to minors) as long as the taking of these drugs poses no threat to anyone else. Drug addiction is a psychological problem to which no present solution exists. Most of the social harm caused by addicts, other than to themselves, is the result of thefts which they perform in order to continue their habit—and then the *legal* crime is the theft, not the addiction. The actual cost of heroin is about ten cents a shot; if it were legalized, the enormous traffic in illegal sale and purchase of it would stop, as well as the accompanying proselytization to get new addicts (to make more money for the pusher) and the thefts performed by addicts who often require eighty dollars a day just to keep up the habit. Addiction would not stop, but the crimes would: it is estimated that 75 percent of the burglaries in New York City today are performed by addicts, and all these crimes could be wiped out at one stroke though the legalization of drugs. (Only when the taking of drugs could be shown to constitute a threat to *others,* should it be prohibited by law. It is only laws protecting people against *themselves* that libertarians oppose.)

Laws should be limited to the second class only: aggression by individuals against other individuals. These are laws whose function is to protect human beings against encroachment by others; and this, as we have seen, is (according to libertarianism) the sole function of government.

Libertarians also reject the third class of laws totally: no one should be forced by law to help others, not even to tell them the time of day if requested, and certainly not to give them a portion of one's weekly paycheck. Governments, in the guise of humanitarianism, have given to some by taking from others (charging a "handling fee" in the process, which, because of the government's waste and inefficiency, sometimes is several hundred percent). And in so doing they have decreased incentive, violated the rights of individuals and lowered the standard of living of almost everyone.

All such laws constitute what libertarians call *moral cannibalism*. A cannibal in the physical sense is a person who lives off the flesh of other human beings. A *moral cannibal* is one who believes he has a right to live off the "spirit" of other human beings—who believes that he has a moral claim on the productive capacity, time, and effort expended by others.

It has become fashionable to claim virtually everything that one needs or desires as one's *right*. Thus, many people claim that they have a right to a job, the right to free medical care, to free food and clothing, to a decent home, and so on. Now if one asks, apart from any specific context, whether it would be desirable if everyone had these things, one might well say yes. But there is a gimmick attached to each of them: *At whose expense?* Jobs, medical care, education, and so on, don't grow on trees. These are goods and services *produced only by men.* Who then is to provide them, and under what conditions?

If you have a right to a job, who is to supply it? Must an employer supply it even if he doesn't want to hire you? What if you are unemployable, or incurably lazy? (If you say "the government must supply it," does that mean that a job must be created for you which no employer needs done, and that you must be kept in it regardless of how much or little you work?) If the employer is forced to supply it at his expense even if he doesn't need you, then isn't *he* being enslaved to that extent? What ever happened to *his* right to conduct his life and his affairs in accordance with his choices?

If you have a right to free medical care, then, since medical care doesn't exist in nature as wild apples do, some people will have to supply it to you for free: that is, they will have to spend their time and money and energy taking care of you whether they want to or not. What ever happened to *their* right to conduct their lives as they see fit? Or do you have a right to violate theirs? Can there be a right to violate rights?

All those who demand this or that as a "free service" are consciously or unconsciously evading the fact that there is in reality no such thing as free services. All man-made goods and services are the result of human expenditure of time and effort. There is no such thing as "something for nothing" in this world. If you demand something free, you are demanding that other men give their time and effort to you without compensation. If they voluntarily choose to do this, there is no problem; but if you demand that they be *forced* to do it, you are interfering with their right not to do it if they so choose. "Swimming in this pool ought to be free!" says the indignant passerby. What he means is that others should build a pool, others should provide the material, and still others should run it and keep it in functioning order, so that *he* can use it without fee. But what right has he to the expenditure of *their* time and effort? To expect something "for free" is to expect it *to be paid for by others* whether they choose to or not.

Many questions, particularly about economic matters, will be generated by the libertarian account of human rights and the role of government. Should government have a role in assisting the needy, in providing social security, in legislating minimum wages, in fixing prices and putting a ceiling on rents, in curbing monopolies, in erecting tariffs, in guaranteeing jobs, in managing the money supply? To these and all similar questions the libertarian answers with an unequivocal no.

"But then you'd let people go hungry!" comes the rejoinder. This, the libertarian insists, is precisely what would not happen; with the restrictions removed, the economy would flourish as never before. With the controls taken off business, existing enterprises would expand and new ones would spring into existence satisfying more and more consumer needs; millions more people would be gainfully employed instead of subsisting on welfare, and all kinds of research and production, released from the stranglehold of govenment, would proliferate, fulfilling man's needs and desires as never before. It has always been so whenever government has permitted men to be free traders on a free market. But *why* this is so, and how the free market is the best solution to all problems relating to the material aspect of man's life, is another and far longer story.

Note

1. Murray Rothbard, "The Great Ecology Issue," *The Individualist,* 2, no. 2 (Feb. 1970), p. 5.

3

From Liberty to Welfare

JAMES P. STERBA

Libertarians today are deeply divided over whether a night watchman state can be morally justified. Some, like Robert Nozick, hold that a night watchman state would tend to arise by an invisible-hand process if people generally respected each other's Lockean rights.[1] Others, like Murray Rothbard, hold that even the free and informed consent of all the members of a society would not justify such a state.[2] Despite this disagreement, libertarians are strongly united in opposition to welfare rights and the welfare state. According to Nozick, "the state may not use its coercive apparatus for the purpose of getting some citizens to aid others."[3] For Rothbard, "the libertarian position calls for the complete abolition of governmental welfare and reliance on private charitable aid."[4] Here I argue that this libertarian opposition to welfare rights and a welfare state is ill-founded. Welfare rights can be given a libertarian justification, and once this is recognized, a libertarian argument for a welfare state, unlike libertarian arguments for the night watchman state, is both straightforward and compelling. . . .

Libertarians have defended their view in basically two different ways. Some libertarians, following Herbert Spencer, have 1) defined liberty as the absence of constraints, 2) taken a right to liberty to be the ultimate political ideal, and 3) derived all other rights from this right to liberty. Other libertarians, following John Locke, have 1) taken a set of rights, including, typically, a right to life or self-ownership and a right to property, to be the ultimate political ideal, 2) defined liberty as the absence

From *Social Theory and Practice*, vol. 11, no. 3 (fall 1985), pp. 285–305.

of constraints in the exercise of these fundamental rights, and 3) derived all other rights, including a right to liberty, from these fundamental rights.

Each of these approaches has its difficulties. The principal difficulty with the first approach is that unless one arbitrarily restricts what is to count as an interference, conflicting liberties will abound, particularly in all areas of social life.[5] The principal difficulty with the second approach is that as long as a person's rights have not been violated, her liberty would not have been restricted either, even if she were kept in prison for the rest of her days.[6] I don't propose to try to decide between these two approaches. What I do want to show, however, is that on either approach welfare rights and a welfare state are morally required.

Spencerian Libertarianism

Thus suppose we were to adopt the view of those libertarians who take a right to liberty to be the ultimate political ideal. According to this view, liberty is usually defined as follows:

> *The Want Conception of Liberty:* Liberty is being unconstrained by other persons from doing what one wants.

This conception limits the scope of liberty in two ways. First, not all constraints whatever their source count as a restriction of liberty; the constraints must come from other persons. For example, people who are constrained by natural forces from getting to the top of Mount Everest do not lack liberty in this regard. Second, constraints that have their source in other persons, but that do not run counter to an individual's wants, constrain without restricting that individual's liberty. Thus, for people who do not want to hear Beethoven's Fifth Symphony, the fact that others have effectively proscribed its performance does not restrict their liberty, even though it does constrain what they are able to do.

Of course, libertarians may wish to argue that even such constraints can be seen to restrict a person's liberty once we take into account the fact that people normally want, or have a general desire, to be unconstrained by others. But other philosophers have thought that the possibility of such constraints points to a serious defect in this conception of liberty,[7] which can only be remedied by adopting the following broader conception of liberty:

> *The Ability Conception of Liberty:* Liberty is being unconstrained by other persons from doing what one is able to do.

Applying this conception to the above example, we find that people's liberty to hear Beethoven's Fifth Symphony would be restricted even if they did not want to hear it (and even if, perchance, they did not want to be unconstrained by others) since other people would still be constraining them from doing what they are able to do. . . .

Of course, there will be numerous liberties determined by the Ability Conception that are not liberties according to the Want Conception. For example, there will be highly talented students who do not want to pursue careers in philosophy, even though no one constrains them from doing so. Accordingly, the Ability Conception but not the Want Conception would view them as possessing a liberty. And even though such liberties are generally not as valuable as those liberties that are common to both conceptions, they still are of some value, even when the manipulation of people's wants is not at issue.

Yet even if we accept all the liberties specified by the Ability Conception, problems of interpretation still remain. The major problem in this regard concerns what is to count as a constraint. On the one hand, libertarians would like to limit constraints to positive acts (that is, acts of commission) that prevent people from doing what they are otherwise able to do. On the other hand, welfare liberals and socialists interpret constraints to include, in addition, negative acts (that is, of omission) that prevent people from doing what they are otherwise able to do. In fact, this is one way to understand the debate between defenders of "negative liberty" and defenders of "positive liberty." For defenders of negative liberty would seem to interpret constraints to include only positive acts of others that prevent people from doing what they otherwise are able to do, while defenders of positive liberty would seem to interpret constraints to include both positive and negative acts of others that prevent people from doing what they are otherwise able to do.[8]

Suppose we interpret constraints in the manner favored by libertarians to include only positive acts by others that prevent people from doing what they are otherwise able to do, and let us consider a typical conflict situation between the rich and the poor.

In this conflict situation, the rich, of course, have more than enough resources to satisfy their basic needs. By contrast, the poor lack the resources to meet their most basic nutritional needs even though they have tried all the means available to them that libertarians regard as legitimate for acquiring such resources. Under circumstances like these, libertarians usually maintain that the rich should have the liberty to use their resources to satisfy their luxury needs if they so wish. Libertarians recognize that this liberty might well be enjoyed at the expense of the satisfaction of the most basic nutritional needs of the poor. Libertarians just think that a right to liberty always has priority over other political ideals, and since they assume that the liberty of the poor is not at stake in such conflict situations, it is easy for them to conclude that the rich should not be required to sacrifice their liberty so that the basic nutritional needs of the poor may be met.

From a consideration of the liberties involved, libertarians claim to derive a number of more specific requirements, in particular, a right to life, a right to freedom of speech, press and assembly, and a right to property.

Here it is important to observe that the libertarian's right to life is not a right to receive from others the goods and resources necessary for preserving one's life; it is simply a right not to be killed unjustly. Correspondingly, the libertarian's right to property is not a right to receive from others the goods and resources necessary for one's welfare, but rather a right to acquire goods and resources either by initial acquisition or by voluntary agreement.

Rights such as these, libertarians claim, can at best support only a limited role for government. That role is simply to prevent and punish initial acts of coercion—the only wrongful actions for libertarians. And, as we noted before, libertarians are deeply divided over whether a government with even such a limited role, that is, a night watchman state, can be morally justified.

Of course, libertarians would allow that it would be nice of the rich to share their surplus resources with the poor. Nevertheless, according to libertarians, such acts of charity should not be coercively required, because the liberty of the poor is not thought to be at stake in such conflict situations.

In fact, however, the liberty of the poor is at stake in such conflict situations. What is at stake is the liberty of the poor to take from the surplus possessions of the rich what is necessary to satisfy their basic nutritional needs. When libertarians are brought to see that this is the case, they are often genuinely surprised, for they had not previously seen the conflict between the rich and the poor as a conflict of liberties.[9]

When the conflict between the rich and the poor is viewed as a conflict of liberties, we can either say that the rich should have the liberty to use their surplus resources for luxury purposes, or we can say that the poor should have the liberty to take from the rich what they require to meet their basic nutritional needs. If we choose one liberty, we must reject the other. What needs to be determined, therefore, is which liberty is morally preferable: the liberty of the rich or the liberty of the poor.

I submit that the liberty of the poor, which is the liberty to take from the surplus resources of others what is required to meet one's basic nutritional needs, is morally preferable to the liberty of the rich, which is the liberty to use one's surplus resources for luxury purposes. To see that this is the case we need only appeal to one of the most fundamental principles of morality, one that is common to all political perspectives, namely, the "ought" implies "can" principle. According to this principle, people are not morally required to do what they lack the power to do or what would involve so great a sacrifice that it would be unreasonable to ask them to perform such an action.[10] For example, suppose I promised to attend a meeting on Friday, but on Thursday I am involved in a serious car accident which puts me into a coma. Surely it is no longer the case that I ought to attend the meeting now that I lack the power to do so. Or suppose instead that on Thursday I develop a severe case of pneumonia for which I am hospitalized. Surely I could legitimately claim that I no longer ought to attend the meeting on the grounds that the risk to my health involved in attending is a sacrifice that it would be unreasonable to ask me to bear.

Now applying the "ought" implies "can" principle to the case at hand, it seems clear that the poor have it within their power to willingly relinquish such an important liberty as the liberty to take from the rich what they require to meet their basic nutritional needs. Nevertheless, it would be unreasonable to require them to make so great a sacrifice. In the extreme case, it would involve requiring the poor to sit back and starve to death. Of course, the poor may have no real alternative to relinquishing this liberty. To do anything else may involve worse consequences for themselves and their loved ones and may invite a painful death. Accordingly, we may expect that the poor would acquiesce, albeit unwillingly, to a political system that denied them the welfare rights supported by such a liberty, at the same time that we recognize that such a system imposed an unreasonable sacrifice upon the poor—a sacrifice that we could not morally blame the poor for trying to evade.[11] Analogously, we might expect that a woman whose life was threatened would submit to a rapist's demands, at the same time that we recognize the utter unreasonableness of those demands.

By contrast, it would not be unreasonable to require the rich to sacrifice the liberty to meet some of their luxury needs so that the poor can have the liberty to meet their basic nutritional needs. Naturally, we might expect that the rich for reasons of self-interest and past contribution might be disinclined to make such a sacrifice. We might even suppose that the past contribution of the rich provides a good reason for not sacrificing their liberty to use their surplus for luxury purposes. Yet, unlike the poor, the rich could not claim that relinquishing such a liberty involved so great a sacrifice that it would be unreasonable to require them to make it; unlike the poor, the rich could be morally blameworthy for failing to make such a sacrifice.

Consequently, if we assume that however else we specify the requirements of morality, they cannot violate the "ought" implies "can" principle, it follows that, despite what libertarians claim, the right to liberty endorsed by libertarians actually favors the liberty of the poor over the liberty of the rich.

Yet couldn't libertarians object to this conclusion, claiming that it would be unreasonable to require the rich to sacrifice the liberty to meet some of their luxury needs so that the poor could have the liberty to meet their basic nutritional needs? As I have pointed out, libertarians don't usually see the situation as a conflict of liberties, but suppose they did. How plausible would such an objection be? Not very plausible at all, I think.

Consider this: what are libertarians going to say about the poor? Isn't it clearly unreasonable to require the poor to sacrifice the liberty to meet their basic nutritional needs so that the rich can have the liberty to meet their luxury needs? Isn't it clearly unreasonable to require the poor to sit back and starve to death? If it is, then there is no resolution of this conflict that would be reasonable to require both the rich and the poor to accept. But that would mean that the libertarian ideal of liberty cannot be a moral ideal that resolves conflicts of interest in ways that it would be reasonable to require everyone affected to accept. Therefore, as long as libertarians think of themselves as putting forth such a moral ideal, they cannot allow that it would be unreasonable both to require the rich to sacrifice the liberty to meet some of their luxury needs in order to benefit the poor and to require the poor to sacrifice the liberty to meet their basic nutritional needs in order to benefit the rich. But I submit that if one of these requests is to be judged reasonable, then, by any neutral assessment, it must be the requirement that the rich sacrifice the liberty to meet some of their luxury needs so that the poor can have the liberty to meet their basic nutritional needs; there is no other plausible resolution, if libertarians intend to be putting forth a moral ideal that reasonably resolves conflicts of interest.

But might not libertarians hold that putting forth a moral ideal means no more than being willing to universalize one's fundamental commitments? Surely we have no difficulty imagining the rich willing to universalize their commitments to relatively strong property rights. Yet, at the same time, we have no difficulty imagining the poor and their advocates willing to universalize their commitments to relatively weak property rights. Consequently, if the libertarian's moral ideal is interpreted in this fashion, it would not be able to provide a basis for reasonably resolving conflicts of interest between the rich and the poor. But without such a basis for conflict resolution, how could societies flourish, as libertarians claim they would, under a minimal state or with no state at all?[12] Surely, in order for societies to flourish in this fashion, the libertarian ideal must resolve conflicts of interest in ways that it would be reasonable to require everyone affected to accept. But, as we have seen, that requirement can only be satisfied if the rich sacrifice the liberty to meet some of their luxury needs so that the poor can have the liberty to meet their basic nutritional needs.

It should also be noted that this case for restricting the liberty of the rich depends upon the willingness of the poor to take advantage of whatever opportunities are available to them for satisfying their basic needs by engaging in mutually beneficial work, so that failure of the poor to take advantage of such opportunities would normally either cancel or at least significantly reduce the obligation of the rich to restrict their own liberty for the benefit of the poor.[13] In addition, the poor would be required to return the equivalent of any surplus possessions they have taken from the rich once they are able to do so and still satisfy their basic needs. Nor would the poor be required to keep the liberty to which they are entitled. They could give up part of it, or all of it, or risk losing it on the chance of gaining a greater share of liberties or other social goods.[14] Consequently, the case for restricting the liberty of the rich for the benefit of the poor is neither unconditional nor inalienable.

Even so, libertarians would have to be disconcerted about what turns out to be the practical upshot of taking a right to liberty to be the ultimate political ideal. For libertarians contend that their political ideal would support welfare rights only when constraints are "illegitimately" interpreted to induce both positive and negative acts by others that prevent people from doing what they are otherwise able to do. By contrast, when constraints are interpreted to include only positive acts, libertarians contend, no such welfare rights can be justified.

Nevertheless, what the foregoing argument demonstrates is that this view is mistaken. For even when the interpretation of constraints favored by libertarians is employed, a moral assessment of the competing liberties still requires an allocation of liberties to the poor that will be generally sufficient to provide them with the goods and resources necessary for satisfying their basic nutritional needs.

One might think that once the rich realize that the poor should have the liberty not to be interfered with when taking from the surplus possessions of the rich what they require to satisfy their basic needs, it would be in the interest of the rich to stop producing any surplus whatsoever. Yet that would only be the case if first, the recognition of the rightful claims of the poor would exhaust the surplus of the rich and second, the poor would never be in a position to be obligated to repay what they appropriated from the rich. Fortunately for the poor both of these conditions are unlikely to obtain.

Of course, there will be cases where the poor fail to satisfy their basic nutritional needs, not because of any direct restriction of liberty on the part of the rich, but because the poor are in such dire need that they are unable even to attempt to take from the rich what they require to meet their basic nutritional needs. Accordingly, in such cases, the rich would not be performing any act of commission that prevents the poor from taking what they require. Yet, even in such cases, the rich would normally be performing acts of commission that prevent other persons from aiding the poor by taking from the surplus possessions of the rich. And when assessed from a moral point of view, restricting the liberty of these other persons would not be morally justified for the very same reason that restricting the liberty of the poor to meet their own basic nutritional needs would not be morally justified: it would not be reasonable to ask all of those affected to accept such a restriction of liberty. . . .

In brief, what this shows is that if a right to liberty is taken to be the ultimate political ideal, then, contrary to what libertarians claim, not only would a system of welfare rights be morally required, but also such a system would clearly benefit the poor.

Lockean Libertarianism

Yet suppose we were to adopt the view of those libertarians who do not take a right to liberty to be the ultimate political ideal. According to this view, liberty is defined as follows:

> *The Rights Conception of Liberty.* Liberty is being unconstrained by other persons from doing what one has a right to do.

The most important ultimate rights in terms of which liberty is specified are, according to this view, a right to life understood as a right not to be killed unjustly and a right to property understood as a right to acquire goods and resources either by initial acquisition or voluntary agreement. In order to evaluate this view, we must determine what are the practical implications of these rights.

Presumably, a right to life understood as a right not to be killed unjustly would not be violated by defensive measures designed to protect one's person from life-threatening attacks. Yet would this right be violated when the rich prevent the poor from taking what they require to satisfy their basic nutritional needs? Obviously, as a consequence of such preventive actions poor people sometimes do starve to death. Have the rich, then, in contributing to this result, killed the poor, or simply let them die; and, if they have killed the poor, have they done so unjustly?

Sometimes the rich, in preventing the poor from taking what they require to meet their basic nutritional needs, would not in fact be killing the poor, but only causing them to be physically or mentally debilitated. Yet since such preventive acts involve resisting the life-preserving activities of the poor, when the poor do die as a consequence of such acts, it seems clear that the rich would be killing the poor, whether intentionally or unintentionally.

Of course, libertarians would want to argue that such killing is simply a consequence of the legitimate exercise of property rights, and hence, not unjust. But to understand why libertarians are mistaken in this regard, let us appeal again to that fundamental principle of morality, the "ought" implies "can" principle. In this context, the principle can be used to assess two opposing accounts of property rights. According to the first account, a right to property is not conditional upon whether other persons have sufficient opportunities and resources to satisfy their basic needs. This view holds that the initial acquisition and voluntary agreement of some can leave others, through no fault of their own, dependent upon charity for the satisfaction of their most basic needs. By contrast, according to the second account, initial acquisition and voluntary agreement can confer title of property on all goods and resources except those surplus goods and resources of the rich that are required to satisfy the basic needs of those poor who through no fault of their own lack opportunities and resources to satisfy their own basic needs.

Clearly, only the first of these two accounts of property rights would generally justify the killing of the poor as a legitimate exercise of the property rights of the rich. Yet it would be unreasonable to require the poor to accept anything other than some version of the second account of property rights. Moreover, according to the second account, it does not matter whether the poor would actually die or are only physically or mentally debilitated as a result of such acts of prevention. Either result would preclude property rights from arising. Of course, the poor may have no real alternative to acquiescing to a political system modeled after the first account of property rights, even though such a system imposes an unreasonable sacrifice upon them—a sacrifice that we could not blame them for trying to evade. At the same time, although the rich would be disinclined to do so, it would not be unreasonable to require them to accept a political system modeled after the second account of property rights—the account favored by the poor.

Consequently, if we assume that however else we specify the requirements of morality, they cannot violate the "ought" implies "can" principle, it follows that, despite what libertarians claim, the right to life and the right to property endorsed by libertarians actually support a system of welfare rights. . . .

Nevertheless, it might be objected that the welfare rights that have been established against the libertarian are not the same as the welfare rights endorsed by welfare liberals. We could mark this difference by referring to the welfare rights that have been established against the libertarian as "action welfare rights" and referring to the welfare rights endorsed by welfare liberals as both "action and recipient welfare rights." The significance of this difference is that a person's action welfare right can be violated only when other people through acts of commission interfere with a person's exercise of that right, whereas a person's action and recipient welfare right can be violated by such acts of commission and by acts of omission as well. However, this difference will have little practical import. For once libertarians come to recognize the legitimacy of action welfare rights, then in order not to be subject to the poor person's discretion in choosing when and how to exercise her action welfare right, libertarians will tend to favor two morally legitimate ways of preventing the exercise of such rights. First, libertarians can provide the poor with mutually beneficial job opportunities. Second, libertarians can institute adequate recipient welfare rights that would take precedence over the poor's action welfare rights. Accordingly, if libertarians adopt either or both of these ways of legitimately preventing the poor from exercising their action welfare rights, libertarians will end up endorsing the same sort of welfare institutions favored by welfare liberals.

Finally, once a system of welfare rights is seen to follow irrespective of whether one takes a right to liberty or rights to life and property as the ultimate political ideal, the jusification for a welfare state become straightforward and compelling. For while it is at least conceivable that rights other than welfare rights could be adequately secured in a society without the enforcement agencies of a state, it is inconceivable that welfare rights themselves could be adequately secured without such enforcement agencies. Only a welfare state would be able to effectively solve the large-scale coordination problem necessitated by the provision of welfare. Consequently, once a system of welfare rights can be seen to have a libertarian justification, the argument for a welfare state hardly seems to need stating.[15]

Notes

1. Robert Nozick, *Anarchy, State and Utopia* (New York: Basic Books, 1974), Part I.

2. Murray Rothbard, *The Ethics of Liberty* (Atlantic Highlands: Humanities Press, 1982), p. 230.

3. Nozick, *Anarchy, State and Utopia*, p. ix.

4. Murray Rothbard, *For a New Liberty* (New York: Collier Books, 1978), p. 148.

5. See, for example, James P. Sterba, "Neo-Libertarianism," *American Philosophical Quarterly* 15 (1978): 17–19; Ernest Loevinsohn, "Liberty and the Redistribution of Property," *Philosophy and Public Affairs* 6 (1977): 226–39; David Zimmerman, "Coercive Wage Offers," *Philosophy and Public Affairs* 10 (1981): 121–45. To limit what is to count as coercive, Zimmerman claims that in order for P's offer to be coercive

   (I)t must be the case that P does more than merely prevent Q *from taking from* P resources necessary for securing Q's strongly preferred preproposal situation; P must prevent Q *from acting on his own* (or with the help of others) *to produce or procure* the strongly preferred preposal situation.

   But this restriction seems arbitrary, and Zimmerman provides little justification for it. See David Zimmerman, "More on Coercive Wage Offers," *Philosophy and Public Affairs* 12 (1983): 67–68.

6. It might seem that this second approach could avoid this difficulty if a restriction of liberty is understood as the curtailment of one's prima facie rights. But in order to avoid the problem of a multitude of conflicting liberties, which plagues the first approach, the specification of prima facie rights must be such that they only can be overridden when one or more of them is violated. And this may involve too much precision for our notion of prima facie rights.

7. Isaiah Berlin, *Four Essays on Liberty* (New York: Oxford University Press, 1969), pp. XXXVIII–XL.

8. On this point, see Maurice Cranston, *Freedom* (New York: Basic Books, 1953), pp. 52–53; C. B. Macpherson, *Democratic Theory* (Oxford: Oxford University Press, 1973), p. 95; Joel Feinberg,

Rights, Justice and the Bounds of Liberty (Princeton, N. J.: Princeton University Press, 1980), Chapter 1.

9. See John Hospers, *Libertarianism* (Los Angeles: Nash Publishing Co., 1971), Chapter 7.

10. Alvin Goldman, *A Theory of Human Action* (Englewood Cliffs, N. J.: Prentice-Hall, 1970), pp. 208–15; William Frankena, "Obligation and Ability," in *Philosophical Analysis,* edited by Max Black (Ithaca, N.Y.: Cornell University Press, 1950), pp. 157–75.

    Judging from some recent discussions of moral dilemmas by Bernard Williams and Ruth Marcus, one might think that the "ought" implies "can" principle would only be useful for illustrating moral conflicts rather than resolving them. (See Bernard Williams, *Problems of the Self* (Cambridge: Cambridge University Press, 1977), Chapters 11 and 12; Ruth Marcus, "Moral Dilemmas and Consistency," *The Journal of Philosophy* 80 (1980): 121–36. See also Terrance C. McConnell, "Moral Dilemmas and Consistency in Ethics," *Canadian Journal of Philosophy* 18 (1978): 269–87. But this is only true if one interprets the "can" in the principle to exclude only "what a person lacks the power to do." If one interprets the "can" to exclude in addition "what would involve so great a sacrifice that it would be unreasonable to ask the person to do it" then the principle can be used to resolve moral conflicts as well as state them. Nor would libertarians object to this broader interpretation of the "ought" implies "can" principle since they do not ground their claim to liberty on the existence of irresolvable moral conflicts.

11. See James P. Sterba, "Is there a Rationale for Punishment?", *The American Journal of Jurisprudence* 29 (1984): 29–44.

12. As further evidence, notice that those libertarians who justify a minimal state do so on the grounds that such a state would arise from reasonable disagreements concerning the application of libertarian rights. They do not justify the minimal state on the grounds that it would be needed to keep in submission large numbers of people who could not come to see the reasonableness of libertarian rights.

13. Obviously, the employment opportunities offered to the poor must be honorable and supportive of self-respect. To do otherwise would be to offer the poor the opportunity to meet some of their basic needs at the cost of denying some of their other basic needs.

14. The poor cannot, however, give up the liberty to which their children are entitled.

15. Of course, someone might still want to object to welfare states on the grounds that they "force workers to sell their labor" (see G. A. Cohen, "The Structure of Proletarian Unfreedom," *Philosophy and Public Affairs* 12 (1982): 3–33) and subject workers to "coercive wage offers." (See Zimmerman, "Coercive Wage Offers.") But for a defense of at least one form of welfare state against such an objection, see James P. Sterba, "A Marxist Dilemma for Social Contract Theory," *American Philosophical Quarterly* 21 (1981): 51–59.

4

The Nonexistence of Basic Welfare Rights

TIBOR MACHAN

James Sterba and others maintain that we all have the right to "receive the goods and resources necessary for preserving" ourselves. This is not what I have argued human beings have a right to. They have the right, rather, not to be killed, attacked, and deprived of their property—by persons in or outside of government. As Abraham Lincoln put it, "no man is good enough to govern another man, without that other's consent."[1]

Sterba claims that various political outlooks would have to endorse these "rights." He sets out to show, in particular, that welfare rights follow from libertarian theory itself.[2] Sterba wishes to show that *if* Lockean libertarianism is correct, then we all have rights to welfare and equal (economic) opportunity. What I wish to show is that since Lockean libertarianism—as developed in this work—is true, and since the rights to welfare and equal opportunity require their violation, no one has these latter rights. The reason some people, including Sterba, believe otherwise is that they have found some very rare instances in which some citizens could find themselves in circumstances that would require disregarding rights altogether. This would be in situations that cannot be characterized to be "where peace is possible."[3] And every major libertarian thinker from Locke to the present has treated these kinds of cases.[4]

Let us be clear about what Sterba sets out to show. It is that libertarians are philosophically unable to escape the welfare-statist implication of their commitment to negative liberty. This means that despite their belief that they are only supporting

Reprinted from *Individuals and Their Rights* by Tibor Machan by permission of The Open Court Publishing Company, La Salle, Illinois.

the enforceable right of every person not to be coerced by other persons, libertarians must accept, by the logic of their own position, that individuals also possess basic enforceable rights to being provided with various services from others. He holds, then, that basic negative rights imply basic positive rights.

To Lockean libertarians the ideal of liberty means that we all, individually, have the right not to be constrained against our consent within our realm of authority—ourselves and our belongings. Sterba states that for such libertarians "Liberty is being unconstrained by persons from doing what one has a right to do."[5] Sterba adds, somewhat misleadingly, that for Lockean libertarians "a right to life [is] a right not to be killed unjustly and a right to property [is] a right to acquire goods and resources either by initial acquisition or voluntary agreement."[6] Sterba does realize that these rights do not entitle one to receive from others the goods and resources necessary for preserving one's life.

A problem with this foundation of the Lockean libertarian view is that political justice—not the justice of Plato, which is best designated in our time as 'perfect virtue'—for natural-rights theorists presupposes individual rights. One cannot then explain rights in terms of justice but must explain justice in terms of rights.

For a Lockean libertarian, to possess any basic right to receive the goods and resources necessary for preserving one's life conflicts with possessing the right not to be killed, assaulted, or stolen from. The latter are rights Lockean libertarians consider to be held by all individual human beings. Regularly to protect and maintain—that is, enforce—the former right would often require the violation of the latter. A's right to the food she has is incompatible with B's right to take this same food. Both the rights could not be fundamental in an integrated legal system. The situation of one's having rights to welfare, and so forth, and another's having rights to life, liberty, and property is thus theoretically intolerable and practically unfeasible. The point of a system of rights is the securing of mutually peaceful and consistent moral conduct on the part of human beings. As Rand observes,

> "Rights" are . . . the link between the moral code of a man and the legal code of a society, between ethics and politics. *Individual rights are the means of subordinating society to moral law.*[7]

Sterba asks us—in another discussion of his views—to consider what he calls "a *typical* conflict situation between the rich and the poor." He says that in his situation "the rich, of course, have more than enough resources to satisfy their basic needs. By contrast, the poor lack the resources to meet their most basic needs even though *they have tried all the means available to them that libertarians regard as legitimate for acquiring such resources*"[8] (my emphasis).

The goal of a theory of rights would be defeated if rights were typically in conflict. Some bureaucratic group would have to keep applying its moral intuitions on numerous occasions when rights claims would *typically* conflict. A constitution is workable if it helps remove at least the largest proportion of such decisions from the realm of arbitrary (intuitive) choice and avail a society of men and women of objective guidelines that are reasonably integrated, not in relentless discord.

Most critics of libertarianism assume some doctrine of basic needs which they invoke to show that whenever basic needs are not satisfied for some people, while others have "resources" which are not basic needs for them, the former have just claims against the latter. (The language of resources of course loads the argument in the critic's favor since it suggests that these goods simply come into being and happen to be in the possession of some people, quite without rhyme or reason, arbitrarily [as John Rawls claims].).[9]

This doctrine is full of difficulties. It lacks any foundation for why the needs of some persons must be claims upon the lives of others. And why are there such needs anyway—to what end are they needs, and whose ends are these and why are not the persons whose needs they are held responsible for supplying the needs? (Needs, as I have already observed, lack any force in moral argument without the prior justification of the purposes they serve, or the goals they help to fulfil. A thief has a basic need of skills and powers that are clearly not justified if theft is morally unjustified. If, however, the justification of basic needs, such as food and other resources, presupposes the value of human life, and if the value of human life justifies, as I have argued earlier, the principle of the natural rights to life, liberty and property, then the attainment or fulfillment of the basic need for food may not involve the violation of these rights.)

Sterba claims that without guaranteeing welfare and equal-opportunity rights, Lockean libertarianism violates the most basic tenets of any morality, namely, that "ought" implies "can." The thrust of "'ought' implies 'can'" is that one ought to do that which one is free to do, that one is morally responsible only for those acts that one had the power either to choose to engage in or to choose not to engage in. (There is debate on just how this point must be phrased—in terms of the will being free or the person being free to will something. For our purposes, however, all that counts is that the person must have [had] a genuine option to do X or not to do X before it can be true that he or she ought to do X or ought to have done X.) If an innocent person is forced by the actions of another to forgo significant moral choices, then that innocent person is not free to act morally and thus his or her human dignity is violated.

This is not so different from the commonsense legal precept that if one is not sound of mind one cannot be criminally culpable. Only free agents, capable of choosing between right and wrong, are open to moral evaluation. This indeed is the reason that many so-called moral theories fail to be anything more than value theories. They omit from consideration the issue of self-determination. If either hard or soft determinism is true, morality is impossible, although values need not disappear.[10]

If Sterba were correct about Lockean libertarianism typically contradicting "'ought' implies 'can,'" his argument would be decisive. (There are few arguments against this principle that I know of and they have not convinced me. They trade on rare circumstances when persons feel guilt for taking actions that had bad consequences even though they could not have avoided them.)[11] It is because Karl Marx's and Herbert Spencer's systems typically, normally, indeed in every case, violate this principle that they are not bona fide moral systems. And quite a few others may be open to a similar charge.[12]

Sterba offers his strongest argument when he observes that "'ought' implies 'can'" is violated "when the rich prevent the poor from taking what they require to satisfy their basic needs even though they have tried all the means available to them that libertarians regard as legitimate for acquiring such resources."[13]

Is Sterba right that such are—indeed, must be—typical conflict cases in a libertarian society? Are the rich and poor, even admitting that there is some simple division of people into such economic groups, in such hopeless conflict all the time? Even in the case of homeless people, many find help without having to resort to theft. The political factors contributing to the presence of helpless people in the United States and other Western liberal democracies are a hotly debated issue, even among utilitarians and welfare-state supporters. Sterba cannot make his argument for the typicality of such cases by reference to history alone. (Arguably, there are fewer helpless poor in near-libertarian, capitalist systems than anywhere else—why else would virtually everyone wish to live in these societies rather than those where welfare is guaranteed, indeed enforced? Not, at least originally, for their welfare-statist features. Arguably, too, the disturbing numbers of such people in these societies could be due, in part, to the lack of consistent protection of all the libertarian natural rights.)

Nonetheless, in a system that legally protects and preserves property rights there will be cases where a rich person prevents a poor person from taking what belongs to her (the rich person)—for example, a chicken that the poor person might use to feed herself. Since after such prevention the poor person might starve, Sterba asks the rhetorical question, "Have the rich, then, in contributing to this result, killed the poor, or simply let them die; and if they have killed the poor, have they done so unjustly?"[14] His answer is that they have. Sterba holds that a system that accords with the Lockean libertarian's idea that the rich person's preventive action is just "imposes an unreasonable sacrifice upon" the poor, one "that we could not blame them for trying to evade." Not permitting the poor to act to satisfy their basic needs is to undermine the precept that "'ought' implies 'can,'" since, as Sterba claims, that precept means, for the poor, that they ought to satisfy their basic needs. This they must have the option to do if they ought to do it. . . .

When people defend their property, what are they doing? They are protecting themselves against the intrusive acts of some other person, acts that would normally deprive them of something to which they have a right, and the other has no right. As such, these acts of protectiveness make it possible for men and women in society to retain their own sphere of jurisdiction intact, protect their own "moral space."[15] They refuse to have their human dignity violated. They want to be sovereigns and govern their own lives, including their own productive decisions and actions. Those who mount the attack, in turn, fail or refuse to refrain from encroaching upon the moral space of their victims. They are treating the victim's life and its productive results as though these were unowned resources for them to do with as they choose.

Now the argument that cuts against the above account is that on some occasions there can be people who, with no responsibility for their situation, are highly unlikely to survive without disregarding the rights of others and taking from them what they need. This is indeed possible. It is no less possible that there be cases in which someone is highly unlikely to survive without obtaining the services of a doctor who is at that moment spending time healing someone else, or in which there is a person who is highly unlikely to survive without obtaining one of the lungs of another person, who wants to keep both lungs so as to be able to run the New York City marathon effectively. And such cases could be multiplied indefinitely.

But are such cases typical? The argument that starts with this assumption about a society is already not comparable to the libertarianism that has emerged in the footsteps of Lockean natural-rights doctrine, including the version advanced in this book. That system is developed for a human community in which "peace is possible." Libertarian individual rights, which guide men and women in such an adequately hospitable environment to act without thwarting the flourishing of others, are thus suitable bases for the legal foundations for a human society. It is possible for people in the world to pursue their proper goals without thwarting a similar pursuit by others.

The underlying notion of society in such a theory rejects the description of human communities implicit in Sterba's picture. Sterba sees conflict as typically arising from some people producing and owning goods, while others having no alternative but to take these goods from the former in order to survive. But these are not the typical conflict situations even in what we today consider reasonably free human communities—most thieves and robbers are not destitute, nor are they incapable of doing something aside from taking other people's property in order to obtain their livelihood.

The typical conflict situation in society involves people who wish to take shortcuts to earning their living (and a lot more) by attacking others, not those who lack any other alternative to attacking others so as to reach that same goal. This may not be evident from all societies that team with human conflict—in the Middle East, or Central and South America, for example. But it must be remembered that these societies are far from being even near-libertarian. Even if the typical conflicts there involved the kind Sterba describes, that would not suffice to make his point. Only if it were true that in comparatively free countries the typical conflict involved the utterly destitute and helpless arrayed against the well-to-do, could his argument carry any conviction.

The Lockean libertarian has confidence in the willingness and capacity of *virtually all persons* to make headway in life in a free society. The very small minority of exceptional cases must be taken care of by voluntary social institutions, not by the government, which guards self-consistent individual rights.

The integrity of law would be seriously endangered if the government entered areas that required it to make very particular judgments and depart from serving the interest of the public as such. We have already noted that the idea of "satisfying basic needs" can involve the difficulty of distinguishing those whose actions are properly to be so characterized. Rich persons are indeed satisfying their basic needs as they protect and preserve their property rights. . . . Private property rights are necessary for a morally decent society.

The Lockean libertarian argues that private property rights are morally justified in part because they are the concrete requirement for delineating the sphere of jurisdiction of each person's moral authority, where her own judgment is decisive.[16] This is a crucial basis for the right to property. And so is the contention that we live in a metaphysically hospitable universe wherein people normally need not suffer innocent misery and deprivation—so that such a condition is usually the result of negligence or the violation of Lockean rights, a violation that has made self-development and commerce impossible. If exceptional emergencies set the agenda for the law, the law itself will disintegrate. (A just legal system makes provision for coping with emergencies that are brought to the attention of the authorities, for example, by way of judicial discretion, without allowing such cases to determine the direction of the system. If legislators and judges don't uphold the integrity of the system, disintegration ensues. This can itself encourage the emergence of strong leaders, demagogues, who promise to do what the law has not been permitted to do, namely, satisfy people's sense of justice. Experience with them bodes ill for such a prospect.)

Normally persons do not "lack the opportunities and resources to satisfy their own basic needs." Even if we grant that some helpless, crippled, retarded, or destitute persons could offer nothing to anyone that would merit wages enabling them to carry on with their lives and perhaps even flourish, there is still the other possibility for most actual, known hard cases, that is, seeking help. I am not speaking here of the cases we know: people who drop out of school, get an unskilled job, marry and have kids, only to find that their personal choice of inadequate preparation for life leaves them relatively poorly off. "'Ought' implies 'can'" must not be treated ahistorically—some people's lack of current options results from their failure to exercise previous options prudently. I refer here to the "truly needy," to use a shop-worn but still useful phrase—those who have never been able to help themselves and are not now helpless from their own neglect. Are such people being treated *unjustly,* rather than at most uncharitably, ungenerously, indecently, pitilessly, or in some other respect immorally—by those who, knowing of the plight of such persons, resist forcible efforts to take from them enough to provide the ill-fated with what they truly need? Actually, if we tried to pry the needed goods or money from the well-to-do, we would not even learn if they would act generously. Charity, generosity, kindness, and acts of compassion presuppose that those well enough off are not coerced to provide help. These virtues cannot flourish, nor can the corresponding vices, of course, without a clearly identified and well-protected right to private property for all.

If we consider the situation as we are more likely to find it, namely, that desperate cases not caused by previous injustices (in the libertarian sense) are rare, then, contrary to what Sterba suggests, there is much that unfortunate persons can and should do in those plausible, non-emergency situations that can be considered typical. They need not resort to violating the private-property rights of those who are better off. The destitute can appeal for assistance both from the rich and from the many voluntary social service agencies which emerge from the widespread compassion of people who know about the mishaps that can at times strike perfectly decent people.

Consider, as a prototype of this situation on which we might model what concerns Sterba, that if one's car breaks down on a remote road, it would be unreasonable to expect one not to seek a phone or some other way of escaping one's unfortunate situation. So one ought to at least try to obtain the use of a phone.

But should one break into the home of a perfect stranger living nearby? Or ought one instead to request the use of the phone as a favor? "'Ought' implies 'can'" is surely fully satisfied here. Actual practice makes this quite evident. When someone is suffering from misfortune and there are plenty of others who are not, and the unfortunate person has no other avenue for obtaining help than to obtain it from others, it would not be unreasonable to expect, morally, that the poor seek such help as surely might be forthcoming. We have no justification for assuming that the rich are all callous, though this caricature is regularly painted by communists and by folklore. Supporting and gaining advantage from the institution of private property by no means implies that one lacks the virtue of generosity. The rich are no more immune to virtue than the poor are to vice. The contrary view is probably a legacy of the idea that only those concerned with spiritual or intellectual matters can be trusted to know virtue—those concerned with seeking material prosperity are too base.

The destitute typically have options other than to violate the rights of the well-off. "'Ought' implies 'can'" is satisfiable by the moral imperative that the poor ought to seek help, not loot. There is then no injustice in the rich preventing the poor from seeking such loot by violating the right to private property. "'Ought' implies 'can'" is fully satisfied if the poor can take the kind of action that could gain them the satisfaction of their basic needs, and this action could well be asking for help.

All along here I have been considering only the helplessly poor, who through no fault of their own, nor again through any rights violation by others, are destitute. I am taking the hard cases seriously, where violation of "'ought' implies 'can'" would appear to be most probable. But such cases are by no means typical. They are extremely rare. And even rarer are those cases in which all avenues regarded as legitimate from the libertarian point of view have been exhausted, including appealing for help.

The bulk of poverty in the world is not the result of natural disaster or disease. Rather it is political oppression, whereby people throughout many of the world's countries are not legally permitted to look out for themselves in production and trade. The famines in Africa and India, the poverty in the same countries and in Central and Latin America, as well as in China, the Soviet Union, Poland, Rumania, and so forth, are not the result of lack of charity but of oppression. It is the kind that those who have the protection of even a seriously compromised document and system protecting individual negative human rights, such as the U.S. Constitution, do not experience. The first requirement for men and women to ameliorate their hardship is to be free of other people's oppression, not to be free to take other people's belongings.

Of course, it would be immoral if people failed to help out when this was clearly no sacrifice for them. But charity or generosity is not a categorical imperative, even for the rich. There are more basic moral principles that might require the rich to refuse to be charitable—for example, if they are using most of their wealth for the protection of freedom or a just society. Courage can be more important than charity or benevolence or compassion. But a discussion of the ranking of moral virtues would take us far afield. One reason that many critics of libertarianism find their own cases persuasive is that they think the libertarian can only subscribe to *political* principles or values. But this is mistaken.[17]

There can be emergency cases in which there is no alternative available to disregarding the rights of others. But these are extremely rare, and not at all the sort invoked by critics such as Sterba. I have in mind the desert-island case found in ethics books where instantaneous action, with only one violent alternative, faces persons–the sort we know from the law books in which the issue is one of immediate life and death. These are not cases, to repeat the phrase quoted from Locke by H. L. A. Hart, "where peace is possible." They are discussed in the libertarian literature and considerable progress has been made in integrating them with the concerns of law and politics. Since we are here discussing law and politics, which are general systematic approaches to how we normally ought to live with one another in human communities, these emergency situations do not help us except as limiting cases. And not surprisingly many famous court cases illustrate just this point as they now and then confront these kinds of instances after they have come to light within the framework of civilized society. . . .

Notes

1. Quoted in Harry V. Jaffa, *How to Think About the American Revolution* (Durham, NC: Carolina Academic Press, 1978), p. 41 (from *The Collected Works of Abraham Lincoln* [R. Basler (ed.), 1953], pp. 108–115).

2. See, in particular, James Sterba, 'A Libertarian Justification for a Welfare State', *Social Theory and Practice*, vol. 11 (Fall 1985), 285–306. I will be referring to this essay as well as a more developed version, titled 'The U.S. Constitution: A Fundamentally Flawed Document' in *Philosophical Reflections on the United States Constitution,* edited by Christopher Gray (1989).

3. H. L. A. Hart, 'Are There Any Natural Rights?' *Philosophical Review,* vol. 64 (1955), 175.

4. See, for my own discussions, Tibor R. Machan, *Human Rights and Human Liberties* (Chicago: Nelson-Hall, 1975), pp. 213–222; 'Prima Facie versus Natural (Human) Rights', *Journal of Value Inquiry,* vol. 10 (1976), 119–131; 'Human Rights: Some Points of Clarification', *Journal of Critical Analysis,* vol. 5 (1973), 30–39.

5. Sterba, op. cit, 'A Libertarian Justification', p. 295.

6. Ibid.

7. Ayn Rand, 'Value and Rights', in J. Hospers, (ed.), *Readings in Introductory Philosophical Analysis* (Englewood Cliffs, NJ: Prentice-Hall, 1968), p. 382.

8. Sterba, 'The U.S. Constitution: A Fundamentally Flawed Document'.

9. John Rawls, *A Theory of Justice* (Cambridge, MA: Harvard University Press, 1971), pp. 101–02. For a discussion of the complexities in the differential attainments of members of various ethnic groups—often invoked as evidence for the injustice of a capitalist system, see Thomas Sowell, *Ethnic America: A History* (New York: Basic Books, 1981). There is pervasive prejudice in welfare-state proponents' writings against crediting people with the ability to extricate themselves from poverty without special political assistance. The idea behind the right to negative liberty is to set people free from others so as to pursue their progressive goals. This is the

ultimate teleological justification of Lockean libertarian natural rights. See Tibor R. Machan, *Human Rights and Human Liberties: A Radical Reconsideration of the American Political Tradition* (Chicago: Nelson-Hall, 1975). Consider also this thought from Herbert Spencer:

The feeling which vents itself in "poor fellow!" on seeing one in agony, excludes the thought of "bad fellow," which might at another time arise. Naturally, then, if the wretched are unknown or but vaguely known, all the demerits they may have are ignored: and thus it happens that when the miseries of the poor are dilated upon, they are thought of as the miseries of the deserving poor, instead of being thought of as the miseries of undeserving poor, which in large measure they should be. Those whose hardships are set forth in pamphlets and proclaimed in sermons and speeches which echo throughout society, are assumed to be all worthy souls, grievously wronged; and none of them are thought of as bearing the penalties of their own misdeeds. (*Man versus the State* [Caldwell, ID: Caxton Printers, 1940], p. 22)

10. Tibor R. Machan, 'Ethics vs. Coercion: Morality of Just Values?' in L. H. Rockwell, Jr. et al., (ed.), *Man, Economy and Liberty: Essays in Honor of Murray N. Rothbard* (Auburn, AL: Ludwig von Mises Institute, 1988), pp. 236–246.

11. John Kekes, '"Ought Implies Can" and Two Kinds of Morality', *The Philosophical Quarterly*, vol. 34 (1984), 459–467.

12. Tibor R. Machan, 'Ethics vs. Coercion'. In a vegetable garden or even in a forest, there can be good things and bad, but no morally good things and morally evil things (apart from people who might be there).

13. Sterba, 'The U.S. Constitution: A Fundamentally Flawed Document'.

14. Sterba, 'A Libertarian Justification', pp. 295–296.

15. Robert Nozick, *Anarchy, State, and Utopia* (New York: Basic Books, 1974), p. 57. See, also, Tibor R. Machan, 'Conditions for Rights, Sphere of Authority', *Journal of Human Relations*, vol. 19 (1971), 184–187, where I argue that "within the context of a legal system where the *sphere of authority* of individuals and groups of individuals cannot be delineated independently of the sphere of authority of the public as a whole, there is an inescapable conflict of rights specified by the same legal system." (186) See, also, Tibor R. Machan, 'The Virtue of Freedom in Capitalism', *Journal of Applied Philosophy*, vol. 3 (1986), 49–58, and Douglas J. Den Uyl, 'Freedom and Virtue', in Tibor R. Machan (ed.), *The Main Debate: Communism versus Capitalism* (New York: Random House, 1987), pp. 200–216. This last essay is especially pertinent to the understanding of the ethical or moral merits of coercion and coerced conduct. Thus it is argued here that 'coercive charity' amounts to an oxymoron.

16. See, Machan, op. cit., 'The Virtue of Freedom in Capitalism' and 'Private Property and the Decent Society', in J. K. Roth and R. C. Whittemore (eds.), *Ideology and American Experience* (Washington, DC: Washington Institute Press, 1986).

17. E.g. James Fishkin, *Tyranny and Legitimacy* (Baltimore, MD: Johns Hopkins University Press, 1979). Cf., Tibor R. Machan, 'Fishkin on Nozick's Absolute Rights', *Journal of Libertarian Studies*, vol. 6 (1982), 317–320.

■■■□□□

PART III

Socialist Justice

5

The Socialist Ideal

KARL MARX AND
FRIEDRICH ENGELS

A spectre is haunting Europe—the spectre of Communism. All the Powers of old Europe have entered into a holy alliance to exorcise this spectre: Pope and Czar, Metternich and Guizot, French Radicals and German police-spies.

Where is the party in opposition that has not been decried as Communistic by its opponents in power? Where the Opposition that has not hurled back the branding reproach of Communism, against the more advanced opposition parties, as well as against its reactionary adversaries?

Two things result from this fact.

I. Communism is already acknowledged by all European Powers to be itself a Power.

II. It is high time that Communists should openly, in the face of the whole world, publish their views, their aims, their tendencies, and meet this nursery tale of the Spectre of Communism with a Manifesto of the party itself . . .

The Communist Program

The Communists do not form a separate party opposed to other working-class parties.

They have no interests separate and apart from those of the proletariat as a whole.

From the *Communist Manifesto,* first published in English by Friedrich Engels in 1888, and the *Critique of the Gotha Program,* edited by C. P. Dutt (1966), pp. 5–11. Reprinted by permission of International Publishers.

They do not set up any sectarian principles of their own, by which to shape and mould the proletarian movement.

The Communists are distinguished from the other working-class parties by this only: (1) In the national struggles of the proletarians of the different countries, they point out and bring to the front the common interests of the entire proletariat, independently of all nationality. (2) In the various stages of development which the struggle of the working class against the bourgeoisie has to pass through they always and everywhere represent the interests of the movement as a whole.

The Communists, therefore, are on the one hand, practically, the most advanced and resolute section of the working-class parties of every country, that section which pushes forward all others; on the other hand, theoretically, they have over the great mass of the proletariat the advantage of clearly understanding the line of march, the conditions, and the ultimate general results of the proletarian movement.

The immediate aim of the Communists is the same as that of all the other proletarian parties: formation of the proletariat into a class, overthrow of the bourgeois supremacy, conquest of political power by the proletariat.

The theoretical conclusions of the Communists are in no way based on ideas or principles that have been invented, or discovered, by this or that would-be universal reformer.

They merely express, in general terms, actual relations springing from an existing class struggle, from a historical movement going on under our very eyes. The abolition of existing property relations is not at all a distinctive feature of Communism.

All property relations in the past have continually been subject to historical change consequent upon the change in historical conditions.

The French Revolution, for example, abolished feudal property in favour of bourgeois property.

The distinguishing feature of Communism is not the abolition of property generally, but the abolition of bourgeois property. But modern bourgeois private property is the final and most complete expression of the system of producing and appropriating products, that is based on class antagonisms, on the exploitation of the many by the few.

In this sense, the theory of the Communists may be summed up in the single sentence: Abolition of private property.

We Communists have been reproached with the desire of abolishing the right of personally acquiring property as the fruit of man's own labour, which property is alleged to be the groundwork of all personal freedom, activity and independence.

Hard-won, self-acquired, self-earned property! Do you mean the property of the petty artisan and of the small peasant, a form of property that preceded the bourgeois form? There is no need to abolish that; the development of industry has to a great extent already destroyed it, and is still destroying it daily.

Or do you mean modern bourgeois private property?

But does wage-labour create any property for the labourer? Not a bit. It creates capital, *i.e.,* that kind of property which exploits wage-labour, and which cannot increase except upon condition of begetting a new supply of wage-labour for fresh exploitation. Property, in its present form, is based on the antagonism of capital and wage-labour. Let us examine both sides of this antagonism.

To be capitalist, is to have not only a purely personal, but a social *status* in production. Capital is a collective product, and only by the united action of many members, nay, in the last resort, only by the united action of all members of society, can it be set in motion.

Capital is, therefore, not a personal, it is a social power.

When, therefore, capital is converted into common property, into the property of all members of society, personal property is not thereby transformed into social property. It is only the social character of the property that is changed. It loses its class-character.

Let us now take wage-labour.

The average price of wage-labour is the minimum wage, *i.e.,* that quantum of the means of subsistence, which is absolutely requisite to keep the labourer in bare existence as a labourer. What, therefore, the wage-labourer appropriates by means of his labour, merely suffices to prolong and reproduce a bare existence. We by no means intend to abolish this personal appropriation of the products of labour, an appropriation that is made for the maintenance and reproduction of human life, and that leaves no surplus wherewith to command the labour of others. All that we want to do away with, is the miserable character of this appropriation, under which the labourer lives merely to increase capital, and is allowed to live only in so far as the interest of the ruling class requires it.

In bourgeois society, living labour is but a means to increase accumulated labour. In Communist society, accumulated labour is but a means to widen, to enrich, to promote the existence of the labourer.

In bourgeois society, therefore, the past dominates the present; in Communist society, the present dominates the past. In bourgeois society capital is independent and has individuality, while the living person is dependent and has no individuality.

And the abolition of this state of things is called by the bourgeois, abolition of individuality and freedom! And rightly so. The abolition of bourgeois individuality, bourgeois independence, and bourgeois freedom is undoubtedly aimed at.

By freedom is meant, under the present bourgeois conditions of production, free trade, free selling and buying.

But if selling and buying disappears, free selling and buying disappears also. This talk about free selling and buying, and all the other "brave words" of our bourgeoisie about freedom in general, have a meaning, if any, only in contrast with restricted selling and buying, with the fettered traders of the Middle Ages, but have no meaning when opposed to the Communistic abolition of buying and selling, of the bourgeois conditions of production, and of the bourgeoisie itself.

You are horrified at our intending to do away with private property. But in your existing society, private property is already done away with for nine-tenths of the population; its existence for the few is solely due to its non-existence in the hands of those nine-tenths. You reproach us, therefore, with intending to do away with a form of property, the necessary condition for whose existence is the non-existence of any property for the immense majority of society.

In one word, you reproach us with intending to do away with your property. Precisely so; that is just what we intend.

From the moment when labour can no longer be converted into capital, money, or rent, into a social power capable of being monopolised, *i.e.,* from the moment when individual property can no longer be transformed into bourgeois property, into capital, from that moment, you say, individuality vanishes.

You must, therefore, confess that by "individual" you mean no other person than the bourgeois, than the middle-class owner of property. This person must, indeed, be swept out of the way, and made impossible.

Communism deprives no man of the power to appropriate the products of society; all that it does is to deprive him of the power to subjugate the labour of others by means of such appropriation.

It has been objected that upon the abolition of private property all work will cease, and universal laziness will overtake us.

According to this, bourgeois society ought long ago to have gone to the dogs through sheer idleness; for those of its members who work, acquire nothing, and those who acquire anything, do not work. The whole of this objection is but another expression of the tautology: that there can no longer be any wage-labour when there is no longer any capital.

All objections urged against the Communistic mode of producing and appropriating material products, have, in the same way, been urged against the Communistic modes of producing and appropriating intellectual products. Just as, to the bourgeois, the disappearance of class property is the disappearance of production itself, so the disappearance of class culture is to him identical with the disappearance of all culture.

That culture, the loss of which he laments, is, for the enormous majority, a mere training to act as a machine.

But don't wrangle with us so long as you apply, to our intended abolition of bourgeois property, the standard of your bourgeois notions of freedom, culture, law, [and so on]. Your very ideas are but the outgrowth of the conditions of your bourgeois production and bourgeois property, just as your jurisprudence is but the will of your class made into a law for all, a will, whose essential character and direction are determined by the economical conditions of existence of your class.

The selfish misconception that induces you to transform into eternal laws of nature and reason, the social forms springing from your present mode of production and form of property—historical relations that rise and disappear in the progress of production—this misconception you share with every ruling class that has preceded you. What you see clearly in the case of ancient property, what you admit in the case of feudal property, you are of course forbidden to admit in the case of your own bourgeois form of property.

Abolition of the family! Even the most radical flare up at this infamous proposal of the Communists.

On what foundation is the present family, the bourgeois family, based? On capital, on private gain. In its completely developed form this family exists only among the bourgeoisie. But this state of things finds its complement in the practical absence of the family among the proletarians, and in public prostitution.

The bourgeois family will vanish as a matter of course when its complement vanishes, and both will vanish with the vanishing of capital.

Do you charge us with wanting to stop the exploitation of children by their parents? To this crime we plead guilty.

But, you will say, we destroy the most hallowed of relations, when we replace home education by social.

And your education! Is not that also social, and determined by the social conditions under which you educate, by the intervention, direct or indirect, of society, by means of schools, [and so on]? The Communists have not invented the intervention of society in education; they do but seek to alter the character of that intervention, and to rescue education from the influence of the ruling class.

The bourgeois clap-trap about the family and education, about the hallowed co-relation of parent and child, becomes all the more disgusting, the more, by the action of Modern Industry, all family ties among the proletarians are torn asunder, and their children transformed into simple articles of commerce and instruments of labour.

But you Communists would introduce community of women, screams the whole bourgeoisie in chorus.

The bourgeois sees in his wife a mere instrument of production. He hears that the instruments of production are to be exploited in common, and, naturally, can come to no other conclusion than that the lot of being common to all will likewise fall to the women.

He has not even a suspicion that the real point aimed at is to do away with the status of women as mere instruments of production.

For the rest, nothing is more ridiculous than the virtuous indignation of our bourgeois at the community of women which, they pretend, is to be openly and officially established by the Communists. The Communists have no need to introduce community of women; it has existed almost from time immemorial.

Our bourgeois, not content with having the wives and daughters of their proletarians at their disposal, not to speak of common prostitutes, take the greatest pleasure in seducing each other's wives.

Bourgeois marriage is in reality a system of wives in common and thus, at the most, what the Communists might possibly be reproached with, is that they desire to introduce, in substitution for a hypocritically concealed, an openly legalised community of women. For the rest, it is self-evident that the abolition of the present system of production must bring with it the abolition of the community of women springing from that system, *i.e.,* of prostitution both public and private.

The Communists are further reproached with desiring to abolish countries and nationality.

The working men have no country. We cannot take from them what they have not got. Since the proletariat must first of all acquire political supremacy, must rise to be the leading class of the nation, must constitute itself *the* nation, it is, so far, itself national, though not in the bourgeois sense of the word.

National differences and antagonisms between peoples are daily more and more vanishing, owing to the development of the bourgeoisie, to freedom of commerce, to the world-market, to uniformity in the mode of production and in the conditions of life corresponding thereto.

The supremacy of the proletariat will cause them to vanish still faster. United action, of the leading civilised countries at least, is one of the first conditions for the emancipation of the proletariat.

In proportion as the exploitation of one individual by another is put an end to, the exploitation of one nation by another will also be put an end to. In proportion as the antagonism between classes within the nation vanishes, the hostility of one nation to another will come to an end.

The charges against Communism made from a religious, a philosophical, and, generally, from an ideological standpoint, are not deserving of serious examination.

Does it require deep intuition to comprehend that man's ideas, views and conceptions, in one word, man's consciousness, changes with every change in the conditions of his material existence, in his social relations and in his social life?

What else does the history of ideas prove, than that intellectual production changes its character in proportion as material production is changed? The ruling ideas of each age have ever been the ideas of its ruling class.

When people speak of ideas that revolutionise society, they do but express the fact, that within the old society, the elements of a new one have been created, and that the dissolution of the old ideas keeps even pace with the dissolution of the old conditions of existence.

When the ancient world was in its last throes, the ancient religions were overcome by Christianity. When Christian ideas succumbed in the 18th century to rationalist ideas, feudal society fought its death battle with the then revolutionary bourgeoisie. The ideas of religious liberty and freedom of conscience merely gave expression to the sway of free competition within the domain of knowledge.

"Undoubtedly," it will be said, "religious, moral, philosophical and juridical ideas have been modified in the course of historical development. But religion, morality, philosophy, political science, and law, constantly survived this change."

"There are, besides, eternal truths, such as Freedom, Justice, etc., that are common to all states of society. But Communism abolishes eternal truths, it abolishes all religion, and all morality, instead of constituting them on a new basis; it therefore acts in contradiction to all past historical experience."

What does this accusation reduce itself to? The history of all past society has consisted in the development of class antagonisms, antagonisms that assumed different forms at different epochs.

But whatever form they may have taken, one fact is common to all past ages, *viz.,* the exploitation of one part of society by the other. No wonder, then, that the social consciousness of past ages, despite all the multiplicity and variety it displays, moves within certain common forms, or general ideas, which cannot completely vanish except with the total disappearance of class antagonisms.

The Communist revolution is the most radical rupture with traditional property relations; no wonder that its development involves the most radical rupture with traditional ideas.

But let us have done with the bourgeois objections to Communism.

We have seen above, that the first step in the revolution by the working class, is to raise the proletariat to the position of ruling class, to win the battle of democracy.

The proletariat will use its political supremacy to wrest, by degrees, all capital from the bourgeoisie, to centralise all instruments of production in the hands of the State, *i.e.,* of the proletariat organised as the ruling class; and to increase the total of productive forces as rapidly as possible.

Of course, in the beginning, this cannot be effected except by means of despotic inroads on the rights of property, and on the conditions of bourgeois production; by means of measures, therefore, which appear economically insufficient and untenable, but which, in the course of the movement, outstrip themselves, necessitate further inroads upon the old social order, and are unavoidable as a means of entirely revolutionising the mode of production.

These measures will of course be different in different countries.

Nevertheless in the most advanced countries, the following will be pretty generally applicable.

1. Abolition of property in land and application of all rents of land to public purposes.
2. A heavy progressive or graduated income tax.
3. Abolition of all right of inheritance.
4. Confiscation of the property of all emigrants and rebels.
5. Centralisation of credit in the hands of the State, by means of a national bank with State capital and an exclusive monopoly.
6. Centralisation of the means of communication and transport in the hands of the State.
7. Extension of factories and instruments of production owned by the State; the bringing into cultivation of waste-lands, and the improvement of the soil generally in accordance with a common plan.
8. Equal liability of all to labour. Establishment of industrial armies, especially for agriculture.
9. Combination of agriculture with manufacturing industries; gradual abolition of the distinction between town and country, by a more equable distribution of the population over the country.
10. Free education for all children in public schools. Abolition of children's factory labour in its present form. Combination of education with industrial production [and so on].

When, in the course of development, class distinctions have disappeared, and all production has been concentrated in the hands of a vast association of the whole nation, the public power will lose its political character. Political power, properly so called, is merely the organised power of one class for oppressing another. If the proletariat during its contest with the bourgeoisie is compelled, by the force of circumstances, to organise itself as a class, if, by means of a revolution, it makes itself the ruling class, and, as such, sweeps away by force the old conditions of production, then it will, along with these conditions, have swept away the conditions for the existence of class antagonisms and of classes generally, and will thereby have abolished its own supremacy as a class.

In place of the old bourgeois society, with its classes and class antagonisms, we shall have an association, in which the free development of each is the condition for the free development of all. . . .

Critique of Social Democracy

In present-day society, the instruments of labour are the monopoly of the capitalist class; the resulting dependence of the working class is the cause of misery and servitude in all its forms.

This sentence, borrowed from the Statutes of the International, is incorrect in this "improved" edition.

In present-day society the instruments of labour are the monopoly of the landowners (the monopoly of property in land is even the basis of the monopoly of capital) *and* the capitalists. In the passage in question, the Statutes of the International do not mention by name either the one or the other class of monopolists. They speak of the *"monopoly of the means of labour, that is the sources of life."* The addition, *"sources of life"* makes it sufficiently clear that land is included in the instruments of labour.

The correction was introduced because Lassalle, for reasons now generally known, attacked *only* the capitalist class and not the landowners. In England, the capitalist is usually not even the owner of the land on which his factory stands.

The emancipation of labour demands the promotion of the instruments of labour to the common property of society, and the co-operative regulation of the total labour with equitable distribution of the proceeds of labour.

"Promotion of the instruments of labour to the common property" ought obviously to read, their "conversion into the common property," but this only in passing.

What are the "proceeds of labour"? The product of labour or its value? And in the latter case, is it the total value of the product or only that part of the value which labour has newly added to the value of the means of production consumed?

The "proceeds of labour" is a loose notion which Lassalle has put in the place of definite economic conceptions.

What is "equitable distribution"?

Do not the bourgeois assert that the present-day distribution is "equitable"? And is it not, in fact, the only "equitable" distribution on the basis of the present-day mode of production? Are economic relations regulated by legal conceptions or do not, on the contrary, legal relations arise from economic ones? Have not also the socialist sectarians the most varied notions about "equitable" distribution?

To understand what idea is meant in this connection by the phrase "equitable distribution," we must take the first paragraph and this one together. The latter implies a society wherein "the instruments of labour are common property, and the total labour is co-operatively regulated," and from the first paragraph we learn that "the proceeds of labour belong undiminished with equal right to all members of society."

"To all members of society"? To those who do not work as well? What remains then of the "undiminished proceeds of labour"? Only to those members of society who work? What remains then of the "equal right" of all members of society?

But "all members of society" and "equal right" are obviously mere phrases. The kernel consists in this, that in this communist society every worker must receive the "undiminished" Lassallean "proceeds of labour."

Let us take first of all the words "proceeds of labour" in the sense of the product of labour, then the co-operative proceeds of labour are the *total social product.*

From this is then to be deducted:

First, cover for replacement of the means of production used up.

Secondly, additional portion for expansion of production.

Thirdly, reserve or insurance fund to provide against mis-adventures, disturbances through natural events, etc.

These deductions from the "undiminished proceeds of labour" are an economic necessity and their magnitude is to be determined by available means and forces, and partly by calculation of probabilities, but they are in no way calculable by equity.

There remains the other part of the total product, destined to serve as means of consumption.

Before this is divided among the individuals, there has to be deducted from it:

First, the general costs of administration not belonging to production.

This part will, from the outset, be very considerably restricted in comparison with present-day society and it diminishes in proportion as the new society develops.

Secondly, that which is destined for the communal satisfaction of needs, such as schools, health services, etc.

From the outset this part is considerably increased in comparison with present-day society and it increases in proportion as the new society develops.

Thirdly, funds for those unable to work, etc., in short, what is included under so-called official poor relief today.

Only now do we come to the "distribution" which the programme, under Lassallean influence, alone has in view in its narrow fashion, namely that part of the means of consumption which is divided among the individual producers of the co-operative society.

The "undiminished proceeds of labour" have already quietly become converted into the "diminished" proceeds, although what the producer is deprived of in his capacity as a private individual benefits him directly or indirectly in his capacity as a member of society.

Just as the phrase "undiminished proceeds of labour" has disappeared, so now does the phrase "proceeds of labour" disappear altogether.

Within the co-operative society based on common ownership of the means of production, the producers do not exchange their products; just as little does the labour employed on the products appear here *as the value* of these products, as a material quality possessed by them, since now, in contrast to capitalist society, individual labour no longer exist in an indirect fashion but directly as a component part of the total labour. The phrase "proceeds of labour," objectionable even today on account of its ambiguity, thus loses all meaning.

What we have to deal with here is a communist society, not as it has *developed* on its own foundations, but, on the contrary, as it *emerges* from capitalist society; which is thus in every respect, economically, morally and intellectually, still stamped with the birthmarks of the old society from whose womb it emerges. Accordingly the individual producer receives back from society—after the deductions have been made—exactly what he gives to it. What he has given to it is his individual amount of labour. For example, the social working day consists of the sum of the individual labour hours; the individual labour time of the individual producer is the part of the social labour day contributed by him, his share in it. He receives a certificate from society that he has furnished such and such an amount of labour (after deducting his labour for the common fund), and with this certificate he draws from the social stock of means of consumption as much as the same amount of labour costs. The same amount of labour which he has given to society in one form, he receives back in another.

Here obviously the same principle prevails as that which regulates the exchange of commodities, as far as this is exchange of equal values. Content and form are changed, because under the altered circumstances no one can give anything except his labour, and because, on the other hand, nothing can pass into the ownership of individuals except individual means of consumption. But, as far as the distribution of the latter among the individual producers is concerned, the same principle prevails as in the exchange of commodity-equivalents, so much labour in one form is exchanged for an equal amount of labour in another form.

Hence, *equal right* here is still in principle—*bourgeois right,* although principle and practice are no longer in conflict, while the exchange of equivalents in commodity exchange only exists on the *average* and not in the individual case.

In spite of this advance, this *equal right* is still stigmatised by a bourgeois limitation. The right of the producers is *proportional* to the labour they supply; the equality consists in the fact that measurement is made with an *equal standard,* labour.

But one man is superior to another physically or mentally and so supplies more labour in the same time, or can labour for a longer time; and labour, to serve as a measure, must be defined by its duration or intensity, otherwise it ceases to be a standard of measurement. This *equal* right is an unequal right for unequal labour.

It recognises no class differences, because everyone is only a worker like everyone else; but it tacitly recognises unequal individual endowment and thus productive capacity as natural privileges. *It is therefore a right of inequality in its content, like every right.* Right by its very nature can only consist in the application of an equal standard; but unequal individuals (and they would not be different individuals if they were not unequal) are only measurable by an equal standard in so far as they are brought under an equal point of view, are taken from one *definite* side only, *e.g.,* in the present case are regarded *only as workers,* and nothing more seen in them, everything else being ignored. Further, one worker is married, another not; one has more children than another and so on and so forth. Thus with an equal output, and hence an equal share in the social consumption fund, one will in fact receive more than another, one will be richer than another, and so on. To avoid all these defects, right, instead of being equal, would have to be unequal.

But these defects are inevitable in the first phase of communist society as it is when it has just emerged after prolonged birth pangs from capitalist society. Right can never be higher than the economic structure of society and the cultural development thereby determined.

In a higher phase of communist society, after the enslaving subordination of individuals under division of labour, and therewith also the antithesis between mental and physical labour, has vanished; after labour, from a mere means of life, has itself become the prime necessity of life; after the productive forces have also increased with the all-round development of the individual, and all the springs of co-operative wealth flow more abundantly—only then can the narrow horizon of bourgeois right be fully left behind and society inscribe on its banners: from each according to his ability, to each according to his needs!

I have dealt more at length with the "undiminished proceeds of labour" on the one hand, and with "equal right" and "equitable distribution" on the other, in order to show what a crime it is to attempt, on the one hand, to force on our party again, as dogmas, ideas which in a certain period had some meaning but have now become obsolete rubbishy phrases, while on the other, perverting the realistic outlook, which has cost so much effort to instill into the party, but which has now taken root in it, by means of ideological nonsense about "right" and other trash common among the democrats and French Socialists.

Quite apart from the analysis so far given, it was in general incorrect to make a fuss about so-called *"distribution"* and put the principal stress on it.

The distribution of the means of consumption at any time is only a consequence of the distribution of the conditions of production themselves. The latter distribution, however, is a feature of the mode of production itself. The capitalist mode of production, for example, rests on the fact that the material conditions of production are in the hands of non-workers in the form of property in capital and land, while the masses are only owners of the personal condition of production, *viz.,* labour power. Once the elements of production are so distributed, then the present-day distribution of the means of consumption results automatically. If the material conditions of production are the co-operative property of the workers themselves, then this likewise results in a different distribution of the means of consumption from the present one. Vulgar socialism (and from it in turn a section of democracy) has taken over from the bourgeois economists the consideration and treatment of distribution as independent of the mode of production and hence the presentation of socialism as turning principally on distribution. After the real position has long been made clear, why go back again?

6

Justice Under Socialism

EDWARD NELL AND ONORA O'NEILL

"From each according to his ability, to each according to his need."

The stirring slogan that ends *The Critique of the Gotha Program* is generally taken as a capsule summary of the socialist approach to distributing the burdens and benefits of life. It can be seen as the statement of a noble ideal and yet be found wanting on three separate scores. First, there is no guarantee that, even if all contribute according to their abilities, all needs can be met: the principle gives us no guidance for distributing goods when some needs must go unmet. Second, if all contribute according to their abilities, there may be a material surplus after all needs are met: again, the principle gives us no guidance for distributing such a surplus. Third, the principle incorporates no suggestion as to why each man would contribute according to his ability: no incentive structure is evident.

These apparent shortcomings can be compared with those of other principles a society might follow in distributing burdens and benefits. Let us call

1. "From each according to his ability, to each according to his need," the *Socialist Principle of Justice*. Its Capitalist counterpart would be
2. From each according to his choice, given his assets, to each according to his contribution. We shall call this the *Laissez-Faire Principle*.

From "Justice Under Socialism," *Dissent,* Vol 18 (1972), pp. 483–491. Reprinted by permission of the authors and Dissent Publishing Corporation.

These two principles will require a good deal of interpretation, but at the outset we can say that in the Socialist Principle of Justice "abilities" and "needs" refer to persons, whereas the "choices" and "contributions" in the Laissez-Faire Principle refer also to the management of impersonal property, the given assets. It goes without saying that some of the "choices," particularly those of the propertyless, are normally made under considerable duress. As "choice" is the ideologically favored term, we shall retain it.

In a society where the Socialist Principle of Justice regulates distribution, the requirement is that everyone use such talents as have been developed in him (though this need not entail any allocation of workers to jobs), and the payment of workers is contingent not upon their contributions but upon their needs. In a laissez-faire society, where individuals may be endowed with more or less capital or with bare labor power, they choose in the light of these assets how and how much to work (they may be dropouts or moonlighters), and/or how to invest their capital, and they are paid in proportion.

None of the three objections raised against the Socialist Principle of Justice holds for the Laissez-Faire Principle. Whatever the level of contribution individuals choose, their aggregate product can be distributed in proportion to the contribution—whether of capital or of labor—each individual chooses to make. The Laissez-Faire Principle is applicable under situations both of scarcity and of abundance, and it incorporates a theory of incentives: people choose their level of contribution in order to get a given level of material reward.

Principles 1 and 2 can be crossfertilized, yielding two further principles:

3. From each according to his ability, to each according to his contribution.
4. From each according to his choice, to each according to his need.

Principle 3 could be called an *Incentive Socialist Principle* of distribution. Like the Socialist Principle of Justice, it pictures a society in which all are required to work in proportion to the talents that have been developed in them. Since unearned income is not available and rewards are hinged to contribution rather than need, all work is easily enforced in an economy based on the Incentive Socialist Principle. This principle, however, covers a considerable range of systems. It holds for a Stalinist economy with an authoritarian job allocation. It also holds for a more liberal, market socialist economy in which there is a more or less free labor market, though without an option to drop out or live on unearned income, or the freedom to choose the level and type of qualification one is prepared to acquire. The Incentive Socialist Principle rewards workers according to their contribution: it is a principle of distribution in which an incentive system—reliance on material rewards—is explicit. Marx believed this principle would have to be followed in the early stages of socialism, in a society "still stamped with the birthmarks of the old society."

Under the Incentive Socialist Principle, each worker receives back the value of the amount of work he contributes to society in one form or another. According to Marx, this is a form of bourgeois right that "tacitly recognizes unequal individual endowments, and thus natural privileges in respect of productive capacity." So this principle holds for a still deficient society where the needs of particular workers, which depend on many things other than their productive capacity, may not be met. Although it may be less desirable than the Socialist Principle of Justice, the Incentive Socialist Principle clearly meets certain criteria the Socialist Principle of Justice cannot meet. It provides a principle of allocation that can be applied equally well to the various situations of scarcity, sufficiency, and abundance. Its material incentive structure explains how under market socialism, given a capital structure and a skill structure, workers will choose jobs and work hard at them—and also why under a Stalinist economy workers will work hard at jobs to which they have been allocated.

Under the Incentive Socialist Principle, workers—whether assigned to menial work or to specific jobs—respond to incentives of the same sort as do workers under the Laissez-Faire Principle. The difference is that, while the Laissez-Faire Principle leaves the measurement of the contribution of a worker to be determined by the level of wage he is offered, the Incentive Socialist Principle relies on a bureaucratically determined weighting that takes into account such factors as the difficulty, duration, qualification level, and risk involved in a given job.

There is another difference between societies living under the Laissez–Faire Principle and those following the Incentive Socialist Principle. Under the Laissez-Faire Principle, there is no central coordination of decisions, for assets are managed according to the choices of their owners. This gives rise to the well-known problems of instability and unemployment. Under the Incentive Socialist Principle, assets are managed by the central government; hence one would expect instability to be eliminated and full employment guaranteed. However, we do not regard this difference as a matter of principle on the same level with others we are discussing. Moreover, in practice some recognizable capitalist societies have managed to control fluctuations without undermining the Laissez-Faire Principle as the principle of distribution.

Let us call Principle 4 the *Utopian Principle of Justice*. It postulates a society without any requirement of contribution or material incentives, but with guaranteed minimal consumption. This principle suffers from the same defect as the Socialist Principle of Justice: it does not determine distributions of benefits under conditions either of scarcity or of abundance, and it suggests no incentive structure to explain why enough should be contributed to its economy to make it possible to satisfy needs. Whether labor is contributed according to choice or according to ability, it is conceivable that the aggregate social product should be such that either some needs cannot be met or that, when all needs are met, a surplus remains that cannot be divided on the basis of needs.

On the surface, this Utopian Principle of Justice excludes the aroma of laissez-faire: though needs will not go unmet in utopia, contributions will be made for no more basic reason than individual whim. They are tied neither to the reliable effects of the incentive of material reward for oneself, nor to those of the noble ideal of filling the needs of others, nor to a conception of duty or self-sacrifice. Instead, contributions will come forth, if they do, according to the free and unconstrained choices of individual economic agents, on the basis of their given preferences. Preferences, however, are not "given"; they develop and change, are learned and unlearned, and follow fashions and fads. Whim, fancy, pleasure, desire, wish are all words suggesting this aspect of consumer choice. By tying the demand for products to needs and the supply of work to choice, the Utopian Principle of Justice ensures stability in the former but does not legislate against fluctuations and unpredictable variability in the latter.

So the Socialist Principle of Justice and the Utopian Principle of Justice suffer from a common defect. There is no reason to suppose these systems will operate at precisely the level at which aggregate output is sufficient to meet all needs without surplus. And since people do not need an income in money terms but rather an actual and quite precisely defined list of food, clothing, housing, etc. (bearing in mind the various alternatives that might be substituted), the *aggregate* measured in value terms could be right, yet the *composition* might still be unable to meet all the people's needs. People might choose or have the ability to do the right amount of work, but on the wrong projects. One could even imagine the economy growing from a situation of scarcity to one of abundance without ever passing through any point at which its aggregate output could be distributed to meet precisely the needs of its population.

So far, we have been considering not the justification or desirability of alternative principles of distribution, but their practicality. It appears that, in this respect, principles hinging reward on contribution rather than on need have a great advantage. They can both provide a general principle of distribution and indicate the pattern of incentives to which workers will respond.

It might be held that these advantages are restricted to the Incentive Socialist Principle in its various versions, since under the Laissez–Faire Principle there is some income—property income—which is not being paid in virtue of any contribution. This problem can be dealt with either, as we indicated above, by interpreting the notion of contribution to cover the contribution of one's assets to the capital market, or by restricting the scope of the Laissez-Faire Principle to cover workers only, or by interpreting the notion of property income so as to regard wages as a return to property, i.e., property in one's labor power. One can say that under capitalism part of the aggregate product is set aside for the owners of capital (and another part, as under market socialism, for government expenditure) and the remainder is distributed according to the Laissez-Faire Principle. Or one may say that property income is paid in virtue of past contributions, whose reward was not consumed at the time it was earned but was stored. Apologists tend to favor interpretations that make the worker a sort of capitalist or the capitalist a sort of slow-consuming worker. Whichever line is taken, it is clear that the Laissez-Faire Principle—however undesirable we may find it—is a principle of distribution that can be of general use in two senses. Appropriately interpreted, it covers the distribution of earned and of unearned income, and it applies in situations both of scarcity and of abundance.

So we seem to have reached the paradoxical conclusion that the principle of distribution requiring that workers' needs be met is of no use in situations of need, since it does not assign priorities among needs, and that the principle demanding that each contribute according to his ability is unable to explain what incentives will lead him to do so. In this view, the Socialist Principle of Justice would have to be regarded as possibly noble but certainly unworkable.

The Socialist Principle Defended

But this view should not be accepted. Marx formulated the Socialist Principle of Justice on the basis of a conception of human abilities and needs that will yield some guidance to its interpretation. We shall now try to see whether the difficulties discussed above can be alleviated when we consider this principle in the light of Marxian theory.

Marx clearly thought that the Socialist Principle of Justice was peculiarly relevant to situations of abundance. In the last section we argued that, on the contrary, it was an adequate principle of distribution only when aggregate output exactly covered total needs. The source of this discrepancy lies in differing analyses of human needs.

By fulfillment of needs we understand at least a subsistence income. Needs are not met when a person lacks sufficient food, clothing, shelter, medical care, or socially necessary training/education. But beyond this biological and social minimum we can point to another set of needs, which men do not have qua men but acquire qua producers. Workers need not merely a biological and social minimum, but whatever other goods—be they holidays or contacts with others whose work bears on theirs or guaranteed leisure, which they need to perform their jobs as well as possible. So a principle of distribution according to needs will not be of use only to a subsistence-level economy. Very considerable goods over and above those necessary for biological subsistence can be distributed according to a principle of need.

But despite this extension of the concept of need the Socialist Principle of Justice still seems to face the three problems listed [earlier]:

1. What guarantees are there that even under abundance the *composition* of the output, with all contributing according to their abilities, will suffice to fill all needs? (There may still be scarcities of goods needed to fill either biological or job-related needs.)
2. What principle can serve to distribute goods that are surplus both to biological and to job-related needs?
3. What system of incentives explains why each will contribute to the full measure of his abilities, though he is not materially rewarded for increments of effort? Whether or not there is authoritative job allocation, job performance cannot be guaranteed.

Marx's solution to these problems does not seem too explicit. But much is suggested by the passage at the end of the *Critique of the Gotha Program* where he describes the higher phase of communist society as one in which "labor is no longer merely a means of life but has become life's principal need."

To most people it sounds almost comic to claim that labor could become life's principal need: it suggests a society of compulsive workers. Labor in the common view is intrinsically undesirable, but undertaken as a means to some further, typically material, end. For Marx this popular view would have been confirmation of his own view of the degree to which most labor under capitalism is alienating. He thought that under capitalism laborers experienced a threefold alienation: alienation from the *product* of their labor, which is for them merely a means to material reward; alienation from the *process* of labor, which is experienced as forced labor rather than as desirable activity; and alienation from *others,* since activities undertaken with others are undertaken as a means to achieving further ends, which are normally scarce and allocated competitively. Laborers cooperate in production but, under capitalism, compete for job and income, and the competition overrides the cooperation. Hence Marx claims (in the *Economic and Philosophical Manuscripts*) that "life itself appears only as a means to life." Though the horror of that situation is apparent in the very words, many people accept that labor should be only a means to life—whose real ends lie elsewhere; whether in religion, consumption, personal relations, or leisure.

Marx, on the other hand, held that labor could be more than a means; it could also be an end of life, for labor in itself—*the activity*—can, like other activities, be something for whose sake one does other things. We would be loath to think that activity itself should appear only as a means to life—on the contrary, life's worth for most people lies in the activities undertaken. Those we call labor do not differ intrinsically from the rest, only in relation to the system of production. In Marx's view a system was possible in which all activities undertaken would be nonalienating. Nobody would have to compete to engage in an activity he found unpleasant for the sake of a material reward. Instead, workers would cooperate in creative and fulfilling activities that provide occasions for the experience of talents, for taking responsibilities, and that result in useful or beautiful products. In such a situation one can see why labor would be regarded as life's greatest need, rather than as its scourge. Nonalienated labor is humanly fulfilling activity.

In the course of switching from the conception of alienating labor to that of nonalienating labor, it might seem that we have moved into a realm for which principles of distribution may be irrelevant. What can the Socialist Principle of Justice tell us about the distribution of burdens and benefits in "the higher phase of Communist society?"

In such a society each is to contribute according to his abilities. In the light of the discussion of nonalienated labor, it is clear that there is no problem of incentives. Each man works at what he wants to work at. He works because that is his need. (This is not a situation in which "moral incentives" have replaced material ones, for both moral and material incentives are based on alienating labor. The situation Marx envisages is one for which incentives of *all* sorts are irrelevant.)

Though this disposes of the problem of incentives under the Socialist Principle of Justice, it is much less clear whether this principle can work for a reasonable range of situations. Can it cope with both the situation of abundance and that of scarcity?

In the case of abundance, a surplus of goods over and above those needed is provided. But if all activities are need-fulfilling, then no work is done that does not fulfill some need. In a sense there is no surplus to be distributed, for nothing needless is being done. Nevertheless, there may be a surplus of material goods that are the by-product of need-fulfilling activity. In a society where everybody fulfills himself by painting pictures, there may be a vast surplus of pictures. If so, the Socialist Principle of Justice gives no indication of the right method for their distribution; they are not the goal for which the task was undertaken. Since they do not fulfill an objective need, the method for their distribution is not important. In this the higher phase of communist society is, as one might expect, the very antithesis of consumerism; rather than fabricate reasons for desiring and so acquiring what is not needed, it disregards anything that is not needed in decisions of distribution.

There, nevertheless, is a problem of distribution the Socialist Principle of Justice does not attempt to solve. Some of the products of need-fulfilling activity may be things other people either desire or detest. When need-fulfilling activity yields works of art or noisy block parties, its distribution cannot be disregarded. Not all planning problems can be solved by the Socialist Principle of Justice. We shall not discuss the merits of various principles that could serve to handle these cases, but shall only try to delimit the scope of the Socialist Principle of Justice.

This brings us to the problem of scarcity. Can the Socialist Principle of Justice explain why, when all contribute to the extent of their abilities, all needs can be met? Isn't it conceivable that everyone should find fulfillment in painting, but nobody find fulfillment in producing either biological necessities or the canvases, brushes, and paints everybody wants to use? Might not incentive payments be needed, even in this higher phase of communist society, to guarantee the production of subsistence goods and job-related necessities? In short, will not any viable system involve some alienating labor?

Marx at any rate guarantees that communism need not involve much alienating labor. He insists that the Socialist Principle of Justice is applicable only in a context of abundance. For only when man's needs can be met is it relevant to insist that they ought to be met. The Socialist Principle of Justice comes into its own only with the development of the forces of production. But, of course, higher productivity does not by itself guarantee the right composition of output. Subsistence goods and job-related services and products might not be provided as the population fulfills itself in painting, poetry, and sculpture. Man cannot live by works of art alone.

This socialist version of the story of Midas should not alarm us too much. The possibility of starvation admidst abundant art works seemed plausible only because we abstracted it from other features of an abundant socialist society. Such a society is a planned society, and part of its planning concerns the ability structure of the population. Such a society would include people able to perform all tasks necessary to maintain a high level of material well-being.

Nevertheless, there may be certain essential tasks in such a society whose performance is not need-fulfilling for anybody. Their allocation presents another planning problem for which the Socialist Principle of Justice, by hypothesis, is not a solution. But the degree of coercion need not be very great. In a highly productive society the amount of labor expended on nonfulfilling tasks is a diminishing proportion of total labor time. Hence, given equitable allocation of this burden (and it is here that the planning decisions are really made), nobody would be prevented from engaging principally in need-fulfilling activities. In the limiting case of abundance, where automation of the production of material needs is complete, nobody would have to do any task he did not find intrinsically worthwhile. To the extent that this abundance is not reached, the Socialist Principle of Justice cannot be fully implemented.

However, the degree of coercion experienced by those who are allocated to necessary but nonfulfilling chores may be reducible if the planning procedure is of a certain sort. To the extent that people participate in planning and that they realize the necessity of the nonfulfilling chores in order for everyone to be able to do also what he finds need-fulfilling, they may find the performance of these chores less burdensome. As they want to achieve the ends, so—once they are informed—they cannot rationally resent the means, provided they perceive the distribution of chores as just.

The point can be taken a step further. Under the Socialist Principle of Justice, households do not put forth productive effort to be rewarded with an aliquot portion of time and means for self-fulfillment. It is precisely this market mentality from which we wish to escape. The miserable toil of society should be

> performed gratis for the benefit of society . . . performed not as a definite duty, not for the purpose of obtaining a right to certain products, not according to previously established and legally fixed quotas, but voluntary labor . . . performed because it has become a habit to work for the common good, and because of a conscious realization (that has become a habit) of the necessity of working for the common good.[1]

Creative work should be done for its own sake, not for any reward. Drudgery should be done for the common good, not in order to be rewarded with opportunity and means for creative work. Of course, the better and more efficient the performance of drudgery, the more will be the opportunities for creative work. To realize this, however, is to understand the necessity of working for the common good, not to be animated by private material incentives. For the possibilities of creative work are opened by the simultaneous and parallel development of large numbers of people. To take the arts, poets need a public, authors readers, performers audiences, and all need (though few want) critics. One cannot sensibly wish, under the Socialist Principle of Justice, to be rewarded *privately* with opportunities and means for nonalienated work.

There is a question regarding the distribution of educational opportunities. Before men can contribute according to their abilities, their abilities must be developed. But in whom should society develop which abilities? If we regard education as consumption, then according to the Socialist Principle of Justice, each should receive it according to his need.

It is clear that all men require some early training to make them viable social beings; further, all men require certain general skills necessary for performing work. But we could hardly claim that some men need to be doctors or economists or lawyers, or need to receive any other specialized or expensive training. If, on the other hand, we regard education as production of those skills necessary for maintaining society and providing the possibility of fulfillment, then the Socialist Principle of Justice can determine a lower bound to the production of certain skills: so-and-so many farmers/doctors/mechanics must be produced to satisfy future subsistence and job-related needs. But the Socialist Principle of Justice cannot determine who shall get which of these educational opportunities. One traditional answer might be that each person should specialize at whatever he is relatively best suited to do. Yet this only makes sense in terms of tasks done as onerous means to desirable ends. Specialization on the basis of comparative advantage minimizes the effort in achieving given ends; but if work is itself fulfilling, it is not an "effort" that must be minimized.

In conditions of abundance, it is unlikely that anyone will be denied training they want and can absorb, though they may have to acquire skills they do not particularly want, since some onerous tasks may still have to be done. For even in conditions of abundance, it may be necessary to compel some or all to undertake certain unwanted training in the interests of the whole. But it is not necessary to supplement the Socialist Principle of Justice with an incentive scheme, whether material or moral. The principle already contains the Kantian maxim: develop your talents to the utmost, for only in this way can a person contribute to the limits of his ability. And if a society wills the end of self-fulfillment, it must will sufficient means. If the members of society take part in planning to maintain and expand the opportunities for everyone's nonalienated activity, they must understand the necessity of allocating the onerous tasks, and so the training for them.

Perhaps we can make our point clearer by looking briefly at Marx's schematic conception of the stages of modern history—feudalism, capitalism, socialism, communism—where each stage is characterized by a higher productivity of labor than the preceding stage. In feudalism, the principle of distribution would be:

5. From each according to his status, to each according to his status—the *Feudal Principles of Justice*.

There is no connection between work and reward. There are no market incentives in the "ideal" feudal system. Peasants grow the stuff for their own subsistence and perform traditional labor services for their lord on domain land. He in turn provides protection and government in traditional fashion. Yet, though labor is not performed as a means to a distant or abstract end, as when it is done for money, it still is done for survival, not for its own sake, and those who do it are powerless to control their conditions of work or their own destinies. Man lives on the edge of famine and is subject to the vagaries of the weather and the dominion of tradition. Only a massive increase in productive powers frees him. But to engender this increase men must come to connect work directly with reward. This provides the incentive to labor, both to take those jobs most needed (moving from the farm to the factory) and to work sufficiently hard once on the job.

But more than work is needed; the surplus of output over that needed to maintain the work force (including managers) and replace and repair the means of production (machines, raw materials) must be put to productive use; it must be reinvested, not consumed. In capitalism, station at birth determines whether one works or owns capital; workers are rewarded for their contribution of work, capitalists for theirs of reinvestment. There is a stick as well as a carrot. Those workers who do not work, starve; those capitalists who fail to reinvest, fail to grow and will eventually be crushed by their larger rivals. Socialism rationalizes this by eliminating the two-class dichotomy and by making reinvestment a function of the institutions of the state, so that the capital structure of the society is the collective property of the citizenry, all of whom must work for reward. In this system the connection between work and reward reaches its fullest development, and labor in one sense is most fully alienated. The transition to communism then breaks this link altogether.

The link between work and rewards serves a historical purpose; namely, to encourage the development of the productive forces. But as the productive forces continue to develop, the demand for additional rewards will tend to decline, while the difficulty of stimulating still further growth in productivity may increase. This, at least, seems to be implied by the principles of conventional economics— diminishing marginal utility and diminishing marginal productivity. Even if one rejects most of the conventional wisdom of economics, a good case can be made for the diminishing efficacy of material incentives as prosperity increases. For as labor productivity rises, private consumption needs will be met, and the most urgent needs remaining will be those requiring *collective* consumption—and, indeed, some of these needs will be generated by the process of growth and technical progress. These last needs, if left unmet, may hinder further attempts to raise the productive power of labor. So the system of material incentives could in principle come to a point where the weakened encouragements to extra productivity offered as private reward for contribution might be offset by the accumulated hindrances generated by the failures to meet collective needs and by the wastes involved in competition. At this point, it becomes appropriate to break the link between work and reward. Breaking the link, however, is not enough. Both the Socialist Principle of Justice and the Utopian Principle of Justice break the link between work and reward. But the Utopian Principle of Justice leaves the distinction between them. Work is a means, the products of work are the ends. Given a high productivity of labor, workers would in principle choose their occupations and work-leisure patterns, yet still producing enough to satisfy everyone's needs. This would be a society devoted to minimizing effort, a sort of high-technology Polynesia. Since it neither makes consumption dependent upon work nor regards work as other than a regrettable means to consumption, it fails to explain why sufficient work to supply basic needs should ever be done. The alienation of labor cannot be overcome by eliminating labor rather than alienation.

Breaking the link between work and reward, while leaving the distinction itself intact, may also lead to the loss of the productive powers of labor. For without reward, and when the object is to work as little as possible, why expend the effort to acquire highly complex skills? What is the motive to education, self-improvement, self-development? A high-technology Polynesia contains an inner contradiction.

By contrast, the Socialist Principle of Justice not only does not make reward depend upon work but denies that there is a distinction between the two. Because man needs fulfilling activity—work that he chooses and wants—men who get it contribute according to their ability.

Yet there still may remain routine and menial, unfulfilling jobs. But who wills the end wills the means. The society must plan to have such jobs done. No doubt many will be mechanized or automated, but the remaining ones will form a burden that must be allocated.

The Socialist Principle of Justice cannot solve this problem of allocation. But everyone has some interest in getting uncoveted but essential work done. Hence it should not be difficult to find an acceptable supplementary principle of distribution for allocating these chores. For instance, the Principle of Comparative Advantage might be introduced to assign each the drudgery at which he is relatively best. There can be no quarrel with this so long as such alienating work is only a small fraction of a man's total activity, conferring no special status. It is only when alienating work takes up the bulk of one's waking hours, and determines status, that specialization inevitably entails some form of class structure.

The Socialist Principle of Justice cannot solve all allocation problems. But once one understands that it is based on a denial of a distinction between work, need, and reward, it is clear that it can solve an enormous range of such problems. In a highly productive society the only allocation problems the Socialist Principle of Justice cannot solve are the distribution of unmechanized and uncoveted chores and of the material by-products of creative endeavor.

Note

1. V. I. Lenin, "From the Destruction of the Old Social System to the Creation of the New," April 11, 1920. From *Collected Works,* English trans., 40 vols. (London: Lawrence & Wishart, 1965), vol. 30, p. 517.

7

Radical Egalitarianism

KAI NIELSON

I

I have talked of equality as a right and of equality as a goal. And I have taken, as the principal thing, to be able to state what goal we are seeking when we say equality is a goal. When we are in a position actually to achieve that goal, then that same equality becomes a right. The goal we are seeking is an equality of basic condition for everyone. Let me say a bit what this is: everyone, as far as possible, should have equal life prospects, short of genetic engineering and the like and the rooting out of any form of the family and the undermining of our basic freedoms. There should, where this is possible, be an equality of access to equal resources over each person's life as a whole, though this should be qualified by people's varying needs. Where psychiatrists are in short supply only people who are in need of psychiatric help should have equal access to such help. This equal access to resources should be such that it stands as a barrier to there being the sort of differences between people that allow some to be in a position to control and to exploit others; such equal access to resources should also stand as a barrier to one adult person having power over other adult persons that does not rest on the revokable consent on the part of the persons over whom he comes to have power. Where, because of some remaining scarcity in a society of considerable productive abundance, we cannot reasonably distribute resources equally, we should first, where considerations of desert are not at issue, distribute according to stringency of need, second according to the strength of unmanipulated preferences and third, and finally, by lottery. We should, in trying to

Abridged from *Equality and Liberty* (1985), pp. 283–292, 302–306, 309. Reprinted by permission of Rowman & Littlefield, Publishers. Notes renumbered.

attain equality of condition, aim at a condition of autonomy (the fuller and the more rational the better) for everyone and at a condition where everyone alike, to the fullest extent possible, has his or her needs and wants satisfied. The limitations on the satisfaction of people's wants should be only where that satisfaction is incompatible with everyone getting the same treatment. Where we have conflicting wants, such as where two persons want to marry the same person, the fair thing to do will vary with the circumstances. In the marriage case, freedom of choice is obviously the fair thing. But generally, what should be aimed at is having everyone have their wants satisfied as far as possible. To achieve equality of condition would be, as well, to achieve a condition where the necessary burdens of the society are equally shared, where to do so is reasonable, and where each person has an equal voice in deciding what these burdens shall be. Moreover, everyone, as much as possible, should be in a position—and should be equally in that position—to control his own life. The goals of egalitarianism are to achieve such equalities.

Minimally, classlessness is something we should all aim at if we are egalitarians. It is necessary for the stable achievement of equalities of the type discussed in the previous paragraph. Beyond that, we should also aim at a statusless society, though not at an undifferentiated society or a society which does not recognize merit. . . . It is only in such a classless, statusless society that the ideals of equality (the conception of equality as a very general goal to be achieved) can be realized. In aiming for a statusless society, we are aiming for a society which, while remaining a society of material abundance, is a society in which there are to be no extensive differences in life prospects between people because some have far greater income, power, authority or prestige than others. This is the *via negativa* of the egalitarian way. The *via postiva* is to produce social conditions, where there is generally material abundance, where well-being and satisfaction are not only maximized (the utilitarian thing) but, as well, a society where this condition, as far as it is achievable, is sought equally for all (the egalitarian thing). This is the underlying conception of the egalitarian commitment to equality of condition.

II

Robert Nozick asks, "How do we decide how much equality is enough?"[1] In the preceding section we gestured in the direction of an answer. I should now like to be somewhat more explicit. Too much equality, as we have been at pains to point out, would be to treat everyone identically, completely ignoring their differing needs. Various forms of "barracks equality" approximating that would also be too much. Too little equality would be to limit equality of condition, as did the old egalitarianism, to achieving equal legal and political rights, equal civil liberties, to equality of opportunity and to a redistribution of gross disparities in wealth sufficient to keep social peace, the rationale for the latter being that such gross inequalities if allowed to stand would threaten social stability. This Hobbesist stance indicates that the old egalitarianism proceeds in a very pragmatic manner. Against the old egalitarianism I would argue that we must at least aim at an equality of whole life prospects, where that is not read simply as the right to compete for scarce positions of advantage, but where there is to be brought into being the kind of equality of condition that would provide everyone equally, as far as possible, with the resources and the social conditions to satisfy their needs as fully as possible compatible with everyone else doing likewise. (Note that between people these needs will be partly the same but will still often be importantly different as well.) Ideally, as a kind of ideal limit for a society of wondrous abundance, a radical egalitarianism would go beyond that to a similar thing for wants. We should, that is, provide all people equally, as far as possible, with the resources and social conditions to satisfy their wants, as fully as possible compatible with everyone else doing likewise. (I recognize that there is a slide between wants and needs. As the wealth of a society increases and its structure changes, things that started out as wants tend to become needs, e.g. someone in the Falkland Islands might merely reasonably want an auto while someone in Los Angeles might not only want it but need it as well. But this does not collapse the distinction between wants and needs. There are things in any society people need, if they are to survive at all in anything like a commodious condition, whether they want them or not, e.g., they need food, shelter, security, companionship and the like. An egalitarian starts with basic needs, or at least with what are taken in the cultural environment in which a given person lives to be basic needs, and moves out to other needs and finally to wants as the productive power of the society increases.)

I qualified my above formulations with "as far as possible" and with "as fully as possible compatible with everyone else doing likewise." These are essential qualifications. Where, as in societies that we know, there are scarcities, even rather minimal scarcities, not everyone can have the resources or at least all the resources necessary to have their needs satisfied. Here we must first ensure that, again as far as possible, their basic needs are all satisfied and then we move on to other needs and finally to wants. But sometimes, to understate it, even in very affluent societies, everyone's needs cannot be met, or at least they cannot be equally met. In such circumstances we have to make some hard choices. I am thinking of a situation where there are not enough dialysis machines to go around so that everyone who needs one can have one. What then should we do? The thing to aim at, to try as far as possible to approximate, if only as a heuristic ideal, is the full and equal meeting of needs and wants of everyone. It is when we have that much equality that we have enough equality. But, of course, "ought implies can," and where we can't achieve it we can't achieve it. But where we reasonably can, we ought to do it. It is something that fairness requires.

The "reasonably can" is also an essential modification: we need situations of sufficient abundance so that we do not, in going for such an equality of condition, simply spread the misery around or spread very Spartan conditions around. Before we can rightly aim for the equality of condition I mentioned, we must first have the productive capacity and resource conditions to support the institutional means that would make possible the equal satisfaction of basic needs and the equal satisfaction of other needs and wants as well.

Such achievements will often not be possible; perhaps they will never be fully possible, for, no doubt, the physically handicapped will always be with us. Consider, for example, situations where our scarcities are such that we cannot, without causing considerable misery, create the institutions and mechanisms that would work to satisfy all needs, even all basic needs. Suppose we have the technology in place to develop all sorts of complicated life-sustaining machines all of which would predictably provide people with a quality of life that they, viewing the matter clearly, would rationally choose if they were simply choosing for themselves. But suppose, if we put such technologies in place, we will then not have the wherewithal to provide basic health care in outlying regions in the country or adequate educational services in such places. We should not, under those circumstances, put those technologies in place. But we should also recognize that where it becomes possible to put these technologies in place without sacrificing other more pressing needs, we should do so. The underlying egalitarian rationale is evident enough: produce the conditions for the most extensive satisfaction of needs for everyone. Where A's need and B's need are equally important (equally stringent) but cannot both be satisfied, satisfy A's need rather than B's if the satisfaction of A's need would be more fecund for the satisfaction of the needs of others than B's, or less undermining of the satisfaction of the needs of others than B's. (I do not mean to say that this is our only criterion of choice but it is the criterion most relevant for us here.) We should seek the satisfaction of the greatest compossible set of needs where the conditions for compossibility are (a) that everyone's needs be considered, (b) that everyone's needs be *equally* considered and where two sets of needs cannot both be satisfied, the more stringent set of needs shall first be satisfied. (Do not say we have no working criteria for what they are. If you need food to keep you from starvation or debilitating malnutrition and I need a vacation to relax after a spate of hard work, your need is plainly more stringent than mine. There would, of course, be all sorts of disputable cases, but there are also a host of perfectly determinate cases indicating that we have working criteria.) The underlying rationale is to seek compossible sets of needs so that we approach as far as possible as great a satisfaction of needs as possible for everyone.

This might, it could be said, produce a situation in which very few people got those things that they needed the most, or at least wanted the most. Remember Nozick with his need for the resources of Widener Library in an annex to his house. People, some might argue, with expensive tastes and extravagant needs, say a need for really good wine, would never, with a stress on such compossibilia, get things they are really keen about.[2] Is that the kind of world we would reflectively want? Well, *if* their not getting them is the price we have to pay for everyone having their basic needs met, then it is a price we ought to pay. I am very fond of very good wines as well as fresh ripe mangoes, but if the price of my having them is that people starve or suffer malnutrition in the Sahel, or indeed anywhere else, then plainly fairness, if not just plain human decency, requires that I forgo them.

In talking about how much equality is enough, I have so far talked of the benefits that equality is meant to provide. But egalitarians also speak of an equal sharing of the necessary burdens of the society as well. Fairness requires a sharing of the burdens, and for a radical egalitarian this comes to an equal sharing of the burdens where people are equally capable of sharing them. Translated into the concrete this does *not* mean that a child or an old man or a pregnant woman are to be required to work in the mines or that they be required to collect garbage, but it would involve something like requiring every able bodied person, say from nineteen to twenty, to take his or her turn at a fair portion of the necessary unpleasant jobs in the world. In that way we all, where we are able to do it, would share equally in these burdens—in doing the things that none of us want to do but that we, if we are at all reasonable, recognize the necessity of having done. (There are all kinds of variations and complications concerning this—what do we do with the youthful wonder at the violin? But, that notwithstanding, the general idea is clear enough.) And, where we think this is reasonably feasible, it squares with our considered judgments about fairness.

I have given you, in effect appealing to my considered judgments but considered judgments I do not think are at all eccentric, a picture of what I would take to be enough equality, too little equality and not enough equality. But how can we know that my proportions are right? I do not think we can avoid or should indeed try to avoid an appeal to considered judgments here. But working with them there are some arguments we can appeal to get them in wide reflective equilibrium. Suppose we go back to the formal principle of justice, namely that we must treat like cases alike. Because it does not tell us *what* are like cases, we cannot derive substantive criteria from it. But it may, indirectly, be of some help here. We all, if we are not utterly zany, want a life in which our needs are satisfied and in which we can live as we wish and do what we want to do. Though we differ in many ways, in our abilities, capacities for pleasure, determination to keep on with a job, we do not differ about wanting our needs satisfied or being able to live as we wish. Thus, *ceterus paribus,* where questions of desert, entitlement and the like do not enter, it is only fair that all of us should have our needs equally considered and that we should, again *ceterus paribus,* all be able to do as we wish in a way that is compatible with others doing likewise. From the formal principle of justice and a few key facts about us, we can get to the claim that *ceterus paribus* we should go for this much equality. But this is the core content of a radical egalitarianism.

However, how do we know that *ceterus* is *paribus* here? What about our entitlements and deserts? Suppose I have built my house with my own hands, from materials I have purchased and on land that I have purchased and that I have lived in it for years and have carefully cared for it. The house is mine and I am entitled to keep it even if by dividing the house into two apartments greater and more equal satisfaction of need would obtain for everyone. Justice requires that such an entitlement be respected here. (Again, there is an implicit *ceterus paribus* clause. In extreme situations, say after a war with housing in extremely short supply, that entitlement could be rightly overridden.)

There is a response on the egalitarian's part similar to a response utilitarianism made to criticisms of a similar logical type made of utilitarians by pluralistic deontologists. One of the things that people in fact need, or at least reflectively firmly want, is to have such entitlements respected. Where they are routinely overridden to satisfy other needs or wants, we would *not* in fact have a society in which the needs of everyone are being maximally met. To the reply, but what if more needs for everyone were met by ignoring or overriding such entitlements, the radical egalitarian should respond that that is, given the way we are, a thoroughly hypothetical situation and that theories of morality cannot be expected to give guidance for all logically possible worlds but only for worlds which are reasonably like what our actual world is or plausibly could come to be. Setting this argument aside for the moment, even if it did turn out that the need satisfaction linked with having other things—things that involved the overriding of those entitlements—was sufficient to make it the case that more need satisfaction all around for *everyone* would be achieved by overriding those entitlements, then, for reasonable people who clearly saw that, these entitlements would not have the weight presently given to them. They either would not have the importance presently attached to them or the need for the additional living space would be so great that their being overridden would seem, everything considered, the lesser of two evils (as in the example of the postwar housing situation).

There are without doubt genuine entitlements and a theory of justice must take them seriously, but they are not absolute. If the need is great enough we can see the merit in overriding them, just as in law as well as morality the right of eminent domain is recognized. Finally, while I have talked of entitlements here, parallel arguments will go through for desert.

III

I want now to relate this articulation of what equality comes to to my radically egalitarian principles of justice. My articulation of justice is a certain spelling out of the slogan proclaimed by Marx "From each according to his ability, to each according to his needs." The egalitarian conception of society argues for the desirability of bringing into existence a world, once the springs of social wealth flow freely, in which everyone's needs are as fully satisfied as possible and in which everyone gives according to his ability. Which means, among other things, that everyone, according to his ability, shares the burdens of society. There is an equal giving and equal responsibility here according to ability. It is here, with respect to giving according to ability and with respect to receiving according to need, that a complex equality of result, i.e., equality of condition, is being advocated by the radical egalitarian. What it comes to is this: each of us, where each is to count for one and none to count for more than one, is to give according to ability and receive according to need.

My radical egalitarian principles of justice read as follows:

(1) Each person is to have an equal right to the most extensive total system of equal basic liberties and opportunities (including equal opportunities for meaningful work, for self-determination and political and economic participation) compatible with a similar treatment of all. (This principle gives expression to a commitment to attain and/or sustain equal moral autonomy and equal self-respect.)

(2) After provisions are made for common social (community) values, for capital overhead to preserve the society's productive capacity, allowances made for

differing unmanipulated needs and preferences, and due weight is given to the just entitlements of individuals, the income and wealth (the common stock of means) is to be so divided that each person will have a right to an equal share. The necessary burdens requisite to enhance human well-being are also to be equally shared, subject, of course, to limitations by differing abilities and differing situations. (Here I refer to different natural environments and the like and not to class position and the like.)

Here we are talking about equality as a right rather than about equality as a goal as has previously been the subject matter of equality in this chapter. These principles of egalitarianism spell out rights people have and duties they have under *conditions of very considerable productive abundance*. We have a right to certain basic liberties and opportunities and we have, subject to certain limitations spelled out in the second principle, a right to an equal share of the income and wealth in the world. We also have a duty, again subject to the qualifications mentioned in the principle, to do our equal share in shouldering the burdens necessary to protect us from ills and to enhance our well-being.

What is the relation between these rights and the ideal of equality of condition discussed earlier? That is a goal for which we can struggle now to bring about conditions which will some day make its achievement possible, while these rights only become rights when the goal is actually achievable. We have no such rights in slave, feudal or capitalist societies or such duties in those societies. In that important way they are not natural rights for they depend on certain social conditions and certain social structures (socialist ones) to be realizable. What we can say is that it is always desirable that socio-economic conditions come into being which would make it possible to achieve the goal of equality of condition so that these rights and duties I speak of could obtain. But that is a far cry from saying we have such rights and duties now.

It is a corollary of this, if these radical egalitarian principles of justice are correct, that capitalist societies (even capitalist welfare state societies such as Sweden) and statist societies such as the Soviet Union or the People's Republic of China cannot be just societies or at least they must be societies, structured as they are, which are defective in justice. (This is not to say that some of these societies are not juster than others. Sweden is juster than South Africa, Canada than the United States and Cuba and Nicaragua than Honduras and Guatemala.) But none of these statist or capitalist societies can satisfy these radical egalitarian principles of justice, for equal liberty, equal opportunity, equal wealth or equal sharing of burdens are not at all possible in societies having their social structure. So we do not have such rights now but we can take it as a goal that we bring such a society into being with a commitment to an equality of condition in which we would have these rights and duties. Here we require first the massive development of productive power.

The connection between equality as a goal and equality as a right spelled out in these principles of justice is this. This equality of condition appealed to in equality as a goal would, if it were actually to obtain, have to contain the rights and duties enunciated in those principles. There could be no equal life prospects between all people or anything approximating an equal satisfaction of needs if there were not in place something like the system of equal basic liberties referred to in the first principle. Furthermore, without the rough equality of wealth referred to in the second principle, there would be disparities in power and self-direction in society which would render impossible an equality of life prospects or the social conditions required for an equal satisfaction of needs. And plainly, without a roughly equal sharing of burdens, there cannot be a situation where everyone has equal life prospects or has the chance equally to satisfy his needs. The principles of radical egalitarian justice are implicated in its conception of an ideally adequate equality of condition.

IV

The principles of radical egalitarian justice I have articulated are meant to apply globally and not just to particular societies. But it is certainly fair to say that not a few would worry that such principles of radical egalitarian justice, if applied globally, would force the people in wealthier sections of the world to a kind of financial hari-kari. There are millions of desperately impoverished people. Indeed millions are starving or malnourished and things are not getting any better. People in the affluent societies cannot but worry about whether they face a bottomless pit. Many believe that meeting, even in the most minimal way, the needs of the impoverished is going to put an incredible burden on people—people of all classes—in the affluent societies. Indeed it will, if acted on non-evasively, bring about their impoverishment, and this is just too much to ask. Radical egalitarianism is forgetting Rawls' admonitions about "the strains of commitment"—the recognition that in any rational account of what is required of us, we must at least give a minimal healthy self-interest its due. We must construct our moral philosophy for human beings and not for saints. Human nature is less fixed than conservatives are wont to assume, but it is not so elastic that we can reasonably expect people to impoverish themselves to make the massive transfers between North and South—the industrialized world and the Third World—required to begin to approach a situation where even Rawls' principles would be in place on a global level, to say nothing of my radical egalitarian principles of justice.[3]

The first thing to say in response to this is that my radical egalitarian principles are meant actually to guide practice, to directly determine what we are to do, only in a world of extensive abundance where, as Marx put it, the springs of social wealth flow freely. If such a world cannot be attained with the undermining of capitalism and the full putting into place, stabilizing, and developing of socialist relations of production, then such radical egalitarian principles can only remain as heuristic ideals against which to measure the distance of our travel in the direction of what would be a perfectly just society.

Aside from a small capitalist class, along with those elites most directly and profitably beholden to it (together a group constituting not more than 5 percent of the world's population), there would, in taking my radical egalitarian principles as heuristic guides, be no impoverishment of people in the affluent societies, if we moved in a radically more egalitarian way to start to achieve a global fairness. There would be massive transfers of wealth between North and South, but this could be done in stages so that, for the people in the affluent societies (capitalist elites apart), there need be no undermining of the quality of their lives. Even what were once capitalist elites would not be impoverished or reduced to some kind of bleak life though they would, the incidental Spartan types aside, find their life styles altered. But their health and general well being, including their opportunities to do significant and innovative work, would, if anything, be enhanced. And while some of the sources of their enjoyment would be a thing of the past, there would still be a considerable range of enjoyments available to them sufficient to afford anyone a rich life that could be lived with verve and zest.

A fraction of what the United States spends on defense spending would take care of immediate problems of starvation and malnutrition for most of the world. For longer range problems such as bringing conditions of life in the Third World more in line with conditions of life in Sweden and Switzerland, what is necessary is the dismantling of the capitalist system and the creation of a socio-economic system with an underlying rationale directing it toward producing for needs—everyone's needs. With this altered productive mode, the irrationalities and waste of capitalist production would be cut. There would be no more built-in obsolescence, no more merely cosmetic changes in consumer durables, no more fashion roulette, no more useless products and the like. Moreover, the enormous expenditures that go into the war industry would be a thing of the past. There would be great transfers from North to South, but it would be from the North's capitalist fat and not from things people in the North really need. (There would, in other words, be no self-pauperization of people in the capitalist world.) . . .

V

It has been repeatedly argued that equality undermines liberty. Some would say that a society in which principles like my radical egalitarian principles were adopted, or even the liberal egalitarian principles of Rawls or Dworkin were adopted, would not be a free society. My arguments have been just the reverse. I have argued that it is only in an egalitarian society that full and extensive liberty is possible.

Perhaps the egalitarian and the anti-egalitarian are arguing at cross purposes? What we need to recognize, it has been argued, is that we have two kinds of rights both of which are important to freedom but to rather different freedoms and which are freedoms which not infrequently conflict.[4] We have rights to *fair terms of cooperation* but we also have rights to non-interference. If a right of either kind is overridden our freedom is diminished. The reason why it might be thought that the egalitarian and the anti-egalitarian may be arguing at cross purposes is that the egalitarian is pointing to the fact that rights to fair terms of cooperation and their associated liberties require equality while the anti-egalitarian is pointing to the fact that rights to noninterference and their associated liberties conflict with equality. They focus on different liberties.

What I have said above may not be crystal clear, so let me explain. People have a right to fair terms of cooperation. In political terms this comes to the equal right of all to effective participation in government and, in more broadly social terms, and for a society of economic wealth, it means people having a right to a roughly equal distribution of the benefits and burdens of the basic social arrangements that affect their lives and for them to stand in such relations to each other such that no one has the power to dominate the life of another. By contrast, rights to non-interference come to the equal right of all to be left alone by the government and more broadly to live in a society in which people have a right peacefully to pursue their interests without interference.

The conflict between equality and liberty comes down to, very essentially, the conflicts we get in modern societies between rights to fair terms of cooperation and rights to noninterference. As Joseph Schumpeter saw and J. S. Mill before him, one could have a thoroughly democratic society (at least in conventional terms) in which rights to noninterference might still be extensively violated. A central anti-egalitarian claim is that we cannot have an egalitarian society in which the very precious liberties that go with the rights to non-interference would not be violated.

Socialism and egalitarianism plainly protect rights to fair terms of cooperation. Without the social (collective) ownership and control of the means of production, involving with this, in the initial stages of socialism at least, a workers' state, economic power will be concentrated in the hands of a few who will in turn, as a result, dominate effective participation in government. Some right-wing libertarians blind themselves to that reality, but it is about as evident as can be. Only an utter turning away from the facts of social life could lead to any doubts about this at all. But then this means that in a workers' state, if some people have capitalistic impulses, that they would have their rights peacefully to pursue their own interests interfered with. They might wish to invest, retain and bequeath in economic domains. In a workers' state these capitalist acts in many circumstances would have to be forbidden, but that would be a violation of an individual's right to non-interference and the fact, if it was a fact, that we by democratic vote, even with vast majorities, had made such capitalist acts illegal would still not make any difference because individuals' rights to noninterference would still be violated.

We are indeed driven, by egalitarian impulses, of a perfectly understandable sort, to accept interference with laissez-faire capitalism to protect non-subordination and non-domination of people by protecting the egalitarian right to fair terms of cooperation and the enhanced liberty that that brings. Still, as things stand, this leads inevitably to violations of the right to non-interference and this brings with it a diminution of liberty. There will be people with capitalist impulses and they will be interfered with. It is no good denying, it will be said, that egalitarianism and particularly socialism will not lead to interference with very precious individual liberties, namely with our right peacefully to pursue our interests without interference.[5]

The proper response to this, as should be apparent from what I have argued throughout, is that to live in any society at all, capitalist, socialist or whatever, is to live in a world in which there will be some restriction or other on our rights peacefully to pursue our interests without interference. I can't lecture in Albanian or even in French in a standard philosophy class at the University of Calgary, I can't jog naked on most beaches, borrow a book from your library without your permission, fish in your trout pond without your permission, take your dog for a walk without your say so and the like. At least some of these things have been thought to be things which I might peacefully pursue in my own interests. Stopping me from doing them is plainly interfering with my peaceful pursuit of my own interests. And indeed it is an infringement on liberty, an interference with my doing what I may want to do.

However, for at least many of these activities, and particularly the ones having to do with property, even right-wing libertarians think that such interference is perfectly justified. But, justified or not, they still plainly constitute a restriction on our individual freedom. However, what we must also recognize is that there will always be some such restrictions on freedom in any society whatsoever, just in virtue of the fact that a normless society, without the restrictions that having norms imply, is a contradiction in terms.[6] Many restrictions are hardly felt as restrictions, as in the attitudes of many people toward seat-belt legislation, but they are, all the same, plainly restriction on our liberty. It is just that they are thought to be unproblematically justified.

To the question would a socialism with a radical egalitarianism restrict some liberties, including some liberties rooted in rights to noninterference, the answer is that it indeed would; but so would laissez-faire capitalism, aristocratic conceptions of justice, liberal conceptions or any social formations at all, with their associated conceptions of justice. The relevant question is which of these restrictions are justified.

The restrictions on liberty preferred by radical egalitarianism and socialism, I have argued, are justified for they, of the various alternatives, give us both the most extensive and the most abundant system of liberty possible in modern conditions with their thorough protection of the right to fair terms of cooperation. Radical egalitarianism will also, and this is central for us, protect our civil liberties and these liberties are, of course, our most basic liberties. These are the liberties which are the most vital for us to protect. What it will not do is to protect our unrestricted liberties to invest, retain and bequeath in the economic realm and it will not protect our unrestricted freedom to buy and sell. There is, however, no good reason to think that these restrictions are restrictions of anything like a basic liberty. Moreover, we are justified in restricting our freedom to buy and sell if such restrictions strengthen, rather than weaken, our total system of liberty. This is in this way justified, for only by such market restrictions can the rights of the vast majority of people to effective participation in government and an equal role in the control of their social lives be protected. I say this because if we let the market run free in this way, power will pass into the hands of a few who will control the lives of the many and determine the fundamental design of the society. The actual liberties that are curtailed in a radically egalitarian social order are inessential liberties whose restriction in contemporary circumstances enhances human well-being and indeed makes for a firmer entrenchment of basic liberties and for their greater extension globally. That is to say, we here restrict some liberty in order to attain more liberty and a more equally distributed pattern of liberty. More people will be able to do what they want and have a greater control over their own lives than in a capitalist world order with its at least implicit inegalitarian commitments.

However, some might say I still have not faced the most central objection to radical egalitarianism, namely its statism. (I would prefer to say its putative statism.) The picture is this. The egalitarian state must be in the redistribution business. It has to make, or make sure there is made, an equal relative contribution to the welfare of every citizen. But this in effect means that the socialist state or, for that matter, the welfare state, will be deeply interventionist in our personal lives. It will be in the business, as one right-winger emotively put it, of cutting one person down to size in order to bring about that person's equality with another person who was in a previously disadvantageous position.[7] That is said to be morally objectionable and it would indeed be deeply morally objectionable in many circumstances. But it isn't in the circumstances in which the radical egalitarian presses for redistribution. (I am not speaking of what might be mere equalizing upwards.) The circumstances are these: Capitalist A gets his productive property confiscated so that he could no longer dominate and control the lives of proletarians B, C, D, E, F, and G. But what is wrong with it where this "cutting down to size"—in reality the confiscation of productive property or the taxation of the capitalist—involves no violation of A's civil liberties or the harming of his actual well-being (health, ability to work, to cultivate the arts, to have fruitful personal relations, to live in comfort and the like) and where B, C, D, E, F, and G will have their freedom and their well-being thoroughly enhanced if such confiscation or taxation occurs? Far from being morally objectionable, it is precisely the sort of state of affairs that people ought to favor. It certainly protects more liberties and more significant liberties than it undermines.

There is another familiar anti-egalitarian argument designed to establish the liberty-undermining qualities of egalitarianism. It is an argument we have touched upon in discussing meritocracy. It turns on the fact that in any society there will be both talents and handicaps. Where they exist, what do we want to do about maintaining equal distribution? Egalitarians, radical or otherwise, certainly do not want to penalize people for talent. That being so, then surely people should be allowed to retain the benefits of superior talent. But this in some circumstances will lead to significant inequalities in resources and in the meeting of needs. To sustain equality there will have to be an ongoing redistribution in the direction of the less talented and less fortunate. But this redistribution from the more to the less talented does plainly penalize the talented for their talent. That, it will be said, is something which is both unfair and an undermining of liberty.

The following, it has been argued, makes the above evident enough.[8] If people have talents they will tend to want to use them. And if they use them they are very likely to come out ahead. Must not egalitarians say they ought not to be able to come out ahead no matter how well they use their talents and no matter how considerable these talents are? But that is intolerably restrictive and unfair.

The answer to the above anti-egalitarian argument is implicit in a number of things I have already said. But here let me confront this familiar argument directly. Part of the answer comes out in probing some of the ambiguities of "coming out ahead." Note, incidentally, that (1) not all reflective, morally sensitive people will be so concerned with that, and (2) that being very concerned with that is a mentality that capitalism inculcates. Be that as it may, to turn to the ambiguities, note that some take "coming out ahead" principally to mean "being paid well for the use of those talents" where "being paid well" is being paid sufficiently well so that it creates inequalities sufficient to disturb the preferred egalitarian patterns. (Without that, being paid well would give one no relative advantage.) But, as we have seen, "coming out ahead" need not take that form at all. Talents can be recognized and acknowledged in many ways. First, in just the respect and admiration of a fine employment of talents that would naturally come from people seeing them so displayed where these people were not twisted by envy; second, by having, because of these talents, interesting and secure work that their talents fit them for and they merit in virtue of those talents. Moreover, having more money is not going to matter much—for familiar marginal utility reasons—where what in capitalist societies would be called the welfare floors are already very high, this being made feasible by the great productive wealth of the society. Recall that in such a society of abundance everyone will be well off and secure. In such a society people are not going to be very concerned about being a little better off than someone else. The talented are in no way, in such a situation, robbed to help the untalented and handicapped or penalized for their talents. They are only prevented from amassing wealth (most particularly productive wealth), which would enable them to dominate the untalented and the handicapped and to control the social life of the world of which they are both a part. . . .

I think that the moral authority for abstract egalitarianism, for the belief that the interests of everyone matters and matters equally, comes from its being the case that it is *required by the moral point of view*.[9] What I am predicting is that a person who has a good understanding of what morality is, has a good knowledge of the facts, is not ideologically mystified, takes an impartial point of view, and has an attitude of impartial caring, would, if not conceptually confused, come to accept the abstract egalitarian thesis. I see no way of arguing someone into such an egalitarianism who does not in this general way have a love of humankind.[10] A hard-hearted Hobbesist is not reachable here. But given that a person has that love of humankind—that impartial and impersonal caring—together with the other qualities mentioned above, then, I predict, that that person would be an egalitarian at least to the extent of accepting the abstract egalitarian thesis. What I am claiming is that if these conditions were to obtain (if they ceased to be just counterfactuals), then there would be a consensus among moral agents about accepting the abstract egalitarian thesis. . . .

Notes

1. See the debate between Robert Nozick, Daniel Bell and James Tobin, "If Inequality Is Inevitable, What Can Be Done About It?", *The New York Times,* January 3, 1982, p. E5. The exchange between

Bell and Nozick reveals the differences between the old egalitarianism and right-wing libertarianism. It is not only that the right and left clash but sometimes right clashes with right.

2. Amartya Sen, "Equality of What?", *The Tanner Lectures on Human Values,* vol. 1 (1980), ed. Sterling M. McMurrin (Cambridge, England: Cambridge University Press, 1980), pp. 198–220.

3. Henry Shue, "The Burdens of Justice," *The Journal of Philosophy* 80, no. 10 (October 1983): 600–601; 606–8.

4. Richard W. Miller, "Marx and Morality," in *Marxism,* eds. J. R. Pennock and J. W. Chapman, Nomos 26 (New York: New York University Press, 1983), pp. 9–11.

5. Ibid., p. 10.

6. This has been argued from both the liberal center and the left. Ralf Dahrendorf, *Essays in the Theory of Society* (Stanford, Calif.: Stanford University Press, 1968), pp. 151–78; and G. A. Cohen, "Capitalism, Freedom and the Proletariat," in *The Idea of Freedom: Essays in Honour of Isaiah Berlin,* ed. Alan Ryan (Oxford: Oxford University Press, 1979).

7. The graphic language should be duly noted. Jan Narveson, "On Dworkinian Equality," *Social Philosophy and Policy* 1, no. 1 (autumn 1983): 4.

8. Ibid., pp. 1–24.

9. Some will argue that there is no such thing as a moral point of view. My differences with him about the question of whether the amoralist can be argued into morality not withstanding, I think Kurt Baier, in a series of articles written subsequent to his *The Moral Point of View,* has clearly shown that there is something reasonably determinate that can, without ethnocentrism, be called "the moral point of view."

10. Richard Norman has impressively argued that this is an essential background assumption of the moral point of view. Richard Norman, "Critical Notice of Rodger Beehler's *Moral Life,*" *Canadian Journal of Philosophy* 11, no. 1 (March 1981): 157–83.

8

How Liberty Upsets Patterns

ROBERT NOZICK

It is not clear how those holding alternative conceptions of distributive justice can reject the entitlement conception of justice in holdings. For suppose a distribution favored by one of these nonentitlement conceptions is realized. Let us suppose it is your favorite one and let us call this distribution D_1; perhaps everyone has an equal share, perhaps shares vary in accordance with some dimension you treasure. Now suppose that Wilt Chamberlain is greatly in demand by basketball teams, being a great gate attraction. (Also suppose contracts run only for a year, with players being free agents.) He signs the following sort of contract with a team: In each home game, twenty-five cents from the price of each ticket of admission goes to him. (We ignore the question of whether he is "gouging" the owners, letting them look out for themselves.) The season starts, and people cheerfully attend his team's games; they buy their tickets, each time dropping a separate twenty-five cents of their admission price into a special box with Chamberlain's name on it. They are excited about seeing him play; it is worth the total admission price to them. Let us suppose that in one season one million persons attend his home games, and Wilt Chamberlain winds up with $250,000, a much larger sum than the average income and larger even than anyone else has. Is he entitled to this income? Is this new distribution D_2, unjust? If so, why? There is *no* question about whether each of the people was entitled to the control over the resources they held in D_1, because that was the distribution (your favorite) that (for the purposes of argument) we assumed was acceptable. Each of these persons *chose* to give twenty-five cents of their money to Chamberlain. They could have spent it on going to the movies, or on candy bars, or on copies of *Dissent* magazine, or of *Monthly Review*. But they all, at least one million of them, converged on giving it to Wilt Chamberlain in exchange for watching him play basketball. If D_1 was a just distribution, and people voluntarily moved from it to D_2 transferring parts of their shares they were given under D_1 (what was it for if not to do something with?), isn't D_2 also just? If people were entitled to dispose of the resources to which they were entitled (under D_1), didn't this include their being entitled to give it to, or exchange it with, Wilt Chamberlain? Can anyone else complain on grounds of justice? Each other person already has his legitimate share under D_1. Under D_1, there is nothing that anyone has that anyone else has a claim of justice against. After someone transfers something to Wilt Chamberlain, third parties *still* have their legitimate shares; *their* shares are not changed. By what process could such a transfer among two persons give rise to a legitimate claim of distributive justice on a portion of what was transferred, by a third party who had no claim of justice on any holding of the others *before* the transfer?[1] To cut off objections irrelevant here, we might imagine the exchanges occurring in a socialist society, after hours: After playing whatever basketball he does in his daily work, or doing whatever other daily work he does, Wilt Chamberlain decides to put in *overtime* to earn additional money. (First his work quota is set; he works time over that.) Or imagine it is a skilled juggler people like to see, who puts on shows after hours.

Why might someone work overtime in a society in which it is assumed their needs are satisfied? Perhaps because they care about things other than needs. I like to write in books that I read, and to have easy access to books for browsing at odd hours. It would be very pleasant and convenient to have the resources of Widener Library in my back yard. No society, I assume, will provide such resources close to each person who would like them as part of his regular allotment (under D_1). Thus, persons either must do without some extra things that they want, or be allowed to do something extra to get some of these things. On what basis could the inequalities that would eventuate be forbidden? Notice also that small factories would spring up in a socialist society, unless forbidden. I melt down some of my personal possessions (under D_1) and build a machine out of the material. I offer you, and others, a philosophy lecture once a week in exchange for your cranking the handle on my machine, whose products I exchange for yet other things, and so on. (The raw materials used by the machine are given to me by others who possess them under D_1, in exchange for hearing lectures.) Each person might participate to gain things over and above their allotment under D_1. Some persons even might want to leave their job in socialist industry and work full time in this private sector. [In any case] I wish merely to note how private property even in means of production would occur in a socialist society that did not forbid people to use as they wished some of the resources they are given under the socialist distribution D_1.[2] The socialist society would have to forbid capitalist acts between consenting adults.

The general point illustrated by the Wilt Chamberlain example and the example of the entrepreneur in a socialist society is that no end-state principle or distributional patterned principle of justice can be continuously realized without continuous interference with people's lives. Any favored pattern would be transformed into one unfavored by the principle, by people choosing to act in various ways; for example, by people exchanging goods and services with other people, or giving things to other people, things the transferrers are entitled to under the favored distributional pattern. To maintain a pattern one must either continually interfere to stop people from transferring resources as they wish to, or continually (or periodically) interfere to take from some persons resources that others for some reason chose to transfer to them. (But if some time limit is to be set on how long people may keep resources others voluntarily transfer to them, why let them keep these resources for *any* period of time? Why not have immediate confiscation?) It might be objected that all persons voluntarily will choose to refrain from actions which would upset the pattern. This presupposes unrealistically (1) that all will most want to maintain the pattern (are those who don't, to be "reeducated" or forced to undergo "self-criticism"?), (2) that each can gather enough information about his own actions and the ongoing activities of others to discover which of his actions will upset the pattern, and (3) that diverse and far-flung persons can coordinate their actions to dovetail into the pattern. Compare the manner in which the market is neutral among persons' desires, as it reflects and transmits widely scattered information via prices, and coordinates persons' activities.

It puts things perhaps a bit too strongly to say that every patterned (or end-state) principle is liable to be thwarted by the voluntary actions of the individual parties transferring some of their shares they recieve under the principle. For perhaps some *very* weak patterns are not so thwarted.[3] Any distributional pattern with any egalitarian component is overturnable by the voluntary actions of individual persons over time, as is every patterned condition with sufficient content so as actually to have been proposed as presenting the central core of distributive justice. Still, given the possibility that some weak conditions or patterns may not be unstable in this way, it would be better to formulate an explicit description of the kind of interesting and contentful patterns under discussion, and to prove a theorem about their instability. Since the weaker the patterning, the more likely it is that the entitlement system itself satisfies it, a plausible conjecture is that any patterning either is unstable or is satisfied by the entitlement system. . . .

Notes

1. Might not a transfer have instrumental effects on a third party, changing his feasible options? (But what if the two parties to the transfer independently had used their holdings in this fashion?) I discuss this question below, but note here that this question concedes the point for distributions of ultimate intrinsic noninstrumental goods (pure utility experiences, so to speak) that are transferable. It also might be objected that the transfer might make a third party more envious because it worsens his position relative to someone else. I find it incomprehensible how this can be thought to involve a claim of justice. . . .

    Here and elsewhere in this chapter, a theory which incorporates elements of pure procedural justice might find what I say acceptable, *if* kept in its proper place; that is, if background institutions exist to ensure the satisfaction of certain conditions on distributive shares. But if these institutions are not themselves the sum or invisible-hand result of people's voluntary (nonaggressive) actions, the constraints they impose require justification. At no point does *our* argument assume any background institutions more extensive than those of the minimal nightwatchman state, a state limited to protecting persons against murder, assault, theft, fraud, and so forth.

2. See the selection from John Henry MacKay's novel, *The Anarchists*, reprinted in Leonard Krimmerman and Lewis Perry, eds., *Patterns of Anarchy* (New York: Doubleday Anchor Books, 1966), in which an individualist anarchist presses upon a communist anarchist the following question: "Would you, in the system of society which you call 'free Communism' prevent individuals from exchanging their labor among themselves by means of their own medium of exchange? And further: Would you prevent them from occupying land for the purpose of personal use?" The novel continues: "[the] question was not to be escaped. If he answered 'Yes!' he admitted that society had the right of control over the individual and threw overboard the autonomy of the individual which he had always zealously defended; if, on the other hand, he answered 'No!' he admitted the right of private property which he had just denied so emphatically. . . . Then he answered, 'In Anarchy any number of men must have the right of forming a voluntary association, and so realizing their ideas in practice. Nor can I understand how anyone could justly be driven from the land and house which he uses and occupies . . . every serious man must declare himself: for Socialism, and thereby for force and against liberty, or for Anarchism, and thereby for liberty and against force.' " In contrast, we find Noam Chomsky writing, "Any consistent anarchist must oppose private ownership of the means of production," "the consistent anarchist then . . . will be a socialist . . . of a particular sort." Introduction to Daniel Guerin, *Anarchism: From Theory to Practice* (New York: Monthly Review Press, 1970), pages xiii, xv.

3. Is the patterned principle stable that requires merely that a distribution be Pareto-optimal? One person might give another a gift or bequest that the second could exchange with a third to their mutual benefit. Before the second makes this exchange there is not Pareto-optimality. Is a stable pattern presented by a principle choosing that among the Pareto-optimal positions that satisfies some further condition C? It may seem that there cannot be a counterexample, for won't any voluntary exchange made away from a situation show that the first situation wasn't Pareto-optimal. (Ignore the implausibility of this last claim for the case of bequests.) But principles are to be satisfied over time, during which new possibilities arise. A distribution that at one time satisfies the criterion of Pareto-optimality might not do so when some new possibilities arise (Wilt Chamberlain grows up and starts playing basketball); and though people's activities will tend to move then to a new Pareto-optimal position, *this* new one need not satisfy the contentful condition C. Continual interference will be needed to insure the continual satisfaction of C. (The theoretical possibility of a pattern's being maintained by some invisible-hand process that brings it back to an equilibrium that fits the pattern when deviations occur should be investigated.)

■■□□□□

PART IV

Welfare Liberal Justice: The Contractarian Perspective

9

The Contractual Basis for a Just Society

Immanuel Kant

Among all the contracts by which a large group of men unites to form a society, . . .
the contract establishing a *civil constitution* . . . is of an exceptional nature. For while,
so far as its execution is concerned, it has much in common with all others that are
likewise directed toward a chosen end to be pursued by joint effort, it is essentially
different from all others in the principle of its constitution. . . . In all social contracts,
we find a union of many individuals for some common end which they all *share.* But
a union as an end in itself which they all *ought to share* and which is thus an absolute
and primary duty in all external relationships whatsoever among human beings
(who cannot avoid mutually influencing one another), is only found in a society
insofar as it constitutes a civil state, i.e. a commonwealth. . . .

The civil state, regarded purely as a lawful state, is based on the following *a priori*
principles:

1. the *freedom* of every member of society as a *human being*
2. the *equality* of each with all the others as a *subject*
3. the *independence* of each member of a commonwealth as a *citizen*

These principles are not so much laws given by an already established state, as
laws by which a state can alone be established in accordance with pure rational
principles of external human right. Thus:

From *Kant's Political Writings,* edited by Hans Reiss and translated by H. B. Nisbet (1970), pp. 73–81.
Reprinted by permission of Cambridge University Press.

1. Man's *freedom* as a human being, as a principle for the constitution of a commonwealth, can be expressed in the following formula. No one can compel me to be happy in accordance with his conception of the welfare of others, for each may seek his happiness in whatever way he sees fit, so long as he does not infringe upon the freedom of others to pursue a similar end which can be reconciled with the freedom of everyone else within a workable general law—i.e., he must accord to others the same right as he enjoys himself. A government might be established on the principle of benevolence toward the people, like that of a father toward his children. Under such a *paternal government* . . . the subjects, as immature children who cannot distinguish what is truly useful or harmful to themselves, would be obliged to behave purely passively and to rely upon the judgement of the head of state as to how they *ought* to be happy, and upon his kindness in willing their happiness at all. Such a government is the greatest conceivable *despotism*, i.e., a constitution which suspends the entire freedom of its subjects, who thenceforth have no rights whatsoever. The only conceivable government for men who are capable of possessing rights, even if the ruler is benevolent, is not a *paternal* but a *patriotic* government. . . . A *patriotic* attitude is one where everyone in the state, not excepting its head, regards the commonwealth as a maternal womb, or the land as the paternal ground from which he himself sprang and which he must leave to his descendants as a treasured pledge. Each regards himself as authorized to protect the rights of the commonwealth by laws of the general will, but not to submit it to his personal use at his own absolute pleasure. This right of freedom belongs to each member of the commonwealth as a human being, insofar as each is a being capable of possessing rights.

2. Man's equality as a subject might be formulated as follows. Each member of the commonwealth has rights of coercion in relation to all the others, except in relation to the head of state. For he alone is not a member of the commonwealth, but its creator or preserver, and he alone is authorized to coerce others without being subject to any coercive law himself. But all who are subject to laws are the subjects of a state, and are thus subject to the right of coercion along with all other members of the commonwealth; the only exception is a single person (in either the physical or the moral sense of the word), the head of state, through whom alone the rightful coercion of all others can be exercised. For if he too could be coerced, he would not be the head of state, and the hierarchy of subordination would ascend infinitely. But if there were two persons exempt from coercion, neither would be subject to coercive laws, and neither could do to the other anything contrary to right, which is impossible.

This uniform equality of human beings as subjects of a state is, however, perfectly consistent with the utmost inequality of the mass in the degree of its possessions, whether these take the form of physical or mental superiority over others, or of fortuitous external property and of particular rights (of which there may be many) with respect to others. Thus the welfare of the one depends very much on the will of the other (the poor depending on the rich), the one must obey the other (as the child its parents or the wife her husband), the one serves (the laborer) while the other pays, etc. Nevertheless, they are all equal as subjects *before the law*, which, as the pronouncement of the general will, can only be single in form, and which concerns the form of right and not the material or object in relation to which I possess rights. For no one can coerce anyone else other than through the public law and its executor, the head of state, while everyone else can resist the others in the same way and to the same degree. No one, however, can lose this authority to coerce others and to have rights toward them except through committing a crime. And no one can voluntarily renounce his rights by a contract or legal transaction to the effect that he has no rights but only duties, for such a contract would deprive him of the right to make a contract, and would thus invalidate the one he had already made.

From this idea of the equality of men as subjects in a commonwealth, there emerges this further formula: every member of the commonwealth must be entitled to reach any degree of rank which a subject can earn through his talent, his industry and his good fortune, And his fellow-subjects may not stand in his way by *hereditary* prerogatives or privileges of rank and thereby hold him and his descendants back indefinitely.

All right consists solely in the restriction of the freedom of others, with the qualification that their freedom can co-exist with my freedom within the terms of a general law; and public right in a commonwealth is simply a state of affairs regulated by a real legislation which conforms to this principle and is backed up by power, and under which a whole people live as subjects in a lawful state. . . . This is what we call a civil state, and it is characterized by equality in the effects and countereffects of freely willed actions which limit one another in accordance with the general law of freedom. Thus the *birthright* of each individual in such a state (i.e., before he has performed any acts which can be judged in relation to right) is absolutely *equal* as regards his authority to coerce others to use their freedom in a way which harmonizes with his freedom. Since birth is not an act on the part of the one who is born, it cannot create any inequality in his legal position and cannot make him submit to any coercive laws except insofar as he is subject, along with all the others, of the one supreme legislative power. Thus no member of the commonwealth can have a hereditary privilege as against his fellow-subjects; and no one can hand down to his descendants the privileges attached to the rank he occupies in the commonwealth, nor act as if he were qualified as a ruler by birth and forcibly prevent others from reaching the higher levels of the hierarchy (which are *superior* and *inferior,* but never *imperans* and *subiectus*) through their own merit. He may hand down everything else, so long as it is material and not pertaining to his person, for it may be acquired and disposed of as property and may over a series of generations create considerable inequalities in wealth among the members of the commonwealth (the employee and the employer, the landowner and the agricultural servants, etc.). But he may not prevent his subordinates from raising themselves to his own level if they are able and entitled to do so by their talent, industry and good fortune. If this were not so, he would be allowed to practise coercion without himself being subject to coercive countermeasures from others, and would thus be more than their fellow-subject. No one who lives within the lawful state of a commonwealth can forfeit this equality other than through some crime of his own, but never by contract or through military force. . . . For no legal transaction on his part or on that of anyone else can make him cease to be his own master. He cannot become like a domestic animal to be employed in any chosen capacity and retained therein without consent for any desired period, even with the reservation (which is at times sanctioned by religion, as among the Indians) that he may not be maimed or killed. He can be considered happy in any condition so long as he is aware that, if he does not reach the same level as others, the fault lies either with himself (i.e., lack of ability or serious endeavour) or with circumstances for which he cannot blame others, and not with the irresistible will of any outside party. For as far as right is concerned, his fellow-subjects have no advantage over him.

3. The *independence* . . . of a member of the commonwealth as a *citizen,* i.e., as a co-legislator, may be defined as follows. In the question of actual legislation, all who are free and equal under existing public laws may be considered equal, but not as regards the right to make these laws. Those who are not entitled to this right are nonetheless obliged, as members of the commonwealth, to comply with these laws, and they thus likewise enjoy their protection (not as *citizens* but as co-beneficiaries of this protection). For all right depends on laws. But a public law which defines for everyone that which is permitted and prohibited by right, is the act of a public will, from which all right proceeds and which must not therefore itself be able to do an injustice to any one. And this requires no less than the will of the entire people (since all men decide for all men and each decides for himself). For only toward oneself can one never act unjustly. But on the other hand, the will of another person cannot decide anything for someone without injustice, so that the law made by this other person would require a further law to limit his legislation. Thus an individual will cannot legislate for a commonwealth. For this requires freedom, equality and *unity* of the will of *all* the members. And the prerequisite for unity, since it necessitates a general vote (if freedom and equality are both present), is independence. The basic law, which can come only from the general, united will of the people, is called the *original contract.*

Anyone who has the right to vote on this legislation is a *citizen* . . . (i.e., citizen of a state). . . . The only qualification required by a citizen (apart, of course, from being an adult male) is that he must be his *own master* . . . , and must have some *property* (which can include any skill, trade, fine art or science) to support himself. In cases where he must earn his living from others, he must earn it only by *selling* that which is his,[1] and not by allowing others to make use of him; for he must in the true sense of the word *serve* no one but the commonwealth. In this respect, artisans and large or small landowners are all equal, and each is entitled to one vote only. As for landowners, we leave aside the questions of how anyone can have rightfully acquired more land than he can cultivate with his own hands (for acquisition by military seizure is not primary acquisition), and how it came about that numerous people who might otherwise have acquired permanent property were thereby reduced to serving someone else in order to live at all. It would certainly conflict with the above principle of equality if a law were to grant them a privileged status so that their descendants would always remain feudal landowners, without their land being sold or divided by inheritance and thus made useful to more people; it would also be unjust if only those belonging to an arbitrarily selected class were allowed to acquire land, should the estates in fact be divided. The owner of a large estate keeps out as many smaller property owners (and their votes) as could otherwise occupy his territories. He does not vote on their behalf, and himself has only *one* vote. It should be left exclusively to the ability, industry and good fortune of each member of the commonwealth to enable each to acquire a part and all to acquire the whole, although this distinction cannot be observed within the general legislation itself. The number of those entitled to vote on matters of legislation must be calculated purely from the number of property owners, not from the size of their properties.

Those who possess this right to vote must agree *unanimously* to the law of public justice, or else a legal contention would arise between those who agree and those who disagree, and it would require yet another higher legal principle to resolve it. An entire people cannot, however, be expected to reach unanimity, but only to show a majority of votes (and not even of direct votes, but simply of the votes of those delegated in a large nation to represent the people). Thus the actual principle of being content with majority decisions must be accepted unanimously and embodied in a contract; and this itself must be the ultimate basis on which a civil constitution is established.

Conclusion

This, then, is an *original contract* by means of which a civil and thus completely lawful constitution and commonwealth can alone be established. But we need by no means assume that this contract . . . , based on a coalition of the wills of all private individuals in a nation to form a common, public will for the purposes of rightful legislation, actually exists as a *fact,* for it cannot possibly be so. Such an assumption would mean that we would first have to prove from history that some nation, whose rights and obligations have been passed down to us, did in fact perform such an act, and handed down some authentic record or legal instrument, orally or in writing, before we could regard ourselves as bound by a preexisting civil constitution. It is in fact merely an *idea* of reason, which nonetheless has undoubted practical reality; for it can oblige every legislator to frame his laws in such a way that they could have been produced by the united will of a whole nation, and to regard each subject, insofar as he can claim citizenship, as if he had consented within the general will. This is the test of the rightfulness of every public law. For if the law is such that a whole people could not *possibly* agree to it (for example, if it stated that a certain class of *subjects* must be privileged as a hereditary *ruling class*), it is unjust; but if it is at least *possible* that a people could agree to it, it is our duty to consider the law as just, even if the people is at present in such a position or attitude of mind that it would probably refuse its consent if it were consulted.[2] But this restriction obviously applies only to the judgment of the legislator, not to that of the subject. Thus if a people, under some existing legislation, were asked to make a judgment which in all probability would prejudice its happiness, what should it do? Should the people not oppose the measure? The only possible answer is that they can do nothing but obey. For we are not concerned here with any happiness which the subject might expect to derive from the institutions or administration of the commonwealth, but primarily with the rights which would thereby be secured for everyone. And this is the highest principle from which all maxims relating to the commonwealth must begin, and which cannot be qualified by any other principles. No generally valid principle of legislation can be based on happiness. For both the current circumstances and the highly conflicting and variable illusions as to what happiness is (and no one can prescribe to others how they should attain it) make all fixed principles impossible, so that happiness alone can never be a suitable principle of legislation. The doctrine that *salus publica suprema civitatis lex est*[3] retains its value and authority un-diminished; but the public welfare which demands *first* consideration lies precisely in that legal constitution which guarantees everyone his freedom within the law, so that each remains free to seek his happiness in whatever way he thinks best, so long as he does not violate the lawful freedom and rights of his fellow subjects at large. If the supreme power makes laws which are primarily directed toward happiness (the affluence of the citizens, increased population, etc.), this cannot be regarded as the end for which a civil constitution was established, but only as a means of *securing the rightful state,* especially against external enemies of the people. The head of state must be authorized to judge for himself whether such measures are necessary for the commonwealth's prosperity, which is required to maintain its strength and stability both internally and against external enemies. The aim is not, as it were, to make the people happy against its will, but only to ensure its continued existence as a commonwealth.[4] The legislator may indeed err in judging whether or not the measures he adopts are *prudent,* but not in deciding whether or not the law harmonizes with the principle of right. For he has ready to hand as an infallible *a priori* standard, the idea of an original contract, and he need not wait for experience to show whether the means are suitable, as would be necessary if they were based on the principle of happiness. For so long as it is not self-contradictory to say that an entire people could agree to such a law, however painful it might seem, then the law is in harmony with right. But if a public law is beyond reproach (i.e., *irreprehensible*) with respect to right, it carries with it the authority to coerce those to whom it applies, and conversely, it forbids them to resist the will of the legislator by violent means. In other words, the power of the state to put the law into effect is also *irresistible,* and no rightfully established commonwealth can exist without a force of this kind to suppress all internal resistance. For such resistance would be dictated by a maxim which, if it became general, would destroy the whole civil constitution and put an end to the only state in which men can possess rights.

Notes

1. He who does a piece of work *(opus)* can sell it to someone else, just as if it were his own property. But guaranteeing one's labor *(praestatio operae)* is not the same as selling a commodity. The domestic servant, the shop assistant, the laborer, or even the barber, are merely laborers *(operarii),* not *artists (artifices,* in the wider sense) or members of the state, and are thus unqualified to be citizens. And although the man to whom I give my firewood to chop and the tailor to whom I give material to make into clothes both appear to have a similar relationship

toward me, the former differs from the latter in the same way as the barber from the wigmaker (to whom I may in fact have given the requisite hair) or the laborer from the artist or tradesman, who does a piece of work which belongs to him until he is paid for it. For the latter, in pursuing his trade, exchanges his property with someone else *(opus),* while the former allows someone else to make use of him. But I do admit that it is somewhat difficult to define the qualifications which entitle anyone to claim the status of being his own master.

2. If, for example, a war tax were proportionately imposed on all subjects, they could not claim, simply because it is oppressive, that it is unjust because the war is in their opinion unnecessary. For they are not entitled to judge this issue, since it is at least *possible* that the war is inevitable and the tax indispensable, so that the tax must be deemed rightful in the judgment of the subjects. But if certain estate owners were oppressed with levies for such a war, while others of the same class were exempted, it is easily seen that a whole people could never agree to a law of this kind, and it is entitled at least to make representations against it, since an unequal distribution of burdens can never be considered just.

3. "The public welfare is the supreme law of the state."

4. Measures of this kind might include certain restrictions on imports, so that the means of livelihood may be developed for the benefit of the subjects themselves and not as an advantage to foreigners or an encouragement for their industry. For without the prosperity of the people, the state would not have enough strength to resist external enemies or to preserve itself as a commonwealth.

10

Justice as Rational Choice Behind a Veil of Ignorance

JOHN RAWLS

My aim is to present a conception of justice which generalizes and carries to a higher level of abstraction the familiar theory of the social contract as found, say, in Locke, Rousseau, and Kant.[1] In order to do this we are not to think of the original contract as one to enter a particular society or to set up a particular form of government. Rather, the guiding idea is that the principles of justice for the basic structure of society are the object of the original agreement. They are the principles that free and rational persons concerned to further their own interests would accept in an initial position of equality as defining the fundamental terms of their association. These principles are to regulate all further agreements; they specify the kinds of social cooperation that can be entered into and the forms of government that can be established. This way of regarding the principles of justice I shall call justice as fairness.

Thus we are to imagine that those who engage in social cooperation choose together, in one joint act, the principles which are to assign basic rights and duties and to determine the division of social benefits. Men are to decide in advance how they are to regulate their claims against one another and what is to be the foundation

From *A Theory of Justice* (1971), pp. 11–22, 60–65, 150–156, 302–303, 252–257. Reprinted by permission of the publishers from *A Theory of Justice* by John Rawls, Cambridge, Mass.: the Belknap Press of Harvard University Press, Copyright © 1971 by the President and Fellows of Harvard College. Notes renumbered.

charter of their society. Just as each person must decide by rational reflection what constitutes his good—that is, the system of ends which it is rational for him to pursue—so a group of persons must decide once and for all what is to count among them as just and unjust. The choice which rational men would make in this hypothetical situation of equal liberty, assuming for the present that this choice problem has a solution, determines the principles of justice.

In justice as fairness the original position of equality corresponds to the state of nature in the traditional theory of the social contract. This original position is not, of course, thought of as an actual historical state of affairs, much less as a primitive condition of culture. It is understood as a purely hypothetical situation characterized so as to lead to a certain conception of justice.[2] Among the essential features of this situation is that no one knows his place in society, his class position or social status, nor does any one know his fortune in the distribution of natural assets and abilities, his intelligence, strength, and the like. I shall even assume that the parties do not know their conceptions of the good or their special psychological propensities. The principles of justice are chosen behind a veil of ignorance. This ensures that no one is advantaged or disadvantaged in the choice of principles by the outcome of natural chance or the contingency of social circumstances. Since all are similarly situated and no one is able to design principles to favor his particular condition, the principles of justice are the result of a fair agreement or bargain. For given the circumstances of the original position, the symmetry of everyone's relations to each other, this initial situation is fair between individuals as moral persons; that is, as rational beings with their own ends and capable, I shall assume, of a sense of justice. The original position is, one might say, the appropriate initial status quo, and thus the fundamental agreements reached in it are fair. This explains the propriety of the name "justice as fairness"; it conveys the idea that the principles of justice are agreed to in an initial situation that is fair. The name does not mean that the concepts of justice and fairness are the same, any more than the phrase "poetry as metaphor" means that the concepts of poetry and metaphor are the same.

Justice as fairness begins, as I have said, with one of the most general of all choices which persons might make together, namely, with the choice of the first principles of a conception of justice which is to regulate all subsequent criticism and reform of institutions. Then, having chosen a conception of justice, we can suppose that they are to choose a constitution and a legislature to enact laws, and so on, all in accordance with the principles of justice initially agreed upon. Our social situation is just if it is such that by this sequence of hypothetical agreements we would have contracted into the general system of rules which defines it. Moreover, assuming that the original position does determine a set of principles (that is, that a particular conception of justice would be chosen), it will then be true that whenever social institutions satisfy these principles those engaged in them can say to one another that they are cooperating on terms to which they would agree if they were free and equal persons whose relations with respect to one another were fair. They could all view their arrangements as meeting the stipulations which they would acknowledge in an initial situation that embodies widely accepted and reasonable constraints on the choice of principles. The general recognition of this fact would provide the basis for a public acceptance of the corresponding principles of justice. No society can, of course, be a scheme of cooperation which men enter voluntarily in a literal sense; each person finds himself placed at birth in some particular position in some particular society, and the nature of this position materially affects his life prospects. Yet a society satisfying the principles of justice as fairness comes as close as a society can to being a voluntary scheme, for it meets the principles which free and equal persons would assent to under circumstances that are fair. In this sense its members are autonomous and the obligations they recognize self-imposed.

One feature of justice as fairness is to think of the parties in the initial situation as rational and mutually disinterested. This does not mean that the parties are egoists; that is, individuals with only certain kinds of interests, say in wealth, prestige, and domination. But they are conceived as not taking an interest in one another's interests. They are to presume that even their spiritual aims may be opposed, in the way that the aims of those of different religions may be opposed. Moreover, the concept of rationality must be interpreted as far as possible in the narrow sense, standard in economic theory, of taking the most effective means to given ends. I shall modify this concept to some extent . . . , but one must try to avoid introducing into it any controversial ethical elements. The initial situation must be characterized by stipulations that are widely accepted.

In working out the conception of justice as fairness one main task clearly is to determine which principles of justice would be chosen in the original position. To do this we must describe this situation in some detail and formulate with care the problem of choice which it presents. It may be observed, however, that once the principles of justice are thought of as arising from an original agreement in a situation of equality, it is an open question whether the principle of utility would be acknowledged. Offhand it hardly seems likely that persons who view themselves as equals, entitled to press their claims upon one another, would agree to a principle which may require lesser life prospects for some simply for the sake of a greater sum of advantages enjoyed by others. Since each desires to protect his interests, his capacity to advance his conception of the good, no one has a reason to acquiesce in an enduring loss for himself in order to bring about a greater net balance of satisfaction. In the absence of strong and lasting benevolent impulses, a rational man would not accept a basic structure merely because it maximized the algebraic sum of advantages irrespective of its permanent effects on his own basic rights and interests. Thus it seems that the principle of utility is incompatible with the conception of social cooperation among equals for mutual advantage. It appears to be inconsistent with the idea of reciprocity implicit in the notion of a well-ordered society. Or, at any rate, so I shall argue.

I shall maintain instead that the persons in the initial situation would choose two rather different principles: the first requires equality in the assignment of basic rights and duties, while the second holds that social and economic inequalities (for example, inequalities of wealth and authority) are just only if they result in compensating benefits for everyone, and in particular for the least advantaged members of society. These principles rule out justifying institutions on the grounds that the hardships of some are offset by a greater good in the aggregate. It may be expedient but it is not just that some should have less in order that others may prosper. But there is no injustice in the greater benefits earned by a few provided that the situation of persons not so fortunate is thereby improved. The intuitive idea is that since everyone's well-being depends upon a scheme of cooperation without which no one could have a satisfactory life, the division of advantages should be such as to draw forth the willing cooperation of everyone taking part in it, including those less well situated. Yet this can be expected only if reasonable terms are proposed. The two principles mentioned seem to be a fair agreement on the basis of which those better endowed, or more fortunate in their social position, neither of which we can be said to deserve, could expect the willing cooperation of others when some workable scheme is a necessary condition of the welfare of all.[3] Once we decide to look for a conception of justice that nullifies the accidents of natural endowment and the contingencies of social circumstance as counters in quest for political and economic advantage, we are led to these principles. They express the result of leaving aside those aspects of the social world that seem arbitrary from a moral point of view.

The problem of the choice of principles, however, is extremely difficult. I do not expect the answer I shall suggest to be convincing to everyone. It is, therefore, worth noting from the outset that justice as fairness, like other contract views, consists of two parts: (1) an interpretation of the initial situation and of the problem of choice posed there, and (2) a set of principles which, it is argued, would be agreed to. One may accept the first part of the theory (or some variant thereof), but not the other, and conversely. The concept of the initial contractual situation may seem reasonable although the particular principles proposed are rejected. To be sure, I want to maintain that the most appropriate conception of this situation does lead to principles of justice contrary to utilitarianism and perfectionism, and therefore that the contract doctrine provides an alternative to these views. Still, one may dispute this contention even though one grants that the contractarian method is a useful way of studying ethical theories and of setting forth their underlying assumptions.

Justice as fairness is an example of what I have called a contract theory. Now there may be an objection to the term "contract" and related expressions, but I think it will serve reasonably well. Many words have misleading connotations which at first are likely to confuse. The terms "utility" and "utilitarianism" are surely no exception. They too have unfortunate suggestions which hostile critics have been willing to exploit; yet they are clear enough for those prepared to study utilitarian doctrine. The same should be true of the term "contract" applied to moral theories. As I have mentioned, to understand it one has to keep in mind that it implies a certain level of abstraction. In particular, the content of the relevant agreement is not to enter a given society or to adopt a given form of government, but to accept certain moral principles. Moreover, the undertakings referred to are purely hypothetical: a contract view holds that certain principles would be accepted in a well-defined initial situation.

The merit of the contract terminology is that it conveys the idea that principles of justice may be conceived as principles that would be chosen by rational persons, and that in this way conceptions of justice may be explained and justified. The theory of justice is a part, perhaps the most significant part, of the theory of rational choice. Furthermore, principles of justice deal with conflicting claims upon the advantages won by social cooperation; they apply to the relations among several persons or groups. The word "contract" suggests this plurality as well as the condition that the appropriate division of advantages must be in accordance with principles acceptable to all parties. The condition of publicity for principles of justice is also connoted by the contract phraseology. Thus, if these principles are the outcome of an agreement, citizens have a knowledge of the principles that others follow. It is characteristic of contract theories to stress the public nature of political principles. Finally there is the long tradition of the contract doctrine. Expressing the tie with this line of thought helps to define ideas and accords with natural piety. There are then several advantages in the use of the term "contract." With due precautions taken, it should not be misleading.

A final remark. Justice as fairness is not a complete contract theory. For it is clear that the contractarian idea can be extended to the choice of more or less an entire ethical system; that is, to a system including principles for all the virtues and not only for justice. Now for the most part I shall consider only principles of justice and others closely related to them; I make no attempt to discuss the virtues in a systematic way. Obviously if justice as fairness succeeds reasonably well, a next step would be to study the more general view suggested by the name "rightness as fairness." But even this wider theory fails to embrace all moral relationships, since it would seem to include only our relations with other persons and to leave out of account how we are to conduct ourselves toward animals and the rest of nature. I do not contend that the contract notion offers a way to approach these questions, which are certainly of the first importance; and I shall have to put them aside. We must recognize the limited scope of justice as fairness and of the general type of view that it exemplifies. How far its conclusions must be revised once these other matters are understood cannot be decided in advance.

The Original Position and Justification

I have said that the original position is the appropriate initial status quo which insures that the fundamental agreements reached in it are fair. This fact yields the name "justice as fairness." It is clear, then, that I want to say that one conception of justice is more reasonable than another, or justifiable with respect to it, if rational persons in the initial situation would choose its principles over those of the other for the role of justice. Conceptions of justice are to be ranked by their acceptability to persons so circumstanced. Understood in this way the question of justification is settled by working out a problem of deliberation: we have to ascertain which principles it would be rational to adopt given the contractual situation. This connects the theory of justice with the theory of rational choice.

If this view of the problem of justification is to succeed, we must, of course, describe in some detail the nature of this choice problem. A problem of rational decision has a definite answer only if we know the beliefs and interests of the parties, their relations with respect to one another, the alternatives between which they are to choose, the procedure whereby they make up their minds, and so on. As the circumstances are presented in different ways, correspondingly different principles are accepted. The concept of the original position, as I shall refer to it, is that of the most philosophically favored interpretation of this initial choice situation for the purposes of a theory of justice.

But how are we to decide what is the most favored interpretation? I assume, for one thing, that there is a broad measure of agreement that principles of justice should be chosen under certain conditions. To justify a particular description of the initial situation one shows that it incorporates these commonly shared presumptions. One argues from widely accepted but weak premises to more specific conclusions. Each of the presumptions should by itself be natural and plausible; some of them may seem innocuous or even trivial. The aim of the contract approach is to establish that taken together they impose significant bounds on acceptable principles of justice. The ideal outcome would be that these conditions determine a unique set of principles; but I shall be satisfied if they suffice to rank the main traditional conceptions of social justice.

One should not be misled, then, by the somewhat unusual conditions which characterize the original position. The idea here is simply to make vivid to ourselves the restrictions that it seems reasonable to impose on arguments for principles of justice, and therefore on these principles themselves. Thus it seems reasonable and generally acceptable that no one should be advantaged or disadvantaged by natural fortune or social circumstances in the choice of principles. It also seems widely agreed that it should be impossible to tailor principles to the circumstances of one's own case. We should ensure further that particular inclinations and aspirations, and persons' conceptions of their good, do not affect the principles adopted. The aim is to rule out those principles that it would be rational to propose for acceptance, however little the chance of success, only if one knew certain things that are irrelevant from the standpoint of justice. For example, if a man knew that he was wealthy, he might find it rational to advance the principle that various taxes for welfare measures be counted unjust; if he knew that he was poor, he would most likely propose the contrary principle. To represent the desired restrictions one imagines a situation in which everyone is deprived of this sort of information. One excludes the knowledge of those contingencies which sets men at odds and allows them to be guided by their prejudices. In this manner the veil of ignorance is arrived at in a natural way. This concept should cause no difficulty if we keep in mind the constraints on arguments that it is meant to express. At any time we can enter the original position, so to speak, simply by following a certain procedure; namely, by arguing for principles of justice in accordance with these restrictions.

It seems reasonable to suppose that the parties in the original position are equal. That is, all have the same rights in the procedure for choosing principles; each can make proposals, submit reasons for their acceptance, and so on. Obviously the purpose of these conditions is to represent equality between human beings as moral persons, as creatures having a conception of their good and capable of a sense of justice. The basis of equality is taken to be similarity in these two respects. Systems of ends are not ranked in value, and each man is presumed to have the requisite ability to understand and to act upon whatever principles are adopted. Together with the veil of ignorance, these conditions define the principles of justice as those which rational persons concerned to advance their interests would consent to as equals when none are known to be advantaged or disadvantaged by social and natural contingencies.

There is, however, another side to justifying a particular description of the original position. This is to see if the principles which would be chosen match our considered convictions of justice or extend them in an acceptable way. We can note whether applying these principles would lead us to make the same judgments about the basic structure of society which we now make intuitively and in which we have the greatest confidence; or whether, in cases where our present judgments are in doubt and given with hesitation, these principles offer a resolution which we can affirm on reflection. There are questions which we feel sure must be answered in a certain way. For example, we are confident that religious intolerance and racial discrimination are unjust. We think that we have examined these things with care and have reached what we believe is an impartial judgment not likely to be distorted by an excessive attention to our own interests. These convictions are provisional fixed points which we presume any conception of justice must fit. But we have much less assurance as to what is the correct distribution of wealth and authority. Here we may be looking for a way to remove our doubts. We can check an interpretation of the initial situation, then, by the capacity of its principles to accommodate our firmest convictions and to provide guidance where guidance is needed.

In searching for the most favored description of this situation we work from both ends. We begin by describing it so that it represents generally shared and preferably weak conditions. We then see if these conditions are strong enough to yield a significant set of principles. If not, we look for further premises equally reasonable. But if so, and these principles match our considered convictions of justice, then so far well and good. But presumably there will be discrepancies. In this case we have a choice. We can either modify the account of the initial situation or we can revise our existing judgments, for even the judgments we take provisionally as fixed points are liable to revision. By going back and forth, sometimes altering the conditions of the contractual circumstances, at others withdrawing our judgments and conforming them to principle, I assume that eventually we shall find a description of the initial situation that both expresses reasonable conditions and yields principles which match our considered judgments duly pruned and adjusted. This state of affairs I refer to as reflective equilibrium.[4] It is an equilibrium because at last our principles and judgments coincide; and it is reflective since we know to what principles our judgments conform and the premises of their derivation. At the moment everything is in order. But this equilibrium is not necessarily stable. It is liable to be upset by further examination of the conditions which should be imposed on the contractual situation and by particular cases which may lead us to revise our judgments. Yet for the time being we have done what we can to render coherent and to justify our convictions of social justice. We have reached a conception of the original position.

I shall not, of course, actually work through this process. Still, we may think of the interpretation of the original position that I shall present as the result of such a hypothetical course of reflection. It represents the attempt to accommodate within one scheme both reasonable philosophical conditions on principles as well as our considered judgments of justice. In arriving at the favored interpretation of the initial situation there is no point at which an appeal is made to self-evidence in the traditional sense either of general conceptions or particular convictions. I do not claim for the principles of justice proposed that they are necessary truths or derivable from such truths. A conception of justice cannot be deduced from self-evident premises or conditions on principles; instead, its justification is a matter of the mutual support of many considerations, of everything fitting together into one coherent view.

A final comment. We shall want to say that certain principles of justice are justified because they would be agreed to in an initial situation of equality. I have emphasized that this original position is purely hypothetical. It is natural to ask why, if this agreement is never actually entered into, we should take any interest in these principles, moral or otherwise. The answer is that the conditions embodied in the description of the original position are ones that we do in fact accept. Or if we do not, then perhaps we can be persuaded to do so by philosophical reflection. Each aspect of the contractual situation can be given supporting grounds. Thus what we shall do is to collect together into one conception a number of conditions on principles that we are ready upon due consideration to recognize as reasonable. These constraints express what we are prepared to regard as limits on fair terms of social cooperation. One way to look at the idea of the original position, therefore, is to see it as an expository device which sums up the meaning of these conditions and helps us to extract their consequences. On the other hand, this conception is also an intuitive notion that suggests its own elaboration, so that led on by it we are drawn to define more clearly the standpoint from which we can best interpret moral relationships. We need a conception that enables us to envision our objective from afar: the intuitive notion of the original position is to do this for us. . . .

Two Principles of Justice

I shall now state in a provisional form the two principles of justice that I believe would be chosen in the original position. In this section I wish to make only the most general comments, and therefore the first formulation of these principles is tentative. As we go on I shall run through several formulations and approximate step by step the final statement to be given much later. I believe that doing this allows the exposition to proceed in a natural way.

The first statement of the two principles reads as follows:

First: each person is to have an equal right to the most extensive basic liberty compatible with a similar liberty for others.

Second: social and economic inequalities are to be arranged so that they are both (a) reasonably expected to be to everyone's advantage, and (b) attached to positions and offices open to all.

There are two ambiguous phrases in the second principle, namely "everyone's advantage" and "open to all." Determining their sense more exactly will lead to a second formulation of the principle. . . .

By way of general comment, these principles primarily apply, as I have said, to the basic structure of society. They are to govern the assignment of rights and duties and to regulate the distribution of social and economic advantages. As their formulation suggests, these principles presuppose that the social structure can be divided into two more or less distinct parts, the first principle applying to the one, the second to the other. They distinguish between those aspects of the social system that define and secure the equal liberties of citizenship and those that specify and establish social and economic inequalities. The basic liberties of citizens are, roughly speaking, political liberty (the right to vote and to be eligible for public office) together with freedom of speech and assembly; liberty of conscience and freedom of thought; freedom of the person along with the right to hold (personal) property; and freedom from arbitrary arrest and seizure as defined by the concept of the rule of law. These liberties are all required to be equal by the first principle, since citizens of a just society are to have the same basic rights.

The second principle applies, in the first approximation, to the distribution of income and wealth and to the design of organizations that make use of differences in authority and responsibility, or chains of command. While the distribution of wealth and income need not be equal, it must be to everyone's advantage, and at the same time, positions of authority and offices of command must be accessible to all. One applies the second principle by holding positions open, and then, subject to this constraint, arranges social and economic inequalities so that everyone benefits.

These principles are to be arranged in a serial order with the first principle prior to the second. This ordering means that a departure from the institutions of equal liberty required by the first principle cannot be justified by, or compensated for, by greater social and economic advantages. The distribution of wealth and income, and the hierarchies of authority, must be consistent with both the liberties of equal citizenship and equality of opportunity.

It is clear that these principles are rather specific in their content, and their acceptance rests on certain assumptions that I must eventually try to explain and justify. A theory of justice depends upon a theory of society in ways that will become evident as we proceed. For the present, it should be observed that the two principles (and this holds for all formulations) are a special case of a more general conception of justice that can be expressed as follows:

All social values—liberty and opportunity, income and wealth, and the bases of self-respect—are to be distributed equally unless an unequal distribution of any, or all, of these values is to everyone's advantage.

Injustice, then, is simply inequalities that are not to the benefit of all. Of course, this conception is extremely vague and requires interpretation.

As a first step, suppose that the basic structure of society distributes certain primary goods, that is, things that every rational man is presumed to want. These goods normally have a use whatever a person's rational plan of life. For simplicity, assume that the chief primary goods at the disposition of society are rights and liberties, powers and opportunities, income and wealth. (Later on . . . the primary good of self-respect has a central place.) These are the social primary goods. Other primary goods such as health and vigor, intelligence and imagination, are natural goods; although their possession is influenced by the basic structure, they are not so directly under its control. Imagine, then, a hypothetical initial arrangement in which all the social primary goods are equally distributed: everyone has similar rights and duties, and income and wealth are evenly shared. This state of affairs provides a benchmark for judging improvements. If certain inequalities of wealth and organizational powers would make everyone better off than in this hypothetical starting situation, then they accord with the general conception.

Now it is possible, at least theoretically, that by giving up some of their fundamental liberties men are sufficiently compensated by the resulting social and economic gains. The general conception of justice imposes no restrictions on what sort of inequalities are permissible; it only requires that everyone's position be improved. We need not suppose anything so drastic as consenting to a condition of slavery. Imagine instead that men forgo certain political rights when the economic returns are significant and their capacity to influence the course of policy by the exercise of these rights would be marginal in any case. It is this kind of exchange which the two principles as stated rule out; being arranged in serial order they do not permit exchanges between basic liberties and economic and social gains. The serial ordering of principles expresses an underlying preference among primary social goods. When this preference is rational so likewise is the choice of these principles in this order.

In developing justice as fairness I shall, for the most part, leave aside the general conception of justice and examine instead the special case of the two principles in serial order. The advantage of this procedure is that from the first the matter of priorities is recognized and an effort made to find principles to deal with it. One is led to attend throughout to the conditions under which the acknowledgment of the absolute weight of liberty with respect to social and economic advantages, as defined by the lexical order of the two principles, would be reasonable. Offhand, this ranking appears extreme and too special a case to be of much interest; but there is more justification for it than would appear at first sight. Or at any rate, so I shall maintain. . . . Furthermore, the distinction between fundamental rights and liberties and economic and social benefits marks a difference among primary social goods that one should try to exploit. It suggests an important division in the social system. Of course, the distinctions drawn and the ordering proposed are bound to be at best only approximations. There are surely circumstances in which they fail. But it is essential to depict clearly the main lines of a reasonable conception of justice; and under many conditions, anyway, the two principles in serial order may serve well enough. When necessary we can fall back on the more general conception.

The fact that the two principles apply to institutions has certain consequences. Several points illustrate this. First of all, the rights and liberties referred to by these principles are those that are defined by the public rules of the basic structure. Whether men are free is determined by the rights and duties established by the major institutions of society. Liberty is a certain pattern of social forms. The first principle simply requires that certain sorts of rules, those defining basic liberties, apply to everyone equally and that they allow the most extensive liberty compatible with a like liberty for all. The only reason for circumscribing the rights defining liberty and making men's freedom less extensive than it might otherwise be is that these equal rights as institutionally defined would interfere with one another.

Another thing to bear in mind is that when principles mention persons, or require that everyone gain from an inequality, the reference is to representative persons holding the various social positions, or offices, or whatever, established by the basic structure. Thus in applying the second principle I assume that it is possible to assign an expectation of well-being to representative individuals holding these positions. This expectation indicates their life prospects as viewed from their social station. In general, the expectations of representative persons depend upon the distribution of rights and duties throughout the basic structure. When this changes, expectations change. I assume, then, that expectations are connected: by raising the prospects of the representative man in one position we presumably increase or decrease the prospects of representative men in other positions. Since it applies to institutional forms, the second principle (or rather the first part of it) refers to the expectations of representative individuals. As I shall discuss below, neither principle applies to distributions of particular goods to particular individuals who may be identified by their proper names. The situation where someone is considering how to allocate certain commodities to needy persons who are known to him is not within the scope of the principles. They are meant to regulate basic institutional arrangements. We must not assume that there is much similarity from the standpoint of justice between an administrative allotment of goods to specific persons and the appropriate design of society. Our common sense intuitions for the former may be a poor guide to the latter.

Now the second principle insists that each person benefit from permissible inequalities in the basic structure. This means that it must be reasonable for each relevant representative man defined by this structure, when he views it as a going concern, to prefer his prospects with the inequality, to his prospects without it. One is not allowed to justify differences in income or organizational powers on the ground that the disadvantages of those in one position are outweighed by the greater advantages of those in another. Much less can infringements of liberty be counterbalanced in this way. Applied to the basic structure, the principle of utility would have us maximize the sum of expectations of representative men (weighted by the number of persons they represent, on the classical view); and this would permit us to compensate for the losses of some by the gains of others. Instead the two principles require that everyone benefit from economic and social inequalities.

The Reasoning Leading to the Two Principles of Justice

It will be recalled that the general conception of justice as fairness requires that all primary social goods be distributed equally unless an unequal distribution would be to everyone's advantage. No restrictions are placed on exchanges of these goods and therefore a lesser liberty can be compensated for by greater social and economic benefits. Now looking at the situation from the standpoint of one person selected arbitrarily, there is no way for him to win special advantages for himself. Nor, on the other hand, are there grounds for his acquiescing in special disadvantages. Since it is not reasonable for him to expect more than an equal share in the division of social goods, and since it is not rational for him to agree to less, the sensible thing for him to do is to acknowledge as the first principle of justice one requiring an equal distribution. Indeed, this principle is so obvious that we would expect it to occur to anyone immediately.

Thus, the parties start with a principle establishing equal liberty for all, including equality of opportunity, as well as an equal distribution of income and wealth. But there is no reason why this acknowledgment should be final. If there are inequalities in the basic structure that work to make everyone better off in comparison with the benchmark of initial equality, why not permit them? The immediate gain which a greater equality might allow can be regarded as intelligently invested in view of its future return. If, for example, these inequalities set up various incentives which succeed in eliciting more productive efforts, a person in the original position may look upon them as necessary to cover the costs of training and to encourage effective performance. One might think that ideally individuals should want to serve one another. But since the parties are assumed not to take an interest in one another's interests, their acceptance of these inequalities is only the acceptance of the relations in which men stand in the circumstances of justice. They have no grounds for complaining of one another's motives. A person in the original position would, therefore, concede the justice of these inequalities. Indeed, it would be shortsighted of him not to do so. He would hesitate to agree to these regularities only if he would be dejected by the bare knowledge or perception that others were better situated; and I have assumed that the parties decide as if they are not moved by envy. In order to make the principle regulating inequalities determinate, one looks at the system from the standpoint of the least advantaged representative man. Inequalities are permissible when they maximize, or at least all contribute to, the long-term expectations of the least fortunate group in society.

Now this general conception imposes no constraints on what sorts of inequalities are allowed, whereas the special conception, by putting the two principles in serial order (with the necessary adjustments in meaning), forbids exchanges between basic liberties and economic and social benefits. I shall not try to justify this ordering here. . . . But roughly, the idea underlying this ordering is that if the parties assume that their basic liberties can be effectively exercised, they will not exchange a lesser liberty for an improvement in economic well-being. It is only when social conditions do not allow the effective establishment of these rights that one can concede their limitation; and these restrictions can be granted only to the extent that they are necessary to prepare the way for a free society. The denial of equal liberty can be defended only if it is necessary to raise the level of civilization so that in due course these freedoms can be enjoyed. Thus in adopting a serial order we are in effect making a special assumption in the original position, namely, that the parties know that the conditions of their society, whatever they are, admit the effective realization of the equal liberties. The serial ordering of the two principles of justice eventually comes to be reasonable if the general conception is consistently followed. This lexical ranking is the long-run tendency of the general view. For the most part I shall assume that the requisite circumstances for the serial order obtain.

It seems clear from these remarks that the two principles are at least a plausible conception of justice. The question, though, is how one is to argue for them more systematically. Now there are several things to do. One can work out their consequences for institutions and note their implications for fundamental social policy. In this way they are tested by a comparison with our considered judgments of justice. . . . But one can also try to find arguments in their favor that are decisive from the standpoint of the original position. In order to see how this might be done, it is useful as a heuristic device to think of the two principles as the maximin solution to the problem of social justice. There is an analogy between the two principles and the maximin rule for choice under uncertainty.[5] This is evident from the fact that the two principles are those a person would choose for the design of a society in which his enemy is to assign him his place. The maximin rule tells us to rank alternatives by their worst possible outcomes: we are to adopt the alternative the worst outcome of which is superior to the worst outcomes of the others. The persons in the original position do not, of course, assume that their initial place in society is decided by a malevolent opponent. As I note below, they should not reason from false premises. The veil of ignorance does not violate this idea, since an absence of information is not misinformation. But that the two principles of justice would be chosen if the parties were forced to protect themselves against such a contingency explains the sense in which this conception is the maximin solution. And this analogy suggests that if the original position has been described so that it is rational for the parties to adopt the conservative attitude expressed by this rule, a conclusive argument can indeed be constructed for these principles. Clearly the maximin rule is not, in general, a suitable guide for choices under uncertainty. But it is attractive in situations marked by certain special features. My aim, then, is to show that a good case can be made for the two principles based on the fact that the original position manifests these features to the fullest possible degree, carrying them to the limit, so to speak.

Consider the gain-and-loss table below. It represents the gains and losses for a situation which is not a game of strategy. There is no one playing against the person making the decision; instead he is faced with several possible circumstances which may or may not obtain. Which circumstances happen to exist does not depend upon what the person choosing decides or whether he announces his moves in advance. The numbers in the table are monetary values (in hundreds of dollars) in comparison with some initial situation. The gain (g) depends upon the individual's decision

(d) and the circumstances (c). Thus $g = f(d,c)$. Assuming that there are three possible decisions and three possible circumstances, we might have this gain-and-loss table.

Decisions	Circumstances		
	C1	C2	C3
d1	−7	8	12
d2	−8	7	14
d3	5	6	8

The maximin rule requires that we make the third decision. For in this case the worst that can happen is that one gains five hundred dollars, which is better than the worst for the other actions. If we adopt one of these we may lose either eight or seven hundred dollars. Thus, the choice of d_3 maximizes $f(d,c)$ for that value of c which for a given d, minimizes f. The term "maximin" means the *maximum minimorum;* and the rule directs our attention to the worst that can happen under any proposed course of action, and to decide in the light of that.

Now there appear to be three chief features of situations that give plausibility to this unusual rule.[6] First, since the rule takes no account of the likelihoods of the possible circumstances, there must be some reason for sharply discounting estimates of these probabilities. Offhand, the most natural rule of choice would seem to be to compute the expectation of monetary gain for each decision and then to adopt the course of action with the highest prospect. (This expectation is defined as follows: let us suppose that g_{ij} represent the numbers in the gain-and-loss table, where i is the row index and j is the column index; and let p_j, $j = 1, 2, 3$, be the likelihoods of the circumstances, with $\Sigma p_j = 1$. Then the expectation for the ith decision is equal to $\Sigma p_j g_{ij}$.) Thus it must be, for example, that the situation is one in which a knowledge of likelihoods is impossible, or at best extremely insecure. In this case it is unreasonable not to be skeptical of probabilistic calculations unless there is no other way out, particularly if the decision is a fundamental one that needs to be justified to others.

The second feature that suggests the maximin rule is the following: the person choosing has a conception of the good such that he cares very little, if anything, for what he might gain above the minimum stipend that he can, in fact, be sure of by following the maximin rule. It is not worthwhile for him to take a chance for the sake of a further advantage, especially when it may turn out that he loses much that is important to him. This last provision brings in the third feature; namely, that the rejected alternatives have outcomes that one can hardly accept. The situation involves grave risks. Of course these features work most effectively in combination. The paradigm situation for following the maximin rule is when all three features are realized to the highest degree. This rule does not, then, generally apply, nor of course is it self-evident. Rather, it is a maxim, a rule of thumb, that comes into its own in special circumstances. Its application depends upon the qualitative structure of the possible gains and losses in relation to one's conception of the good, all this against a background in which it is reasonable to discount conjectural estimates of likelihoods.

It should be noted, as the comments on the gain-and-loss table say, that the entries in the table represent monetary values and not utilities. This difference is significant since for one thing computing expectations on the basis of such objective values is not the same thing as computing expected utility and may lead to different results. The essential point, though, is that in justice as fairness the parties do not know their conception of the good and cannot estimate their utility in the ordinary sense. In any case, we want to go behind de facto preferences generated by given conditions. Therefore expectations are based upon an index or primary goods and the parties make their choice accordingly. The entries in the example are in terms of money and not utility to indicate this aspect of the contract doctrine.

Now, as I have suggested, the original position has been defined so that it is a situation in which the maximin rule applies. In order to see this, let us review briefly the nature of this situation with these three special features in mind. To begin with, the veil of ignorance excludes all but the vaguest knowledge of likelihoods. The parties have no basis for determining the probable nature of their society, or their place in it. Thus they have strong reasons for being wary of probability calculations if any other course is open to them. They must also take into account the fact that their choice of principles should seem reasonable to others, in particular their descendants, whose rights will be deeply affected by it. There are further grounds for discounting that I shall mention as we go along. For the present it suffices to note that these considerations are strengthened by the fact that the parties know very little about the gain-and-loss table. Not only are they unable to conjecture the likelihoods of the various possible circumstances, they cannot say much about what the possible circumstances are, much less enumerate them and foresee the outcome of each alternative available. Those deciding are much more in the dark than the illustration by a numerical table suggests. It is for this reason that I have spoken of an analogy with the maximin rule.

Several kinds of arguments for the two principles of justice illustrate the second feature. Thus, if we can maintain that these principles provide a workable theory of social justice, and that they are compatible with reasonable demands of efficiency, then this conception guarantees a satisfactory minimum. There may be, on reflection, little reason for trying to do better. Thus much of the argument . . . is to show, by their application to the main questions of social justice, that the two principles are a satisfactory conception. These details have a philosophical purpose. Moreover, this line of thought is practically decisive if we can establish the priority of liberty, the lexical ordering of the two principles. For this priority implies that the persons in the original position have no desire to try for greater gains at the expense of the equal liberties. The minimum assured by the two principles in lexical order is not one that the parties wish to jeopardize for the sake of greater economic and social advantages. . . .

Finally, the third feature holds if we can assume that other conceptions of justice may lead to institutions that the parties would find intolerable. For example, it has sometimes been held that under some conditions the utility principle (in either form) justifies, if not slavery or serfdom, at any rate serious infractions of liberty for the sake of greater social benefits. We need not consider here the truth of this claim, or the likelihood that the requisite conditions obtain. For the moment, this contention is only to illustrate the way in which conceptions of justice may allow for outcomes which the parties may not be able to accept. And having the ready alternative of the two principles of justice which secure a satisfactory minimum, it seems unwise, if not irrational, for them to take a chance that these outcomes are not realized.

So much, then, for a brief sketch of the features of situations in which the maximin rule comes into its own and of the way in which the arguments for the two principles of justice can be subsumed under them. . . .

The Final Formulation of the Principles of Justice

. . . I now wish to give the final statement of the two principles of justice for institutions. For the sake of completeness, I shall give a full statement including earlier formulations.

First Principle
Each person is to have an equal right to the most extensive total system of equal basic liberties compatible with a similar system of liberty for all.

Second Principle
Social and economic inequalities are to be arranged so that they are both:
(a) to the greatest benefit of the least advantaged, consistent with the just savings principle, and
(b) attached to offices and positions open to all under conditions of fair equality of opportunity.

First Priority Rule (The Priority of Liberty)
The principles of justice are to be ranked in lexical order and therefore liberty can be restricted only for the sake of liberty. There are two cases:
(a) a less extensive liberty must strengthen the total system of liberty shared by all;
(b) a less than equal liberty must be acceptable to those with the lesser liberty.

Second Priority Rule (The Priority of Justice over Efficiency and Welfare)
The second principle of justice is lexically prior to the principle of efficiency and to that of maximizing the sum of advantages; and fair opportunity is prior to the difference principle. There are two cases:
(a) an inequality of opportunity must enhance the opportunities of those with the lesser opportunity;
(b) an excessive rate of saving must on balance mitigate the burden of those bearing this hardship.

General Conception
All social primary goods—liberty and opportunity, income and wealth, and the bases of self-respect—are to be distributed equally unless an unequal distribution of any or all of these goods is to the advantage of the least favored.

By way of comment, these principles and priority rules are no doubt incomplete. Other modifications will surely have to be made, but I shall not further complicate the statement of the principles. It suffices to observe that when we come to nonideal theory, we do not fall back straightway upon the general conception of justice. The lexical ordering of the two principles, and the valuations that this ordering implies, suggest priority rules which seem to be reasonable enough in many cases. By various examples I have tried to illustrate how these rules can be used and to indicate their plausibility. Thus the ranking of the principles of justice in ideal theory reflects back and guides the application of these principles to nonideal situations. It identifies which limitations need to be dealt with first. The drawback of the general conception of justice is that it lacks the definite structure of the two principles in serial order. In more extreme and tangled instances of nonideal theory there may be no alternative to it. At some point the priority of rules for nonideal cases will fail; and indeed, we may be able to find no satisfactory answer at all. But we must try to postpone the day of reckoning as long as possible, and try to arrange society so that it never comes. . . .

The Kantian Interpretation

Kant held, I believe, that a person is acting autonomously when the principles of his action are chosen by him as the most adequate possible expression of his nature as a free and equal rational being. The principles he acts upon are not adopted because of his social position or natural endowments, or in view of the particular kind of society in which he lives or the specific things that he happens to want. To act on such principles is to act heteronomously. Now the veil of ignorance deprives the persons in the original position of the knowledge that would enable them to choose heteronomous principles. The parties arrive at their choice together as free and equal rational persons knowing only that those circumstances obtain which give rise to the need for principles of justice.

To be sure, the argument for these principles does add in various ways to Kant's conception. For example, it adds the feature that the principles chosen are to apply to the basic structure of society; and premises characterizing this structure are used in deriving the principles of justice. But I believe that this and other additions are natural enough and remain fairly close to Kant's doctrine, at least when all of his ethical writings are viewed together. Assuming, then, that the reasoning in favor of the principles of justice is correct, we can say that when persons act on these principles they are acting in accordance with principles that they would choose as rational and independent persons in an original position of equality. The principles of their actions do not depend upon social or natural contingencies, nor do they reflect the bias of the particulars of their plan of life or the aspirations that motivate them. By acting from these principles persons express their nature as free and equal rational beings subject to the general conditions of human life. For to express one's nature as a being of a particular kind is to act on the principles that would be chosen if this nature were the decisive determining element. Of course, the choice of the parties in the original position is subject to the restrictions of that situation. But when we knowingly act on the principles of justice in the ordinary course of events, we deliberately assume the limitations of the original position. One reason for doing this, for persons who can do so and want to, is to give expression to one's nature.

The principles of justice are also categorical imperatives in Kant's sense. For by a categorical imperative Kant understands a principle of conduct that applies to a person in virtue of his nature as a free and equal rational being. The validity of the principle does not presuppose that one has a particular desire or aim. Whereas a hypothetical imperative by contrast does assume this: it directs us to take certain steps as effective means to achieve a specific end. Whether the desire is for a particular thing, or whether it is for something more general, such as certain kinds of agreeable feelings or pleasures, the corresponding imperative is hypothetical. Its applicability depends upon one's having an aim which one need not have as a condition of being a rational human individual. The argument for the two principles of justice does not assume that the parties have particular ends, but only that they desire certain primary goods. These are things that it is rational to want whatever else one wants. Thus given human nature, wanting them is part of being rational; and while each is presumed to have some conception of the good, nothing is known about his final ends. The preference for primary goods is derived, then, from only the most general assumptions about rationality and the conditions of human life. To act from the principles of justice is to act from categorical imperatives in the sense that they apply to us whatever in particular our aims are. This simply reflects the fact that no such contingencies appear as premises in their derivation.

We may note also that the motivational assumption of mutual disinterest accords with Kant's notion of autonomy, and gives another reason for this condition. So far this assumption has been used to characterize the circumstances of justice and to provide a clear conception to guide the reasoning of the parties. We have also seen that the concept of benevolence, being a second-order notion, would not work out well. Now we can add that the assumption of mutual disinterest is to allow for freedom in the choice of a system of final ends.[7] Liberty in adopting a conception of the good is limited only by principles that are deduced from a doctrine which imposes no prior constraints on these conceptions. Presuming mutual disinterest in the original position carries out this idea. We postulate that the parties have opposing claims in a suitably general sense. If their ends were restricted in some specific way, this would appear at the outset as an arbitrary restriction on freedom. Moreover, if the parties were conceived as altruists, or as pursuing certain kinds of pleasures, then the principles chosen would apply, as far as the argument would have shown, only to persons whose freedom was restricted to choices compatible with altruism or hedonism. As the argument now runs, the principles of justice cover all persons with rational plans of life, whatever their content, and these principles represent the appropriate restrictions on freedom. Thus it is possible to say that the constraints on conceptions of the good are the result of an interpretation of the contractual situation that puts no prior limitations on what men may desire. There are a variety of reasons, then, for the motivational premise of mutual disinterest. This premise is not only a matter of realism about the circumstances of justice or a way to make the theory manageable. It also connects up with the Kantian idea of autonomy. . . .

The original position may be viewed, then, as a procedural interpretation of Kant's conception of autonomy and the categorical imperative. The principles regulative of the kingdom of ends are those that would be chosen in this position, and the description of this situation enables us to explain the sense in which acting from these principles expresses our nature as free and equal rational persons. No longer are these notions purely transcendent and lacking explicable connections with human conduct, for the procedural conception of the original position allows us to make these ties. . . .

Notes

1. As the text suggests, I shall regard Locke's *The Second Treatise of Government,* Rousseau's *Social Contract,* and Kant's ethical works beginning with *The Foundations of the Metaphysics of Morals* as definitive of the contract tradition. For all of its greatness, Hobbes's *Leviathan* raises special problems. A general historical survey is provided by J. W. Gough, *The Social Contract,* 2nd ed. (Oxford, The Clarendon Press, 1957), and Otto Gierke, *Natural Law and the Theory of Society,* trans. with an introduction by Ernest Barker (Cambridge, The University Press, 1934). A presentation of the contract view as primarily an ethical theory is to be found in G. R. Grice, *The Grounds of Moral Judgment* (Cambridge, The University Press, 1967). . . .

2. Kant is clear that the original agreement is hypothetical. See *The Metaphysics of Morals,* pt. I *(Rechtslehre),* especially §§ 47, 52; and pt. II of the essay "Concerning the Common Saying: This May Be True in Theory But It Does Not Apply in Practice," in *Kant's Political Writings,* ed. Hans Reiss and trans. by H. B. Nisbet (Cambridge, The University Press, 1970), pp. 73–87. See Georges Vlachos, *La Pensée politique de Kant* (Paris, Presses Universitaires de France, 1962), pp. 326–335; and J. G. Murphy, *Kant: The Philosophy of Right* (London, Macmillan, 1970), pp. 109–112, 133–136, for a further discussion.

3. For the formulation of this intuitive idea I am indebted to Allan Gibbard.

4. The process of mutual adjustment of principles and considered judgments is not peculiar to moral philosophy. See Nelson Goodman, *Fact, Fiction, and Forecast* (Cambridge, Mass., Harvard University Press, 1955), pp. 65–68, for parallel remarks concerning the justification of the principles of deductive and inductive inference.

5. An accessible discussion of this and other rules of choice under uncertainty can be found in W. J. Baumol, *Economic Theory and Operations Analysis,* 2nd ed. (Englewood Cliffs, N. J., Prentice-Hall, 1965), ch. 24. Baumol gives a geometric interpretation of these rules, including the diagram used . . . to illustrate the difference principle. See pp. 558–562. See also R. D. Luce and Howard Raiffa, *Games and Decisions* (New York, John Wiley and Sons, Inc., 1957), ch. XIII, for a fuller account.

6. Here I borrow from William Fellner, *Probability and Profit* (Homewood, Ill., Richard D. Irwin, 1965), pp. 140–142, where these features are noted.

7. For this point I am indebted to Charles Fried.

11

Hypothetical Contracts and Rights

RONALD DWORKIN

I trust that it is not necessary to describe John Rawls's famous idea of the original position in any great detail.[1] It imagines a group of men and women who come together to form a social contract. Thus far it resembles the imaginary congresses of the classical social contract theories. The original position differs, however, from these theories in its description of the parties. They are men and women with ordinary tastes, talents, ambitions, and convictions, but each is temporarily ignorant of these features of his own personality, and must agree upon a contract before his self-awareness returns.

Rawls tries to show that if these men and women are rational, and act only in their own self-interest, they will choose his two principles of justice. These provide, roughly, that every person must have the largest political liberty compatible with a like liberty for all, and that inequalitites in power, wealth, income, and other resources must not exist except insofar as they work to the absolute benefit of the worst-off members of society. Many of Rawls's critics disagree that men and women in the original position would inevitably choose these two principles. The principles are conservative, and the critics believe they would be chosen only by men who were conservative by temperament, and not by men who were natural gamblers. I do not think this criticism is well taken, but in this essay, at least, I mean to ignore the point. I am interested in a different issue.

Suppose that the critics are wrong, and that men and women in the original

From *Taking Rights Seriously* (1977), pp. 150–159, 177–183. Reprinted by permission of the author.

position would in fact choose Rawls's two principles as being in their own best interest. Rawls seems to think that that fact would provide an argument in favor of these two principles as a standard of justice against which to test actual political institutions. But it is not immediately plain why this should be so.

If a group contracted in advance that disputes amongst them would be settled in a particular way, the fact of that contract would be a powerful argument that such disputes should be settled in that way when they do arise. The contract would be an argument in itself, independent of the force of the reasons that might have led different people to enter the contract. Ordinarily, for example, each of the parties supposes that a contract he signs is in his own interest; but if someone has made a mistake in calculating his self-interest, the fact that he did contract is a strong reason for the fairness of holding him nevertheless to the bargain.

Rawls does not suppose that any group ever entered into a social contract of the sort he describes. He argues only that if a group of rational men did find themselves in the predicament of the original position, they would contract for the two principles. His contract is hypothetical, and hypothetical contracts do not supply an independent argument for the fairness of enforcing their terms. A hypothetical contract is not simply a pale form of an actual contract; it is no contract at all.

If, for example, I am playing a game, it may be that I would have agree to any number of ground rules if I had been asked in advance of play. It does not follow that these rules may be enforced against me if I have not, in fact, agreed to them. There must be reasons, of course, why I would have agreed if asked in advance, and these may also be reasons why it is fair to enforce these rules against me even if I have not agreed. But my hypothetical agreement does not count as a reason, independent of these other reasons, for enforcing the rules against me, as my actual agreement would have.

Suppose that you and I are playing poker and we find, in the middle of a hand, that the deck is one card short. You suggest that we throw the hand in, but I refuse because I know I am going to win and I want the money in the pot. You might say that I would certainly have agreed to that procedure had the possibility of the deck being short been raised in advance. But your point is not that I am somehow committed to throwing the hand in by an agreement I never made. Rather you use the device of a hypothetical agreement to make a point that might have been made without that device, which is that the solution recommended is so obviously fair and sensible that only someone with an immediate contrary interest could disagree. Your main argument is that your solution is fair and sensible, and the fact that I would have chosen it myself adds nothing of substance to that argument. If I am able to meet the main argument nothing remains, rising out of your claim that I would have agreed, to be answered or excused.

In some circumstances, moreover, the fact that I would have agreed does not even suggest an independent argument of this character. Everything depends on your reasons for supposing that I would have agreed. Suppose you say that I would have agreed, if you had brought up the point and insisted on your solution, because I very much wanted to play and would have given in rather than miss my chance. I might concede that I would have agreed for that reason, and then add that I am lucky that you did not raise the point. The fact that I would have agreed if you had insisted neither adds nor suggests any argument why I should agree now. The point is not that it would have been unfair of you to insist on your proposal as a condition of playing; indeed, it would not have been. If you had held out for your proposal, and I had agreed, I could not say that my agreement was in any way nullified or called into question because of duress. But if I had not in fact agreed, the fact that I would have in itself means nothing.

I do not mean that it is never relevant, in deciding whether an act affecting someone is fair, that he would have consented if asked. If a doctor finds a man unconscious and bleeding, for example, it might be important for him to ask whether the man would consent to a transfusion if he were conscious. If there is every reason to think that he would, the fact is important in justifyin g the transfusion if the patient later, perhaps because he has undergone a religious conversion, condemns the doctor for having proceeded. But this sort of case is beside the present point, because the patient's hypothetical agreement shows that his will was inclined toward the decision at the time and in the circumstances that the decision was taken. He has lost nothing by not being consulted at the appropriate time, because he would have consented if he had been. The original position argument is very different. If we take it to argue for the fairness of applying the two principles we must take it to argue that because a man would have consented to certain principles if asked in advance, it is fair to apply those principles to him later, under different circumstances, when he does not consent.

But that is a bad argument. Suppose I did not know the value of my painting on Monday; if you had offered me $100 for it then I would have accepted. On Tuesday I discovered it was valuable. You cannot argue that it would be fair for the courts to make me sell it to you for $100 on Wednesday. It may be my good fortune that you did not ask me on Monday, but that does not justify coercion against me later.

We must therefore treat the argument from the original position as we treat your argument in the poker game; it must be a device for calling attention to some independent argument for the fairness of the two principles—an argument that does not rest on the false premise that a hypothetical contract has some pale binding force. What other argument is available? One might say that the original position shows that the two principles are in the best interests of every member of any political community, and that it is fair to govern in accordance with them for that reason. It is true that if the two principles could be shown to be in everyone's interest, that would be a sound argument for their fairness, but it is hard to see how the original position can be used to show that they are.

We must be careful to distinguish two senses in which something might be said to be in my interest. It is in my *antecedent* interest to make a bet on a horse that, all things considered, offers the best odds, even if, in the event, the horse loses. It is in my *actual* interest to bet on the horse that wins, even if the bet was, at the time I made it, a silly one. If the original position furnishes an argument that it is in everyone's interest to accept the two principles over other possible bases for a constitution, it must be an argument that uses the idea of antecedent and not actual interest. It is not in the actual best interests of everyone to choose the two principles, because when the veil of ignorance is lifted some will discover that they would have been better off if some other principle, like the principle of average utility, had been chosen.

A judgment of antecedent interest depends upon the circumstances under which the judgment is made, and, in particular, upon the knowledge available to the man making the judgment. It might be in my antecedent interest to bet on a certain horse at given odds before the starting gun, but not, at least at the same odds, after he has stumbled on the first turn. The fact, therefore, that a particular choice is in my interest at a particular time, under conditions of great uncertainty, is not a good argument for the fairness of enforcing that choice against me later under conditions of much greater knowledge. But that is what, on this interpretation, the original position argument suggests, because it seeks to justify the contemporary use of the two principles on the supposition that, under conditions very different from present conditions, it would be in the antecedent interest of everyone to agree to them. If I have bought a ticket on a longshot it might be in my antecedent interest, before the race, to sell the ticket to you for twice what I paid; it does not follow that it is fair for you to take it from me for that sum when the longshot is about to win.

Someone might now say that I have misunderstood the point of the special conditions of uncertainty in the original position. The parties are made ignorant of their special resources and talents to prevent them from bargaining for principles that are inherently unfair because they favor some collection of resources and talents over others. If the man in the original position does not know his special interests, he cannot negotiate to favor them. In that case, it might be said, the uncertainty of the original position does not vitiate the argument from antecedent interest as I have suggested, but only limits the range within which self-interest might operate. The argument shows that the two principles are in everyone's interest once obviously unfair principles are removed from consideration by the device of uncertainty. Since the only additional knowledge contemporary men and women have over men and women in the original position is knowledge that they ought not to rely upon in choosing principles of justice, their antecedent interest is, so far as it is relevant, the same, and if that is so the original position argument does offer a good argument for applying the two principles to contemporary politics.

But surely this confuses the argument that Rawls makes with a different argument that he might have made. Suppose his men and women had full knowledge of their own talents and tastes, but had to reach agreement under conditions that ruled out, simply by stipulation, obviously unfair principles like those providing special advantage for named individuals. If Rawls could show that, once such obviously unfair principles had been set aside, it would be in the interest of everyone to settle for his two principles, that would indeed count as an argument for the two principles. My point—that the antecedent self-interest of men in the original position is different from that of contemporary men—would no longer hold because both groups of men would then have the same knowledge about themselves, and be subject to the same moral restrictions against choosing obviously unfair principles.

Rawls's actual argument is quite different, however. The ignorance in which his men must choose affects their calculations of self-interest, and cannot be described merely as setting boundaries within which these calculations must be applied. Rawls supposes, for example, that his men would inevitably choose conservative principles because this would be the only rational choice, in their ignorance, for self-interested men to make. But some actual men, aware of their own talents, might well prefer less conservative principles that would allow them to take advantage of the resources they know they have. Someone who considers the original position an argument for the conservative principles, therefore, is faced with this choice. If less conservative principles, like principles that favor named individuals, are to be ruled out as obviously unfair, then the argument for the conservative principles is complete at the outset, on grounds of obvious fairness alone. In that case neither the original position nor any considerations of self-interest it is meant to demonstrate play any role in the argument. But if less conservative principles cannot be ruled out in advance as obviously unfair, then imposing ignorance on Rawls's men, so that they prefer the more conservative principles, cannot be explained simply as ruling out obviously unfair choices. And since this affects the antecedent self-interest of these men, the argument that the original position demonstrates the antecedent self-interest of actual men must therefore fail. This same dilemma can, of course, be constructed for each feature of the two principles.

I recognize that the argument thus far seems to ignore a distinctive feature of Rawls's methodology, which he describes as the technique of seeking a "reflective equilibrium" between our ordinary, unreflective moral beliefs and some theoretical structure that might unify and justify these ordinary beliefs.[2] It might now be said that the idea of an original position plays a part in this reflective equilibrium, which we will miss if we insist, as I have, on trying to find a more direct, one-way argument from the original position to the two principles of justice.

The technique of equilibrium does play an important role in Rawls's argument, and it is worth describing that technique briefly here. The technique assumes that Rawls's readers have a sense, which we draw upon in our daily life, that certain particular political arrangements or decisions, like conventional trials, are just and others, like slavery, are unjust. It assumes, moreover, that we are each able to arrange these immediate intuitions or convictions in an order that designates some of them as more certain than others. Most people, for example, think that it is more plainly unjust for the state to execute innocent citizens of its own than to kill innocent foreign civilians in war. They might be prepared to abandon their position on foreign civilians in war, on the basis of some argument, but would be much more reluctant to abandon their view on executing innocent countrymen.

It is the task of moral philosophy, according to the technique of equilibrium, to provide a structure of principles that supports these immediate convictions about which we are more or less secure, with two goals in mind. First, this structure of principles must explain the convictions by showing the underlying assumptions they reflect; second, it must provide guidance in those cases about which we have either no convictions or weak or contradictory convictions. If we are unsure, for example, whether economic institutions that allow great disparity of wealth are unjust, we may turn to the principles that explain our confident convictions, and then apply these principles to that difficult issue.

But the process is not simply one of finding principles that accommodate our more or less settled judgments. These principles must support, and not merely account for, our judgments, and this means that the principles must have independent appeal to our moral sense. It might be, for example, that a cluster of familiar moral convictions could be shown to serve an undeserving policy—perhaps, that the standard judgments we make without reflection serve the purpose of maintaining one particular class in political power. But this discovery would not vouch for the principle of class egoism; on the contrary, it would discredit our ordinary judgments, unless some other principle of a more respectable sort could be found that also fits our intuitions, in which case it would be this principle and not the class-interest principle that our intuitions would recommend.

It might be that no coherent set of principles could be found that has independent appeal and that supports the full set of our immediate convictions; indeed it would be surprising if this were not often the case. If that does happen, we must compromise, giving way on both sides. We might relax, though we could not abandon, our initial sense of what might be an acceptable principle. We might come to accept, for example, after further reflection, some principle that seemed to us initially unattractive, perhaps the principle that men should sometimes be made to be free. We might accept this principle if we were satisfied that no less harsh principle could support the set of political convictions we were especially reluctant to abandon. On the other hand, we must also be ready to modify or adjust, or even to give up entirely, immediate convictions that cannot be accommodated by any principle that meets our relaxed standards; in adjusting these immediate convictions we will use our initial sense of which seem to us more and which less certain, though in principle no immediate conviction can be taken as immune from reinspection or abandonment if that should prove necessary. We can expect to proceed back and forth between our immediate judgments and the structure of explanatory principles in this way, tinkering first with one side and then the other, until we arrive at what Rawls calls the state of reflective equilibrium in which we are satisfied, or as much satisfied as we can reasonably expect.

It may well be that, at least for most of us, our ordinary political judgments stand in this relation of reflective equilibrium with Rawls's two principles of justice, or, at least, that they could be made to do so through the process of adjustment just described. It is nevertheless unclear how the idea of the original position fits into this structure or, indeed, why it has any role to play at all. The original position is not among the ordinary political convictions that we find we have, and that we turn to reflective equilibrium to justify. If it has any role, it must be in the process of justification, because it takes its place in the body of theory we construct to bring our convictions into balance. But if the two principles of justice are themselves in reflective equilibrium with our convictions, it is unclear why we need the original position to supplement the two principles on the theoretical side of the balance. What can the idea contribute to a harmony already established?

We should consider the following answer. It is one of the conditions we impose on a theoretical principle, before we allow it to figure as a justification of our convictions, that the people the principle would govern would have accepted that principle, at least under certain conditions, if they had been asked, or at least that the principle can be shown to be in the antecedent interest of every such person. If this is so, then the original position plays an essential part in the process of justification through equilibrium. It is used to show that the two principles conform to this established standard of acceptability for political principles. At the same time, the fact that the two principles, which do conform to that standard, justify our ordinary convictions in reflective equilibrium reinforces our faith in the standard and encourages us to apply it to other issues of political or moral philosophy.

This answer does not advance the case that the original position furnishes an argument for the two principles, however; it merely restates the ideas we have already considered and rejected. It is certainly not part of our established political traditions or ordinary moral understanding that principles are acceptable only if they would be chosen by men in the particular predicament of the original position. It is, of course, part of these traditions that principles are fair if they have in fact been chosen by those whom they govern, or if they can at least be shown to be in their antecedent common interest. But we have already seen that the original position device cannot be used to support either of these arguments in favor of applying the two principles to contemporary politics. If the original position is to play any role in a structure of principles and convictions in reflective equilibrium, it must be by virtue of assumptions we have not yet identified.

It is time to reconsider an earlier assumption. So far I have been treating the original position construction as if it were either the foundation of Rawls's argument or an ingredient in a reflective equilibrium established between our political intuitions and his two principles of justice. But, in fact, Rawls does not treat the original position that way. He describes the construction in these words:

> I have emphasized that this original position is purely hypothetical. It is natural to ask why, if this agreement is never actually entered into, we should take any interest in these principles, moral or otherwise. The answer is that the conditions embodied in the description of the original position are ones that we do in fact accept. Or if we do not, then perhaps we can be persuaded to do so by philosophical reflection. Each aspect of the contractual situation can be given supporting grounds. . . . On the other hand, this conception is also an intuitive notion that suggests its own elaboration, so that led on by it we are drawn to define more clearly the standpoint from which we can best interpret moral relationships. We need a conception that enables us to envision our objective from afar: the intuitive notion of the original position is to do this for us.[3]

This description is taken from Rawls's first statement of the original position. It is recalled and repeated in the very last paragraph of [his] book.[4] It is plainly of capital importance, and it suggests that the original position, far from being the foundation of his argument, or an expository device for the technique of equilibrium, is one of the major substantive products of the theory as a whole. Its importance is reflected in another crucial passage. Rawls describes his moral theory as a type of psychology. He wants to characterize the structure of our (or, at least, one person's) capacity to make moral judgments of a certain sort; that is, judgments about justice. He thinks that the conditions embodied in the original position are the fundamental "principles governing our moral powers, or more specifically, our sense of justice."[5] The original position is therefore a schematic representation of a particular mental process of at least some, and perhaps most, human beings, just as depth grammar, he suggests, is a schematic presentation of a different mental capacity.

All this suggests that the original position is an intermediate conclusion, a halfway point in a deeper theory that provides philosophical arguments for its conditions. In the next part of this essay I shall try to describe at least the main outlines of this deeper theory. I shall distinguish three features of the surface argument of the book—the technique of equilibrium, the social contract, and the original position itself—and try to discern which of various familiar philosophical principles or positions these represent.

First, however, I must say a further word about Rawls's exciting, if imprecise, idea that the principles of this deeper theory are constitutive of our moral capacity. That idea can be understood on different levels of profundity. It may mean, at its least profound, that the principles that support the original position as a device for reasoning about justice are so widely shared and so little questioned within a particular community, for whom the book is meant, that the community could not abandon these principles without fundamentally changing its patterns of reasoning and arguing about political morality. It may mean, at its most profound, that these principles are innate categories of morality common to all men, imprinted in their neural structure, so that man could not deny these principles short of abandoning the power to reason about morality at all.

I shall be guided, in what follows, by the less profound interpretation, though what I shall say, I think, is consistent with the more profound. I shall assume, then, that there is a group of men and women who find, on reading Rawls, that the original position does strike them as a proper "intuitive notion" from which to think about problems of justice, and who would find it persuasive, if it could be demonstrated that the parties to the original position would in fact contract for the two principles he describes. I suppose, on the basis of experience and the literature, that this group contains a very large number of those who think about justice at all, and I find that I am a member myself. I want to discover the hidden assumptions that bend the inclinations of this group that way, and I shall do so by repeating the question with which I began. Why does Rawls's argument support his claim that his two principles are principles of justice? My answer is complex and it will take us, at times, far from his text, but not, I think, from its spirit. . . .

The Original Position

I said that the use of a social contract, in the way that Rawls uses it, presupposes a deep theory that assumes natural rights. I want now to describe, in somewhat more detail, how the device of a contract applies that assumption. It capitalizes on the idea, mentioned earlier, that some political arrangements might be said to be in the antecedent interest of every individual even though they are not, in the event, in his actual interest.

Everyone whose consent is necessary to a contract has a veto over the terms of that contract, but the worth of that veto, to him, is limited by the fact that his judgment must be one of antecedent rather than actual self-interest. He must commit himself, and so abandon his veto, at a time when his knowledge is sufficient only to allow him to estimate the best odds, not to be certain of his bet. So the contract situation is in one way structurally like the situation in which an individual with specific political rights confronts political decisions that may disadvantage him. He had a limited, political right to veto these, a veto limited by the scope of the rights he has. The contract can be used as a model for the political situation by shaping the degree of character of a party's ignorance in the contractual situation so that this ignorance has the same force on his decision as the limited nature of his rights would have in the political situation.

This shaping of ignorance to suit the limited character of political rights is most efficiently done simply by narrowing the individual goals that the parties to the contract know they wish to pursue. If we take Hobbes's deep theory, for example, to propose that men have a fundamental natural right to life, so that it is wrong to take their lives, even for social goals otherwise proper, we should expect a contract situation of the sort he describes. Hobbes's men and women, in Rawls's phrase, have lexically ordered security of life over all other individual goals; the same situation would result if they were simply ignorant of any other goals they might have and unable to speculate about the chances that they have any particular one or set of these.

The ignorance of the parties in the original position might thus be seen as a kind of limiting case of the ignorance that can be found, in the form of a distorted or eccentric ranking of interests, in classical contract theories and that is natural to the contract device. The original position is a limiting case because Rawls's men are not simply ignorant of interests beyond a chosen few; they are ignorant of all the interests they have. It would be wrong to suppose that this makes them incapable of any judgments of self-interest. But the judgments they make must nevertheless be very abstract; they must allow for any combination of interests, without the benefit of any supposition that some of these are more likely than others.

The basic right of Rawls's deep theory, therefore, cannot be a right to any particular individual goal, like a right to security of life, or a right to lead a life according to a particular conception of the good. Such rights to individual goals may be produced by the deep theory, as rights that men in the original position would stipulate as being in their best interest. But the original position cannot itself be justified on the assumption of such a right, because the parties to the contract do not know that they have any such interest or rank it lexically ahead of others.

So the basic right of Rawls's deep theory must be an abstract right, that is, not a right to any particular individual goal. There are two candidates, within the familiar concepts of political theory, for this role. The first is the right to liberty, and it may strike many readers as both plausible and comforting to assume that Rawls's entire structure is based on the assumption of a fundamental natural right to liberty—

plausible because the two principles that compose his theory of justice give liberty an important and dominant place, and comforting because the argument attempting to justify that place seems uncharacteristically incomplete.[6]

Nevertheless, the right to liberty cannot be taken as the fundamental right in Rawls's deep theory. Suppose we define general liberty as the overall minimum possible constraints, imposed by government or by other men, on what a man might want to do.[7] We must then distinguish this general liberty from particular liberties, that is, freedom from such constraints on particular acts thought specially important, like participation in politics. The parties to the original position certainly have, and know that they have, an interest in general liberty, because general liberty will, *pro tanto,* improve their power to achieve any particular goals they later discover themselves to have. But the qualification is important, because they have no way of knowing that general liberty will in fact improve this power overall, and every reason to suspect that it will not. They know that they might have other interests, beyond general liberty, that can be protected only by political constraints on acts of others.

So if Rawlsian men must be supposed to have a right to liberty of some sort, which the contract situation is shaped to embody, it must be a right to particular liberties. Rawls does name a list of basic liberties, and it is these that his men do choose to protect through their lexically ordered first principle of justice.[8] But Rawls plainly casts this principle as the product of the contract rather than as a condition of it. He argues that the parties to the original position would select these basic liberties to protect the basic goods they decide to value, like self-respect, rather than taking these liberties as goals in themselves. Of course they might, in fact, value the activities protected as basic liberties for their own sake, rather than as means to some other goal or interest. But they certainly do not know that they do.

The second familiar concept of political theory is even more abstract than liberty. This is equality, and in one way Rawlsian men and women cannot choose other than to protect it. The state of ignorance in the original position is so shaped that the antecedent interest of everyone must lie, as I said, in the same solution. The right of each man to be treated equally without regard to his person or character or tastes is enforced by the fact that no one else can secure a better position by virtue of being different in any such respect. In other contract situations, when ignorance is less complete, individuals who share the same goal may nevertheless have different antecedent interests. Even if two men value life above everything else, for example, the antecedent interest of the weaker might call for a state monopoly of force rather than some provision for private vengeance, but the antecedent interest of the stronger might not. Even if two men value political participation above all else, the knowledge that one's views are likely to be more unorthodox or unpopular than those of the other will suggest that his antecedent interest calls for different arrangements. In the original position no such discrimination of antecedent interests can be made.

It is true that, in two respects, the principles of justice that Rawls thinks men and women would choose in the original position may be said to fall short of an egalitarian ideal. First, they subordinate equality in material resources, when this is necessary, to liberty of political activity, by making the demands of the first principle prior to those of the second. Second, they do not take account of relative deprivation, because they justify any inequality when those worse off are better off than they would be, in absolute terms, without that inequality.

Rawls makes plain that these inequalities are required, not by some competing notion of liberty or some overriding goal, but by a more basic sense of equality itself. He accepts a distinction between what he calls two conceptions of equality:

> Some writers have distinguished between equality as it is invoked in connection with the distribution of certain goods, some of which will almost certainly give higher status or prestige to those who are more favored, and equality as it applies to the respect which is owed to persons irrespective of their social position. Equality of the first kind is defined by the second principle of justice. . . . But equality of the second kind is fundamental.[9]

We may describe a right to equality of the second kind, which Rawls says is fundamental, in this way. We might say that individuals have a right to equal concern and respect in the design and administration of the political institutions that govern them. This is a highly abstract right. Someone might argue, for example, that it is satisfied by political arrangements that provide equal opportunity for office and position on the basis of merit. Someone else might argue, to the contrary, that it is satisfied only by a system that gurantees absolute equality of income and status, without regard to merit. A third man might argue that equal concern and respect is provided by that system, whatever it is, that improves the average welfare of all citizens counting the welfare of each on the same scale. A fourth might argue, in the name of this fundamental equality, for the priority of liberty, and for the other apparent inequalities of Rawls's two principles.

The right to equal concern and respect, then, is more abstract than the standard conceptions of equality that distinguish different political theories. It permits arguments that this more basic right requires one or another of these conceptions as a derivative right or goal.

The original position may now be seen as a device for testing these competing arguments. It supposes, reasonably, that political arrangements that do not display equal concern and respect are those that are established and administered by powerful men and women who, whether they recognize it or not, have more concern and respect for members of a particular class, or people with particular talents or ideals, than they have for others. It relies on this supposition in shaping the ignorance of the parties to the contract. Men who do not know to which class they belong cannot design institutions, consciously or unconsciously, to favor their own class. Men who have no idea of their own conception of the good cannot act to favor those who hold one ideal over those who hold another. The original position is well designed to enforce the abstract right to equal concern and respect, which must be understood to be the fundamental concept of Rawls's deep theory.

It this is right, then Rawls must not use the original position to argue for this right in the same way that he uses it, for example, to argue for the rights to basic liberties embodied in the first principle. The text confirms that he does not. It is true that he once says that equality of respect is "defined" by the first principle of justice.[10] But he does not mean, and in any case he does not argue, that the parties choose to be respected equally in order to advance some more basic right or goal. On the contrary, the right to equal respect is not, on his account, a product of the contract, but a condition of admission to the original position. This right, he says, is "owed to human beings as moral persons," and follows from the moral personality that distinguishes humans from animals. It is possessed by all men who can give justice, and only such men can contract.[11] This is one right, therefore, that does not emerge from the contract, but is assumed, as the fundamental right must be, in its design.

Rawls is well aware that his argument for equality stands on a different footing from his argument for the other rights within his theory:

> Now of course none of this is literally argument. I have not set out the premises from which this conclusion follows, as I have tried to do, albeit not very rigorously, with the choice of conceptions of justice in the original position. Nor have I tried to prove that the characterization of the parties must be used as the basis of equality. Rather this interpretation seems to be the natural completion of justice as fairness.[12]

It is the "natural completion," that is to say, of the theory as a whole. It completes the theory by providing the fundamental assumption that charges the original position, and makes it an "intuitive notion" for developing and testing theories of justice.

We may therefore say that justice as fairness rests on the assumption of a natural right of all men and women to equality of concern and respect, a right they possess not by virtue of birth or characteristic or merit or excellence but simply as human beings with the capacity to make plans and give justice. Many readers will not be surprised by this conclusion, and it is, as I have said, reasonably clear from the text. It is an important conclusion, nevertheless, because some forms of criticism of the theory, already standard, ignore it. I shall close this long essay with one example.

One form of criticsm has been expressed to me by many colleagues and students, particularly lawyers. They point out that the particular political institutions and arrangements that Rawls says men in the original position would choose are merely idealized forms of those now in force in the United States. They are the institutions, that is, of liberal constitutional democracy. The critics conclude that the fundamental assumptions of Rawls's theory must, therefore, be the assumptions of classical liberalism, however they define these, and that the original position, which appears to animate the theory, must somehow be an embodiment of these assumptions. Justice as fairness therefore seems to them, in its entirety, as particularly subtle rationalization of the political status quo, which may safely be disregarded by those who want to offer a more radical critique of the liberal tradition.

If I am right, this point of view is foolish, and those who take it lose an opportunity, rare for them, to submit their own political views to some form of philosophical examination. Rawls's most basic assumption is not that men have a right to certain liberties that Locke or Mill thought important, but that they have a right to equal respect and concern in the design of political institutions. This assumption may be contested in many ways. It will be denied by those who believe that some goal, like utility or the triumph of a class or the flowering of some conception of how men should live, is more fundamental than any individual right, including the right to equality. But it cannot be denied in the name of any more radical concept of equality, because none exists.

Rawls does argue that this fundamental right to equality requires a liberal constitution, and supports an idealized form of present economic and social structures. He argues, for example, that men in the original position would protect the basic liberties in the interest of their right to equality, once a certain level of material comfort has been reached, because they would understand that a threat to self-respect, which the basic liberties protect, is then the most serious threat to equal respect. He also argues that these men would accept the second principle in preference to material equality because they would understand that sacrifice out of envy for another is a form of subordination to him. These arguments may, of course, be wrong. I have certainly said nothing in their defense here. But the critics of liberalism now have the responsibility to show that they are wrong. They cannot say that Rawls's basic assumptions and attitudes are too far from their own to allow a confrontation.

Notes

1. John Rawls, *A Theory of Justice* (Cambridge, Mass.: Harvard University Press, 1971).
2. pp. 48 ff.
3. pp. 21–2
4. p. 587.
5. p. 51.
6. See Hart, 'Rawls on Liberty and Its Priority,' 40 *U. Chi. L. Rev.* 534 (1973).
7. Cf. Rawls's definition of liberty at p. 202.
8. p. 61.
9. p. 511.
10. Id.
11. Chapter 77.
12. p. 509.

12

Rawls and Marxism

RICHARD MILLER

In *A Theory of Justice,* John Rawls claims that all of the most fundamental questions about justice, including questions about an individual's duty to help achieve justice, can be settled from the standpoint of the original position.[1] He proposes, as a criterion of social justice, the so-called "difference principle," the principle that basic institutions ought to maximize the life prospects of the worst off.[2] And he presents this standard as a morally realistic one, in that people in societies that do not yet fulfill it ought to accept advances toward it (at least if these advances do not conflict with the maximization of equal basic liberties or with fair equality of opportunity), and ought, to some extent, to help achieve such advances.[3]

I shall try to show that these claims, taken together, presuppose a relatively low estimate of the extent and consequences of social conflict. In particular, if a Marxist analysis of social conflict is right in certain respects, a commitment to accept advances toward the difference principle in societies that do not embody it would not emerge from the original position. Thus, if these Marxist ideas are correct, either the difference principle is unrealistic, in that people do not have a duty to accept and to further its realization, or there are fundamental issues concerning justice (for example, this issue of moral realism), that cannot be resolved from the standpoint of the original position.

In Rawls's "ideal contractualism," principles concerning justice are seen as agreements that would be made by rational deliberants seeking to pursue their interests behind a veil of ignorance which excludes knowledge of what one's place in society and one's special interests are. This is, of course, a very rough statement, but most

From "Rawls and Marxism," *Philosophy and Public Affairs* 3 (1974), pp. 167–180. Reprinted by permission of the author and Princeton University Press.

refinements on it go beyond the needs of this essay. There are, however, a few details of Rawls's theory that need further elaboration, for the sake of my subsequent arguments.

In the original position, one does not know what one's social position or one's special needs and interests are. And in deciding the most general questions about justice, one does not know what particular form of society (e.g., slave-holding, feudal, capitalist) one lives in.[4] But one does know "the general facts about human society."[5] Thus, if Marxist social theory is correct, the general facts contained in this theory would be known in the original position, and could affect its outcome.

In defining the agreements Rawls believes would emerge from the original position, it will be helpful to distinguish the outcomes Rawls thinks he *has* established in his book, from the outcomes he thinks *can* be established by ideal contractualism. In particular, Rawls claims to have actually derived a commitment to support the difference principle in circumstances of "strict compliance," i.e., in any society the basic institutions of which conform to the difference principle and the members of which regard the latter as a principle of justice and willingly do what it requires.[6] But he surely regards it as *possible* to derive a commitment to accept and, to some extent, to further advances toward the difference principle in any society within the "circumstances of justice," i.e., in any society with respect to which questions of justice can appropriately be raised. For he says the difference principle applies throughout the circumstances of justice.[7] As noted before, he regards it as a duty to help realize principles of justice. And he sees all fundamental questions concerning justice as being decidable by determining what commitments would emerge from the original position. Thus some commitment to uphold the difference principle, even when strict compliance has not been achieved, ought to emerge from the original position.

Of course, that the text of Rawls's book implies a commitment to there being an ideal contractualist account of the duty to uphold Rawlsian justice does not show that this commitment is central to Rawls's theory. But in fact this claim of Rawls cannot be rejected without casting doubt on the whole ideal contractualist approach. To begin with, the view that people in less than just societies have no duty to help achieve justice, or even to accept advances in this direction, is monstrous, and more than a bit absurd. After all, a slave owner who refuses to let his slaves go free, when this would require only moderate financial losses, would not be a just man because he believed slavery to be an unjust institution. Indeed, we would regard this belief as playing a trivial role in his sense of justice. But if the assertion of principles of justice for institutions must be accompanied by the requirement that these principles be upheld, a moral outlook appealed to in support of the former claim should provide support for the latter. Certainly, if ideal contractualism is supposed to tell us how basic institutions should operate, but must be abandoned when we ask how people should behave in less than ideal circumstances, it cannot be the satisfactory end result of moral reflection that Rawls wants it to be. Thus, the importance of the idea of an ideal contractualists account of the duty to help achieve justice is much greater than might be thought from the few paragraphs Rawls devotes directly to this claim.

I shall be arguing that certain aspects of Marxism (and not very hard-line ones) would preclude the requisite agreement to uphold the difference principle throughout the circumstances of justice. In particular, I shall argue that this commitment would not be made if *some* societies in the circumstances of justice display the following three features: no social arrangement that is acceptable to the best-off class is acceptable to the worst-off class; the best-off class is a ruling class, i.e., one whose interests are served by the major political and ideological institutions; the need for weatlth and power typical of the best-off class is much more acute than that typical of the rest of society. This piece of Marxism is, of course, less controversial than Marx's whole theory, in which these features are said to hold true of all nonprimitive societies. But certain of the claims I have sketched can be so understood that it is implausible that they should hold true of any society. And, of course, the question of whether there is an obligation to uphold the difference principle in a society like our own will be an implicit concern in my arguments, even though I do not explicitly address myself to it. For these reasons, I would like to spell out in more detail the ways in which the above three properties might obtain in various societies.

To begin with, Marx claims that in any society, from the dissolution of primitive communism to the overthrow of capitalism, there is no social contract that the best-off class and the worst-off one will acquiesce in, except as a result of defeat in class struggle or a tactical retreat to perserve long-term advantages. For example, Marx would say that no aristocracy has reduced feudal obligations, no bourgeoisie has reduced the length or pace of the working day, except in response to the actual or potential militancy of peasants or of workers, usually in alliance with other classes. And no peasantry or proletariat has accepted an economic arrangement for long without fighting against it, whether in peasant uprisings, militant strikes, or revolutions. For Marx, this determination of social affairs by what Rawls would call "threat advantage" reflects people's rational pursuit of their self-interests. Moreover, improvements in the relative position of the worst-off class cannot, in Marx's view, be brought about by appeals to any universal sense of justice. Even when such a sense exists, no appropriate consensus can be achieved as to whether the demands of justice have in fact been fulfilled. For instance, capitalists, as a class, have always insisted that a proposed reduction of the working day, e.g., from twelve or more hours to ten, would do immeasurable harm to workers by destroying the capitalist economy on whose existence workers' welfare depends.[8]

The second Marxist idea I shall emphasize is the notion that the best-off class is a ruling class, one whose interests are served by all major institutions. Marx and Engels emphasize two aspects of this rule, the repressive and the ideological. In their view, the official instruments of coercion are employed, in almost all crucial instances of class conflict, in favor of the best-off class. Thus, to take some dramatic examples, the police, the army, and the courts were used in the United States and Great Britain to break up meetings in support of the ten-hour day, not meetings against it. In the fight for industrial unionism in this country in the twenties and thirties, they were used to protect strikebreakers and threaten sit-down strikers, not the other way around. In addition to institutions of repression, ideological institutions, in the Marxist view, help to maintain the special status of the best-off class. For example, in the Middle Ages, the Church tended to teach that submission to the dominant social order was an expression of piety. In nineteenth-century England, according to Marx, as class struggle became more intense, academic economists mostly became "hired prizefighters" of the bourgeoisie,[9] arguing, e.g., that abolishing tariffs on grain would immensely enrich workers and that a ten-hour workday would reduce profits to zero.[10] To take a present-day American example, many Marxists would now argue that the media and the schools foster anti-Black racism because it serves to divide those having common interests against American big business.

The third Marxist idea to which I shall refer is, strictly speaking, an extrapolation from Marx's writings, and not taken directly from them. Marx seems to regard a typical member of the best-off class in an exploitive society as having an especially acute need for wealth and power. He would, I think, have accepted the following estimate of how acute these needs usually are: the need for wealth and power of a typical member of the best-off class is sufficiently great that such a person would be miserable if his society were transformed to accord with the egalitarian demands of the difference principle. Indeed, this misery would be so great that the possibility of such unhappiness would dissuade someone in the original position from committing himself to help realize the difference principle, when the veil of ignorance is lifted. (I shall spell out this claim in more detail later on.)

While this specific estimate of ruling-class needs cannot, of course, be found in Marx, it is, I think, a reasonable extrapolation from Marx's writings. Some such radical estimate of how much greater a lord's needs are than a serf's, or how much greater a capitalist's are than a worker's, is suggested by Marx's comments on the immense differences between what workers in different societies regard as "necessities of life."[11] It also seems implicit in his historical writings. For example, in Marx's account, the factions of the French bourgeoisie who overthrew Louis Philippe risked large-scale social disorder to escape a subordination to other factions that allowed the worst-off factions wealth and power beyond the dreams of most of the French working class, or indeed, most workers in the Paris Commune, twenty years later. The general idea that classes differ in their needs, and not just in the degree to which their needs are satisfied, is almost explicitly stated in one of Marx's last writings, his notes on Wagner's *Lehrbuch der politischen Oekonomie,* when he criticizes some remarks of Wagner's on the "natural" needs of Man: "[If 'Man'] means Man, as a category, he has . . . no . . . needs at all. If it means man confronting nature by himself, one has in mind a non-social animal. If it means a man who is already to be found in some form of society . . . one must begin by presenting the particular character of this social man, i.e., the particular character of the community in which he lives, since here production, and thus *the means by which he maintains his existence* already have a social character."[12] This idea is, in turn, a special case of Marx's general thesis that "the social being [of men] determines their consciousness."[13]

If some societies in the circumstances of justice have the three features I have sketched, then, I shall try to show, no commitment to uphold the difference principle throughout the circumstances of justice would emerge from the original position.[14] To organize my argument, I shall take advantage of a certain feature of Rawls's exposition. His arguments for the difference principle often look like arguments for a commitment to participate in the immediate realization of the difference principle, once the veil of ignorance is lifted.[15] As I have mentioned, I do not think Rawls actually means to put forward such an argument within the confines of his book. He means only to argue for a commitment to uphold the difference principle in a society in which the principle has already been stably realized and everyone has a psychology supporting compliance with it. Nevertheless, the considerations Rawls brings forward in these arguments, considerations concerning the strains of commitment, rationality, self-respect, and stability, seem the ones that would be appealed to in support of a commitment to uphold the difference principle in less than ideal circumstances. In fact, it will be helpful to examine Rawls's arguments in turn, first taking each as if it *were* an argument for a commitment to realize the difference principle as soon as possible, then seeing if such an argument could be modified so as to generate a commitment to gradual realization. It might seem that working in this way I will tie my arguments too closely to special features of Rawls's text. But I think the reader will find that if the putative arguments I construct conflict with Marxist social theory, it seems quite unlikely that any argument for a commitment to uphold the difference principle throughout the circumstances of justice could accord with relevant aspects of Marxism.

One final comment may be necessary, before setting out my main arguments, in order for their import not to be misundertood. I shall be maintaining that Rawls is tacitly committed to a social hypothesis than can reasonably be argued either way, i.e., that the Marxist analysis I have just sketched is wrong throughout the circumstances of justice. I should note that I do not at all intend to criticize Rawls for developing a moral theory based on controversial factual assumptions. Indeed, it seems unlikely he could have written a book of such merit and importance if he had not been willing to commit himself to empirical claims. My intention in this essay is, rather, to show what some of Rawls's implicit assumptions are. By that token, I shall be arguing that some of his claims must be rejected if these assumptions are held to be false.

On the Derivation of the Difference Principle

I shall now consider Rawls's main attempts to derive the difference principle from the original position. In the chapter entitled "Some Main Grounds for the Two Principles of Justice" Rawls begins with the argument that his standard of social justice uniquely satisfies the following constraint:" . . . they [the bargainers in the original position] consider the strains of commitment. They cannot enter into agreements that may have consequences they cannot accept. They will avoid those that they can adhere to only with great difficulty."[16] Rawls argues along these lines against the principle of utility, noting that it will probably be a standard one cannot adhere to if it turns out to demand that one make great sacrifices simply to create more happiness for mankind as a whole.

Taken as an argument for a commitment to realize the difference principle as soon as possible, such reasoning from the strains of commitment seems subject to the charge Rawls makes against utilitarianism. It might be said that the best-off people will generally find it intolerable to give up great advantages in order to maximize the situation of the worst-off. This is, of course, a claim that Marxists would make. They would claim that the best-off people in any exploitive society cannot be made to give up their privileges except by force. In support of this claim, they would argue, for example, that no dominant exploitive class has voluntarily given up its rule, no matter how unjust. If Marxist social theory is right, at least when applied to some societies, someone in the original position would foresee that the difference principle may be intolerable for him, if he turns out to be a typical member of a dominant exploitive class. Thus, he could not accept, as grounds for a commitment to help realize the difference principle, an argument that this commitment, unlike its rivals, will be one he can live up to, no matter what social position he turns out to occupy.

In his book Rawls advances certain considerations that might be taken to show that in the original position one can foresee oneself as fulfilling a commitment to the difference principle, even if one turns out to be among the best-off. Most notably, in the chapter "On the Tendency to Equality," Rawls argues, in the following terms, that the difference principle is a "principle of mutual benefit":

> to begin with, it is clear that the well-being of each [i.e., both the best-off and the worst-off] depends on a scheme of social cooperation without which no one could have a satisfactory life. Secondly, we can ask for the willing cooperation of everyone only if the terms of the scheme are reasonable. The difference principle, then, seems to be a fair basis on which those better endowed, or more fortunate in their social circumstances, could expect others to collaborate with them when some workable arrangement is a necessary condition of the good of all.[17]

Such a line of reasoning is inadequate to establish the tolerability of commitment to the difference principle, if the best-off are a *ruling class* in an exploitive society. In a system which is in fact thoroughly exploitive, a ruling class can, for centuries, maintain as much willing cooperation as it needs, because ideological institutions serve its interests, while restraining most who do not cooperate and dissuading most who are tempted not to, by employing the coercive apparatus of the state. In such a situation, the rewards of exploitation for the ruling class far outweigh the costs to it of maintaining cooperation in an exploitive society. (Note that most of these costs are not supplied by the ruling class at all, but by workers who supply taxes and, in times of war, their lives.) Thus, if the best-off are sometimes a ruling class, of the sort just described, someone in the original position would foresee that if he turns out to be one of the best-off, his interests may not lie in the realization of Rawls's standard of social justice.

Of course, there is nothing in Marxist social theory to indicate one is *likely* to find it impossible to live up to a commitment to help realize the difference principle. To the contrary, the sort of exploitive ruling class I have described is supposed to be a small minority in any society. But an argument that one is quite unlikely to find commitment to the difference principle intolerable could not be successfully advanced behind the veil of ignorance. For, as Rawls indicates on several occasions, if reasoning from the respective likelihoods of one's occupying various social positions were admitted in the original position, the social ideal chosen would be some version of the principle of average utility.[18] Thus, if probabilistic reasoning were admitted (and Rawls thinks it should not be), the resultant commitment would be to help maximize the welfare of the average person, or something of the sort.

Let us suppose that if the sort of exploitive ruling class Marx describes has, at times, existed, the reasoning about the strains of commitment that Rawls uses against utilitarianism would also count against a commitment to help realize the difference principle immediately, or, in any case, as soon as possible after the veil of ignorance is lifted. It might still seem possible that the argument from the strains of commitment might persuade one to help maintain some *gradual* course of development toward full realization. Ideal contractualism might thus lead to a view according to which one sometimes has a duty to accept (and, perhaps, to promote) a certain incremental advance toward the realization of the difference principle, without having a duty to accept any advance beyond this increment. An example of such a gradualist moral claim, though admittedly an extreme one, is the view that slaveholders are obliged to accept emancipation with compensation, but not to accept uncompensated emancipation involving considerable financial sacrifice.

One thing to be said about the gradualist position is that it is repugnant to many people's considered moral judgments. Many would say that if the difference principle defines the requirements of perfect social justice, everyone should willingly accept its immediate realization. Indeed, many would say that everyone who can be helpful in realizing perfect social justice should take an active part in this process, if no great effort is involved.

In any case, an argument from the strains of commitment would not in fact support a gradualist commitment to the difference principle, if exploitive classes such as Marx describes have existed. For on the latter assumption every course of development leading to the difference principle will be more than some social class can willingly accept. Roughly speaking, there will be at least some circumstances in which any rate of change is either too fast for the best-off or too slow for the worst-off. The gradual realization of Rawls's principle will require a narrowing of the gap between best-off and worst-off, until Rawls's standard is satisfied. In the process, wealth, power, and status of the best-off will be progressively reduced. There are, presumably, definite limits to the size of the reduction an upper class can be expected to accept willingly in a given generation. They may accept a greater advance toward equality as a concession to force or the prospect of it. (Thus, the prospect of further social turmoil is sometimes said to be the cause of ultimate corporate acceptance of New Deal legislation.) But in a society for which a Marxist analysis holds true, the best-off will not accept an advance toward equality beyond a certain limit as a voluntary expression of their sense of justice. On the other hand, there are definite lower limits to the rate of advance typical members of the worst-off class find acceptable. They may settle for less out of fear, or a misguided perception of social reality, but not out of a feeling that in the actual social setting justice requires no quicker rate of progress. According to the view of class conflict characteristic of, though by no means special to, Marxist social theory, these two ranges of tolerability do not, as a rule, intersect. An advance that is not too much for the best-off class is, characteristically, too little for the worst-off class. Thus, Marx (e.g., in the beginning of Part I of the *Manifesto*) characterizes the whole course of social development as a more or less veiled civil war. And a great many people who do not discern such conflict in the most advanced societies would still claim that in some less advanced societies (where the circumstances of justice obtain) there is no course of action that is relevantly tolerable to all classes. Given such assumptions as these, the reasoning from the strains of commitment that Rawls directs against utilitarianism could also be directed against a commitment to accept any course of development leading to the difference principle.

It should be noted that there is a second sort of objection that might be raised against a gradualist version of Rawls's tolerability argument. Assuming that upper class needs do not change as the gap between best-off and worst-off narrows, the question of tolerability is simply postponed, since the cumulative results of change will eventually become intolerable from the standpoint of the best-off. Marxists and many others would reject the possibility of an appropriate gradual reduction of upper-class needs. They would, for example, point to many upper classes of the past that have responded more and more vigorously as their status has been eroded, even entering when necessary into civil wars. They would also claim that no substantial long-run decline in upper-class needs is to be discerned over the course of history. It might be replied that for the purposes of a strict-compliance theory, it is enough that upper-class needs might be gradually reduced by modifying educational institutions, in the broadest sense of the phrase, to make a representative member of each new upper-class generation less demanding in his needs than his forebears. But it is hard to see how this educational process could effectively obtain without the constant threat to the upper class of intolerable reductions in self-respect. After all, seeing that one's children are successfully and intentionally taught what one takes to be false-hoods, and that their basic needs and desires are systematically changed from one's own is never a small burden (cf. Rawls's discussion of self-respect and liberty of conscience in chapter 33). Thus, gradualism would be seen as at best a postpone-ment of problems of intolerability.

I have tried to show that if Marxist social theory precludes a certain argument for a commitment to the immediate realization of the difference principle, it precludes the use of this argument in support of a gradualist commitment, as well. While this discussion of gradualism as a putative "way out" has been tied to reasoning from the strains of commitment, analogous considerations can readily be developed in con-nection with arguments we shall subsequently examine, which concern rationality, self-respect, and stability. In considering these arguments, rather than repeating my discussion of gradualism, I shall, on the whole, assume that gradualism does not remove conflicts between Rawls and Marxist social theory.

One further objection to my arguments about tolerability concerns supposed strains of pursuing something less than justice. I have assumed that members of an exploitive ruling class would oppose the changes that the difference principle requires, even if they had a sense of justice defined by Rawls's principles. It might be felt that this would produce a considerable burden of either self-hatred or self-deception, a burden so great that it would not, in fact, be in one's interests to resist the consequences of the difference principle, if on leaving the original position one turns out to be a member of an exploitive ruling class. The answer to this, I think, is that while the ruling class does, in a sense, practice considerable self-deception, this self-deception is of a peculiarly unburdensome kind.

In the following sense, the capacity for self-deception of an exploitive ruling class would be said by Marx to be practically infinite: The long-term nonmoral interests of a typical member of such a class often sharply conflict with the moral principles which he puts forward without conscious hypocrisy; and when this conflict obtains, no reasoning from those moral principles can, in a typical case, dissuade an exploiter from doing what his nonmoral interests demand. Thus, suppose a decision to speed up the pace of work without installing safety equipment will keep profits up at the cost of hundreds of workers' lives. According to Marx, a typical capitalist will make the decision that serves the needs of profit, in spite of an appeal to common principles of justice, even if that appeal is backed by the best arguments in the world. It should also be noted that the emotional strain associated with the instances of self-deception most of us have encountered will typically be lacking in such cases. In Marx's view, the unresponsiveness of members of an exploitive ruling class to arguments conflicting with their class interests is supported by falsehoods, e.g., "What's good for Business (or—what preserves feudal bonds) is good for everyone," which the immense variety of ideological institutions operating in the interests of the ruling class promote, and which everyone in the social circle of a typical member of that class acknowledges. Indeed, even if a revolution were to destroy the basic institutions that contribute to these falsehoods, the survival of bourgeois ideologues, and of bourgeois ideas among many people, including working people, together with the suvival of exclusive networks of social acquaintance, would continue to insulate a member of the bourgeoisie from the truths on which the correct application of principles of justice depends. Thus, if one wants to speak of self-deception in situations like the one described (where the self gets so much help in its deception) it is not the sort of self-deception that imposes such strains as to make it preferable for a member of the exploitive ruling class to accept the objective fulfillment of his sense of justice.

I have sketched some reasons for rejecting the claim that the realization of Rawls's standard of social justice would be tolerable to a typical member of every income group. In particular I tried to show how a Rawlsian argument from a common interest in social cooperation conflicts with the conception of the best-off group in society as a ruling class. . . .

Notes

1. John Rawls, *A Theory of Justice* (Cambridge, Mass., 1971), pp. 11, 17, 115, 333f. Otherwise unidentified page references in the notes that follow are to this volume.

2. Pp. 60f., 75ff.

3. Pp. 115, 246, 288f., 334. On the priority of the principles of equal liberties and equal opportunity, see note 7, below.

4. P. 137.

5. *Ibid.* Rawls goes on to say, "They understand political affairs and the principles of economic theory. . . . Indeed the parties are presumed to know whatever general facts affect the choice of the principles of justice."

6. The derivation is contained in sections 26, 29, and 51. For the restriction to circumstances of strict compliance, see pp. 8, 288f., 334. This restriction was also imposed in unpublished comments of Rawls in response to David Lyons's paper at the 1972 A.P.A. symposium on *A Theory of Justice*. I should add that a reader who favors a less restrictive interpretation of Rawls's claims will find the conflict I sketch between Rawls and Marx all the more acute.

7. Pp. 125, 126. Strictly speaking, the difference principle is always to be fulfilled insofar as this does not conflict with the principle of greatest equal liberty or the principle of fair equality of opportunity (pp. 61, 302f.). Also, an expanded version of the difference principle, in which liberty, opportunity, and self-respect are counted among the relevant goods, holds universally (pp. 62f.). In this essay, all discussions of the difference principle are to be understood as bearing on these two restricted claims. There is little danger of resulting oversimplification, for we shall not be concerned with conflicts between the (narrower) difference principle and principles that override it.

8. See Karl Marx, *Capital* (Moscow, n.d.), 1, chap. 9. sec. 3, "Senior's 'Last Hour.'"

9. *Ibid.,* 1, "Preface to the Second German Edition," p. 25.

10. *Ibid.,* 1, p. 25 and chap. 9, sec. 3.

11. See, for example, *ibid.,* 1, chap. 6, "The Buying and Selling of Labor-Power," p. 168: "On the other hand, the number and extent of his [the wage-laborer's] so-called necessary wants, as also the modes of satisfying them, are themselves the product of historical development, and depend therefore to a great extent on the degree of civilization of a country, more particularly on the conditions under which, and consequently on the habits and degree of comfort in which, the class of free laborers has been formed."

There is a discussion to the same effect in *Wages, Price and Profit,* in which Marx speaks of "a *traditional standard of life*" as "the satisfaction of certain wants springing from the social conditions in which people are placed and reared up," and contrasts "the English standard of life" with "the Irish standard," "the standard of life of a German peasant" with that "of a Livonian peasant" (*Selected Works in One Volume* [New York, 1970], p. 225). See also *Wage-Labor and Capital, ibid.,* pp. 84f.

12. Marx's emphasis. See Marx and Engels, *Werke* (Berlin, 1958), 19, p. 362. The idea that needs differ significantly among different classes or socio-economic groups is not, of course, by any means confined to Marxist or left-wing writers. See, for example, Emile Durkheim, "Anomic Suicide," in *Suicide* (New York, 1951), pp. 249ff.

13. Preface to the *Critique of Political Economy,* in Marx and Engles, *Selected Works,* p. 182.

14. One clear and immediate corollary will be that if present-day society has these features, no commitment to uphold the difference principle in the present day would emerge.

15. These arguments, in sections 26 and 29, are actually presented as arguments for Rawls's two principles of justice, in serial order. But they are fairly characterized as "Rawls's arguments for the difference principle," since no other derivation of that principle is given in Rawls's book.

16. P. 176.

17. P. 103.

18. Pp. 154, 164f., 168.

Welfare Liberal Justice: The Utilitarian Perspective

13

On the Connection Between Justice and Utility

JOHN STUART MILL

In all ages of speculation one of the strongest obstacles to the reception of the doctrine that utility or happiness is the criterion of right and wrong has been drawn from the idea of justice. The powerful sentiment and apparently clear perception which that word recalls with a rapidity and certainty resembling an instinct have seemed to the majority of thinkers to point to an inherent quality in things; to show that the just must have an existence in nature as something absolute, generically distinct from every variety of the expedient and, in idea, opposed to it, though (as is commonly acknowledged) never, in the long run, disjoined from it in fact.

In the case of this, as of our other moral sentiments, there is no necessary connection between the question of its origin and that of its binding force. That a feeling is bestowed on us by nature does not necessarily legitimate all its promptings. The feeling of justice might be a peculiar instinct, and might yet require, like our other instincts, to be controlled and enlightened by a higher reason. If we have intellectual instincts leading us to judge in a particular way, as well as animal instincts that prompt us to act in a particular way, there is no necessity that the former should be more infallible in their sphere than the latter in theirs; it may as well happen that wrong judgments are occasionally suggested by those, as wrong actions by these. But though it is one thing to believe that we have natural feelings of justice, and another

From *Utilitarianism,* Chapter V. First published 1863.

to acknowledge them as an ultimate criterion of conduct, these two opinions are very closely connected in point of fact. Mankind is always predisposed to believe that any subjective feeling, not otherwise accounted for, is a revelation of some objective reality. Our present object is to determine whether the reality to which the feeling of justice corresponds is one which needs any such special revelation, whether the justice or injustice of an action is a thing intrinsically peculiar and distinct from all its other qualities or only a combination of certain of those qualities presented under a peculiar aspect. For the purpose of this inquiry it is practically important to consider whether the feeling itself, of justice and injustice, is *sui generis* like our sensations of color and taste or a derivative feeling formed by a combination of others. And this it is the more essential to examine, as people are in general willing enough to allow that objectively the dictates of justice coincide with a part of the field of general expediency; but inasmuch as the subjective mental feeling of justice is different from that which commonly attaches to simple expediency, and, except in the extreme cases of the latter, is far more imperative in its demands, people find it difficult to see in justice only a particular kind or branch of general utility, and think that its superior binding force requires a totally different origin.

To throw light upon this question, it is necessary to attempt to ascertain what is the distinguishing character of justice, or of injustice; what is the quality, or whether there is any quality, attributed in common to all modes of conduct designated as unjust (for justice, like many other moral attributes, is best defined by its opposite), and distinguishing them from such modes of conduct as are disapproved, but without having that particular epithet of disapprobation applied to them. If in everything which men are accustomed to characterize as just or unjust some one common attribute or collection of attributes is always present, we may judge whether this particular attribute or combination of attributes would be capable of gathering round it a sentiment of that peculiar character and intensity by virtue of the general laws of our emotional constitution, or whether the sentiment is inexplicable and requires to be regarded as a special provision of nature. If we find the former to be the case, we shall, in resolving this question, have resolved also the main problem; if the latter, we shall have to seek for some other mode of investigating it.

To find the common attributes of a variety of objects, it is necessary to begin by surveying the objects themselves in the concrete. Let us therefore advert successively to the various modes of action and arrangements of human affairs which are classed, by universal or widely spread opinion, as just or as unjust. The things well known to excite the sentiments associated with those names are of a very multifarious character. I shall pass them rapidly in review, without studying any particular arrangement.

In the first place, it is mostly considered unjust to deprive anyone of his personal liberty, his property, or any other thing which belongs to him by law. Here, therefore, is one instance of the application of the terms "just" and "unjust" in a perfectly definite sense, namely, that it is just to respect, unjust to violate, the *legal rights* of anyone. But this judgment admits of several exceptions, arising from the other forms in which the notions of justice and injustice present themselves. For example, the person who suffers the deprivation may (as the phrase is) have *forfeited* the rights which he is so deprived of—a case to which we shall return presently. But also—

Secondly, the legal rights of which he is deprived may be rights which *ought* not to have belonged to him; in other words, the law which confers on him these rights may be a bad law. When it is or when (which is the same thing for our purpose) it is supposed to be so, opinions will differ as to the justice or injustice of infringing it. Some maintain that no law, however bad, ought to be disobeyed by an individual citizen; that his opposition to it, if shown at all, should only be shown in endeavoring to get it altered by competent authority. This opinion (which condemns many of the most illustrious benefactors of mankind, and would often protect pernicious institutions against the only weapons which, in the state of things existing at the time, have any chance of succeeding against them) is defended by those who hold it on grounds of expediency, principally on that of the importance to the common interest of mankind, of maintaining inviolate the sentiment of submission to law. Other persons, again, hold the directly contrary opinion that any law, judged to be bad, may blamelessly be disobeyed, even though it be not judged to be unjust but only inexpedient, while others would confine the license of disobedience to the case of unjust laws; but, again, some say that all laws which are inexpedient are unjust, since every law imposes some restriction on the natural liberty of mankind, which restriction is an injustice unless legitimated by tending to their good. Among these diversities of opinion it seems to be universally admitted that there may be unjust laws, and that law, consequently, is not the ultimate criterion of justice, but may give to one person a benefit, or impose on another an evil, which justice condemns. When, however, a law is thought to be unjust, it seems always to be regarded as being so in the same way in which a breach of law is unjust; namely, by infringing somebody's right, which, as it cannot in this case be a legal right, receives a different appellation and is called a moral right. We may say, therefore, that a second case of injustice consists in taking or withholding from any person that to which he has a *moral right.*

Thirdly, it is universally considered just that each person should obtain that (whether good or evil) which he *deserves,* and unjust that he should obtain a good or be made to undergo an evil which he does not deserve. This is, perhaps, the clearest and most emphatic form in which the idea of justice is conceived by the general mind. As it involves the notion of desert, the question arises, what constitutes desert? Speaking in a general way, a person is understood to deserve good if he does right, evil if he does wrong; and in a more particular sense, to deserve good from those to whom he does or has done good, and evil from those to whom he does or has done evil. The precept of returning good for evil has never been regarded as a case of the fulfillment of justice, but as one in which the claims of justice are waived, in obedience to other considerations.

Fourthly, it is confessedly unjust to *break faith* with anyone: to violate an engagement, either express or implied, or disappoint expectations raised by our own conduct, at least if we have raised those expectations knowingly and voluntarily. Like the other obligations of justice already spoken of, this one is not regarded as absolute, but as capable of being overruled by a stronger obligation of justice on the other side, or by such conduct on the part of the person concerned as is deemed to absolve us from our obligation to him and to constitute a *forfeiture* of the benefit which he has been led to expect.

Fifthly, it is, by universal admission, inconsistent with justice to be *partial*—to show favor or preference to one person over another in matters to which favor and preference do not properly apply. Impartiality, however, does not seem to be regarded as a duty in itself, but rather as instrumental to some other duty; for it is admitted that favor and preference are not always censurable, and, indeed, the cases in which they are condemned are rather the exception than the rule. A person would be more likely to be blamed than applauded for giving his family or friends no superiority in good offices over strangers when he could do so without violating any other duty; and no one thinks it unjust to seek one person in preference to another as a friend, connection, or companion. Impartiality where rights are concerned is of course obligatory, but this is involved in the more general obligations of giving to everyone his right. A tribunal, for example, must be impartial because it is bound to award, without regard to any other consideration, a disputed object to the one of two parties who has the right to it. There are other cases in which impartiality means being solely influenced by desert, as with those who, in the capacity of judges, preceptors, or parents, administer reward and punishment as such. There are cases, again, in which it means being solely influenced by considerations for the public interest, as in making a selection among candidates for a government employment. Impartiality, in short, as an obligation of justice, may be said to mean being exclusively influenced by the considerations which it is supposed ought to influence the particular case in hand, and resisting solicitation of any motives which prompt to conduct different from what those considerations would dictate.

Nearly allied to the idea of impartiality is that of *equality,* which often enters as a component part of both into the conception of justice and into the practice of it, and, in the eyes of many persons, constitutes its essence. But in this, still more than in any other case, the notion of justice varies in different persons, and always conforms in its variations to their notion of utility. Each person maintains that equality is the dictate of justice, except where he thinks that expediency requires inequality. The justice of giving equal protection to the rights of all is maintained by those who support the most outrageous inequality in the rights themselves. Even in slave countries it is theoretically admitted that the rights of the slave, such as they are, ought to be as sacred as those of the master, and that a tribunal which fails to enforce them with equal strictness is wanting in justice; while, at the same time, institutions which leave to the slave scarcely any rights to enforce are not deemed unjust because they are not deemed inexpedient. Those who think that utility requires distinctions of rank do not consider it unjust that riches and social privileges should be unequally dispensed; but those who think this inequality inexpedient think it unjust also. Whoever thinks that government is necessary sees no injustice in as much inequality as is constituted by giving to the magistrate powers not granted to other people. Even among those who hold leveling doctrines, there are differences of opinion about expediency. Some communists consider it unjust that the produce of the labor of the community should be shared on any other principle than that of exact equality;

others think it just that those should receive most whose wants are greatest; while others hold that those who work harder, or who produce more, or whose services are more valuable to the community, may justly claim a larger quota in the division of the produce. And the sense of natural justice may be plausibly appealed to in behalf of every one of these opinions.

Among so many diverse applications of the term "justice," which yet is not regarded as ambiguous, it is a matter of some difficulty to seize the mental link which holds them together, and on which the moral sentiment adhering to the term essentially depends. Perhaps, in this embarrassment, some help may be derived from the history of the word, as indicated by its etymology.

In most if not all languages, the etymology of the word which corresponds to "just" points distinctly to an origin connected with the ordinances of law. *Justum* is a form of *jussum*, that which has been ordered. *Dikaion* comes directly from *dike*, a suit at law. *Recht,* from which came *right* and *righteous,* is synonymous with law. The courts of justice, the administration of justice, are the courts and the administration of law. *La justice,* in French, is the established term for judicature. I am not committing the fallacy, imputed with some show of truth to Horne Tooke, of assuming that a word must still continue to mean what it originally meant. Etymology is slight evidence of what the idea now signified is, but the very best evidence of how it sprang up. There can, I think, be no doubt that the *idée mère,* the primitive element, in the formation of the notion of justice was conformity to law. It constituted the entire idea among the Hebrews, up to the birth of Christianity; as might be expected in the case of a people whose laws attempted to embrace all subjects on which precepts were required, and who believed those laws to be a direct emanation from the Supreme Being. But other nations, and in particular the Greeks and Romans, who knew that their laws had been made originally, and still continued to be made, by men, were not afraid to admit that those men might make bad laws; might do, by law, the same things, and from the same motives, which if done by individuals without the sanction of law would be called unjust. And hence the sentiment of injustice came to be attached, not to all violations of law, but only to violations of such laws as *ought* to exist, including such as ought to exist but do not, and to laws themselves if supposed to be contrary to what ought to be law. In this manner the idea of law and of its injunctions was still predominant in the notion of justice, even when the laws actually in force ceased to be accepted as the standard of it.

It is true that mankind consider the idea of justice and its obligations as applicable to many things which neither are, nor is it desired that they should be, regulated by law. Nobody desires that laws should interfere with the whole detail of private life; yet everyone allows that in all daily conduct a person may and does show himself to be either just or unjust. But even here, the idea of the breach of what ought to be law still lingers in a modified shape. It would always give use pleasure, and chime in with our feelings of fitness, that acts which we deem unjust should be punished, though we do not always think it expedient that this should be done by the tribunals. We forego that gratification on account of incidental inconveniences. We should be glad to see just conduct enforced and injustice repressed, even in the minutest details, if we were not, with reason, afraid of trusting the magistrate with so unlimited an amount of power over individuals. When we think that a person is bound in justice to do a thing, it is an ordinary form of language to say that he ought to be compelled to do it. We should be gratified to see the obligation enforced by anybody who had the power. If we see that its enforcement by law would be inexpedient, we lament the impossibility, we consider the impunity given to injustice as an evil and strive to make amends for it by bringing a strong expression of our own and the public disapprobation to bear upon the offender. Thus the idea of legal constraint is still the generating idea of the notion of justice, though undergoing several transformations before that notion as it exists in an advanced state of society becomes complete.

The above is, I think, a true account, as far as it goes, of the origin and progressive growth of the idea of justice. But we must observe that it contains as yet nothing to distinguish that obligation from moral obligation in general. For the truth is that the idea of penal sanction, which is the essence of law, enters not only into the conception of injustice, but into that of any kind of wrong. We do not call anything wrong unless we mean to imply that a person ought to be punished in some way or other for doing it—if not by law, by the opinion of his fellow creatures; if not by opinion, by the reproaches of his own conscience. This seems the real turning point of the distinction between morality and simple expediency. It is a part of the notion of duty in every one of its forms that a person may rightfully be compelled to fulfill it. Duty is a thing which may be *exacted* from a person, as one exacts a debt. Unless we think that it may be exacted from him, we do not call it his duty. Reasons of prudence, or the interest of other people, may militate against actually exacting it, but the person himself, it is clearly understood, would not be entitled to complain. There are other things, on the contrary, which we wish that people should do, which we like or admire them for doing, perhaps dislike or despise them for not doing, but yet admit that they are not bound to do; it is not a case of moral obligation; we do not blame them; that is, we do not think that they are proper objects of punishment. How we come by these ideas of deserving and not deserving punishment will appear, perhaps, in the sequel; but I think there is no doubt that this distinction lies at the bottom of the notions of right and wrong; that we call any conduct wrong, or employ, instead, some other term of dislike or disparagement, according as we think that the person ought, or ought not, to be punished for it; and we say it would be right to do so and so, or merely that it would be desirable or laudable, according as we would wish to see the person whom it concerns compelled, or only persuaded and exhorted, to act in that manner.

Justice Correlated with Certain Rights

This, therefore, being the characteristic difference which marks off, not justice, but morality in general from the remaining provinces of expediency and worthiness, the character is still to be sought which distinguishes justice from other branches of morality. Now it is known that ethical writers divide moral duties into two classes, denoted by the ill-chosen expressions, duties of perfect and of imperfect obligation; the latter being those in which, though the act is obligatory, the particular occasions of performing it are left to our choice, as in the case of charity or beneficence, which we are indeed bound to practice but not toward any definite person, nor at any prescribed time. In the more precise language of philosophic jurists, duties of perfect obligation are those duties in virtue of which a correlative *right* resides in some person or persons; duties of imperfect obligation are those moral obligations which do not give birth to any right. I think it will be found that this distinction exactly coincides with that which exists between justice and the other obligations of morality. In our survey of the various popular acceptations of justice, the term appeared generally to involve the idea of a personal right—a claim on the part of one or more individuals, like that which the law gives when it confers a proprietary or other legal right. Whether the injustice consists in depriving a person of a possession, or in breaking faith with him, or in treating him worse than he deserves, or worse than other people who have no greater claims—in each case the supposition implies two things: a wrong done, and some assignable person who is wronged. Injustice may also be done by treating a person better than others; but the wrong in this case is to his competitors, who are also assignable persons. It seems to me that this feature in the case—a right in some person, correlative to the moral obligation—constitutes a specific difference between justice and generosity or beneficence. Justice implies something which it is not only right to do, and wrong not to do, but which some individual person can claim from us as his moral right. No one has a moral right to our generosity or beneficence because we are not morally bound to practice those virtues toward any given individual. And it will be found with respect to this as to every correct definition that the instances which seem to conflict with it are those which most confirm it. For if a moralist attempts, as some have done, to make out that mankind generally, though not any given individual, have a right to all the good we can do them, he at once, by that thesis, includes generosity and beneficence within the category of justice. He is obliged to say that our utmost exertions are *due* to our fellow creatures, thus assimilating them to a debt; or that nothing less can be a sufficient *return* for what society does for us, thus classing the case as one of gratitude; both of which are acknowledged cases of justice, and not of the virture of beneficence; and whoever does not place the distinction between justice and morality in general, where we have now placed it, will be found to make no distinction between them at all, but to merge all morality in justice. . . . When we call anything a person's right, we mean that he has a valid claim on society to protect him in the possession of it, either by the force of law or by that of education and opinion. If he has what we consider a sufficient claim, on whatever account, to have something guaranteed to him by society, we say that he has a right to it. If we desire to prove that anything does not belong to him by right, we think this done as soon as it is admitted that society ought not to take measures for securing it to him, but should leave him to chance or to his own exertions. Thus a person is said to have a right to what he can earn in fair professional competition, because society ought not to allow any other person to hinder him from endeavoring to earn in that manner as much as he can. But he has not a right to three hundred a year, though he may happen to be earning it; because society is not called on to provide that he shall earn that sum. On the contrary, if he owns ten thousand pounds three-per-cent stock, he *has* a right to three hundred a year because society has come under an obligation to provide him with an income of that amount.

To have a right, then, is, I conceive, to have something which society ought to defend me in the possession of. If the objector goes on to ask why it ought, I can give him no other reason than general utility. If that expression does not seem to convey a sufficient feeling of the strength of the obligation, nor to account for the peculiar energy of the feeling, it is because there goes to the composition of the sentiment, not a rational only but also an animal element—the thirst for retaliation; and this thirst derives its intensity, as well as its moral justification, from the extraordinarily important and impressive kind of utility which is concerned. The interest involved is that of security, to everyone's feelings the most vital of all interests. All other earthly benefits are needed by one person, not needed by another; and many of them can, if necessary, be cheerfully foregone or replaced by something else; but security no human being can possibly do without; on it we depend for all our immunity from evil and for the whole value of all and every good, beyond the passing moment, since nothing but the gratification of the instant could be of any worth to us if we could be deprived of everything the next instant by whoever was momentarily stronger than ourselves. Now this most indispensable of all necessaries, after physical nutriment, cannot be had unless the machinery for providing it is kept unintermittedly in active play. Our notion, therefore, of the claim we have on our fellow creatures to join in making safe for us the very groundwork of our existence gathers feelings around it so much more intense than those concerned in any of the more common cases of utility that the difference in degree (as is often the case in psychology) becomes a real difference in kind. The claim assumes that character of absoluteness, that apparent infinity and incommensurability with all other considerations which constitute the distinction between the feeling of right and wrong and that of ordinary expediency and inexpediency. The feelings concerned are so powerful, and we count so positively on finding a responsive feeling in others (all being alike interested) that *ought* and *should* grow into *must,* and recognized indispensability becomes a moral necessity, analogous to physical, and often not inferior to it in binding force.

Justice and Utility

If the preceding analysis, or something resembling it, be not the correct account of the notion of justice—if justice be totally independent of utility, and be a standard *per se,* which the mind can recognize by simple retrospection of itself—it is hard to understand why that internal oracle is so ambiguous, and why so many things appear either just or unjust, according to the light in which they are regarded.

We are continually informed that utility is an uncertain standard, which every different person interprets differently, and that there is no safety but in the immutable, ineffaceable, and unmistakable dictates of justice, which carry their evidence in themselves and are independent of the fluctuations of opinion. One would suppose from this that on questions of justice there could be no controversy; that, if we take that for our rule, its application to any given case could leave us in as little doubt as a mathematical demonstration. So far is this from being the fact that there is as much difference of opinion, and as much discussion, about what is just as about what is useful to society. Not only have different nations and individuals different notions of justice, but in the mind of one and the same individual, justice is not some one rule, principle, or maxim, but many which do not always coincide in their dictates, and, in choosing between which, he is guided either by some extraneous standard or by his own personal predilections. . . . [to take an] example from a subject already once referred to. In cooperative industrial association, is it just or not that talent or skill should give a title to superior remuneration? On the negative side of the question it is argued that whoever does the best he can deserves equally well, and ought not in justice to be put in a position of inferiority for no fault of his own; that superior abilities have already advantages more than enough, in the admiration they excite, the personal influence they command, and the internal sources of satisfaction attending them, without adding to these a superior share of the world's goods; and that society is bound in justice rather to make compensation to the less favored for this unmerited inequality of advantages than to aggravate it. On the contrary side it is contended that society receives more from the more efficient laborer; that, his services being more useful, society owes him a larger return for them; that a greater share of the joint result is actually his work, and not to allow his claim to it is a kind of robbery; that, if he is only to receive as much as others, he can only be justly required to produce as much, and to give a smaller amount of time and exertion, proportioned to his superior efficiency. Who shall decide between these appeals to conflicting principles of justice? Justice has in this case two sides to it, which it is impossible to bring into harmony, and the two disputants have chosen opposite sides; the one looks to what it is just that the individual should receive, the other to what it is just that the community should give. Each, from his own point of view, is unanswerable; and any choice between them, on the grounds of justice, must be perfectly arbitrary. Social utility alone can decide the preference.

How many, again, and how irreconcilable are the standards of justice to which reference is made in discussing the repartition of taxation. One opinion is that the payment to the state should be in numerical proportion to pecuniary means. Others think that justice dictates what they term graduated taxation—taking a higher percentage from those who have more to spare. In point of natural justice a strong case might be made for disregarding means altogether, and taking the same absolute sum (whenever it could be got) from everyone; as the subscribers to a mess or to a club all pay the same sum for the same privileges, whether they can all equally afford it or not. Since the protection (it might be said) of law and government is afforded to and is equally required by all, there is no injustice in making all buy it at the same price. It is reckoned justice, not injustice, that a dealer should charge to all customers the same price for the same article, not a price varying according to their means of payment. This doctrine, as applied to taxation, finds no advocates because it conflicts so strongly with man's feelings of humanity and of social expediency; but the principle of justice which it invokes is as true and as binding as those which can be appealed to against it. Accordingly it exerts a tacit influence on the line of defense employed for other modes of assessing taxation. People feel obliged to argue that the state does more for the rich man than for the poor, as a justification for its taking more from them, though this is in reality not true, for the rich would be far better able to protect themselves, in the absence of law or government, than the poor, and indeed would probably be successful in converting the poor into their slaves. Others, again, so far defer to the same conception of justice as to maintain that all should pay an equal capitation tax for the protection of their persons (these being of equal value to all), and an unequal tax for the protection of their property, which is unequal. To this others reply that the all of one man is as valuable to him as the all of another. From these confusions there is no other mode of extrication than the utilitarian.

Is, then, the difference between the just and the expedient a merely imaginary distinction? Have mankind been under a delusion in thinking that justice is a more sacred thing than policy, and that the latter ought only to be listened to after the former has been satisfied? By no means. The exposition we have given of the nature and origin of the sentiment recognizes a real distinction; and no one of those who profess the most sublime contempt for the consequences of actions as an element in their morality attaches more importance to the distinction than I do. While I dispute the pretensions of any theory which sets up an imaginary standard of justice not grounded on utility, I account the justice which is grounded on utility to be the chief part, and incomparably the most sacred and binding part, of all morality. Justice is a name for certain classes of moral rules which concern the essentials of human well-being more nearly, and are therefore of more absolute obligation, than any other rules for the guidance of life; and the notion which we have found to be of the essence of the idea of justice—that of a right residing in an individual—implies and testifies to this more binding obligation.

The moral rules which forbid mankind to hurt one another (in which we must never forget to include wrongful interference with each other's freedom) are more vital to human well-being than any maxims, however important, which only point out the best mode of managing some department of human affairs. They have also the peculiarity that they are the main element in determining the whole of the social feelings of mankind. It is their observance which alone preserves peace among human beings; if obedience to them were not the rule, and disobedience the exception, everyone would see in everyone else an enemy against whom he must be perpetually guarding himself. What is hardly less important, these are the precepts which mankind have the strongest and the most direct inducements for impressing upon one another. By merely giving to each other prudential instruction or exhortation, they may gain, or think they gain, nothing; in inculcating on each other the duty of positive beneficence, they have an unmistakable interest, but far less in degree; a person may possibly not need the benefits of others, but he always needs that they should not do him hurt. Thus the moralities which protect every individual from being harmed by others, either directly or by being hindered in his freedom of pursuing his own good, are at once those which he himself has most at heart and those which he has the strongest interest in publishing and enforcing by word and deed. It is by a person's observance of these that his fitness to exist as one of the fellowship of human beings is tested and decided; for on that depends his being a nuisance or not to those with whom he is in contact. Now it is these moralities primarily which compose the obligations of justice. The most marked cases of injustice, and those which give the tone to the feeling of repugnance which characterizes the sentiment, are acts of wrongful aggression or wrongful exercise of power over someone; the next are those which consist in wrongfully withholding from him something which is his due—in both cases inflicting on him a positive hurt, either in the form of direct suffering or of the privation of some good which he had reasonable ground, either of a physical or of a social kind, for counting upon.

The same powerful motives which command the observance of these primary moralities enjoin the punishment of those who violate them; and as the impulses of self-defense, of defense of others, and of vengeance are all called forth against such persons, retribution, or evil for evil, becomes closely connected with the sentiment of justice, and is universally included in the idea. Good for good is also one of the dictates of justice; and this, though its social utility is evident, and though it carries with it a natural human feeling, has not at first sight that obvious connection with hurt or injury which, existing in the most elementary cases of just and unjust, is the source of the characteristic intensity of the sentiment. But the connection, though less obvious, is not less real. He who accepts benefits and denies a return of them when needed inflicts a real hurt by disappointing one of the most natural and reasonable of expectations, and one which he must at least tacitly have encouraged, otherwise the benefits would seldom have been conferred. The important rank, among human evils and wrongs, of the disappointment of expectation is shown in the fact that it constitutes the principal criminality of two such highly immoral acts as a breach of friendship and a breach of promise. Few hurts which human beings can sustain are greater, and none wound more, than when that on which they habitually and with full assurance relied fails them in the hour of need; and few wrongs are greater than this mere withholding of good; none excite more resentment, either in the person suffering or in a sympathizing spectator. The principle, therefore, of giving to each what they deserve, that is, good for good as well as evil for evil, is not only included within the idea of justice as we have defined it, but is a proper object of that intensity of sentiment which places the just in human estimation above the simply expedient.

Most of the maxims of justice current in the world, and commonly appealed to in its transactions, are simply instrumental to carrying into effect the principles of justice which we have now spoken of. That a person is only responsible for what he has done voluntarily, or could voluntarily have avoided; that it is unjust to condemn any person unheard; that the punishment ought to be proportioned to the offense; and the like, are maxims intended to prevent the just principle of evil for evil from being perverted to the infliction of evil without that justification. The greater part of these common maxims have come into use from the practice of courts of justice, which have been naturally led to a more complete recognition and elaboration than was likely to suggest itself to others, of the rules necessary to enable them to fulfill their double function—of inflicting punishment when due, and of awarding to each person his right.

That first of judicial virtues, impartiality, is an obligation of justice, partly for the reason last mentioned, as being a necessary condition of the fulfillment of other obligations of justice. But this is not the only source of the exalted rank, among human obligations, of those maxims of equality and impartiality which, both in popular estimation and in that of the most enlightened, are included among the precepts of justice. In one point of view, they may be considered as corollaries from the principles already laid down. If it is a duty to do to each according to his deserts, returning good for good, as well as repressing evil by evil, it necessarily follows that we should treat all equally well (when no higher duty forbids) who have deserved equally well of *us,* and that society should treat all equally well who have deserved equally well of *it,* that is, who have deserved equally well absolutely. This is the highest abstract standard of social and distributive justice, toward which all in-stitutions and the efforts of all virtuous citizens should be made in the utmost possible degree to converge. But this great moral duty rests upon a still deeper foundation, being a direct emanation from the first principle of morals, and not a mere logical corollary from secondary or derivative doctrines. It is involved in the very meaning of utility, or the greatest happiness principle. That principle is a mere form of words without rational signification unless one person's happiness, sup-posed equal in degree (with the proper allowance made for kind), is counted for exactly as much as another's. Those conditions being supplied, Bentham's dictum, "everybody to count for one, nobody for more than one," might be written under the principle of utility as an explanatory commentary.[1] The equal claim of everybody to happiness, in the estimation of the moralist and of the legislator, involves an equal claim to all the means of happiness except insofar as the inevitable conditions of human life and the general interest in which that of every individual is included set limits to the maxim; and those limits ought to be strictly construed. As every other maxim of justice, so this is by no means applied or held applicable universally; on the contrary, as I have already remarked, it bends to every person's ideas of social expediency. But in whatever case it is deemed applicable at all, it is held to be the dictate of justice. All persons are deemed to have a *right* to equality of treatment, except when some recognized social expediency requires the reverse. And hence all social inequalities which have ceased to be considered expedient assume the character, not of simple inexpediency, but of injustice, and appear so tyrannical that people are apt to wonder how they ever could have been tolerated—forgetful that they themselves, perhaps, tolerate other inequalities under an equally mistaken notion of expediency, the correction of which would make that which they approve seem quite as monstrous as what they have at last learned to condemn. The entire history of social improvement has been a series of transitions by which one custom or institution after another, from being a supposed primary necessity of social existence, has passed into the rank of a universally stigmatized injustice and tyranny. So it has been with the distinctions of slaves and freemen, nobles and serfs, patricians and plebeians; and so it will be, and in part already is, with the aristocra-cies of color, race, and sex.

It appears from what has been said that justice is a name for certain moral requirements which, regarded collectively, stand higher in the scale of social utility, and are therefore of more paramount obligation, than any others, though particular cases may occur in which some other social duty is so important as to overrule any one of the general maxims of justice. Thus, to save a life, it may not only be allowable, but a duty, to steal or take by force the necessary food or medicine, or to kidnap and compel to officiate the only qualified medical practitioner. In such cases, as we do not call anything justice which is not a virtue, we usually say, not that justice must give way to some other moral principle, but that what is just in ordinary cases is, by reason of that other principle, not just in the particular case. By this useful accommodation of language, the character of indefeasibility attributed to justice is kept up, and we are saved from the necessity of maintaining that there can be laudable injustice.

The considerations which have now been adduced resolve, I conceive, the only real difficulty in the utilitarian theory of morals. It has always been evident that all cases of justice are also cases of expediency; the difference is in the peculiar sentiment which attaches to the former, as contradistinguished from the latter. If this characteristic sentiment has been sufficiently accounted for; if there is no necessity to assume for it any peculiarity of origin; if it is simply the natural feeling of resentment, moralized by being made co-extensive with the demands of social good; and if this feeling not only does but ought to exist in all the classes of cases to which the idea of justice corresponds—that idea no longer presents itself as a stumbling block to the utilitarian ethics. Justice remains the appropriate name for certain social utilities which are vastly more important, and therefore more absolute and imperative, than any others are as a class (though not more so than others may be in particular cases); and which, therefore, ought to be, as well as naturally are, guarded by a sentiment, not only different in degree, but also in kind; distinguished from the milder feeling which attaches to the mere idea of promoting human pleasure or convenience at once by the more definite nature of its commands and by the sterner character of its sanctions.

Notes

1. This implication, in the first principle of the utilitarian scheme, of perfect impartiality between persons is regarded by Mr. Herbert Spencer (in his *Social Statics*) as a disproof of the pretensions of utility to be a sufficient guide to right; since (he says) the principle of utility presupposes the anterior principle that everybody has an equal right to happiness. It may be more correctly described as supposing that equal amounts of happiness are equally desirable, whether felt by the same or different persons. This, however, is not a *pre*supposition, not a premise needful to support the principle of utility, but the very principle itself; for what is the principle of utility if it be not that "happiness" and "desirable" are synonymous terms? If there is any anterior principle implied, it can be no other than this, that the truths of arithmetic are applicable to the valuation of happiness, as of all other measurable quantities.

   (Mr. Herbert Spencer, in a private communication on the subject of the preceding note, objects to being considered an opponent of utilitarianism and states that he regards happiness as the ultimate end of morality; but deems that end only partially attainable by empirical generalizations from the observed results of conduct, and completely attainable only by deducing, from the laws of life and the conditions of existence, what kinds of action necessarily tend to produce happiness, and what kinds to produce unhappiness. With the exception of the word "necessarily," I have no dissent to express from this doctrine; and (omitting that word) I am not aware that any modern advocate of utilitarianism is of a different opinion. Bentham, certainly, to whom in the *Social Statics* Mr. Spencer particularly referred, is, least of all writers, chargeable with unwillingness to deduce the effect of actions on happiness from the laws of human nature and the universal conditions of human life. The common charge against him is of relying too exclusively upon such deductions and declining altogether to be bound by the generalizations from specific experience which Mr. Spencer thinks that utilitarians generally confine themselves to. My own opinion (and, as I collect, Mr. Spencer's) is that in ethics, as in all other branches of scientific study, the concilience of the results of both these processes, each corroborating and verifying the other, is requisite to give to any general proposition the kind and degree of evidence which constitutes scientific proof.)

14

Justice and Equality

R. M. HARE

There are several reasons why a philosopher of my persuasion should wish to write about justice. The first is the general one that ethical theory ought to be applied to practical issues, both for the sake of improving the theory and for any light it may shed on the practical issues, of which many of the most important involve questions of justice. This is shown by the frequency with which appeals are made to justice and fairness and related ideals when people are arguing about political or economic questions (about wages for example, or about schools policy or about relations between races or sexes). If we do not know what "just" and "fair" mean (and it looks as if we do not) and therefore do not know what would settle questions involving these concepts, then we are unlikely to be able to sort out these very difficult moral problems. I have also a particular interest in the topic: I hold a view about moral reasoning which has at least strong affinities with utilitarianism;[1] and there is commonly thought to be some kind of antagonism between justice and utility or, as it is sometimes called, expediency. I have therefore a special need to sort these questions out.

We must start by distinguishing between different kinds of justice, or between different senses or uses of the word "just" (the distinction between these different ways of putting the matter need not now concern us). In distinguishing between different kinds of justice we shall have to make crucial use of a distinction between different levels of moral thinking which I have explained at length in other places.[2] It is perhaps simplest to distinguish three levels of thought, one ethical or meta-ethical and two moral or normative-ethical. At the meta-ethical level we try to establish the

From "Justice and Equality," *Justice and Economic Distribution,* edited by John Arthur and William Shaw (1978), pp. 116–131. Reprinted by permission of the author.

meanings of the moral words, and thus the formal properties of the moral concepts, including their logical propertise. Without knowing these a theory of normative moral reasoning cannot begin. Then there are two levels of (normative) moral thinking which have often been in various ways distinguished. I have myself in the past called them "level 2" and "level 1"; but for ease of remembering I now think it best to give them names, and propose to call level 2 the *critical* level and level 1 the *intuitive* level. At the intuitive level we make use of *prima facie* moral principles of a fairly simple general sort, and do not question them but merely apply them to cases which we encounter. This level of thinking cannot be (as intuitionists commonly suppose) self-sustaining; there is a need for a critical level of thinking by which we select the *prima facie* principles for use at the intuitive level, settle conflicts between them, and give to the whole system of them a justification which intuition by itself can never provide. It will be one of the objects of this paper to distinguish those kinds of justice whose place is at the intuitive level and which are embodied in *prima facie* principles from those kinds which have a role in critical and indeed in meta-ethical thinking.

The principal result of meta-ethical enquiry in this field is to isolate a sense or kind of justice which has come to be known as "formal justice." Formal justice is a property of all moral principles (which is why Professor Rawls heads his chapter on this subject not "Formal constraints of the concept of *just*" but "Formal constraints of the concept of *right*,"[3] and why his disciple David Richards is able to make a good attempt to found the whole of morality, and not merely a theory of justice, on a similar hypothetical-contract basis).[4] Formal justice is simply another name for the formal requirement of universality in moral principles on which, as I have explained in detail elsewhere,[5] golden-rule arguments are based. From the formal, logical properties of the moral words, and in particular from the logical prohibition of individual references in moral principles, it is possible to derive formal canons of moral argument, such as the rule that we are not allowed to discriminate morally between individuals unless there is some qualitative difference between them which is the ground for the discrimination; and the rule that the equal interests of different individuals have equal moral weight. Formal justice consists simply in the observance of these canons in our moral arguments; it is widely thought that this observance by itself is not enough to secure justice in some more substantial sense. As we shall see, one is not offending against the first rule if one says that extra privileges should be given to people just because they have white skins; and one is not offending against either rule if one says that one should take a cent from everybody and give it to the man with the biggest nose, provided that he benefits as much in total as they lose. The question is, How do we get from formal to substantial justice?

This question arises because there are various kinds of material or substantial justice whose content cannot be established directly by appeal to the uses of moral words or the formal properties of moral concepts (we shall see later how much can be done indirectly by appeal to these formal properties *in conjunction with* other premises or postulates or presuppositions). There is a number of different kinds of substantial justice, and we can hardly do better than begin with Aristotle's classification of them,[6] since it is largely responsible for the different senses which the word "just" still has in common use. This is a case where it is impossible to appeal to common use, at any rate of the word "just" (the word "fair" is better) in order to settle philosophical disputes, because the common use is itself the product of past philosophical theories. The expressions "distributive" and "retributive" justice go back to Aristotle,[7] and the word "just" itself occupies the place (or places) that it does in our language largely because of its place in earlier philosophical discussions.

Aristotle first separated off a generic sense of the Greek word commonly translated "just," a sense which had been used a lot by Plato: the sense in which justice is the whole of virtue in so far as it concerns our relations with other people.[8] The last qualification reminds us that this is not the most generic sense possible. Theognis had already used it to include the whole of virtue, full stop.[9] These very generic senses of the word, as applied to men and acts, have survived into modern English to confuse philosophers. One of the sources of confusion is that, in the less generic sense of "just" to be discussed in most of this paper, the judgment that an act would be unjust is sometimes fairly easily overridden by other moral considerations ("unjust," we may say, "but right as an act of mercy"; or "unjust, but right because necessary in order to avert an appalling calamity"). It is much more difficult for judgments that an act is required by justice in the generic sense, in which "unjust" is almost equivalent to "not right," to be overridden in this way.

Adherents of the *"fiat justitia ruat caelum"*[10] school seldom make clear whether, when they say "Let justice be done though the heavens fall," they are using a more or less generic sense of "justice"; and they thus take advantage of its non-overridability in the more generic sense in order to claim unchallengeable sanctity for judgments made using one of the less generic senses. It must be right to do the just thing (whatever that may be) in the sense (if there still is one in English) in which "just" *means* "right." In this sense, if it were right to cause the heavens to fall, and therefore just in the most generic sense, it would of course be right. But we might have to take into account, in deciding whether it would be right, the fact that the heavens would fall (that causing the heavens to fall would be one of the things we were doing if we did the action in question). On the other hand, if it were merely the just act in one of the less generic senses, we might hold that, though just, it was not right, because it would not be right to cause the heavens to fall merely in order to secure justice in this more limited sense; perhaps some concession to mercy, or even to common sense, would be in order.

This is an application of the "split-level" structure of moral thinking sketched above. One of the theses I wish to maintain is that principles of justice in these less generic senses are all *prima facie* principles and therefore overridable. I shall later be giving a utilitarian account of justice which finds a place, at the intuitive level, for these *prima facie* principles of justice. At this level they have great importance and utility, but it is in accordance with utilitarianism, as indeed with common sense, to claim that they can on unusual occasions be overridden. Having said this, however, it is most important to stress that this does *not* involve conceding the overridability of either the generic kind of justice, which has its place at the critical level, or of formal justice, which operates at the meta-ethical level. These are preserved intact, and therefore defenders of the sanctity of justice ought to be content, since these are the core of justice as of morality. We may call to mind here Aristotle's[11] remarks about the "better justice" or "equity" which is required in order to rectify the crudities, giving rise to unacceptable results in particular cases, of a justice whose principles are, as they have to be, couched in general (i.e. simple) terms. The lawgiver who, according to Aristotle, "would have" given a special prescription if he had been present at this particular case, and to whose prescription we must try to conform if we can, corresponds to the critical moral thinker, who operates under the constraints of formal justice and whose principles are not limited to simple general rules but can be specific enough to cover the peculiarities of unusual cases.

Retributive and Distributive Justice

After speaking briefly of generic justice, Aristotle goes on[12] to distinguish two main kinds of justice in the narrower or more particular sense in which it means "fairness." He calls these retributive and distributive justice. They have their place, respectively, in the fixing of penalties and rewards for bad and good actions, and in the distribution of goods and the opposite between the possible recipients. One of the most important questions is whether these two sorts of justice are reducible to a single sort. Rawls, for example, thinks that they are, and so do I. By using the expression "justice as fairness," he implies that all justice can be reduced to kinds of distributive justice, which itself is founded on procedural justice (i.e. on the adoption of fair procedures) in distribution.[13]

We may (without attempting complete accuracy in exposition) explain how Rawls might effect this reduction as follows. The parties in his 'original position' are prevented by his "veil of ignorance" from knowing what their own positions are in the world in which they are to live; so they are unable when adopting principles of justice to tailor them to suit their own individual interests. Impartiality (a very important constituent, at least, of justice) is thus secured. Therefore the principles which govern *both* the distribution of wealth and power and other good things *and* the assignment of rewards and penalties (and indeed all other matters which have to be regulated by principles of justice) will be impartial as between individuals, and in this sense just. In this way Rawls in effect reduces the justice of acts of retribution to justice in distributing between the affected parties the good and bad effects of a system of retributions, and reduces this distributive justice in turn to the adoption of a just procedure for selecting the system of retributions to be used.

This can be illustrated by considering the case of a criminal facing a judge (a case which has been thought to give trouble to me too, though I dealt with it adequately, on the lines which I am about to repeat here, in my book *Freedom and Reason*).[14] A Rawlsian judge, when sentencing the criminal, could defend himself against the charge of injustice or unfairness by saying that he was faithfully observing the principles of justice which would be adopted in the original position, whose conditions are procedurally fair. What these principles would be requires, no doubt, a great deal of discussion, in the course of which I might find myself in disagreement with Rawls. But my own view on how the judge should justify his action is, in its formal properties, very like his. On my view likewise, the judge can say that, when he asks himself what universal principles he is prepared to adopt for situations exactly like the one he is in, and considers examples of such logically possible situations in which *he* occupies, successively, the positions of judge, and of criminal, and of all those who are affected by the administration and enforcement of the law under which he is sentencing the criminal, including, of course, potential victims of possible future crimes—he can say that when he asks himself this, he has no hesitation in accepting the principle which bids him impose such and such a sentence in accordance with the law.

I am assuming that the judge is justifying himself at the critical level. If he were content with justifying himself at the intuitive level, his task would be easier, because, we hope, he, like most of us, has intuitions about the proper administration of justice in the courts, embodying *prima facie* principles of a sort whose inculcation in judges and in the rest of us has a high social utility. I say this while recognizing that *some* judges have intuitions about these matters which have a high social *dis*utility. The question of what intuitions judges ought to have about retributive justice is a matter for *critical* moral thinking.

On both Rawls' view and mine retributive justice has thus been reduced to distributive; on Rawls' view the principles of justice adopted are those which *distribute* fairly between those affected the good and the evil consequences of having or not having certain enforced criminal laws; on my own view likewise it is the impartiality secured by the requirement to universalize one's prescriptions which makes the judge say what he says, and here too it is an impartiality in distributing good and evil consequences between the affected parties. For the judge to let off the rapist would not be *fair* to all those who would be raped if the law were not enforced. I conclude that retributive justive can be reduced to distributive, and that therefore we shall have done what is required of us if we can give an adequate account of the latter.

What is common to Rawls' method and my own is the recognition that to get solutions to particular questions about what is just or unjust, we have to have a way of selecting principles of justice to answer such questions, and that to ask them in default of such principles is senseless. And we both recognize that the method for selecting the principles has to be founded on what he calls "the formal constraints of the concept of right." This measure of agreement can extend to the method of selecting principles of distributive justice as well as retributive. Neither Rawls nor I need be put off our stride by an objector who says that we have not addressed ourselves to the question of what acts are just, but have divagated on to the quite different question of how to select principles of justice. The point is that the first question cannot be answered without answering the second. Most of the apparently intractable conflicts about justice and rights that plague the world have been generated by taking certain answers to the first question as obvious and requiring no argument. We shall resolve these conflicts only by asking what arguments are available for the principles by which questions about the justice of individual acts are to be answered. In short, we need to ascend from intuitive to critical thinking; as I have argued in my review of his book, Rawls is to be reproached with not *completing* the ascent.[15]

Nozick, however, seems hardly to have begun it.[16] Neither Rawls nor I have anything to fear from him, so long as we stick to the formal part of our systems which we in effect share. When it comes to the application of this formal method to produce substantial principles of justice, I might find myself in disagreement with Rawls, because he relies much too much on his own intuitions which are open to question. Nozick's intuitions differ from Rawls', and sometimes differ from, sometimes agree with mine. This sort of question is simply not to be settled by appeal to intuitions, and it is time that the whole controversy ascended to a more serious, critical level. At this level, the answer which both Rawls and I should give to Nozick is that whatever sort of principles of justice we are after, whether structural principles, as Rawls thinks, or historical principles, as Nozick maintains, they have to be supported by critical thinking, of which Nozick seems hardly to see the necessity. This point is quite independent of the structural-historical disagreement.

For example, if Nozick thinks that it is just for people to retain whatever property they have acquired by voluntary exchange which benefited all parties, starting from a position of equality but perhaps ending up with a position of gross inequality, and if Rawls, by contrast, thinks that such inequality should be rectified in order to make the position of the least advantaged in society as good as possible, how are we to decide between them? Not by intuition, because there seems to be a deadlock between their intuitions. Rawls has a procedure, which *need* not appeal to intuition, for justifying distributions; this would give him the game, if he were to base the procedure on firm logical grounds, and if he followed it correctly. Actually he does not so base it, and mixes up so many intuitions in the argument that the conclusions he reaches are not such as the procedure really justifies. But Nozick has no procedure at all: only a variety of considerations of different sorts, all in the end based on intuition. Sometimes he seems to be telling us what arrangments in society would be arrived at if bargaining took place in accordance with games-theory between mutually disinterested parties; sometimes what arrangments would maximize the welfare of members of society; and sometimes what arrangments would strike them as fair. He does not often warn us when he is switching from one of these grounds to another; and he does little to convince us by argument that the arrangements so selected would be in accordance with justice. He hopes that we will think what he thinks; but Rawls at least thinks otherwise.

Formal Justice and Substantial Equality

How then do we get from formal to substantial justice? We have had an example of how this is done in the sphere of retributive justice; but how is this method to be extended to cover distributive justice as a whole, and its relation, if any, to equality in distribution? The difficulty of using formal justice in order to establish principles of substantial justice can indeed be illustrated very well by asking whether, and in what sense, justice demands equality in distribution. The complaint is often made that a certain distribution is unfair or unjust because unequal; so it looks, at least, as if the substantial principle that goods ought to be distributed equally in default of reasons to the contrary forms part of some people's conception of justice. Yet, it is argued, this substantial principle cannot be established simply on the basis of the formal notions we have mentioned. The following kind of schematic example is often adduced: consider two possible distributions of a given finite stock of goods, in one of which the goods are distributed equally, and in the other of which a few of the recipients have nearly all the goods, and the rest have what little remains. It is claimed with some plausibility that the second distribution is unfair, and the first fair. But it might also be claimed that impartiality and formal justice alone will not establish that we ought to distribute the goods equally.

There are two reasons which might be given for this second claim, the first of them a bad one, the other more cogent. The bad reason rests on an underestimate of the powers of golden-rule arguments. It is objected, for example, that people with white skins, if they claimed privileges in distribution purely on the ground of skin-colour, would not be offending against the formal principle of impartiality or universalizability, because no individual reference need enter into the principle to which they are appealing. Thus the principle that blacks ought to be subservient to whites is impartial as between *individuals;* any individual whatever who has the bad luck to find himself with a black skin or the good luck to find himself with a white skin is impartially placed by the principle in the appropriate social rank. This move receives a brief answer in my *Freedom and Reason,*[17] and a much fuller one in a forthcoming paper.[18] If the whites are faced with the decision, not merely of whether to frame this principle, but of whether to prescribe its adoption universally in all cases, including hypothetical ones in which their own skins turn black, they will at once reject it.

The other, more cogent-sounding argument is often used as an argument against utilitarians by those who think that justice has a lot to do with equality. It could also, at first sight, be used as an argument against the adequacy of formal justice or impartiality as a basis for distributive justice. That the argument could be leveled against both these methods is no accident; as I have tried to show elsewhere,[19] utilitarianism of a certain sort is the embodiment of—the method of moral reasoning which fulfills in practice—the requirement of universalizability or formal justice. Having shown that neither of these methods can produce a direct justification for equal distribution, I shall then show that both can produce indirect justifications, which depend, not on a priori reasoning alone, but on likely assumptions about what the world and the people in it are like.

The argument is this. Formal impartiality only requires us to treat everybody's interest as of equal weight. Imagine, then, a situation in which utilities are equally distributed. (There is a complication here which we can for the moment avoid by choosing a suitable example. Shortly I shall be mentioning the so-called principle of diminishing marginal utility, and shall indeed be making important use of it. But for now let us take a case in which it does not operate, so that we can, for ease of illustration, treat money as a linear measure of utility.) Suppose that we can vary the equal distribution that we started with by taking a dollar each away from everybody in the town, and that the loss of purchasing power is so small that they hardly notice it, and therefore the utility enjoyed by each is not much diminished. However, when we give the resulting large sum to one man, he is able to buy himself a holiday in Acapulco, which gives him so much pleasure that his access of utility is equal to the sum of the small losses suffered by all the others. Many would say that this redistribution was unfair. But we were, in the required sense, being impartial between the equal interests of all the parties; we were treating an equal access or loss of utility to any party as of equal value or disvalue. For, on our suppositions, the taking away of a dollar from one of the unfortunate parties deprived him of just as much utility as the addition of that dollar gave to the fortunate one. But if we are completely impartial, we have to regard *who has* that dollar or that access of utility as irrelevant. So there will be nothing to choose, from an impartial point of view, between our original equal distribution and our later highly unequal one, in which everybody else is deprived of a dollar in order to give one person a holiday in Acapulco. And that is why people say that formal impartiality alone is not enough to secure social justice, nor even to secure impartiality itself in some more substantial sense.

What is needed, in the opinion of these people, is some principle which says that it is unjust to give a person more when he already has more than the others—some sort of egalitarian principle. Egalitarian principles are only one possible kind of principles of distributive justice; and it is so far an open question whether they are to be preferred to alternative inegalitarian principles. It is fairly clear as a matter of history that different principles of justice have been accepted in different societies. As Aristotle says, "everybody agrees that the just distribution is one in accordance with desert of some kind; but they do not call desert the same thing, but the democrats say it is being a free citizen, the oligarchs being rich, others good lineage, and the aristocrats virtue."[20] It is not difficult to think of some societies in which it would be thought unjust for one man to have privileges not possessed by all men, and of others in which it would be thought unjust for a slave to have privileges which a free man would take for granted, or for a commoner to have the sort of house which a nobleman could aspire to. Even Aristotle's democrats did not think that slaves, but only citizens, had equal rights; and Plato complains of democracy that it "bestows equality of a sort on equals and unequals alike."[21] We have to ask, therefore, whether there are any reasons for preferring one of these attitudes to another.

At this point some philosophers will be ready to step in with their intuitions, and tell us that some distributions or ways of achieving distributions are *obviously* more just than others, or that *everyone will agree on reflection* that they are. These philosophers appeal to our intuitions or prejudices in support of the most widely divergent methods or patterns of distribution. But this is a way of arguing which should be abjured by anybody who wishes to have rational grounds for his moral judgments. Intuitions prove nothing; general consensus proves nothing; both have been used to support conclusions which *our* intuitions and our consensus may well find outrageous. We want arguments, and in this field seldom get them.

However, it is too early to despair of finding some. The utilitarian, and the formalist like me, still have some moves to make. I am supposing that we have already made the major move suggested above, and have ruled out discrimination on grounds of skin colour and the like, in so far as such discrimination could not be accepted by all for cases where they were the ones discriminated against. I am supposing that our society has absorbed this move, and contains no racists, sexists or in general discriminators, but does still contain economic men who do not think it wrong, in pursuit of Nozickian economic liberty, to get what they can, even if the resulting distribution is grotesquely unequal. Has the egalitarian any moves to make against them, and are they moves which can be supported by appeal to formal justice, in conjunction with the empirical facts?

Two Arguments for Equal Distribution

He has two. The first is based on that good old prop of egalitarian policies, the diminishing marginal utility, within the ranges that matter, of money and of nearly all goods. Almost always, if money or goods are taken away from someone who has a lot of them already, and given to someone who has little, total utility is increased, other things being equal. As we shall see, they hardly ever are equal; but the principle is all right. Its ground is that the poor man will get more utility out of what he is given than the rich man from whom it is taken would have got. A millionaire minds less about the gain or loss of a dollar than I do, and I than a pauper.

It must be noted that this is not an *a priori* principle. It is an empirical fact (if it is) that people are so disposed. The most important thing I have to say in this paper is that when we are, as we now are, trying to establish *prima facie* principles of distributive justice, it is enough if they can be justified in the world as it actually is, among people as they actually are. It is a wholly illegitimate argument against formalists or utilitarians that states of society or of the people in it could be *conceived of* in which gross inequalities could be justified by formal or utilitarian arguments. We are seeking principles for practical use in the world as it is. The same applies when we ask what qualifications are required to the principles.

Diminishing marginal utility is the firmest support for policies of progressive taxation of the rich and other egalitarian measures. However, as I said above, other things are seldom equal, and there are severe empirical, practical restraints on the equality that can sensibly be imposed by governments. To mention just a few of these hackneyed other things: the removal of incentives to effort may diminish the total stock of goods to be divided up; abrupt confiscation or even very steep progressive taxation may antagonize the victims so much that a whole class turns from a useful element in society to a hostile and dangerous one; or, even if that does not happen, it may merely become demoralized and either lose all enterprise and readiness to take business risks, or else just emigrate if it can. Perhaps one main cause of what is called the English sickness is the alienation of the middle class. It is an empirical question, just when egalitarian measures get to the stage of having these effects; and serious political argument on this subject should concentrate on such empirical questions, instead of indulging in the rhetoric of equal (or for that matter of unequal) rights. Rights are the offspring of *prima facie,* intuitive principles, and I have nothing against them; but the question is, What *prima facie* principles ought we to adopt? What intuitions ought we to have? On these questions the rhetoric of rights sheds no light whatever, any more than do appeals to intuition (i.e. to prejudice, i.e. to the *prima facie* principles, good or bad, which our upbringings happen to have implanted in us). The worth of intuitions is to be known by their fruits; as in the case of the principles to be followed by judges in administering the law, the best principles are those with the highest acceptance-utility, i.e. those whose general acceptance maximizes the furtherance of the interests, in sum, of all the affected parties, treating all those interests as of equal weight, i.e. impartially, i.e. with formal justice.

We have seen that, given the empirical assumption of diminishing marginal utility, such a method provides a justification for moderately egalitarian policies. The justification is strengthened by a second move that the egalitarian can make. This is to point out that inequality itself has a tendency to produce envy, which is a disagreeable state of mind and leads people to do disagreeable things. It makes no difference to the argument whether the envy is a good or a bad quality, nor whether it is justified or unjustified—any more than it makes a difference whether the alienation of the middle class which I mentioned above is to be condemned or excused. These states of mind are facts, and moral judgments have to be made in the light of the facts as they are. We have to take account of the actual state of the world and of the people in it. We can very easily think of societies which are highly unequal, but in which the more fortunate members have contrived to find some real or metaphorical opium of some Platonic noble lie[22] to keep the people quiet, so that the people feel no envy of privileges which we should consider outrageous. Imagine, for example, a society consisting of happy slave-owners and of happy slaves, all of whom know their places and do not have ideas above their station. Since there is *ex hypothesi* no envy, this source of disutility does not exist, and the whole argument from envy collapses.

It is salutary to remember this. It may make us stop looking for purely formal, *a priori* reasons for demanding equality, and look instead at the actual conditions which obtain in particular societies. To make the investigation more concrete, albeit oversimplified, let us ask what would have to be the case before we ought to be ready to push this happy slaveowning society into a revolution—peaceful or violent—which would turn the slaves into free and moderately equal wage-earners. I shall be able only to sketch my answer to this question, without doing nearly enough to justify it.

Arguments For and Against Egalitarian Revolutions

First of all, as with all moral questions, we should have to ask what would be the actual consequences of what we were doing—which is the same as to ask what we should be *doing,* so that accusations of "consequentialism"[23] need not be taken very seriously. Suppose, to simplify matters outrageously, that we can actually predict the consequences of the revolution and what will happen during its course. We can then consider two societies (one actual and one possible) and a possible process of transition from one to the other. And we have to ask whether the transition from one to the other will, all in all, promote the interest of all those affected more than to stay as they are, or rather, to develop as they would develop if the revolution did not occur. The question can be divided into questions about the process of transition and questions about the relative merits of the actual society (including its probably subsequent "natural" development) and the possible society which would be produced by the revolution.

We have supposed that the slaves in the existing society feel no envy, and that therefore the disutility of envy cannot be used as an argument for change. If there *were* envy, as in actual cases is probable, this argument *could* be employed; but let us see what can be done without it. We have the fact that there is gross inequality in the actual society and much greater equality in the possible one. The principle of diminishing marginal utility will therefore support the change, provided that its effects are not outweighed by a reduction in total utility resulting from the change and the way it comes about. But we have to be sure that this condition is fulfilled. Suppose, for example, that the actual society is a happy bucolic one and is likely to remain so, but that the transition to the possible society initiates the growth of an industrial economy in which everybody has to engage in a rat-race and is far less happy. We might in that case pronounce the actual society better. In general it is not self-evident that the access of what is called wealth makes people happier, although they nearly always think that it will.

Let us suppose, however, that we are satisfied that the people in the possible society will be better off all round than in the actual. There is also the point that there will be more generations to enjoy the new regime than suffer in the transition from the old. At least, this is what revolutionaries often say; and we have set them at liberty to say it by assuming, contrary to what is likely to be the case, that the future state of society is predictable. In actual fact, revolutions usually produce states of society very different from, and in most cases worse than, what their authors expected—which does not always stop them being better than what went before, once things have settled down. However, let us waive these difficulties and suppose that the future state of society can be predicted, and that it is markedly better than the existing state, because a greater equality of distribution has, owing to diminishing marginal utility, resulted in greater total utility.

Let us also suppose that the more enterprising economic structure which results leads to increased production without causing a rat-race. There will then be more wealth to go round and the revolution will have additional justification. Other benefits of the same general kind may also be adduced; and what is perhaps the greatest benefit of all, namely liberty itself. That people like having this is an empirical fact; it may not be a fact universally, but it is at least *likely* that by freeing slaves we shall *pro tanto* promote their interests. Philosophers who ask for *a priori* arguments for liberty or equality often talk as if empirical facts like this were totally irrelevant to the question. Genuine egalitarians and liberals ought to abjure the aid of these philosophers, because they have taken away the main ground for such views, namely the fact that people are as they are.

The arguments so far adduced support the call for a revolution. They will have to be balanced against the disutilities which will probably be caused by the process of transition. If heads roll, that is contrary to the interests of their owners; and no doubt the economy will be disrupted at least temporarily, and the new rulers, whoever they are, may infringe liberty just as much as the old, and possibly in an even more arbitrary manner. Few revolutions are pleasant while they are going on. But if the revolution can be more or less smooth or even peaceful, it may well be that (given the arguments already adduced about the desirability of the future society thereby achieved) revolution can have a utilitarian justification, and therefore a justification on grounds of formal impartiality between people's interests. But it is likely to be better for all if the same changes can be achieved less abruptly by an evolutionary process, and those who try to persuade us that this is not so are often merely giving way to impatience and showing a curious indifference to the interests of those for whom they purport to be concerned.

The argument in favour of change from a slave-owning society to a wage-earning one has been extremely superficial, and has served only to illustrate the lines on which a utilitarian or a formalist might argue. If we considered instead the transition from a capitalist society to a socialist one, the same forms of argument would have to be employed, but might not yield the same result. Even if the introduction of a fully socialist economy would promote greater equality, or more equal liberties (and I can see no reason for supposing this, but rather the reverse; for socialism tends to produce very great inequalities of *power*), it needs to be argued what the consequences would be, and then an assessment has to be made of the relative benefits and harms accruing from leaving matters alone and from having various sorts of bloody or bloodless change. Here again the rhetoric of rights will provide nothing but inflammatory material for agitators on both sides. It is designed to lead to, not to resolve, conflicts.

Remarks About Methods

But we must now leave this argument and attend to a methodological point which has become pressing. We have not, in the last few pages, been arguing about what state of society would be just, but about what state of society would best promote the interests of its members. All the arguments have been utilitarian. Where then does justice come in? It is likely to come into the propaganda of revolutionaries, as I have already hinted. But so far as I can see it has no direct bearing on the question of what would be the better society. It has, however, an important indirect bearing which I shall now try to explain. Our *prima facie* moral principles and intuitions are, as I have already said, the products of our upbringings; and it is a very important question *what* principles and intuitions it is best to bring up people to have. I have been arguing on the assumption that this question is to be decided by looking at the consequences for society, and the effects on the interests of people in society, of inculcating different principles. We are looking for the set of principles with the highest acceptance-utility.

Will these include principles of justice? The answer is obviously "Yes," if we think that society and the people in it are better off with *some* principles of justice than without any. A "land without justice" (to use the title of Milovan Djilas' book)[24] is almost bound to be an unhappy one. But what are the principles to be? Are we, for example, to inculcate the principle that it is just for people to perform the duties of their station and not envy those of higher social rank? Or the principle that all inequalities of any sort are unjust and ought to be removed? For my part, I would think that neither of these principles has a very high acceptance-utility. It may be that the principle with the highest acceptance-utility is one which makes just reward vary (but not immoderately) with desert, and assesses desert according to service to the interests of one's fellow-men. It would have to be supplemented by a principle securing equality of opportunity. But it is a partly empirical question what principles would have the highest acceptance-utility, and in any case beyond the scope of this paper. If some such principle is adopted and inculcated, people will *call* breaches of it unjust. Will they *be* unjust? Only in the sense that they will be contrary to a *prima facie* principle of distributive justice which we ought to adopt (not because it is itself a just principle, but because it is the best principle). The only sense that can be given to the question of whether it is a just principle (apart from the purely circular or tautological question of whether the principle obeys itself), is by asking whether the procedure by which we have selected the principle satisfies the logical requirements of critical moral thinking, i.e. is *formally* just. We might add that the adoption of such a formally just procedure and of the principles it selects is just in the *generic* sense mentioned at the beginning of this paper: it is the right thing to do; we morally ought to do it. The reason is that critical thinking, because it follows the requirements of formal justice based on the logical properties of the moral concepts, especially "ought" and "right," can therefore not fail, if pursued correctly in the light of the empirical facts, to lead to principles of justice which are in accord with morality. But because the requirements are all formal, they do not by themselves determine the content of the principles of justice. We have to do the thinking.

What principles of justice are best to try to inculcate will depend on the circumstances of particular societies, and especially on psychological facts about their members. One of these facts is their readiness to accept the principles themselves. There might be a principle of justice which it would be highly desirable to inculcate, but which we have no chance of successfully inculcating. The best principles for a society to *have* are, as I said, those with the highest acceptance-utility. But the best principles to *try to inculcate* will not necessarily be these, if these are impossible to inculcate. Imagine that in our happy slave-society both slaves and slave-owners are obstinately conservative and know their places, and that the attempt to get the slaves to have revolutionary or egalitarian thoughts will result only in a very few of them becoming discontented, and probably going to the gallows as a result, and the vast majority merely becoming unsettled and therefore more unhappy. Then we ought not to try to inculcate such an egalitarian principle. On the other hand, if, as is much more likely, the principle stood a good chance of catching on, and the revolution was likely to be as advantageous as we have supposed, then we ought. The difference lies in the dispositions of the inhabitants. I am not saying that the probability of being accepted is the same thing as acceptance-utility; only that the rationality of trying to inculcate a principle (like the rationality of trying to do anything else) varies with the likelihood of success. In this sense the advisability of trying to inculcate principles of justice (though not their merit) is relative to the states of mind of those who, it is hoped, will hold them.

It is important to be clear about the extent to which what I am advocating is a kind of relativism. It is certainly not relativistic in any strong sense. Relativism is the doctrine that the truth of some moral statement depends on whether people accept it. A typical example would be the thesis that if in a certain society people think that they ought to get their male children circumcised, then they ought to get them circumcised, full stop. Needless to say, I am not supporting any such doctrine, which is usually the result of confusion, and against which there are well-known arguments. It is, however, nearly always the case that among the facts relevant to a moral decision are facts about people's thoughts or dispositions. For example, if I am wondering whether I ought to take my wife for a holiday in Acapulco, it is relevant to ask whether she would like it. What I have been saying is to be assimilated to this last example. If we take as given certain dispositions in the members of society (namely dispositions not to accept a certain principle of justice however hard we work at propagating it) then we have to decide whether, in the light of these facts, we ought to propagate it. What principles of justice we ought to propagate will vary with the probable effects of propagating them. The answer to this "ought"-question is not relative to what we, who are asking it, think about the matter; it is to be arrived at by moral thought on the basis of the facts of the situation. But among these facts are facts about the dispositions of people in the society in question.

The moral I wish to draw from the whole argument is that ethical reasoning *can* provide us with a way of conducting political arguments about justice and rights rationally and with hope of agreement; that such rational arguments have to rest on an understanding of the concepts being used, *and* of the facts of our actual situation. The key question is "What principles of justice, what attitudes towards the distribution of goods, what ascriptions of rights, are such that their acceptance is in the general interest?" I advocate the asking of this question as a substitute for one which is much more commonly asked, namely "What rights do I have?" For people who ask this latter question will, being human, nearly always answer that they have just those rights, whatever they are, which will promote a distribution of goods which is in the interest of their own social group. The rhetoric of rights, which is engendered by this question, is a recipe for class war, and civil war. In pursuit of these rights, people will, because they have convinced themselves that justice demands it, inflict almost any harms on the rest of society and on themselves. To live at peace, we need principles such as critical thinking can provide, based on formal justice and on the facts of the actual world in which we have to live. It is possible for all to practise this critical thinking in cooperation, if only they would learn how; for all share the same moral concepts with the same logic, if they could understand them and follow it.

Notes

1. See my "Ethical Theory and Utilitarianism" *(ETU),* in *Comtemporary British Philosophy* 4, ed. H. D. Lewis (London, 1976).

2. See, e.g., my "Principles," *Ar. Soc.* 72 (1972/3), "Rules of War and Moral Reasoning," *Ph. and Pub. Aff.* 1 (1972) and *ETU.*

3. Rawls, J., *A Theory of Justice* (Cambridge, Mass., 1971), p. 130.

4. Richards, D. A. J., *A Theory of Reasons for Action* (Oxford, 1971).

5. See my *Freedom and Reason,* pt. II (Oxford, 1963) and *ETU.*

6. *Nicomachean Ethics,* bk. V.

7. ib. 1130 b 31, 1131 b 25.

8. ib. 1130 a 8.

9. Theognis 147; also attr. to Phocylides by Aristotle, ib. 1129 b 27.

10. The earliest version of this tag is attr. by the *Oxford Dictionary of Quotations* to the Emperor Ferdinand I (1503–64).

11. ib. 1137 b 8.

12. ib. 1130 a 14 ff.

13. *A Theory of Justice,* p. 136.

14. Pp. 115–7, 124.

15. *Ph. Q.* 23 (1973), repr. in *Reading Rawls,* ed. N. Daniels (Oxford, 1975).

16. Nozick, R. D., *Anarchy, State and Utopia* (New York, 1974).

17. Pp. 106f.

18. "Relevance," in a volume in *Values and Morals,* eds. A. Goldman and J. Kim (Reidel, 1978).

19. See note 2 above.

20. ib. 1131 a 25.

21. *Republic* 558 c.

22. ib. 414 b.

23. See, e.g., Anscombe, G. E. M., "Modern Moral Philosophy," *Philosophy* 33 (1958), and Williams, B. A. O., in Smart, J. J. C., and Williams, B. A. O., *Utilitarianism: For and Against* (Cambridge, Eng., 1973), p. 82.

24. Djilas, M., *Land without Justice* (London, 1958).

15

Utilitarianism and the Distinction Between Persons

JOHN RAWLS

There are many forms of utilitarianism, and the development of the theory has continued in recent years. I shall not survey these forms here, nor take account of the numerous refinements found in contemporary discussions. My aim is to work out a theory of justice that represents an alternative to utilitarian thought generally and so to all of these different versions of it. I believe that the contrast between the contract view and utilitarianism remains essentially the same in all these cases. Therefore I shall compare justice as fairness with familiar variants of intuitionism, perfectionism, and utilitarianism in order to bring out the underlying differences in the simplest way. With this end in mind, the kind of utilitarianism I shall describe here is the strict classical doctrine which receives perhaps its clearest and most accessible formulation in Sidgwick. The main idea is that society is rightly ordered, and therefore just, when its major institutions are arranged so as to achieve the greatest net balance of satisfaction summed over all the individuals belonging to it.[1]

We may note first that there is, indeed, a way of thinking of society which makes it easy to suppose that the most rational conception of justice is utilitarian. For consider: each man in realizing his own interests is certainly free to balance his own

From *A Theory of Justice* (1971), pp. 22–27. Reprinted by permission of the publishers from *A Theory of Justice* by John Rawls, Cambridge, Mass.: The Belknap Press of Harvard University Press. Copyright © 1971 by the President and Fellows of Harvard College.

losses against his own gains. We may impose a sacrifice on ourselves now for the sake of a greater advantage later. A person quite properly acts, at least when others are not affected, to achieve his own greatest good, to advance his rational ends as far as possible. Now why should not a society act on precisely the same principle applied to the group and therefore regard that which is rational for one man as right for an association of men? Just as the well-being of a person is constructed from the series of satisfactions that are experienced at different moments in the course of his life, so in very much the same way the well-being of society is to be constructed from the fulfillment of the systems of desires of the many individuals who belong to it. Since the principle for an individual is to advance as far as possible his own welfare, his own system of desires, the principle for society is to advance as far as possible the welfare of the group, to realize to the greatest extent the comprehensive system of desire arrived at from the desires of its members. Just as an individual balances present and future gains against present and future losses, so a society may balance satisfactions and dissatisfactions among different individuals. And so by these reflections one reaches the principle of utility in a natural way: a society is properly arranged when its institutions maximize the net balance of satisfaction. The principle of choice for an association of men is interpreted as an extension of the principle of choice for one man. Social justice is the principle of rational prudence applied to an aggregative conception of the welfare of the group.[2] . . .

This idea is made all the more attractive by a further consideration. The two main concepts of ethics are those of the right and the good; the concept of a morally worthy person is, I believe, derived from them. The structure of an ethical theory is, then, largely determined by how it defines and connects these two basic notions. Now it seems that the simplest way of relating them is taken by teleological theories: the good is defined independently from the right, and then the right is defined as that which maximizes the good.[3] More precisely, those institutions and acts are right which, of the available alternatives, produce the most good, or at least as much good as any of the other institutions and acts open as real possibilities (a rider needed when the maximal class is not a singleton). Teleological theories have a deep intuitive appeal since they seem to embody the idea of rationality. It is natural to think that rationality is maximizing something and that in morals it must be maximizing the good. Indeed, it is tempting to suppose that it is self-evident that things should be arranged so as to lead to the most good.

It is essential to keep in mind that in a teleological theory the good is defined independently from the right. This means two things. First, the theory accounts for our considered judgments as to which things are good (our judgments of value) as a separate class of judgments intuitively distinguishable by common sense, and then proposes the hypothesis that the right is maximizing the good as already specified. Second, the theory enables one to judge the goodness of things without referring to what is right. For example, if pleasure is said to be the sole good, then presumably pleasures can be recognized and ranked in value by criteria that do not presuppose any standards of right, or what we would normally think of as such. Whereas if the distribution of goods is also counted as a good, perhaps a higher order one, and the theory directs us to produce the most good (including the good of distribution among others), we no longer have a teleological view in the classical sense. The problem of distribution falls under the concept of right as one intuitively understands it, and so the theory lacks an independent definition of the good. The clarity and simplicity of classical teleological theories derive largely from the fact that they factor our moral judgments into two classes, the one being characterized separately while the other is then connected with it by a maximizing principle.

Teleological doctrines differ, pretty clearly, according to how the conception of the good is specified. If it is taken as the realization of human excellence in the various forms of culture, we have what may be called perfectionism. This notion is found in Aristotle and Nietzsche, among others. If the good is defined as pleasure, we have hedonism; if as happiness, eudaimonism, and so on. I shall understand the principle of utility in its classical form as defining the good as the satisfaction of desire, or perhaps better, as the satisfaction of rational desire. This accords with the view in all essentials and provides, I believe, a fair interpretation of it. The appropriate terms of social cooperation are settled by whatever in the circumstances will achieve the greatest sum of satisfaction of the rational desires of individuals. It is impossible to deny the initial plausibility and attractiveness of this conception.

The striking feature of the utilitarian view of justice is that it does not matter, except indirectly, how this sum of satisfactions is distributed among individuals any more than it matters, except indirectly, how one man distributes his satisfactions over time. The correct distribution in either case is that which yields the maximum fulfillment. Society must allocate its means of satisfaction whatever these are, rights and duties, opportunities and privileges, and various forms of wealth, so as to achieve this maximum if it can. But in itself no distribution of satisfaction is better than another except that the more equal distribution is to be preferred to break ties.[4] It is true that certain common sense precepts of justice, particularly those which concern the protection of liberties and rights, or which express the claims of desert, seem to contradict this contention. But from a utilitarian standpoint the explanation of these precepts and of their seemingly stringent character is that they are those precepts which experience shows should be strictly respected and departed from only under exceptional circumstances if the sum of advantages is to be maximized.[5] Yet, as with all other precepts, those of justice are derivative from the one end of attaining the greatest balance of satisfaction. Thus there is no reason in principle why the greater gains of some should not compensate for the lesser losses of others; or more importantly, why the violation of the liberty of a few might not be made right by the greater good shared by many. It simply happens that under most conditions, at least in a reasonably advanced stage of civilization, the greatest sum of advantages is not attained in this way. No doubt the strictness of common sense precepts of justice has a certain usefulness in limiting men's propensities to injustice and to socially injurious actions, but the utilitarian believes that to affirm this strictness as a first principle of morals is a mistake. For just as it is rational for one man to maximize the fulfillment of his system of desires, it is right for a society to maximize the net balance of satisfaction taken over all of its members.

The most natural way, then, of arriving at utilitarianism (although not, of course, the only way of doing so) is to adopt for society as a whole the principle of rational choice for one man. Once this is recognized, the place of the impartial spectator and the emphasis on sympathy in the history of utilitarian thought is readily understood. For it is by the conception of the impartial spectator and the use of sympathetic identification in guiding our imagination that the principle for one man is applied to society. It is this spectator who is conceived as carrying out the required organization of the desires of all persons into one coherent system of desire; it is by this construction that many persons are fused into one. Endowed with ideal powers of sympathy and imagination, the impartial spectator is the perfectly rational individual who identifies with and experiences the desires of others as if these desires were his own. In this way, he ascertains the intensity of these desires and assigns them their appropriate weight in the one system of desire the satisfaction of which the ideal legislator then tries to maximize by adjusting the rules of the social system. On this conception of society separate individuals are thought of as so many different lines along which rights and duties are to be assigned and scarce means of satisfaction allocated in accordance with rules so as to give the greatest fulfillment of wants. The nature of the decision made by the ideal legislator is not, therefore, materially different from that of an entrepreneur deciding how to maximize his profit by producing this or that commodity, or that of a consumer deciding how to maximize his satisfaction by the purchase of this or that collection of goods. In each case there is a single person whose system of desires determines the best allocation of limited means. The correct decision is essentially a question of efficient administration. This view of social cooperation is the consequence of extending to society the principle of choice for one man, and then, to make this extension work, conflating all persons into one through the imaginative acts of the impartial sympathetic spectator. Utilitarianism does not take seriously the distinction between persons.

Notes

1. I shall take Henry Sidgwick's *The Methods of Ethics,* 7th ed. (London, 1907), as summarizing the development of utilitarian moral theory. Book III of his *Principles of Political Economy* (London, 1883) applies this doctrine to questions of economic and social justice, and is a precursor of A. C. Pigou, *The Economics of Welfare* (London, Macmillan, 1920). Sidgwick's *Outlines of the History of Ethics,* 5th ed. (London, 1902), contains a brief history of the utilitarian tradition. We may follow him in assuming, somewhat arbitrarily, that it begins with Shaftesbury's *An Inquiry Concerning Virtue and Merit* (1711) and Hutcheson's *An Inquiry Concerning Moral Good and Evil* (1725). Hutcheson seems to have been the first to state clearly the principle of utility. He says in *Inquiry,* sec. III, §8, that "that action is best, which procures the greatest happiness for the greatest numbers; and that, worst, which, in like manner, occasions misery." Other major eighteenth-century works are Hume's *A Treatise of Human Nature* (1739), and *An Enquiry Concerning the Principles of Morals* (1751); Adam Smith's *A Theory of the Moral Sentiments* (1759); and Bentham's *The Principles of Morals and Legislation* (1789). To these we must add the writings of J. S. Mill represented by *Utilitarianism* (1863) and F. Y. Edgeworth's *Mathematical Psychics* (London, 1888).

    The discussion of utilitarianism has taken a different turn in recent years by focusing on what we may call the coordination problem and related questions of publicity. This development stems from the essays of R. F. Harrod, "Utilitarianism Revised," *Mind,* vol. 45 (1936); J. D. Mabbott, "Punishment," *Mind,* vol. 48 (1939); Jonathan Harrison, "Utilitarianism, Universalisation, and Our

Duty to Be Just," *Proceedings of the Aristotelian Society,* vol. 53 (1952–53): and J. O. Urmson, "The Interpretation of the Philosophy of J. S. Mill," *Philosophical Quarterly,* vol. 3 (1953). See also J. J. C. Smart, "Extreme and Restricted Utilitarianism," *Philosophical Quarterly,* vol. 6 (1956), and his *An Outline of a System of Utilitarian Ethics* (Cambridge, The University Press, 1961). For an account of these matters, see David Lyons, *Forms and Limits of Utilitarianism* (Oxford, The Clarendon Press, 1965); and Allan Gibbard, "Utilitarianisms and Coordination" (dissertation, Harvard University, 1971). The problems raised by these works, as important as they are, I shall leave aside as not bearing directly on the more elementary question of distribution which I wish to discuss.

Finally, we should note here the essays of J. C. Harsanyi, in particular, "Cardinal Utility in Welfare Economics and in the Theory of Risk-Taking," *Journal of Political Economy,* 1953, and "Cardinal Welfare, Individualistic Ethics, and Interpersonal Comparisons of Utility," *Journal of Political Economy,* 1955; and R. B. Brandt, "Some Merits of One Form of Rule—Utilitarianism," *University of Colorado Studies* (Boulder, Colorado, 1967). . . .

2. On this point see also D. P. Gauthier, *Practical Reasoning* (Oxford, Clarendon Press, 1963), pp. 126f. The text elaborates the suggestion found in "Constitutional Liberty and the Concept of Justice," *Nomos VI: Justice,* ed. C. J. Friedrich and J. W. Chapman (New York, Atherton Press, 1963), pp. 124f, which in turn is related to the idea of justice as a higher-order administrative decision. See "Justice as Fairness," *Philosophical Review,* 1958, pp. 185–187. . . . That the principle of social integration is distinct from the principle of personal integration is stated by R. B. Perry, *General Theory of Value* (New York, Longmans, Green, and Company, 1926), pp. 674–677. He attributes the error of overlooking this fact to Emile Durkheim and others with similar views. Perry's conception of social integration is that brought about by a shared and dominant benevolent purpose. . . .

3. Here I adopt W. K. Frankena's definition of teleological theories in *Ethics* (Englewood Cliffs, N.J., Prentice Hall, Inc., 1963), p. 13.

4. On this point see Sidgwick, *The Methods of Ethics,* pp. 416f.

5. See J. S. Mill, *Utilitarianism,* ch. V, last two parts.

PART V

Communitarian Justice

16

The Nature of Justice

ARISTOTLE

With regard to justice[1] and injustice, the points we have to consider are—with what class of actions are they connected, in what sense is justice a middle state, and between what extremes is that which is just intermediate? Our enquiry shall follow the same procedure as our previous investigations.

We observe that by the term justice everybody means that state of character which renders men disposed to act justly, and which causes them to do and to wish what is just; and similarly by injustice they mean the disposition that makes men do and wish what is unjust. Let us then accept these definitions to go upon as broadly correct.

The fact is that it is not the same with a state of character as with the sciences and faculties. It appears that the same science or faculty deals with opposite objects;[2] but a state that produces one result does not also produce the opposite result—for instance, health does not cause us to do actions that are the reverse of healthy, but only those that are healthy: A sound gait in walking means walking like a man in good health, not walking lame.

Hence it is often possible to infer one of two opposite states from the other, and often states can be identified from the subjects that exhibit them. Thus if we find out what constitutes good bodily condition we learn what bad condition is as well; but we can also learn what good bodily condition is from actual persons that are in good condition, while from knowing what good condition is we can recognize things that produce good condition. If good condition is firmness of flesh, bad condition must necessarily be flabbiness of flesh, and also 'wholesome' must mean productive of firmness of flesh. Also if one of two opposite terms has more than one meaning,

From Chapter V of *Aristotle's Ethics for English Readers,* rendered from the Greek of the *Nicomachean Ethics* by H. Rackham (1943). Reprinted by permission of Basil Blackwell, Publisher.

it follows as a rule that the other also has more than one meaning—for instance, the terms "just" and "unjust." And "justice" and "injustice" appear to have more than one meaning, but owing to their two meanings not being widely separate, the ambiguity escapes notice and is not rather obvious, as it is in the case of two meanings that are widely separate. Let us then take the different senses in which the word "unjust" is used. A man who breaks the law is unjust, and so also is a man who is grasping and unfair; so that obviously a law-abiding man and a man who is fair in business are both of them just. "Just" therefore denotes both what is lawful and what is fair, and "unjust" denotes both what is unlawful and what is unfair.

As the unjust man is grasping, his injustice will be exercised in regard to things that are good—not all of them but those with which good and bad fortune are concerned, which though always good in the absolute sense are not always good for a particular person. These are the goods that men pray for and seek after, although they ought not to do so; they ought to pray that the things which are good in the absolute sense may also be good for themselves, though choosing the things that are good for themselves. The unjust man does not always choose the larger share—in the case of things that are bad absolutely he chooses the smaller share; but because the smaller quantity of a bad thing seems to be good in a sense, and a grasping nature means that one grasps something good, this makes him appear to be grasping. Let us call him "unfair," as that term includes taking too much of good things and taking too little of bad ones, and covers both.

We saw that the man who breaks the law is unjust and the law-abiding man just. This shows that all that is lawful is just in a sense, since it is the business of legislature to define what is lawful, and the various decisions of the legislature are what we term the principles of justice. Now all the edicts of the laws are aimed either at the common advantage of everybody or at the interest of a ruling class selected by merit or in some other similar way. Consequently in one sense we apply the word "just" to things which produce and preserve happiness, and the things that form part of happiness for the community. And the law prescribes certain conduct: the conduct of a brave man (for instance, not to desert one's post, not to run away in battle, not to throw down one's arms); that of a self-controlled man (for instance, not to commit adultery or violent assault); that of a good-tempered man (for instance, not to strike a person or to use abusive language), and similarly as to all the other forms of virtue—some acts the law enjoins and others it forbids, rightly if the law has been rightly framed and not so well if it has been drafted carelessly.

Justice in this sense then is perfect virtue, though with the qualification that it is virtue in relation to our neighbors. Because of this the view is often held that in the list of virtues justice occupies the top place, and that

Neither the evening nor the morning star[3]

is so sublime; and we have the proverb:

The whole of virtue is comprised in justice.[4]

Justice is perfect because it is our mode of practicing perfect virtue; and it is supremely perfect because its possessor can use it in his relations with others and not only by himself. There are plenty of people who can practice virtue in their personal affairs but who are incapable of displaying it in their relations with others. This shows the truth of the saying of Bias,[5] "Office will show a real man"; when somebody obtains a position of authority he is brought into contact with other people, and is a member of a partnership. For this same reason, justice alone among the virtues is thought to be "another person's good,"[6] because it is exercised in relation to one's neighbors; it does what is in the interest of somebody else, a superior or a partner. The wickedest man therefore is he who exercises his wickedness in his relations with his friends and not merely in his personal affairs; and the best man is the one who practices his virtue not in regard to himself but in relation to someone else, as that is a difficult thing to do.

Justice thus understood therefore is not a part of virtue, but the whole of it; and its opposite, injustice, in not a part of vice, but the whole. The distinction between justice in this sense and virtue is clear from what has been said; they are the same quality of character but differently viewed: what as exercised in relation to others is justice, considered simply as a disposition of a certain sort is virtue.

Justice as a Part of Virtue

But it is justice as a particular part of virtue that we are investigating, that being as we say one sort of justice; and similarly we are considering injustice as a particular vice, not in the sense of wickedness in general.

That there is such a vice is indicated by the following considerations: When a man practices one of the other vices (for instance, when owing to cowardice he throws away his shield,[7] or owing to ill-temper uses abusive language, or owing to meanness refuses to help a friend out of a difficulty with money), he is committing an injustice but he is not taking an unfair share of something. But when he takes an unfair share, he is not displaying one of the vices of the kind specified, and certainly not all of them, but clearly he does display a vice of some sort, as we blame his conduct—in fact he displays injustice. Therefore there is another sort of injustice which is a part of injustice as a whole, and there is a form of unjust action which is a subdivision of unjust and illegal conduct in general. Again, suppose that A commits adultery for gain and gets something by it, whereas B does it out of inclination and loses by his indulgence. B would appear to be self-indulgent rather than avaricious, whereas A would seem unjust but not self-indulgent at all. It is clear then that A's motive would be profit. And yet another reason—whereas all other offenses are always attributed to some particular vice; for instance, adultery is ascribed to self-indulgence, desertion of a comrade in battle to cowardice, assault to anger—an offense out of which a man has made a profit is not put down to any other vice but injustice.

Hence it is clear that beside injustice in the wide sense there is another kind of injustice which is a particular form of vice. It bears the same name because it comes under the same general definition—both forms of injustice being exercised in our relations with other people; but injustice in the special sense is concerned with honor or money or security, or perhaps all of these things included under some general term, and its motive is the pleasure derived from gain, whereas injustice in the wide sense is concerned with the whole of the things in relation to which virtue is displayed.

The next step is to ascertain the nature and the attributes of justice in this special sense of the term, as distinct from justice denoting the whole of virtue.

Now we have distinguished two meanings of the term "unjust"—namely, unlawful and unequal or unfair; and we have shown that "just" means both lawful and equal or fair. Injustice of the kind mentioned above corresponds with "unlawful." But the unfair is not the same thing as the unlawful, but is related to it as part to whole—everything unfair is unlawful, but not everything unlawful is unfair. Consequently the unjust and injustice in the special sense are not the same as the unjust and injustice in the wide sense; although they also are related to each other as part to whole—injustice in this sense is a part of injustice in the wide sense, and likewise justice in this sense is a part of justice in the wide sense. We must consequently discuss justice and injustice, and what is just and unjust, in the special sense also. We may therefore leave on one side that form of justice which is coextensive with virtue as a whole, and the corresponding form of injustice—namely, the exercise of the whole of virtue and of vice in our relations with another person.

It is also clear how we should define what is just and what unjust in the corresponding senses; for almost a majority of the actions ordained by law are those which are prescribed on the basis of virtue taken as a whole, since the law specifies the particular virtues which we are to practice and the particular vices which we are to avoid; and the means for producing virtue as a whole are the regulations laid down by law for education in the duties of a citizen. But in regard to our education as individuals, which renders us simply good *men,* the question whether this is the concern of politics or of another art will have to be decided later,[8] for perhaps to be a good man is not the same thing as to be a good citizen of some particular state.

Special justice, on the other hand, and that which is just in the sense corresponding to it, is of two kinds. One kind is the principle that regulates distributions of honor or money or the other divisible assets of the community, which may be divided among its members in equal or unequal shares. The other kind is that which regulates private transactions. The latter form of justice has two divisions, inasmuch as some transactions are voluntary and others nonvoluntary.[9] Instances of voluntary transactions are selling, buying, lending at interest, lending free of interest, pledging, depositing, letting for hire: these are called voluntary because they are voluntarily entered upon. Of nonvoluntary transactions some are clandestine, such as theft, adultery, poisoning, procuring, enticing slaves to leave their owners, assassination, giving false witness; and some are violent, such as assault, imprisonment, murder, rape, mutilation, abusive language, contumelious treatment.

Distributive and Corrective Justice

Now as an unjust man is unfair and an unjust thing unequal, it is clear that corresponding to the unequal there is a middle point or mean; namely, that which is equal; for any kind of action admitting of more or less also admits what is equal. If then what is unjust is unequal, what is just is equal, as everyone will agree without argument; and since the equal is a mean, the just will be a sort of mean too. Now equality involves at least two terms; it follows therefore not only that the just is a mean and equal, but also that (1) as a mean it implies two extremes, the more and the less, (2) as equal it implies two equal shares, and (3) as just it implies certain persons for whom it is just. Consequently justice involves at least four terms, two persons for whom it is just and two shares which are just. And there will be the same equality between the shares as between the persons, that is, the ratio between the shares will be the same as the ratio between the persons. If the persons are not equal, they will not have equal shares; it is when equals possess or are assigned unequal shares, or persons who are not equal equal shares, that quarrels and complaints arise.

Moreover the same point also clearly follows from the principle of assignment by merit. Everybody agrees that just distribution must be in accordance with merit of some sort, though everybody does not mean the same sort of merit. Democrats take merit to mean free status, adherents of oligarchy take it to mean wealth or noble birth, supporters of aristocracy excellence.

The just then is that which is proportionate and the unjust is that which runs counter to proportion; the man who acts unjustly has too much, and the man who is unjustly treated too little, of the good. In the case of evil, it is the other way about, as the lesser evil is accounted as good in comparison with the greater evil, because the lesser evil is more desirable than the greater, and what is desirable is a good, and what is more desirable a greater good.

This then is one species of justice.

The species of justice that remains is the justice of redress, which operates in the case of voluntary and involuntary transactions. This form of justice has a different specific character from the preceding one. The justice that distributes common property always follows the kind of proportion mentioned above (because in the case of distribution from the common funds of a partnership it will follow the same ratio as that existing between the sums put into the business by the partners); and the unjust that is opposed to this form of the just is that which violates that proportion. But justice in transactions between individuals, although it is equality of a sort, and injustice inequality, does not go by the kind of proportion mentioned, but by arithmetical proportion.[10] It makes no difference[11] whether a good man has defrauded a bad one or a bad man a good one, nor whether a good man or a bad man has committed adultery; the law only looks at the nature of the injury, and treats the parties as equal if one has done and the other suffered a wrong or if one has inflicted and the other sustained damage. Consequently, in such cases the judge tries to equalize this injustice, which consists in inequality—for even in a case where one person has received and the other has inflicted a blow, or where one has killed and the other been killed, the suffering and the action have been distributed in unequal shares, while the judge's endeavor is to make them equal by means of the penalty he inflicts, taking something away from the gain of the assailant. The term "gain" is applied to such cases in a general sense, even though to some, for instance a person who has inflicted a wound, it is not specially appropriate, and the term "loss" is applied to the sufferer; at all events the terms "gain" and "loss" are employed when the amount of the suffering inflicted has been assessed. Consequently, while equal is intermediate between more and less, gain and loss are at once both more and less in contrary ways—more of what is good and less of what is bad are gain, and more of what is bad and less of what is good are loss, intermediate between them being, as we said, the equal, which we pronounce to be just. Consequently the justice of redress will be what is intermediate between loss and gain. This is why when a dispute arises the parties have recourse to a judge; to go to a judge is to appeal to the just, inasmuch as a judge is virtually justice personified;[12] and they have recourse to a judge as intermediary—indeed, in some countries judges are called "mediators"— on the ground that if the litigants get the medium amount they will get what is just. Thus justice is a sort of medium, as the judge is a medium between the litigants. What he does is to restore equality; it is as if there were a line divided into two unequal parts, and he took away the amount by which the larger segment exceeded half the line and added it to the smaller segment. When the whole has been divided into two equal parts, people say that they "have got their own," having got an equal share. This is the arithmetical mean between the greater amount and the less.

Therefore the just is intermediate between gain and loss due to breach of contract; it consists in having an equal amount both before and after the transaction.

Justice in Exchange

Some people hold the view that mere reciprocity is justice. But reciprocity does not coincide with either distributive justice or with corrective justice; it often conflicts with them—for example, if an officer strikes a man, it is wrong for the man to hit back, but if a man strikes an officer, not only should the officer hit him but he must be punished as well. Further, there is a wide distinction between an act done with the consent of the other party and one done without consent. But in association for exchange this sort of justice, reciprocity, is the bond uniting the parties; but it must be reciprocity on a basis of proportion and not of equality. It is proportionate requital that keeps the state together. Men seek to return either evil for evil, failing which they feel themselves mere slaves, or good for good, in default of which no exchange of goods and services takes place; but it is exchange which holds society together. This is why men build a shrine of the Graces in their cities, as a reminder that favors should be returned, since to return favors received is a characteristic of grace. When somebody has done one a service, it behoves one not only to do him a service in return but also on the next occasion to take the initiative in doing him a service oneself.

Proportional requital is achieved by diagonal conjunction. Let A be a builder, B a shoemaker, C a house, and D a pair of shoes. Then the builder has to take from the shoemaker a part of the produce of his labor and give him in return a part of his own product. If proportionate equality between the products be first established, and then reciprocation takes place, the condition indicated will have been satisfied. But if this is not done, the bargain is not equal, and does not hold, since it may happen that the work of one party is worth more than that of the other, so that they have to be equalized. For two doctors do not combine to exchange their services, but a doctor and a farmer, and in general persons who are different and who may be unequal, but in that case they need to be equated. Consequently exchange of commodities requires that the commodities must be in some way commensurable; and it was to achieve this that money was invented. Money serves as a sort of middle term, as it measures all things, and so indicates their superior or inferior value—just how many shoes are the equivalent of a house or a certain quantity of food. The number of shoes exchanged for a house must correspond to the ratio between a builder and a shoemaker. Failing this, there will be no exchange, and no business will be done. And this cannot be secured unless the goods are equated in some way.

It is therefore necessary to have some one standard of measurement for all commodities, as was said before. And this standard is in reality demand; it is demand which keeps commerce together, since if people were to cease to have wants or if their wants were to alter, exchange will not go on, or it will be on different lines. But it has been agreed to accept money as representing demand. Money is a convention, and we can alter the currency if we choose, rendering the old coinage useless. Thus reciprocity will be achieved when the factors have been equated, bringing it about that as farmer is to shoemaker so the amount of shoemaker's work is to the amount of farmer's work exchanged for it.

That demand serves as a single factor holding commerce together is shown by the fact that when there is no demand for mutual service in the case of both parties or at least of one of the two, exchange of services does not take place. And money serves us as a security for future exchange, if we do not need a thing now; money guarantees that we shall have it if we do need it, as we shall be able to get it by producing the money. Now money fluctuates in value, just like goods; but it tends to be steadier. Consequently all goods must have a price given to them, as then exchange of goods will always be possible, and consequently association between men. Currency therefore is a sort of measure, which equates goods by making them commensurable. In fact there would be no association between man and man if there were no exchange, and no exchange if there were no equalization of values, and no equalization of values if there were no commensurability. No doubt it is not really possible for articles that are so different to be made exactly commensurable in value, but they can be made sufficiently commensurable for the practical purpose of exchange. That is why there has to be a single standard fixed by agreement, making all commodities commensurable; for everything can be measured by money. Let A be a house, B 20 minae and C a bedstead. Then $A = B/2$ (supposing a house to be worth—that is, equal to—5 minae) and C (the bedstead) $= B/10$. We can now say how many bedsteads are equal to one house; namely, five. Obviously before money existed this is how the rate of exchange was quoted—five beds for a house; there is no real difference between bartering five bedsteads for a house and buying the house for the price of five bedsteads.

We have now defined "just" and "unjust"; and our definitions show that just action is intermediate between doing injustice and suffering injustice, since the former is to get too much and the latter is to get too little. Justice is a sort of middle state, but not in the same manner as the other virtues are middle states; it is middle because it attaches to a middle amount, injustice being the quality of extremes. Also justice is the virtue which disposes the just man to resolve to act justly, and which leads him, when distributing things between himself and another, not to give himself a larger portion and his neighbor a smaller one of what is desirable, and the other way about in regard to what is detrimental, but to allot shares that are proportionately equal; and similarly when making a distribution between two other persons. Injustice on the contrary stands in the same relation to what is unjust, this being disproportionate excess or deficiency of something useful or harmful. Thus injustice is excess and deficiency in the sense of being productive of excess and deficiency, in one's own case excess of what is simply useful and deficiency of what is harmful, and in the case of others taken as a whole it is the same as in one's own case, but the disproportion may be in either direction.[13] In an unjust distribution to get too little is to suffer injustice and to get too much is to do injustice.

Political Justice and Analogous Kinds of Justice

But it must be borne in mind that what we are investigating is not only justice in the abstract but also political justice. This exists between men living in a community for the purpose of satisfying their needs, men who are free and who enjoy either absolute or proportional equality. Between men who do not fulfill these conditions no political justice exists, but only justice in a special sense and so called by analogy. Justice exists between those whose mutual relations are regulated by law; and law exists for those between whom there is a possibility of injustice, the administration of the law being the discrimination of what is just and what is unjust. Persons therefore between whom may be injustice may act unjustly toward each other (although unjust action does not necessarily imply injustice); and unjust action means appropriating too large a share of things essentially good and taking too small a share of things essentially bad. On this account we do not allow a man to govern, but only the law, because a human ruler governs in his own interest and becomes a tyrant; whereas the true function of a ruler is to be the guardian of justice, and therefore of equality. A just ruler, we think, gets no profit out of his office, as he does not assign to himself the larger share of what is essentially good unless such a share is proportionate to his merits. So he labors for the sake of others: this explains the saying "Justice is other men's good." Consequently it is necessary to give him some recompense in the form of honor and privilege. Rulers not content with such rewards become tyrants.

The justice of a master or a father is not the same thing as absolute justice or political justice, but only analogous to them; for there is no such thing as injustice in the absolute sense toward things that belong to one. Slaves, who are a man's chattels, and also children till they reach a certain age and start an independent life, are in a manner part of oneself, and nobody deliberately does harm to himself, so that there is no such thing as being unjust to oneself. Therefore justice and injustice in the political sense are not exercised in these relations, because they are regulated by law, as we saw, and exist between persons naturally governed by law, who, as we saw, are people who have an equal share in governing and being governed. Consequently justice exists in a fuller degree between a man and his wife than between a man and his children and chattels; it is in fact domestic justice. But this also is different from political justice.

Natural and Conventional Justice

Civic justice is partly natural and partly conventional.[14] A natural rule of justice is one which has the same validity everywhere, independently of whether people accept it or not. A conventional rule is a practice that at the outset may equally well be settled one way or the other, but which when once enacted becomes a regulation—for instance, the rule that the ransom for a prisoner of war shall be a mina, or that a certain sacrifice shall consist of one goat or two sheep; as well as enactments dealing with particular cases; for instance, the sacrifice celebrated in honor of Brasidas;[15] and special regulations promulgated by decree. Some people hold that all justice is a matter of fixed regulations, because a law of nature never alters and has the same validity everywhere—for instance, fire burns both here and in Persia—but they see men's conceptions of justice changing. This is not absolutely true, but only with qualifications—among the gods indeed it is perhaps not true at all. But among us, although there is such a thing as natural justice, nevertheless all rules can be altered. For instance, the right hand is naturally stronger than the left, but anybody can train himself to be ambidextrous. And in all other matters the same distinction will apply. But among things which admit of variation, it is not clear what kind is natural and what is not natural but due to convention and based on agreement, as both kinds alike are equally susceptible of change. But nevertheless it is the case that one thing is natural and another not natural. Rules of justice fixed by agreement and for the sake of expediency are like weights and measures. Wine and corn measures are not the same everywhere, but are larger in wholesale and smaller in retail markets. Similarly those rules of justice which are not due to nature but are enacted by man are not the same everywhere, since the constitution of the state is not the same everywhere; yet there is only one form of constitution which is everywhere in accordance with nature, namely the best form. . . .

Justice and Equity

The next subject to discuss is equity and its relation to justice. They appear on examination to be neither absolutely identical nor yet different in kind. Sometimes, it is true, we praise equity and the equitable man, and virtually employ the word as a term of general approval, using "more equitable" to mean merely "better."[16] But sometimes, when we think the matter out, it seems curious that the equitable should be praiseworthy if it is something different from what is just. If they are different, either the just or the equitable is not good, or if both are good, they are the same thing.

These then more or less are the considerations that make the meaning of "equity" a difficult problem. In one way, however, all the different uses of the term are correct, and there is no real inconsistency between them. Although equity is superior to one kind of justice, it is not better than justice as being generically different from it. Justice and equity are the same thing, and both are good, although equity is the better of the two.

The problem arises from the fact that equity, although just, is not justice as enacted by law, but a rectification of legal justice. The reason of this is that all law is universal, but there are some things about which it is not possible to make a universal statement which will be correct. In matters therefore in which a universal statement is necessary but it is not possible for it to be absolutely correct, the law follows the line that is valid as a general rule—though with full recognition of the error involved. Nevertheless this does not make it bad law, for the error does not lie in the law nor in the lawgiver, but in the nature of the case: the material of practical affairs is essentially irregular. When therefore the law lays down a general rule and afterwards a case arises that is not covered by the rule, the proper course is to rectify the omission in the law where it is defective and where it errs by oversimplification, and to insert the provision which the author of the law would himself suggest if he were present, and would have inserted if he had been cognizant of the case in question. Therefore while equity is just, and is better than one kind of justice, it is not superior to absolute justice, but only to the error that is caused by the absolute statement of what is just. This is the essential nature of equity—it is a rectification of the law where it is defective owing to its universality. Indeed this is the reason why law does not cover everything: there are some things for which it is impossible to provide by legislation, and consequently they require a special decree. When a thing is indefinite the rule dealing with it is also indefinite, like the mason's rule made of lead that is used by builders in Lesbos. This is not rigid but can be bent to fit the shape of the stone; and similarly a special decree can be adapted to suit the circumstances of the case.

The nature of equity has now been explained, and it has been shown to be just, and to be superior to one kind of justice. And from this it is clear what the equitable man is: he is a man who is of set purpose and habitually does what is equitable, and does not stand on his rights unduly but is ready to accept less than his share although he has the law on his side. This quality of character is equity; it is a special kind of justice, not an entirely distinct quality.

Can a Man Treat Himself Unjustly?

The foregoing remarks supply an answer to the question, is it possible for a man to do an injustice to himself? One class of just acts consists of those acts, in conformity with one of the virtues, which are ordained by law. For instance, the law does not sanction suicide, and any form of homicide which it does not expressly permit it must be understood to forbid. Further, when a man in violation of the law voluntarily injures another man (not in retaliation), he acts unjustly ("voluntarily" meaning with a knowledge of the person affected and the instrument employed). Now a man who in a fit of anger stabs himself commits voluntarily an injury that is not a legitimate act of retaliation, and this the law does not permit. He is therefore committing an unjust offense. But against whom? Presumably against the state, not himself, for he suffers the act voluntarily, and no one is voluntarily treated unjustly. Moreover it is for this that the state inflicts a penalty: suicide is punished by certain marks of dishonor, as an offense against the state.[17]

Secondly, in one sense a man who "acts unjustly" is merely unjust, and not wicked in every way; and in this sense it is not possible to act unjustly toward oneself (this is a different sense of the term from the one above; in one sense injustice is a particular evil quality, and does not imply complete wickedness, so that the unjust act specified does not display general wickedness). For, (1) that would imply that a quality was both present and absent in the same person at the same time, which is impossible. Justice and injustice must always belong to different people. Moreover, (2) to be unjust an act must be voluntary and deliberate, and also unprovoked: a man who retaliates and does to another what that other has done to him is not thought to commit an injustice. But one who does harm to himself is both doing and suffering the same thing at the same time. Again, (3) if it were possible for a man to inflict an injustice on himself, it would be possible voluntarily to suffer injustice. And in addition, (4) acting unjustly means committing a particular act of injustice; for instance, adultery, burglary, theft; but a man cannot commit adultery with his own wife or steal his own property. And broadly speaking, the question "Can a man act unjustly toward himself?" is solved by our answer to the question about suffering injustice voluntarily.

(It is also clear that although both doing and receiving injustice are bad things, the former meaning to have more and the latter to have less than the medium amount, which corresponds to health in the art of medicine and to good bodily condition in the art of athletic training, yet to act unjustly is the worse of the two. For it involves wickedness and deserves reprehension, and its wickedness is complete or nearly complete; but to suffer injustice does not involve wickedness, viz., injustice, in the victim. In itself therefore to suffer injustice is the lesser evil, although it may well be the greater evil incidentally. But with this science is not concerned: it pronounces pleurisy to be a more serious malady than a sprain, in spite of the fact that a sprain might on occasion be a more serious mishap, if owing to it you stumbled in a battle and were taken prisoner and killed by the enemy.)

But in a metaphorical and analogical sense there is such a thing as justice not toward oneself but between the different parts of one's nature, not indeed justice in the full sense of the term but such as exists between master and servant or the head of a household and the members of his family. For in the discourses on these questions[18] distinction is made between the rational and irrational parts of the soul; and this has suggested the view that there is such a thing as injustice toward oneself, because these parts of the self may thwart each other in their respective desires, and consequently there is a sort of mutual justice between them as there is between ruler and subject.

Notes

1. The Greek term normally thus rendered is stated in what follows to have two senses, the wider sense of righteousness in general, any right conduct in relation to others, and the narrower sense of right conduct in matters involving gain or loss to the agent or to others. It is justice in the latter sense that this chapter deals with; in some places we should rather term it honesty.
2. For instance, medicine studies both health and disease.
3. A quotation from a play of Euripides that has not come down to us.
4. From the poet Theognis.
5. One of the Seven Sages.
6. Plato, *Republic* 343 c.—the definition given by the sophist Thrasymachus.
7. I.e., so as to be able to run away quickly.
8. It is discussed in Aristotle's *Politics,* Book III.
9. Viz., lacking the consent of one of the parties.
10. I.e., two pairs of terms (e.g., 1, 3, 7, 9) the second of which exceeds the first by the same amount as the fourth exceeds the third. We do not call this proportion, but if the third term also exceeds the second by the same amount (e.g., 1, 3, 5, 7), an arithmetical progression.
11. For corrective justice the merits of the parties are immaterial.
12. Cf. our expressions "Mr. Justice So-and-so," "Justice of the Peace."
13. When A makes an unjust distribution not between himself and B but between B and C, the result for either B or C may be either too large or too small a share of something beneficial and either too small or too large a share of something detrimental.
14. The word thus rendered also means "legal."
15. This Spartan general won the city of Amphipolis from the Athenian Empire, 424 B.C., and fell in defending it two years later. He was consecrated as a local hero, and an annual celebration was held in his honor, with sacrifices and races (for the Greeks races had religious associations).
16 In English "reasonable" is similarly used as a term of general approval.
17. At Athens a suicide's hand, as the guilty instrument, was cut off and buried separately from the body.
18. Plato's *Republic* and the writings of Plato's pupils in the Academy.

17

Morality and the Liberal Ideal

MICHAEL J. SANDEL

Liberals often take pride in defending what they oppose—pornography, for example, or unpopular views. They say the state should not impose on its citizens a preferred way of life, but should leave them as free as possible to choose their own values and ends, consistent with a similar liberty for others. This commitment to freedom of choice requires liberals constantly to distinguish between permission and praise, between allowing a practice and endorsing it. It is one thing to allow pornography, they argue, something else to affirm it.

Conservatives sometimes exploit this distinction by ignoring it. They charge that those who would allow abortions favor abortion, that opponents of school prayer, oppose prayer, that those who defend the rights of Communists sympathize with their cause. And in a pattern of argument familiar in our politics, liberals reply by invoking higher principles; it is not that they dislike pornography less, but rather that they value toleration, or freedom of choice, or fair procedures more.

But in contemporary debate, the liberal rejoinder seems increasingly fragile, its moral basis increasingly unclear. Why should toleration and freedom of choice prevail when other important values are also at stake? Too often the answer implies some version of moral relativism, the idea that it is wrong to "legislate morality" because all morality is merely subjective. "Who is to say what is literature and what is filth? That is a value judgment, and whose values should decide?"

Relativism usually appears less as a claim than as a question. "Who is to judge?"

From "Morality and the Liberal Ideal," *New Republic* (May 7, 1984), pp. 15–17. Reprinted by permission of *The New Republic*. © 1984, The New Republic, Inc.

But it is a question that can also be asked of the values that liberals defend. Toleration and freedom and fairness are values too, and they can hardly be defended by the claim that no values can be defended. So it is a mistake to affirm liberal values by arguing that all values are merely subjective. The relativist defense of liberalism is no defense at all.

What, then, can be the moral basis of the higher principles the liberal invokes? Recent political philosophy has offered two main alternatives—one utilitarian, the other Kantian. The utilitarian view, following John Stuart Mill, defends liberal principles in the name of maximizing the general welfare. The state should not impose on its citizens a preferred way of life, even for their own good, because doing so will reduce the sum of human happiness, at least in the long run; better that people choose for themselves, even if, on occasion, they get it wrong. "The only freedom which deserves the name," writes Mill in *On Liberty,* "is that of pursuing our own good in our own way so long as we do not attempt to deprive others of theirs, or impede their efforts to obtain it." He adds that his argument does not depend on any notion of abstract right, only on the principle of the greatest good for the greatest number. "I regard utility as the ultimate appeal on all ethical questions; but it must be utility in the largest sense, grounded on the permanent interests of man as a progressive being."

Many objections have been raised against utilitarianism as a general doctrine of moral philosophy. Some have questioned the concept of utility, and the assumption that all human goods are in principle commensurable. Others have objected that by reducing all values to preferences and desires, utilitarians are unable to admit qualitative distinctions of worth, unable to distinguish noble desires from base ones. But most recent debate has focused on whether utilitarianism offers a convincing basis for liberal principles, including respect for individual rights.

In one respect, utilitarianism would seem well suited to liberal purposes. Seeking to maximize overall happiness does not require judging people's values, only aggregating them. And the willingness to aggregate preferences without judging them suggests a tolerant spirit, even a democratic one. When people go to the polls we count their votes, whatever they are.

But the utilitarian calculus is not always as liberal as it first appears. If enough cheering Romans pack the Coliseum to watch the lion devour the Christian, the collective pleasure of the Romans will surely outweigh the pain of the Christian, intense though it be. Or if a big majority abhors a small religion and wants it banned, the balance of preferences will favor suppression, not toleration. Utilitarians sometimes defend individual rights on the grounds that respecting them now will serve utility in the long run. But this calculation is precarious and contingent. It hardly secures the liberal promise not to impose on some of the values of others. As the majority will is an inadequate instrument of liberal politics—by itself it fails to secure individual rights—so the utilitarian philosophy is an inadequate foundation for liberal principles.

The case against utilitarianism was made most powerfully by Immanuel Kant. He argued that empirical principles, such as utility, were unfit to serve as basis for the moral law. A wholly instrumental defense of freedom and rights not only leaves rights vulnerable, but fails to respect the inherent dignity of persons. The utilitarian calculus treats people as means to the happiness of others, not as ends in themselves, worthy of respect.

Contemporary liberals extend Kant's argument with the claim that utilitarianism fails to take seriously the distinction between persons. In seeking above all to maximize the general welfare, the utilitarian treats society as a whole as if it were a single person, it conflates our many, diverse desires into a single system of desires. It is indifferent to the distribution of satisfactions among persons, except insofar as this may affect the overall sum. But this fails to respect our plurality and distinctness. It uses some as means to the happiness of all, and so fails to respect each as an end in himself.

In the view of modern day Kantians, certain rights are so fundamental that even the general welfare cannot override them. As John Rawls writes in his important work, *A Theory of Justice*, "Each person possesses an inviolability founded on justice that even the welfare of society as a whole cannot override. . . . The rights secured by justice are not subject to political bargaining or to the calculus of social interests."

So Kantian liberals need an account of rights that does not depend on utilitarian considerations. More than this, they need an account that does not depend on any particular conception of the good, that does not presuppose the superiority of one way of life over others. Only a justification neutral about ends could preserve the liberal resolve not to favor any particular ends, or to impose on its citizens a preferred way of life. But what sort of justification could this be? How is it possible to affirm certain liberties and rights as fundamental without embracing some vision of the good life, without endorsing some ends over others? It would seem we are back to the relativist predicament—to affirm liberal principles without embracing any particular ends.

The solution proposed by Kantian liberals is to draw a distinction between the "right" and the "good"—between a framework of basic rights and liberties, and the conceptions of the good that people may choose to pursue within the framework. It is one thing for the state to support a fair framework, they argue, something else to affirm some particular ends. For example, it is one thing to defend the right to free speech so that people may be free to form their own opinions and choose their own ends, but something else to support it on the grounds that a life of political discussion is inherently worthier than a life unconcerned with public affairs, or on the grounds that free speech will increase the general welfare. Only the first defense is available in the Kantian view, resting as it does on the ideal of a neutral framework.

Now, the commitment to a framework neutral with respect to ends can be seen as a kind of value—in this sense the Kantian liberal is no relativist—but its value consists precisely in its refusal to affirm a preferred way of life or conception of the good. For Kantian liberals, then, the right is prior to the good, and in two senses. First, individual rights cannot be sacrificed for the sake of the general good; and second, the principles of justice that specify these rights cannot be premised on any particular vision of the good life. What justifies the rights is not that they maximize the general welfare or otherwise promote the good, but rather that they comprise a fair framework within which individuals and groups can choose their own values and ends, consistent with a similar liberty for others.

Of course, proponents of the rights-based ethic notoriously disagree about what rights are fundamental, and about what political arrangements the ideal of the neutral framework requires. Egalitarian liberals support the welfare state, and favor a scheme of civil liberties together with certain social and economic rights—rights to welfare, education, health care, and so on. Libertarian liberals defend the market economy, and claim that redistributive policies violate peoples' rights; they favor a scheme of civil liberties combined with a strict regime of private property rights. But whether egalitarian or libertarian, rights-based liberalism begins with the claim that we are separate, individual persons, each with our own aims, interests, and conceptions of the good; it seeks a framework of rights that will enable us to realize our capacity as free moral agents, consistent with a similar liberty for others.

Within academic philosophy, the last decade or so has seen the ascendance of the rights-based ethic over the utilitarian one, due in large part to the influence of Rawls's *A Theory of Justice*. The legal philosopher H. I. A. Hart recently described the shift from "the old faith that some form of utilitarianism must capture the essence of political morality" to the new faith that "the truth must lie with a doctrine of basic humans rights, protecting specific basic liberties and interests of individuals. . . . Whereas not so long ago great energy and much ingenuity of many philosophers were devoted to making some form of utilitarianism work, latterly such energies and ingenuity have been devoted to the articulation of theories of basic rights."

But in philosophy as in life, the new faith becomes the old orthodoxy before long. Even as it has come to prevail over its utilitarian rival, the rights-based ethic has recently faced a growing challenge from a different direction, from a view that gives fuller expression to the claims of citizenship and community than the liberal vision allows. The communitarian critics, unlike modern liberals, make the case for a politics of the common good. Recalling the arguments of Hegel against Kant, they question the liberal claim for the priority of the right over the good, and the picture of the freely choosing individual it embodies. Following Aristotle, they argue that we cannot justify political arrangements without reference to common purposes and ends, and that we cannot conceive of ourselves without reference to our role as citizens, as participants in a common life.

This debate reflects two contrasting pictures of the self. The rights-based ethic, and the conception of the person it embodies, were shaped in large part in the encounter with utilitarianism. Where utilitarians conflate our many desires into a single system of desire, Kantians insist on the separateness of persons. Where the utilitarian self is simply defined as the sum of its desires, the Kantian-self is a choosing self, independent of the desires and ends it may have at any moment. As Rawls writes, "The self is prior to the ends which are affirmed by it, even a dominant end must be chosen from among numerous possibilities."

The priority of the self over its ends means I am never defined by my aims and attachments, but always capable of standing back to survey and assess and possibly to revise them. This is what it means to be a free and independent self, capable of choice. And this is the vision of the self that finds expression in the ideal of the state as a neutral framework. On the rights-based ethic, it is precisely because we are essentially separate, independent selves that we need a neutral framework, a framework of rights that refuses to choose among competing purposes and ends. If the self is prior to its ends, then the right must be prior to the good.

Communitarian critics of rights-based liberalism say we cannot conceive ourselves as independent in this way, as bearers of selves wholly detached from our aims and attachments. They say that certain of our roles are partly constitutive of the persons we are—as citizens of a country, or members of a movement, or partisans of a cause. But if we are partly defined by the communities we inhabit, then we must also be implicated in the purposes and ends characteristic of those communities. As Alasdair MacIntyre writes in his book, *After Virtue*, "What is good for me has to be the good for one who inhabits these roles." Open-ended though it be, the story of my life is always embedded in the story of those communities from which I derive my identity—whether family or city, tribe or nation, party or cause. In the communitarian view, these stories make a moral difference, not only a psychological one. They situate us in the world and give our lives their moral particularity.

What is at stake for politics in the debate between unencumbered selves and situated ones? What are the practical differences between a politics of rights and a politics of the common good? On some issues, the two theories may produce different arguments for similar policies. For example, the civil rights movement of the 1960s might be justified by liberals in the name of human dignity and respect for persons, and by communitarians in the name of recognizing the full membership of fellow citizens wrongly excluded from the common life of the nation. And where liberals might support public education in hopes of equipping students to become autonomous individuals, capable of choosing their own ends and pursuing them effectively, communitarians might support public education in hopes of equipping students to become good citizens, capable of contributing meaningfully to public deliberations and pursuits.

On other issues, the two ethics might lead to different policies. Communitarians would be more likely than liberals to allow a town to ban pornographic book stores, on the grounds that pornography offends its way of life and the values that sustain it. But a politics of civic virtue does not always part company with liberalism in favor of conservative policies. For example, communitarians would be more willing than some rights-oriented liberals to see states enact laws regulating plant closings, to protect their communities from the disruptive effects of capital mobility and sudden industrial change. More generally, where the liberal regards the expansion of individual rights and entitlements as unqualified moral and political progress, the communitarian is troubled by the tendency of liberal programs to displace politics from smaller forms of association to more comprehensive ones. Where libertarian liberals defend the private economy and egalitarian liberals defend the welfare state, communitarians worry about the concentration of power in both the corporate economy and the bureaucratic state, and the erosion of those intermediate forms of community that have at times sustained a more vital public life.

Liberals often argue that a politics of the common good, drawing as it must on particular loyalties, obligations, and traditions, opens the way to prejudice and intolerance. The modern nation-state is not the Athenian polis, they point out; the scale and diversity of modern life have rendered the Aristotelian political ethic nostalgic at best and dangerous at worst. Any attempt to govern by a vision of the good is likely to lead to a slippery slope of totalitarian temptations.

Communitarians reply, rightly in my view, that intolerance flourishes most where forms of life are dislocated, roots unsettled, traditions undone. In our day, the totalitarian impulse has sprung less from the convictions of confidently situated selves than from the confusions of atomized, dislocated, frustrated selves, at sea in a world where common meanings have lost their force. As Hannah Arendt has written, "What makes mass society so difficult to bear is not the number of people involved, or at least not primarily, but the fact that the world between them has lost its power to gather them together, to relate and to separate them." Insofar as our public life has withered, our sense of common involvement diminished, we lie vulnerable to the mass politics of totalitarian solutions. So responds the party of the common good to the party of rights. If the party of the common good is right, our most pressing moral and political project is to revitalize those civic republican possibilities implicit in our tradition but fading in our time.

18

The Basic Requirements of Practical Reasonableness

JOHN FINNIS

1. The Good of Practical Reasonableness Structures Our Pursuit of Goods

There is no reason to doubt that each of the basic aspects of human well-being is worth seeking to realize. But there are many such basic forms of human good; I identified seven.* And each of them can be participated in, and promoted, in an inexhaustible variety of ways and with an inexhaustible variety of combinations of

---

*Editor's Note: The seven basic forms of human good are life, knowledge, play, aesthetic experience, friendship, religion, and practical reasonableness.
© John Finnis 1980. Reprinted from *Natural Law and Natural Rights* by John Finnis (1980) by permission of Oxford University Press.

John Finnis has since developed his account of the requirements of practical reasonableness, including his critique of "consequentialism," here given without his supporting arguments, in: Finnis, *Fundamentals of Ethics* (Oxford: Oxford University Press, and Washington, D. C.: Georgetown University Press, 1983); Finnis, Boyle and Grisez, *Nuclear Deterrence, Morality and Realism* (Oxford and New York: Oxford University Press, 1987).

emphasis, concentration, and specialization. To participate thoroughly in any basic value calls for skill, or at least a thoroughgoing commitment. But our life is short.

By disclosing a horizon of attractive possibilities for us, our grasp of the basic values thus creates, not answers, the problem for intelligent decision: What is to be done? What may be left undone? What is not to be done? We have, in the abstract, no reason to leave any of the basic goods out of account. But we do have good reason to choose commitments, projects, and actions, knowing that choice effectively rules out many alternative reasonable or possible commitment(s), project(s), and action(s).

To have this choice between commitment to concentration upon one value (say, speculative truth) and commitment to others, and between one intelligent and reasonable project (say, understanding this book) and other eligible projects for giving definite shape to one's participation in one's selected value, and between one way of carrying out that project and other appropriate ways, is the primary respect in which we can call ourselves both free and responsible.

For amongst the basic forms of good that we have no good reason to leave out of account is the good of practical reasonableness, which is participated in precisely by shaping one's participation in the other basic goods, by guiding one's commitments, one's selection of projects, and what one does in carrying them out.

The principles that express the general ends of human life do not acquire what would nowadays be called a "moral" force until they are brought to bear upon definite ranges of project, disposition, or action, or upon particular projects, dispositions, or actions. How they are thus to be brought to bear *is* the problem for practical reasonableness. "Ethics," as classically conceived, is simply a recollectively and/or prospectively reflective expression of this problem and of the general lines of solutions which have been thought reasonable.

How does one tell that a decision is practically reasonable? This question is the subject-matter of the present chapter. The classical exponents of ethics (and of theories of natural law) were well aware of this problem of criteria and standards of judgment. They emphasize that an adequate response to that problem can be made only by one who has experience (both of human wants and passions and of the conditions of human life) and intelligence and a desire for reasonableness stronger than the desires that might overwhelm it. Even when, later, Thomas Aquinas clearly distinguished a class of practical principles which he considered self-evident to anyone with enough experience and intelligence to understand the words by which they are formulated, he emphasized that moral principles such as those in the Ten Commandments are *conclusions from* the primary self-evident principles, that reasoning to such conclusions requires good judgment, and that there are many other more complex and particular moral norms to be followed and moral judgments and decisions to be made, all requiring a degree of practical wisdom which (he says) few men in fact possess.

Now, you may say, it is all very well for Aristotle to assert that ethics can be satisfactorily expounded only by and to those who are experienced and wise and indeed of good habits,[1] and that these characteristics are only likely to be found in societies that already have sufficiently sound standards of conduct,[2] and that the popular morality of such societies (as crystallized and detectable in their language of praise and blame, and their lore) is a generally sound pointer in the elaboration of ethics.³ He may assert that what is right and morally good is simply *seen* by the man (the *phronimos*, or again the *spoudaios*) who is right-minded and morally good,⁴ and that what such a man thinks and does *is* the criterion of sound terminology and correct conclusions in ethics (and politics).⁵ Such assertions can scarcely be denied. But they are scarcely helpful to those who are wondering whether their own view of what is to be done is a reasonable view *or not.* The notion of "the mean," for which Aristotle is perhaps too well known, seems likewise to be accurate but not very helpful (though its classification of value-words doubtless serves as a reminder of the dimensions of the moral problem). For what is "the mean and best, that is characteristic of virtue"? It is "to feel [anger, pity, appetite, etc.] when one ought to, and in relation to the objects and persons that one ought to, and with the motives and in the manner that one ought to. . . ."⁶ Have we no more determinate guide than this?

In the two millennia since Plato and Aristotle initiated formal inquiry into the content of practical reasonableness, philosophical reflection has identified a considerable number of requirements of *method* in practical reasoning. Each of these requirements has, indeed, been treated by some philosopher with exaggerated respect, as if it were the exclusive controlling and shaping requirement. For, as with each of the basic forms of good, each of these requirements is fundamental, underived, irreducible, and hence is capable when focused upon of seeming the most important.

Each of these requirements concerns what one *must* do, or think, or be if one is to participate in the basic value of practical reasonableness. Someone who lives up to these requirements is thus Aristotle's *phronimos;* he has Aquinas's *prudentia;* they are requirements of reasonableness or practical wisdom, and to fail to live up to them is irrational. But, secondly, reasonableness both *is* a basic aspect of human well-being and *concerns* one's participation in all the (other) basic aspects of human well-being. Hence its requirements concern fullness of well-being (in the measure in which any one person can enjoy such fullness of well-being in the circumstances of his lifetime). So someone who lives up to these requirements is also Aristotle's *spoudaios* (mature man), his life is *eu zen* (well-living) and, unless circumstances are quite against him, we can say that he has Aristotle's *eudaimonia* (the inclusive all-round flouishing or well-being—not safely translated as "happiness"). But, thirdly, the basic forms of good are opportunities of *being;* the more fully a man participates in them the more he is what he can be. And for this state of being fully what one can be, Aristotle appropriated the word *physis,* which was translated into Latin as *natura.* So Aquinas will say that these requirements are requirements not only of reason, and of goodness, but also (by entailment) of (human) nature.

Thus, speaking very summarily, we could say that the requirements to which we now turn express the "natural law method" of working out the (moral) "natural law" from the first (pre-moral) "principles of natural law." Using only the modern terminology (itself of uncertain import) of "morality," we can say that the following sections of this chapter concern the sorts of reasons why (and thus the ways in which) there are things that morally ought (not) to be done.

2. A Coherent Plan of Life

First, then, we should recall that, though they correspond to urges and inclinations which can make themselves felt prior to any intelligent consideration of what is worth pursuing, the basic aspects of human well-being are discernible only to one who thinks about his opportunities, and thus are realizable only by one who intelligently directs, focuses, and controls his urges, inclinations, and impulses. In its fullest form, therefore, the first requirement of practical reasonableness is what John Rawls calls a rational plan of life.[7] Implicitly or explicitly one must have a harmonious set of purposes and orientations, not as the "plans" or "blueprints" of a pipe-dream, but as effective commitments. (Do not confuse the adoption of a set of basic personal or social commitments with the process, imagined by some contemporary philosophers, of "choosing basic values"!) It is unreasonable to live merely from moment to moment, following immediate cravings, or just drifting. It is also irrational to devote one's attention exclusively to specific projects which can be carried out completely by simply deploying defined means to defined objectives. Commitment to the practice of medicine (for the sake of human life), or to scholarship (for the sake of truth), or to any profession, or to a marriage (for the sake of friendship and children) . . . all require both direction and control of impulses, and the undertaking of specific projects; but they also require the redirection of inclinations, the reformation of habits, the abandonment of old and adoption of new projects, as circumstances require, and, overall, the harmonization of all one's deep commitments—for which there is no recipe or blueprint, since basic aspects of human good are not like the definite objectives of particular projects, but are *participated in.* . . .

The content and significance of this first requirement will be better understood in the light of the other requirements. For indeed, all the requirements are interrelated and capable of being regarded as aspects one of another.

3. No Arbitrary Preferences Amongst Values

Next, there must be no leaving out of account, or arbitrary discounting or exaggeration, of any of the basic human values. Any commitment to a coherent plan of life is going to involve some degree of concentration on one or some of the basic forms of good, at the expense, temporarily or permanently, of other forms of good. But the commitment will be rational only if it is on the basis of one's assessment of one's capacities, circumstances, and even of one's tastes. It will be unreasonable if it is on the basis of a devaluation of any of the basic forms of human excellence, or if it is on the basis of an overvaluation of such merely derivative and supporting or instrumental goods as wealth or 'opportunity' or of such merely secondary and conditionally valuable goods as reputation or (in a different sense of secondariness) pleasure.

A certain scholar may have little taste or capacity for friendship, and may feel that life for him would have no savour if he were prevented from pursuing his commitment to knowledge. None the less, it would be unreasonable for him to deny that, objectively, human life (quite apart from truth-seeking and knowledge) and friendship are good in themselves. It is one thing to have little capacity and even no "taste" for scholarship, or friendship, or physical heroism, or sanctity; it is quite another thing, and stupid or arbitrary, to think or speak or act as if these were not real forms of good.

So, in committing oneself to a rational plan of life, and in interacting with other people (with their own plans of life), one must not use Rawls's "thin theory of the good." For the sake of a "democratic"[8] impartiality between differing conceptions of human good, Rawls insists that, in selecting principles of justice, one must treat as primary goods only liberty, opportunity, wealth, and self-respect, and that one must not attribute intrinsic value to such basic forms of good as truth, or play, or art, or friendship. Rawls gives no satisfactory reason for this radical emaciation of human good, and no satisfactory reason is available: the "thin theory" is arbitrary. It is quite reasonable for many men to choose not to commit themselves to any real pursuit of knowledge, and it is quite unreasonable for a scholar-statesman or scholar-father to demand that all his subjects or children should conform themselves willy-nilly to the modes and standards of excellence that he chooses and sets for himself. But it is even more unreasonable for anyone to deny that knowledge *is* (and is to be treated as) a form of excellence, and that error, illusion, muddle, superstition, and ignorance are evils that no one should wish for, or plan for, or encourage in himself or in others. If a statesman or father or any self-directing individual treats truth or friendship or play or any of the other basic forms of good as of no account, and never asks himself whether his life-plan(s) makes reasonable allowance for participation in those intrinsic human values (and for avoidance of their opposites), then he can be properly accused both of irrationality and of stunting or mutilating himself and those in his care.

4. No Arbitrary Preferences Amongst Persons

Next, the basic goods are human goods, and can in principle be pursued, realized, and participated in by any human being. Another person's survival, his coming to know, his creativity, his all-round flourishing, may not interest me, may not concern me, may in any event be beyond my power to affect. But have I any *reason* to deny that they are really good, or that they are fit matters of interest, concern, and favour by that man and by all those who have to do with him? The questions of friendship, collaboration, mutual assistance, and justice are the ·subject of the next chapters. Here we need not ask just who is responsible for whose well-being. But we can add, to the second requirement of fundamental impartiality of recognition of each of the basic forms of good, a third requirement: of fundamental impartiality among the human subjects who are or may be partakers of those goods.

My own well-being (which, as we shall see, includes a concern for the well-being of others, my friends; but ignore this for the moment) is reasonably the first claim on my interest, concern, and effort. Why can I so regard it? Not because it is of more value than the well-being of others, simply because it is mine: intelligence and reasonableness can find no basis in the mere fact that A is A and is not B (that I am I and am not you) for evaluating his (our) well-being differentially. No: the only *reason* for me to prefer my well-being is that it is through *my* self-determined and self-realizing participation in the basic goods that I can do what reasonableness suggests and requires, viz. favour and realize the forms of human good indicated in the first principles of practical reason.

There is, therefore, reasonable scope for self-preference. But when all allowance is made for that, this third requirement remains, a pungent critique of selfishness, special pleading, double standards, hypocrisy, indifference to the good of others whom one could easily help ("passing by on the other side"), and all the other manifold forms of egoistic and group bias. So much so that many have sought to found ethics virtually entirely on this principle of impartiality between persons. In the modern philosophical discussion, the principle regularly is expressed as a requirement that one's moral judgments and preferences be *universalizable*.

The classical non-philosophical expression of the requirement is, of course, the so-called Golden Rule formulated not only in the Christian gospel but also in the sacred books of the Jews, and not only in didactic formulae but also in the moral appeal of sacred history and parable. It needed no drawing of the moral, no special traditions of moral education, for King David (and every reader of the story of his confrontation with Nathan the prophet) to feel the rational conclusiveness of Nathan's analogy between the rich man's appropriation of the poor man's ewe and the King's appropriation of Uriah the Hittite's wife, and thus the rational necessity for the King to extend his condemnation of the rich man to himself. "You are the man" (2 Samuel 12:7).

"Do to (or for) others what you would have them do to (or for) you." Put yourself in your neighbor's shoes. Do not condemn others for what you are willing to do yourself. Do not (without special reason) prevent others getting for themselves what you are trying to get for yourself. These are requirements of reason, because to ignore them is to be arbitrary as between individuals.

But what are the bounds of reasonable self-preference, of reasonable discrimination in favour of myself, my family, my group(s)? In the Greek, Roman, and Christian traditions of reflection, this question was approached via the heuristic device of adopting the viewpoint, the standards, the principles of justice, of one who sees the whole arena of human affairs and who has the interests of each participant in those affairs equally at heart and equally in mind—the "ideal observer." Such an impartially benevolent "spectator" would condemn some but not all forms of self-preference, and some but not all forms of competition. The heuristic device helps one to attain impartiality as between the possible subjects of human well-being (persons) and to exclude mere bias in one's practical reasoning. It permits one to be impartial, too, among inexhaustibly many of the life-plans that differing individuals may choose. But, of course, it does not suggest "impartiality" about the basic aspects of human good. It does not authorize one to set aside the second requirement of practical reason by indifference to death and disease, by preferring trash to art, by favouring the comforts of ignorance and illusion, by repressing all play as unworthy of man, by praising the ideal of self-aggrandizement and condemning the ideal of friendship, or by treating the search for the ultimate source and destiny of things as of no account or as an instrument of statecraft or a plaything reserved for leisured folk . . .

Therein lies the contrast between the classical heuristic device of the benevolently divine viewpoint and the equivalent modern devices for eliminating mere bias, notably the heuristic concept of the social contract. Consider Rawls's elaboration of the social contract strategy, an elaboration which most readily discloses the purpose of that strategy as a measure and instrument of practical reason's requirement of interpersonal impartiality. Every feature of Rawls's construction is designed to guarantee that if a supposed principle of justice is one that would be unanimously agreed on, behind the "veil of ignorance," in the "Original Position," then it must be a principle that is fair and unbiased as between persons. Rawls's heuristic device is thus of some use to anyone who is concerned for the third requirement of practical reasonableness, and in testing its implications. Unfortunately, Rawls disregards the second requirement of practical reasonableness, viz. that each basic or intrinsic human good be treated as a basic and intrinsic good. The conditions of the Original Position are designed by Rawls to guarantee that no principle of justice will systematically favour any life-plan simply because that life-plan participates more fully in human well-being in any or all of its basic aspects (e.g. by favouring knowledge over ignorance and illusion, art over trash, etc.).

And it simply does not follow, from the fact that a principle chosen in the Original Position would be unbiased and fair as between individuals, that a principle which would *not* be chosen in the Original Position must be unfair or not a proper principle of justice in the real world. For in the real world, as Rawls himself admits, intelligence can discern intrinsic basic values and their contraries.[9] Provided we make the distinctions mentioned in the previous section, between basic practical principles and mere matters of taste, inclination, ability, etc., we are able (and are required in reason) to favour the basic forms of good and to avoid and discourage their contraries. In doing so we are showing no improper favour to individuals as such, no unreasonable "respect of persons," no egoistic or group bias, no partiality opposed to the Golden Rule or to any other aspect of this third requirement of practical reason.

5. Detachment and Commitment

The fourth and fifth requirements of practical reasonableness are closely complementary both to each other and to the first requirement of adopting a coherent plan of life, order of priorities, set of basic commitments.

In order to be sufficiently open to all the basic forms of good in all the changing circumstances of a lifetime, and in all one's relations, often unforeseeable, with other persons, and in all one's opportunities of effecting their well-being or relieving hardship, one must have a certain detachment from all the specific and limited projects which one undertakes. There is no good reason to take up an attitude to any of one's particular objectives, such that if one's project failed and one's objective eluded one, one would consider one's life drained of meaning. Such an attitude irrationally devalues and treats as meaningless the basic human good of authentic and reasonable self-determination, a good in which one meaningfully participates simply by trying to do something sensible and worthwhile, whether or not that sensible and worthwhile project comes to nothing. Moreover, there are often straightforward and evil consequences of succumbing to the temptation to give one's particular project the overriding and unconditional significance which only a basic value and a general commitment can claim: they are the evil consequences that we call to mind when we think of fanaticism. So the fourth requirement of practical reasonableness can be called detachment.

The fifth requirement establishes the balance between fanaticism and dropping out, apathy, unreasonable failure or refusal to "get involved" with anything. It is simply the requirement that having made one's general commitments one must not abandon them lightly (for to do so would mean, in the extreme case, that one would fail ever to really participate in any of the basic values). And this requirement of fidelity has a positive aspect. One should be looking creatively for new and better ways of carrying out one's commitments, rather than restricting one's horizon and one's effort to the projects, methods, and routines with which one is familiar. Such creativity and development shows that a person, or a society, is really living on the level of practical *principle,* not merely on the level of conventional rules of conduct, rules of thumb, rules of method, etc., whose real appeal is not to reason (which would show up their inadequacies) but to the sub-rational complacency of habit, mere urge to conformity, etc.

6. The (Limited) Relevance of Consequences: Efficiency, Within Reason

The sixth requirement has obvious connections with the fifth, but introduces a new range of problems for practical reason, problems which go to the heart of "morality." For this is the requirement that one bring about good in the world (in one's own life and the lives of others) by actions that are efficient for their (reasonable) purpose(s). One must not waste one's opportunities by using inefficient methods. One's actions should be judged by their effectiveness, by their fitness for their purpose, by their utility, their consequences . . .

There is a wide range of contexts in which it is possible and only reasonable to calculate, measure, compare, weigh, and assess the consequences of alternative decisions. Where a choice must be made it is reasonable to prefer human good to the good of animals. Where a choice must be made it is reasonable to prefer basic human goods (such as life) to merely instrumental goods (such as property). Where damage is inevitable, it is reasonable to prefer stunning to wounding, wounding to maiming, maiming to death: i.e. lesser rather than greater damage to one-and-the-same basic good in one-and-the-same instantiation. Where one way of participating in a human good includes *both* all the good aspects and effects of its alternative, *and* more, it is reasonable to prefer that way: a remedy that both relieves pain and heals is to be preferred to the one that merely relieves pain. Where a person or a society has created a personal or social hierarchy of practical norms and orientations, through reasonable choice of commitments, one can in many cases reasonably measure the benefits and disadvantages of alternatives. (Consider a man who has decided to become a scholar, or a society that has decided to go to war.) Where one is considering objects or activities in which there is reasonably a market, the market provides a common denominator (currency) and enables a comparison to be made of prices, costs, and profits. Where there are alternative techniques or facilities for achieving definite objectives, cost–benefit analysis will make possible a certain range of reasonable comparisons between techniques or facilities. Over a wide range of preferences and wants, it is reasonable for an individual or society to seek to maximize the satisfaction of those preferences or wants.

But this sixth requirement is only one requirement among a number. The first, second, and third requirements require that in seeking to maximize the satisfaction of preferences one should discount the preferences of, for example, sadists (who follow the impulses of the moment, and/or do not respect the value of life, and/or do not universalize their principles of action with impartiality). The first, third, and (as we shall see) seventh and eighth requirements require that cost–benefit analysis be contained within a framework that excludes any project involving certain intentional killings, frauds, manipulations of personality, etc. And the second requirement requires that one recognize that each of the basic aspects of human well-being is equally basic, that none is objectively more important than any of the others, and thus that none can provide a common denominator or single yardstick for assessing the utility of all projects: they are incommensurable, and any calculus of consequences that pretends to commensurate them is irrational.

As a general strategy of moral reasoning, utilitarianism or consequentialism is irrational. The utilitarian or (more generally) the consequentialist claims that (i) one should always choose the act that, so far as one can see, will yield the greatest net good on the whole and in the long run ("act-utilitarianism"), or that (ii) one should always choose according to a principle or rule the adoption of which will yield the greatest net good on the whole and in the long run ("rule-utilitarianism"). Each of these claims is not so much false as senseless (in a sense of "senseless" that will shortly be explained). For no plausible sense can be given, here, to the notion of a "greatest net good," or to any analogous alternative notions such as "best consequences," "lesser evil," "smallest net harm," or "greater balance of good over bad than could be expected from any available alternative action". . . .

The sixth requirement—of efficiency in pursuing the definite goals which we adopt for ourselves and in avoiding the definite harms which we choose to regard as unacceptable—is a real requirement, with indefinitely many applications in "moral" (and hence in legal) thinking. But its sphere of proper application has limits, and every attempt to make it the exclusive or supreme or even the central principle of practical thinking is irrational and hence immoral. Still, we ought not to disguise from ourselves the *ultimate* (and hence inexplicable, even "strange"[10]) character of the basic principles and requirements of reasonableness (like the basic aspects of the world . . .) once we go beyond the intellectual routines of calculating cost–benefit and efficiency.

7. Respect for Every Basic Value in Every Act

The seventh requirement of practical reasonableness can be formulated in several ways. A first formulation is that one should not choose to do any act which *of itself does nothing but* damage or impede a realization or participation of any one or more of the basic forms of human good. For the only "reason" for doing such an act, other than the non-reason of some impelling desire, could be that the good *consequences* of the act *outweigh* the damage done in and through the act itself. But, outside merely technical contexts, consequentialist "weighing" is always and necessarily arbitrary and delusive for the reasons indicated in the preceding section. . . .

The basic values, and the practical principles expressing them, are the only guides we have. Each is objectively basic, primary, incommensurable with the others in point of objective importance. If one is to act intelligently at all one must choose to realize and participate in some basic value or values rather than others, and this inevitable concentration of effort will indirectly impoverish, inhibit, or interfere with the realization of those other values. If I commit myself to truthful scholarship, then I fail to save the lives I could save as a doctor, I inhibit the growth of the production of material goods, I limit my opportunities for serving the community through politics, entertainment, art, or preaching. And within the field of science and scholarship, my research into K means that L and M go as yet undiscovered. These unsought but unavoidable side-effects accompany every human choice, and their consequences are incalculable. But it is always reasonable to leave some of them, and often reasonable to leave all of them, out of account. Let us for brevity use the word "damage" to signify also impoverishment, inhibition, or interference, and the word "promote" to signify also pursuit or protection. Then we can say this: to indirectly damage any basic good (by choosing an act that directly and immediately promotes either that basic good in some other aspect or participation, or some other basic good or goods) is obviously quite different, rationally and thus morally, from directly and immediately damaging a basic good in some aspect or participation by choosing an act which in and of itself simply (or, we should now add, primarily) damages that good in some aspect or participation but which indirectly, *via* the mediation of expected consequences. is to promote either that good in some other aspect or participation, or some other basic good(s).

To choose an act which in itself simply (or primarily) damages a basic good is thereby to engage oneself willy-nilly (but directly) in an act of opposition to an incommensurable value (an aspect of human personality) which one treats as if it were an object of measurable worth that could be outweighed by commensurable objects of greater (or cumulatively greater) worth. To do this will often accord with our feelings, our generosity, our sympathy, and with our commitments and projects in the forms in which we undertook them. But it can never be justified in reason. We must choose rationally (and this rational judgment can often promote a shift in our perspective and consequently a realignment of initial feelings and thus of our commitments and projects). Reason requires that every basic value be at least respected in each and every action. If one could ever rightly choose a single act which *itself* damages and *itself* does not promote some basic good, then one could rightly choose whole programmes and institutions and enterprises that themselves damage and do not promote basic aspects of human well-being, for the sake of their "net beneficial consequences." Now we have already seen that consequences, even to the extent that they can be "foreseen as certain," cannot be commensurably *evaluated,* which means that "net beneficial consequences" is a literally absurd general objective or criterion. It only remains to note that a man who thinks that his rational responsibility to be always doing and pursuing good is satisfied by a commitment to act always for best consequences is a man who treats every aspect of human personality (and indeed, therefore, treats himself) as a utensil. He holds himself ready to do *anything* (and thus makes himself a tool for all those willing to threaten sufficiently bad consequences if he does not cooperate with them).

But the objection I am making to such choices is not that programmes of mass killing, mass deception, etc. would then be more eligible (though they would) and indeed morally required (though they would), but that no sufficient reason can be found for treating any act as immune from the only direction which we have, viz. the direction afforded by the basic practical principles. These each direct that a form of good is to be pursued and done; and each of them bears not only on all our large-scale choices of general orientations and commitments, and on all our medium-scale choices of projects (in which attainment of the objective will indeed be the good consequence of successful deployment of effective means), but also on each and every choice of an act which itself is a complete act (whether or not it is also a step in a plan or phase in a project). The incommensurable value of an aspect of personal full-being (and its corresponding primary principle) can never be rightly subordinated to any project or commitment. But such an act of subordination inescapably occurs at least whenever a distinct choice-of-act has in *itself* no meaning save that of damaging that basic value (thus violating that primary principle).

Such, in highly abstract terms, is the seventh requirement, the principle on which alone rests . . . the strict inviolability of basic human rights. There is no human right that will not be overridden if feelings (whether generous and unselfish, or mean and self-centred) are allowed to govern choice, or if cost–benefit considerations are taken outside their appropriate technical sphere and allowed to govern one's direct engagement (whether at the level of commitment, project, or individual act) with basic goods. And the perhaps unfamiliar formulation which we have been consider-ing should not obscure the fact that this "seventh requirement" is well recognized, in other formulations: most loosely, as "the end does not justify the means"; more precisely, though still ambiguously, as "evil may not be done that good might follow therefrom"; and with a special Enlightenment flavour, as Kant's "categorical imperative": Act so that you treat humanity, whether in your own person or in that of another, always as an end and never as a means only."[11]

Obviously, the principal problem in considering the implications of this requirement is the problem of individuating and characterizing actions, to determine what is one complete act-that-itself-does-nothing-but-damage-a-basic-good. Human acts are to be individuated primarily in terms of those factors which we gesture towards with the word "intention." Fundamentally, a human act is a that-which-is-decided-upon (or -chosen) and its primary proper description is as what-is-chosen. A human action, to be humanly regarded, is to be characterized in the way it was characterized in the conclusion to the relevant train of practical reasoning of the man who chose to do it. On the other hand, the world with its material (including our bodily selves) and its structures of physical and psycho-physical causality is not indefinitely malleable by human intention. The man who is deciding what to do cannot reasonably shut his eyes to the causal structure of his project; he cannot characterize his plans *ad lib*. One can be engaged willy-nilly but directly, in act, with a basic good, such as human life.

Perhaps the consequences of one's act seem likely to be very good and would themselves directly promote further basic human good. Still, these expected goods will be realized (if at all) not as aspects of one-and-the-same act, but as aspects or consequences of other acts (by another person, at another time and place, as the upshot of another free decision . . .). So, however "certainly foreseeable" they may be, they cannot be used to characterize the act itself as, *in and of itself,* anything other than an intentional act of, say, man-killing. This is especially obvious when a blackmailer's price for sparing his hostages is "killing that man"; the person who complies with the demand, in order to save the lives of the many, cannot deny that he is choosing an act which of itself does nothing but kill.

Sometimes, however, the "good effects" are really aspects of one-and-the-same act, and can form part of the description of what it is in and of itself. Then we cannot characterize the act as in and of itself *nothing but* damaging to human good. But is it rationally justifiable? Not necessarily; the seventh requirement is not an isolated requirement, and such a choice may flout the second, third, fourth, and fifth requirements. The choice a man makes may be one he would not make if he were sufficiently detached from his impulses and his peculiar project to avoid treating a particular act or project as if it were itself a basic aspect of human well-being; or if he were *creatively* open to all the basic goods and thus careful to adjust his projects so as to minimize their damaging "side-effects" and to avoid substantial and irreparable harms to persons. The third requirement here provides a convenient test of respect for good: would the person acting have thought the act reasonable had *he* been the person harmed? Considerations such as these are woven into the notion of *directly* choosing against a basic value. And for most practical purposes this seventh requirement can be summarized as: Do not choose directly against a basic value. . . .

8. The Requirements of the Common Good

Very many, perhaps even most, of our concrete moral responsibilities, obligations, and duties have their basis in the eighth requirement. We can label this the requirement of favouring and fostering the common good of one's communities. The sense and implications of this requirement are complex and manifold.

9. Following One's Conscience

The ninth requirement might be regarded as a particular aspect of the seventh (that no basic good may be directly attacked in any act), or even as a summary of all the requirements. But it is quite distinctive. It is the requirement that one should not do what one judges or thinks or "feels"-all-in-all should not be done. That is to say one must act "in accordance with one's conscience."

This chapter has been in effect a reflection on the workings of conscience. If one were by inclination generous, open, fair, and steady in one's love of human good, or if one's milieu happened to have settled on reasonable *mores,* then one would be able, without solemnity, rigmarole, abstract reasoning, or casuistry, to make the particular practical judgments (i.e. judgments of conscience) that reason requires. If one is not so fortunate in one's inclinations or upbringing, then one's conscience will mislead one, unless one strives to be reasonable and is blessed with a pertinacious intelligence alert to the forms of human good yet undeflected by the sophistries which intelligence so readily generates to rationalize indulgence, time-serving, and self-love. (The stringency of these conditions is the permanent ground for the possibility of authority in morals, i.e. of authoritative guidance, by one who meets those conditions, acknowledged willingly by persons of conscience.)

The first theorist to formulate this ninth requirement in all its unconditional strictness seems to have been Thomas Aquinas: if one chooses to do what one judges to be in the last analysis unreasonable, or if one chooses not to do what one judges to be in the last analysis required by reason, then one's choice is unreasonable (wrongful), however erroneous one's judgments of conscience may happen to be. (A *logically* necessary feature of such a situation is, of course, that one is ignorant of one's mistake.)

This dignity of even the mistaken conscience is what is expressed in the ninth requirement. It flows from the fact that practical reasonableness is not simply a mechanism for producing correct judgments, but an aspect of personal full-being, to be respected (like all the other aspects) in every act as well as "over-all"—whatever the consequences.

10. The Product of These Requirements: Morality

Now we can see why some philosophers have located the essence of "morality" in the reduction of harm, others in the increase of well-being, some in social harmony, some in universalizability of practical judgment, some in the all-round flourishing of the individual, others in the preservation of freedom and personal authenticity. Each of these has a place in rational choice of commitments, projects, and particular actions. Each, moreover, contributes to the sense, significance, and force of terms such as "moral," "[morally] ought," and "right"; not every one of the nine requirements has a direct role in every moral judgment, but some moral judgments do sum up the bearing of each and all of the nine on the questions in hand, and every moral judgment sums up the bearing of one or more of the requirements. . . .

If, finally, we look back over the complex of basic principles and basic requirements of practical reasonableness, we can see how "natural" is that diversity of moral opinion which the sceptic makes such play of. It is a diversity which has its source in too exclusive attention to some of the basic value(s) and/or some basic requirement(s), and inattention to others. Sometimes, no doubt, the distortion or deflection is most immediately explicable by reference to an uncritical, unintelligent spontaneity; sometimes, by reference to the bias and oversight induced by conventions of language, social structure, and social practice; and sometimes (and always, perhaps, most radically) by the bias of self-love or of other emotions and inclinations that resist the concern to be simply reasonable.

Notes

1. *Nic. Eth.* I, 3: 1095a7–11; 4: 1095b5–13; X, 9: 1179b27–30.

2. *Nic. Eth.* X, 9: 1179b27–1180a5.

3. See *Nic. Eth.* VI, 5: 1140a24–25; II, 5: 1105b30–31; III, 6: 1115a20; III, 10: 1117b32; cf. X, 2: 1173a1.

4. *Nic. Eth.* VI, 11: 1143a35–1143b17.

5. *Nic. Eth.* X, 10: 1176a17–18; cf, III, 6: 1113a33; IX, 4: 1166a12–13: see also I.4, above.

6. *Nic. Eth.* II, 6: 1106b21–24.

7. *Theory of Justice,* pp. 408–23, adopting the terminology of W. F. R. Hardie, "The Final Good in Aristotle's Ethics," (1965) 60 *Philosophy* 277.

8. Cf. *Theory of Justice,* p. 527.

9. *Theory of Justice,* p. 328.

10. Thus Brian Barry rightly begins his "Justice Between Generations," *Essays,* pp. 269–84, by asking (quoting Wilfred Beckerman) "Suppose that, as a result of using up all the world's resources, human life did come to an end. So what?" and concludes a thorough analysis of the issues for practical reasonableness by saying ". . . the continuation of human life into the future is something to be sought (or at least not sabotaged) even if it does not make for the maximum total happiness. Certainly, if I try to analyse the source of my own strong conviction that we should be wrong to take risks with the continuation of human life, I find that it does not lie in any sense of injury to the interests of people who will not get born but rather in a sense of its cosmic impertinence—that we should be grossly abusing our position by taking it upon ourselves to put a term on human life and its possibilities" (p. 284).

11. Kant, *Foundations of the Metaphysics of Morals* (1785; trans. Beck, Indianapolis: 1959), p. 47.

19

The Privatization of Good

ALASDAIR MACINTYRE

When in 1879 in the encyclical *Aeterni Patris* Leo XIII contrasted the moral and political philosophy of Aquinas with that of the secular liberalism of the late nineteenth century, he directed our attention to an area of conflict whose importance has not diminished in the succeeding century. Nowhere is this conflict more evident or persistent than in the radical disagreement between Aquinas and the moral philosophy of modern liberalism over the question of the relationship between how the human good is to be conceived and achieved and how those rules, obedience to which is required for morally right action, are to be formulated, understood and justified.

For Aquinas, as for Aristotle, we can only understand the right in the light afforded by the good. The good for the members of each species is that end to which, *qua* members of that species, those members move in achieving their specific perfection. The rules for right action for rational animals are those rules intentional conformity to which is required if their specific perfection is to be achieved. The content of those rules, their exceptionless character and their authority all derive from the end which obedience to them serves. But they are not to be understood as specifying types of actions the performance of which as a matter of merely contingent fact will bring about some particular type of end-state. They are not specifications of means *externally* related to an end. They are rather rules partially constitutive of a form of life, the living out of which is the peculiar function of human beings as rational

Reprinted by permission of the publisher from Alasdair MacIntyre, "The Privatization of Good," *Review of Politics* 52 (Summer 1990), p. 3.

animals, and the completion of which lies in that activity which is itself supreme happiness and which makes of the life of which it is the completion of a happy life. So to disobey such rules in any way and to any degree is in that way and to that degree to separate oneself from one's good. And, insofar as anyone lacks knowledge of his or her true good, such a person is also deprived of the only sound reasons for right action.

This is not of course to imply that, either for Aristotle or for Aquinas, human beings do or are able to begin with a fully-fledged knowledge of the good and from it deduce the rules of right action. Each of us learns how to articulate his or her own initial inner capacity for comprehending what the good is in the course of also learning from others about rules and about virtues, so that, through a dialectical process of questioning the ways in which rules, virtues, goods and *the* good are interrelated, we gradually come to understand the unity of the deductive structures of practical reasoning. But what we thus come to understand is in part that, to the extent that what we take to be the case about the human good is false or confused, to that extent our understanding of the rules defining right action will also be apt to be false and confused and that, to the extent to which we ignore or put out of mind or otherwise fail to take account of the distinctive character of the human good, to that extent we shall be unable to provide an adequately determinate or authoritative formulation of those same rules. Adequate knowledge of moral rules is inseparable from and cannot be had without genuine knowledge of human good.

It follows that on any substantively Artistotelian or Thomistic view rational agreement on moral rules always presupposes rational agreement on the nature of the human good. Any political society therefore, which possesses a shared stock of adequately determinate and rationally defensible moral rules, publicly recognized to be the rules to which characteristically and generally unproblematic appeals may be made, will therefore, implicitly or explicitly, be committed to an adequately determinate and rationally justifiable conception of the human good. And insofar as the rational justification of particular moral stances is a feature of its public life, that conception will have had to be made explicit in a way and to a degree which will render general allegiance to that particular conception itself a matter of public concern.

This is not of course how things are in the contemporary advanced societies of Western modernity. What shared moral rules there are—and later I shall need to enquire how far there are in fact shared moral rules in such societies—are and cannot but be invoked and upheld independently of any corresponding shared conception of *the* human good. For as to the nature of the human good, as to whether there is indeed any such thing as the human good, disagreements are numerous and fundamental. This socially embodied divorce between rules defining right action on the one hand and conceptions of the human good on the other is one of those aspects of such societies in virtue of which they are entitled to be called liberal. For it is a central tenet of recent liberal moral and political theory that public institutions and more especially the institutions of government should be systematically neutral as between rival conceptions of what the human good is. Allegiance to any particular conception of human good ought, on this liberal view, to be a matter of private individual preference and choice, and it is contrary to rationality to require of anyone that he or she should agree with anyone else in giving his or her allegiance to some particular view.

In this respect the status of conceptions of the human good is very different from that of moral rules. Moral rules, on this modern liberal view, prescribe those actions and those refrainings from action which any rational person may require of any other. About them, about their content, about their binding force, and presumably about the appropriate ways of responding to their breach, agreement among rational persons is therefore required. The type of agreement required about moral rules by liberals and the type of disagreement permitted and expected by those same liberals about conceptions of the good can both be characterized in terms of one and the same understanding of the relationship of freedom to reason. The autonomy of a free and rational individual, according to liberalism, is not infringed by, but requires that individual to assent to the deliverances of reason, where these are unequivocal; and so it is with assent to moral rules. But where the state of the argument is such that there are alternative and incompatible views on some matter, and rational argument currently does not, and provides no prospect of being able to provide unequivocal support for only one set of conclusions out of those which are in contention, the autonomy of a free and rational individual can be exercised in embracing any one of the contending views. It is in the light of this contrast that concerns about elaborating, defending and living out particular conceptions of the good are, on this type of liberal view, to be assigned to and restricted to the sphere of the private life of individuals, while concerns about obedience to what are taken to be the moral rules required of every rational person can be legitimately pursued in the public realm. So appeals to particular moral rules always provide *relevant,* although not necessarily *sufficient* grounds for advocating legislation of various kinds, while appeals to particular conceptions of the human good never do. Insofar as it is this liberal view which has been embodied in social practice in contemporary advanced societies, the good has been privatized.

There are of course important differences between liberal theorists in the ways in which they articulate their positions, but there is also a remarkable degree of concurrence. So Virginia Held, who expresses the contrast between the right and the good in terms of principles defining rights asserts that "We can agree that persons' conceptions of the good will diverge and that, although not all such conceptions will be equally admirable, persons can legitimately pursue a pluralism of admirable goals. But their recognition of principles of freedom, justice, and equality yielding a system of rights for human beings is not a matter of preference, or choice between goods. . . . That all persons ought as moral beings to adhere to principles assuring respect for rights can be asserted and defended" (*Rights and Goals* [Chicago: University of Chicago Press, 1984], p. 19).

Ronald Dworkin had earlier identified a distinctively liberal theory of equality as one which "supposes that political decisions must be, so far as is possible, independent of any particular conception of the good life, or of what gives value to life. Since the citizens of a society differ in their conceptions, the government does not treat them as equals if it prefers one conception to another, either because the officials believe that one is intrinsically superior, or because one is held by the more numerous or more powerful group" ("Liberalism," in *Public and Private Morality*, ed. S. Hampshire [Cambridge: Cambridge University Press, 1978], p. 127). And John Rawls had already gone further than either Held or Dworkin in contending not only that "agreement upon the principles of rational choice" is presupposed in arriving at principles of justice, while in the case of planning one's life in the light of some conception of the good, "unanimity concerning the standards of rationality is not required," since "each person is free to plan his life as he pleases (so long as his intentions are consistent with the principles of justice)," but also that "variety in conceptions of the good is itself a good thing" (*A Theory of Justice* [Cambridge, MA: Harvard University press, 1971], pp. 447–48).

Notice that for liberalism understood in this way everything turns on two contentions: first, that in the debate between particular rival and alternative conceptions of the human good, not only has none established a claim to decisive rational superiority over its rivals, but that it should not even be a matter of public, as against private interest how we ought to proceed in evaluating the rational merits of rival claims in this area; and secondly that rational agreement on moral rules can be—and indeed, given the liberal case, must already have been—somehow or other secured in a way which deserves to secure the consent and compliance of all rational persons, and that this agreement is available or can be made available as a key point of reference in public debate and decision-making. It is with this last claim that I am going to be first of all concerned in this lecture. For it is a claim that we have the strongest of reasons to doubt.

It is not that we do not have a variety of recommended methods for arriving at rational agreement of the kind required. It is rather that we have all too many such methods, each of them incompatible in important ways with some of the others, not only in the type of argument proposed as appropriate for settling disputes about the nature and content of moral rules, but also in the substantive conclusions arrived at about the nature and content of such rules. So we have a range of types of Kantianism, a similar range of types of utilitarianism, and of intuitionism, contractarianism and various blends of these. And since each of these rival and competing views claims to supply the *ultimate* principles by which disputed questions in this area are to be adjudicated, we lack any further rational court of appeal, whose verdicts might settle such questions. Radical and *de facto* ineliminable disagreement confronts us.

Moreover what these various types of philosophical theory mirror are just the types of reasoning upon which ordinary nonphilosophical reflective persons in our culture rely in their moral reasoning. Universalizability arguments, utilitarian attention to consequences, intuitionist appeals to not further to be argued for principles of duty and invocations of contractarian thoughts are as much part of the common currency of everyday practical argument as they are of the academic study of moral philosophy. So that we should expect to find the same range of disagreements at the level of everyday morality. But recently Jeffrey Stout has argued that this is in fact not the case, that disagreements do of course occur on some major issues, but that we have a stock of agreements embodied in what Stout calls "moral platitudes," learned as children in the nursery (*Ethics After Babel* [Boston: Beacon Press, 1988], p. 211). Disagreements presuppose a background of agreement, for "we are initiated into a moral consensus as very young children" (p. 43). Such differences as there may be in modes of reasoning do not at least on many fundamental topics issue in significant differences in moral conclusions.

Against Stout I want to suggest that he is indeed right in thinking that there is a consensus of platitudes in our moral culture, but that this belongs to the rhetorical surface of that culture, and not to its substance. The rhetoric of shared values is of great ideological importance, but it disguises the truth about how action is guided and directed. For what we genuinely share in the way of moral maxims, precepts and principles is insufficiently determinate to guide action and what is sufficiently determinate to guide action is not shared. And this after all is what we might expect, if it were the case *both* that the variety and heterogeneity of the types of moral reasoning recognized among us issued in as wide a range of disparate normative conclusions in everyday practical life as it does in the realm of moral theory *and* that a refusal, or perhaps a failure, to allow that this is so was a prerequisite for the effective functioning of our central political, legal and educational institutions. I take as a test case for deciding the issue between Stout and myself, not those much debated issues such as the wrongness of abortion or the nature of a just war by focussing on which, so Stout claims, I have in the past exaggerated the degree of conflict in our culture, but the subject matter of one of the maxims—platitudes in Stout's idiom—which constitute the moral consensus into which children are initiated, the matter of truth-telling and lying.

What is the shared maxim, so far as there is one, by which children are instructed in this area by parents, teachers and other authoritative adults? It runs as follows: "Never tell a lie" (this first part is uttered loudly and firmly) "except when" (and here the adult voice tends to drop) and there then follows a list of exceptions of varying types ending with an "etc." We all agree on the maxim; where we disagree is first of all upon which types of exception are to be included in the appended list. Is it permissible to lie when the utterance of the truth will be discourteous? Is it permissible or perhaps obligatory to lie when an innocent human life is immediately at stake? Is it permissible to lie when a lie just *might* contribute to the future saving of such a life? Is it permissible to lie to save face? Is it permissible or even obligatory to lie to help a friend out of a difficulty? If I am in fact the best candidate for a job, but I will only get it if I lie, may I lie? If it will serve the national interest or if some highly placed official says that it will serve the national interest, ought I to lie? If it furthers the cause of the National Rifle Association, the ACLU or the girl scouts, should I lie? If doing my job as journalist, a private detective, or an investigator of insurance claims involves lying, should I change my employment?

There is no socially established agreement on the answers to these questions. And both between and within different influential moral and religious traditions, Catholic, Protestant, Jewish and secular, rival and conflicting answers are defended. But our disagreements are not confined to the question of which types of lie, if any, are permissible. For even when it is agreed by some large number of persons that a particular type of lie is impermissible, there will still be extensive disagreements as to how serious an offence it is to tell that type of lie. We disagree as to how to rank order offenses against truth-telling in terms of their gravity. But even this is not all. For we also disagree about how lies, when exposed as such, ought to be responded to by the exposed liar, by those who have been lied to and by members of the society at large. Is it guilt or shame that the offender should feel if exposed in various types of lie, and to what degree, and what kind of subsequent conduct is to be required of the guilty or the ashamed? When, if ever, is the liar to be punished or, if not punished, reproached or shunned and by whom and for how long? From membership in what bodies should proven liars be excluded? Once again we have a range of questions to which different and incompatible answers are given.

Nor is it the case that different individuals each give one clear and consistent set of answers to each of these questions, albeit disagreeing with other individuals. To some significant, even if unmeasured extent these disagreements seem to occur within individuals, one and the same individual hovering between two or more rival opinions, inclining to one on some occasions and in some contexts, to another on others. Only thus can the inconsistency and instability of our shared public responses to lying be made fully intelligible. For what is apparently one and the same type of lie will among the same groups of people or in the same political institution be treated as a grave offence on some occasions, as a minor offence upon others and upon yet others be simply ignored. In our public and political life there are strange oscillations between wild outbursts of self-righteous indignation on the one hand and complacent silences on the other. We do know from empirical psychological research that lying is endemic in the population at large: Bella de Paulo, a psychologist at the University of Virginia, who studies lying by having her experimental subjects keep a diary of the lies which they tell, has concluded that "People tell about two lies a day, or at least that is how many they will admit to" (*New York Times,* 12 February 1985, p. 17). And the indeterminancy of our shared public maxims and the unpredictability of our public responses about truth-telling point to widespread uncertainties about both our own behavior and that of others.

There have been in the past and there are now rival and contending moral traditions about what a strict determinate rule about truth-telling and lying should in fact be. But these disagreements were and are rooted in more fundamental disagreements about the place and purpose of speech and writing within that kind of life which it is best for human beings beings to lead. The determinate character of such rules in each case arises from their relationship to and their implementation of some particular determinate conception of the good and the best. And whatever rational authority each may possess, that in virtue of which rational persons ought to treat it as binding is derived from whatever rational authority that particular conception of human good may possess.

As against Stout, therefore, and indeed against contemporary liberal theory in general I initially conclude that a necessary precondition for a political community's possession of adequately determinate shared rationally founded moral rules is the shared possession of a rationally justifiable conception of human good. And that insofar as appeals to moral rules are to play a part in the public life of such a community, respect for and allegiance to that shared conception of the human good will have had to be institutionalized in the life of that community. On this issue then a Thomistic Aristotelianism is so far vindicated. Notice that it is in an important way a specifically Thomistic Aristotelianism which is thus vindicated. In what way becomes clear when we consider a rival attempt to render Aristotle's ethics of virtue relevant to the debates of contemporary moral philosophy, one undertaken in different versions by a number of thinkers who agree in recognizing the superiority of Aristotelianism to Kantianism and utilitarianism, but who aspire to do this in a way compatible with a modern liberal allegiance. It is this latter which leads them to substitute for the single and unitary, if complex, final good conceived by Aristotle a multiplicity of goods, each *qua* good worthy of being pursued, and each, at least in certain circumstances and perhaps as such, incommensurable with the others. Which good or set of good any particular individual pursues is to be determined by that particular individual's preferences. And the choice of any one such good or set of goods will characteristically exclude the choice of certain others.

When Aristotle is thus emended however, practical reasoning, as understood by Aristotle, ceases to yield unambiguous directives for action. For the first premise of such reasoning—often of course left tacit—is, as Aristotle remarks, of the form "Since the *telos* and the best is such and such" (*Nicomachean Ethics* vi, 1144a32–33), and where there are alternative and competing goods, each of which may equally be treated as the *telos* and the best, there will also in particular situations be alternative and competing practical syllogisms with alternative and competing courses of action as their conclusions. So it will be equally rational to act in any one out of a number of different and incompatible ways and nonrational preference will have become sovereign in decision-making.

It is not then surprising that, while Aristotle found no need to discuss practical dilemmas, this kind of would-be-Aristotelian characteristically finds them of notable importance in the moral life, for practical rationality thus reconceived renders systematically indeterminate what is required of us in just too many types of situation. So that if this were indeed a faithful rendering of Aristotle, Aristotelianism would afford us no resources with which to challenge the indeterminacy of public shared moral rules in contemporary culture. It is only Aristotelianism understood as specifying in adequate outline a single and unitary, albeit complex, conception of the human good, Aristotelianism, that is, understood very much as Thomists have understood it, which is capable of challenging effectively the privatization of conceptions of the good, their exclusion from the public realm, that privatization which precludes the possession of an adequately determinate, rationally justifiable morality. But this is not all that it precludes.

For there are certain issues of the moral life which cannot get raised at all in any adequately systematic way in the public realm, if appeal to conceptions of the overall human good is excluded from that realm. Consider two areas of concern often considered separately in our society: on the one hand, the horrifying infant mortality rate in the United States, one which comes close in some parts of the country to ranking it with Third World rather than other advanced countries, and on the other the condemnation of the old in our society to boredom, nursing homes, and Alzheimer's disease. What these together represent is a distribution of resources, such that more and more has been directed to the mindless extension of the length of human life by medical science into a more and more mindless old age, while the unborn and the very young have continued to be radically deprived. And this maldistribution of resources represents an answer to a set of questions which have not yet been systematically asked, let alone answered.

Aristotle makes it clear that what the living out of the best life for human beings requires of us is not the same at every period of life; and in specifying what participation in which activities is required at each stage in the movement from early childhood to old age—on an Aristotelian view each age has its tasks and functions, including old age; no period of life is functionless—and in what the relationship between older and younger is at each stage, one would have had to have made considerable progress in specifying what the best life for human beings is. Conversely, without some determinate conception of the good and the best it would be impossible to provide adequate answers to these questions. So answering questions in any systematic way, which could be implemented in practice, concerning the overall relationships of the very young, the adolescent, the working adult and the old within families, parishes, schools, clinics, work places and local neighborhood communities, so that we can agree in recognizing what the old owe to the young and the young to the old, is a task inseparable from that of formulating a conception of the good and the best. And when that task is one excluded from the public realm, then it will become impossible to ask and answer such questions, let alone questions about a just distribution of resources between the young and the old. The privatization of the good thus ensures not only that we are deprived of adequately determinate shared moral rules, but that central areas of moral concern cannot become the subject of anything like adequate public shared systematic discourse or enquiry.

Morality is thereby diminished in scope. And hence in part the sterility of much public debate, on issues which *are* admitted to the public realm, such as that of abortion. For what one holds rationally about abortion is inseparable from what one holds about the point and purpose of family life, about the place of the conception and upbringing of children in that life and about the relationship of family ties to other social ties. To abstract the issue of abortion from these contexts is necessarily to obscure what is at issue. Moral questions treated one by one piecemeal in isolation from larger contexts of argument and of practice always begin to appear rationally unanswerable; and since, when morality is defined independently of the good, the relationships between different moral rules disappears from view, one result is that moral questions tend to be presented as a grab bag of separable, isolable and so insoluble problems.

So we confront a situation in which there is great danger and great difficulty. The danger arises from our inhabiting a political and economic system in which a rhetoric of moral consensus masks fundamental dissensus and moral inpoverishment. The difficulty arises from the fact that a standard liberal retort to the arguments which I have advanced is at first inspection highly plausible. It runs as follows.

Even if it were the case that the absence of a shared conception of the human good both rendered our shared moral rules indeterminate and impoverished the definition of our moral concerns, we could not find a remedy in the adoption of such a shared conception, for in our culture radical disagreement about the nature of the good does seem to be ineliminable among rational persons. We need do no more than point to the range and diversity and incompatability of widely held rival and conflicting conceptions of the good for this to be evident. But what ought we to conclude from this range and diversity and incompatibility? Is it the case that there has been somewhere or other in our past history a prolonged and systematic rational debate, whose procedures were fair and impartial, between such conceptions, whose outcome was a failure on the part of each contending party to defeat its rivals, so that by the best test which the resources of rationality can afford radical disagreement and conflict has indeed proved ineliminable? The answer to this question is "No." It is a piece of false mythology to suppose that our fundamental disagreements have either emerged from or been tested by prolonged rational debate. Even such debate as has occurred has been defective in at least three ways.

First what have in fact taken place over the past two hundred years have been at best a series of particular and intermittent engagements of relatively sporadic and unsustained kinds on particular, local issues and problems practical or theoretical. There have been few occasions, perhaps none, in which one point of view, presenting itself systematically and as a whole, has been able to engage with its major rivals, also presented systematically and as a whole. And it is easy to understand why this should be so. The genres of debate, the institutionalizations of the expressions of disagreement, either restrict it to the piecemeal treatment of isolable issues in the more serious academic journals or to relatively brief and rhetorically insinuating treatments in other media.

Secondly liberalism has played two roles in the modern world. It has been and is one of the contending parties with respect to theories of the good. But it has also by and large controlled the terms of both public and academic debate. Other points of view have generally been invited to debate with liberalism only within a framework of procedures whose presuppositions were already liberal. But, important as these two points are, they are much less crucial than a third.

Fundamental disagreement over the nature of the good is not only a matter of theoretical contention, but also and essentially of practice. It is rival conceptions of practical rationality, of the relationship of human beings to the good in their actions, of the practically embodied rules and virtues which are specific to each rival conception of the good, which are in contention. And practical claims cannot be made in exclusively theoretical ways. Certainly the theory of practice is important, but only as in key part arising reflectively from, throwing light upon and being vindicated or failing to be vindicated by the practice of which it is the theory. Hence there can be no genuine abstract, merely theoretical debate between rival conceptions of the good. Such conceptions only confront one another in any decisive way, when presented within the embodied life of particular communities which exemplify each specific conception. It is in key part in the lives of families, parishes, schools, clinics, work places and local neighborhood communities that any particular conception of the good achieves recognizable form.

So just as we only know what a particular conception of the good and the corresponding conceptions of virtues, intellectual and moral, and of rules really amount to when we encounter them to some significant degree embodied in the particularities of social life, so also genuine debate between rival conceptions only occurs when the actualities of one mode of social life, embodying one such conception, are matched against the actualities of its rivals. It is as it is concretely lived out that one fundamental standpoint is or is not vindicated against its rivals. And my earlier criticism of liberalism was expressed in a way that was designed to recognize this. My accusation was not or not only that liberal theory involves a fundamental indeterminateness in respect of moral rules and of impoverishment in respect of moral concerns; it was that as such theory is lived out in practice, this indeterminateness and this impoverishment are exemplified in social reality. And correlatively if it is, as it is, a Thomistic contention that the Thomistic conception of human good can supply a more adequate determinateness in respect of rules and a more adequate specification of moral concerns, that contention too can be vindicated only insofar as it can be translated into the actualities of social life.

To say this is not of course to deny that any particular social embodiment of any particular standpoint about the goods, virtues and rules is always a more or less imperfect embodiment. But it is crucial to note that a central aspect of any such social embodiment is the institutionalization of standard responses to rule-breaking, whether mild or flagrant, and to what are taken to be vices and errors about the good; indeed without such responses there can be no adequate institutionalization of rule-observance or of the recognition of virtues or goods. So what would it be for us here now to give particularized social form to a Thomistic conception of the good and of those virtues the cultivation of which and those rules the observance of which are integral to the achievement of the good thus conceived? And how would that conception, when thus socially embodied, contrast with the actualities of recent liberalism? These are large questions and here I can only gesture toward them. But even such a gesture may be worthwhile. So let me focus attention on the same two issues which I identified as relevant to the critique of liberalism: truth-telling and lying, and the relationship of the young to the old.

Aquinas, like Augustine before him and Kant after him, but unlike John Chrysostom, Benjamin Constant and John Stuart Mill, held that lying is unconditionally and exceptionlessly prohibited. Not all lies are equally grave offenses, but all lying defects from what is required of us by the virtue of justice. If I lie to someone else, I fail to give to him or to her what is his or her due as a rational being. And since rational beings can only achieve their good and the good in and through a variety of social relationhsips, familial and political, informed by friendship, it follows that I both injure those relationships and put in crucial danger my relationship to the good whenever I lie. The virtue of justice and the rules of truth-telling, which partly specify that virtue, are not of course means external to the end toward which rational beings move; they are partially constitutive of that end. So that, if and when I lie, it is not that I have been inefficient in my choice of means to achieve my good; it is rather that I have temporarily at least put my good and the good out of mind and renounced them. And if someone lies to me, they have thereby affronted me by denying my status as a rational being, and ought to be responded to accordingly. There is no room for indeterminateness here, either in action or in response.

It is not of course possible to observe justice in speech merely by refraining from lying. No moral rule, no particular precept of the natural law, can be adequately understood in isolation from other such precepts or from that good, movement toward the achievment of which gives to obedience to such rules their point and purpose. Hence we always need to supply a good deal more than the statement of some particular rule itself supplies in order to understand that rule. What else is it then that we need to understand, if we are to make adequately intelligible the rule which prohibits lying, and to do so in such a way as to know how to institutionalize it in our practices?

Someone would certainly not have understood that rule adequately who supposed that, while we are required to speak and write truthfully, utterance in other respects can be allowed to be whatever we want it to be. It is to the place and purpose of utterance in human life as a whole that this rule is addressed. The ethics of conversation, as understood by Aquinas, is a complex matter and there are some important aspects of it with which I shall not be concerned here. Aquinas, for example, devotes no less than eight questions of the IIa–IIae of the *Summa* to types of use of language which sin against charity and justice, characteristically uses informed by either malice or negligence. And it is of course, on Aquinas's view, the adding of malice to lying which makes of lying a mortal sin. Nonetheless it is lying as such that is prohibited.

Moreover, Aquinas holds that the human good cannot be achieved without games, jokes and dramatic entertainment—even inaugural lectures perhaps—and failure either to engage in these, or to be responsive to and appreciative of others so engaging, is both vicious and sinful. So an institutionalization of any Thomistic conception of the moral and political life will have to be one which provides both for negative responses to malice and for positive responses to wit and to laughter. And once again such wit and laughter and the responses to them will, as Aquinas notes explicitly, have to be truthful. But what gives to this continuous insistence upon truthfulness its point?

A care for truth as a standard of rectitude in life, says Aquinas, following Jerome, is a constitutive part of all the virtues. And although truthfulness is a special virtue and an aspect of the virtue of justice (*Summa Theologiae* IIa-IIae 109, 2, 3) the detail of Aquinas's discussions makes it clear that all the virtues involve truthfulness as part of their exercise. For all the virtues, moral as well as intellectual, have to be developed throughout one's entire life, and this development requires a lifelong process of learning and imparting truths, learning in which reflection upon experience needs initially to be guided by teachers who enable one to learn from experience and so, later on in one's interactions with others, to contribute to their learning as well as to one's own, and in so doing to learn from them.

So mutual relationships of teaching and learning inform all well-ordered relationships and consistent truthfulness is therefore an essential ingredient of all such relationships. There is an informative analogy between the high value which the modern scientific community sets on truthfulness within the community of scientific enquirers, a value expressed in the penalties imposed upon those who falsify data, and the value which, on a Thomistic view, is to be set on truthfulness within any human community. For, on a Thomistic view, every human community is a community of practical enquiry, the subject-matter of whose enquiry consists of everything actually and potentially relevant to the relationship of the individuals who compose it and of the community itself to its and their good. Hence it is precisely as enquirers, as rational beings, that the truth is part of what we owe to one another. And this enquiry is lifelong, having at each particular stage of life its own peculiar tasks, tasks which involve the contribution which those at each such stage have to make both to each other and to those at other stages of life.

To spell out in full what this view of the relationships of those of different ages to each other involves would of course be an immense task, one in which Aristotle's brief, but illuminating remarks on this matter would have to be developed in a way appropriate to our own very different circumstances. But for the purposes of my present argument I need only consider two related implications of this standpoint. One is that we have to think of the old, those approaching and at retirement from earning their living, as both learners and teachers, as people who owe it to the young in a variety of ways to transmit what they have learned and are still learning. The grandparent and the great aunt and the elderly neighbor have to be once again thought of as teachers, so reconstituting one older type of family. How *are* they to do this? In part it will be through telling stories, in part through instructing in the performance of tasks, through making the past present and restoring those various links to the past which modern social mobility and the increasing brevity of the modern attention span all too often break.

Another implication is that we have to stop thinking of teaching and learning as activities restricted to specialized, compartmentalized areas of life within schools, colleges and universities. Of course schools, colleges and universities have their own highly specific tasks, but these tasks need to be defined in terms of their contribution to lifelong learning and teaching, most of it carried out in nonscholastic and nonacademic contexts. We need, that is, to think of formal academic education not primarily as a preparation for something else, a life of work, which terminates when that life of work begins, but rather as itself the beginning of, and the providing of skills, virtues and resources for, a lifelong education directed toward and informed by the achievement of the good.

We need, for example, to teach our students to read, so that they go on reading throughout their lives. We need to make such reading a way of illuminating their social relationships, so that their familial and communal lives continue to be enriched by a stock of common reading. We need to rethink the time-scale of education so that we make one of the tests of the adequacy of what we teach now the answer to the question: "What will our students be reading when they are forty, sixty, seventy-five?" and to accept that if they are not then returning to the *Republic* and the *Confessions,* to *Don Quixote* and Dostoievski and Borges, we will have failed as teachers.

It is within this kind of overall perspective that moral questions about truthfulness and moral questions about the relationship of the old to the young can be seen to be rationally answerable together or not at all. And this exemplifies what I have already suggested is true of moral questions in general, that we cannot expect anything but frustration from a problem by problem or issue by issue approach. To do so will be sterile just because adequately determinate moral rules can only be identified and characterized as parts of the specification of some particular overall conception of the human good and how it is to be achieved. Hence rational debate about what our shared moral rules are to be will always inescapably be also debate about the competing claims of rival conceptions of that good.

To this claim I have added another. It is that even such debate can still be sterile, if it is restricted to competing statements and arguments at the level of a theory which isolates itself from practice. The central weaknesses of recent liberalism are, on the view which I have advanced, only to be understood in the light of those in-stitutionalized practices of contemporary American society which give concrete and particularized expression to the present condition of liberalism. And correspondingly the strengths of an Aristotelian and Thomistic position will only become clear insofar as it too is seen to be embodied in particularized forms of practice in a variety of local modes of communal activity, in teaching and learning, in farming, in craftsmanship of various kinds. Debate and conflict as to the best forms of practice have to be debate and conflict between rival institutions and not merely between rival theories.

Not everyone who contributes to the making and sustaining of the type of practices and institutions which Aristotelianism and Thomism require will of course think of themselves as Aristotelian or Thomist. What, for exmple, Andrew Lytle and Wendell Berry, neither of whom thinks of himself as such, have written and done for the practices of farming and writing provide as good examples of what I am saying as any available. And to a Thomist this should not be in the least surprising. For it is Aquinas's view that rational persons, who are able to develop their practical rational-ity in undistorted ways, become natural Thomists without having had to read Aquinas. But in our culture—indeed in any culture—how relatively few of such persons there are!

The argument of this lecture began from reflections on the consequences for contemporary society of the modern liberal attempt to render our public shared morality independent of conceptions of the human good. I have tried to explain why this attempt is bound to fail, but indicating what kinds of argument would have to be developed and sustained in detail, both in theory and practice, to make an alternative view, one drawing upon Aristotle and Aquinas, rather than upon Hume and Kant and Mill, compelling. Notice however that the remaking and the sustaining of our own local institutions and practices, which, on the view which I have been developing, is a necessary first step in the transformation of public debate, let alone of public moral practice, are primarily activities wothwhile in themselves and immensely so, and only secondarily a means to further outcomes. As to whether we can even contrive a reopening of genuine public debate about rival conceptions of the good in contem-porary America, let alone bring such a debate to an effective conclusion, the evidence, as I understand it, suggests that we ought to be as deeply pessimistic as is compatible with a belief in Divine Providence. But as to that remaking of ourselves and our own local practices and institutions through a better understanding of what it is that, in an Aristotelian and Thomistic perspective, the unity of moral theory and practice now require of us, we have as much to hope for as we have to do, and not least within the community of this university.

20

Liberal Individualism and Liberal Neutrality

WILL KYMLICKA

A distinctive feature of contemporary liberal theory is its emphasis on "neutrality"—the view that the state should not reward or penalize particular conceptions of the good life but, rather, should provide a neutral framework within which different and potentially conflicting conceptions of the good can be pursued. Liberal neutrality has been criticized from many angles, but I will be concerned here only with the connection critics draw between neutrality and individualism, particularly in the context of Rawls's theory of justice. One of the most persistent criticisms of Rawls's theory is that it is excessively individualistic, neglecting the way that individual values are formed in social contexts and pursued through communal attachments. I will distinguish three different ways that critics have attempted to connect neutrality and individualism and argue that all rest on misinterpretations of Rawls's theory. However, there are important aspects of the relationship between individual values and social contexts which Rawls does not discuss, and I hope to show that the dispute over liberal neutrality would be more fruitful if both sides moved away from general questions of "individualism" toward more specific questions about the relationship between state, society, and culture in liberal democracies.

Defining Liberal Neutrality

What sort of neutrality is present, or aspired to, in Rawls's theory? Raz distinguishes two principles which he believes are present, and inadequately distinguished, in liberal writings on neutrality. One, which Raz calls "neutral political concern,"

From *Ethics,* vol. 99 (July 1989), 883–905. © 1989 by the University of Chicago. Reprinted by permission.

requires that the state seek to help or hinder different life-plans to an equal degree—that is, government action should have neutral consequences. The other, which Raz calls the "exclusion of ideals," allows that government action may help some ways of life more than others but denies that government should act in order to help some ways of life over others. The state does not take a stand on which ways of life are most worth living, and the desire to help one way of life over another is precluded as a justification of government action. The first requires neutrality in the consequences of government policy; the second requires neutrality in the justification of government policy. I will call these two conceptions consequential and justificatory neutrality, respectively.

Which conception does Rawls defend? Raz argues that Rawls endorses consequential neutrality,[1] and some of Rawls's formulations are undoubtedly consistent with that interpretation. But there are two basic tenets of Rawls's theory which show that he could not have endorsed consequential neutrality. First, respect for civil liberties will necessarily have nonneutral consequences. Freedom of speech and association allow different groups to pursue and advertise their way of life. But not all ways of life are equally valuable, and some will have difficulty attracting or maintaining adherents. Since individuals are free to choose between competing visions of the good life, civil liberties have nonneutral consequences—they create a marketplace of ideas, as it were, and how well a way of life does in this market depends on the kinds of goods it can offer to prospective adherents. Hence, under conditions of freedom, satisfying and valuable ways of life will tend to drive out those which are worthless and unsatisfying.

Rawls endorses such a cultural marketplace, despite its nonneutral consequences. Moreover, the prospect that trivial and degrading ways of life fare less well in free competition is not something he regrets or views as an unfortunate side effect. On the contrary, the liberal tradition has always endorsed civil liberties precisely because they make it possible "that the worth of different modes of life should be proved practically."[2]

Consequential neutrality is also inconsistent with Rawls's explanation of the role of "primary goods." They are supposed to be employable in the pursuit of diverse conceptions of the good. But not all ways of life have the same costs, and so an equal distribution of resources will have nonneutral consequences. Those who choose expensive ways of life—valuing leisure over work, or champagne over beer—will get less welfare out of an equal bundle of resources than will people with more modest tastes. This is unlike an equality of welfare scheme, in which those with expensive tastes would be subsidized by others in order to achieve equality of welfare. On an equality of welfare scheme, resources would be unequally distributed so that every way of life is equally helped, no matter how expensive—those who wish champagne get enough money for champagne.

Rawls favors equality of resources, despite its nonneutral consequences and, indeed, because it prohibits excess demands on resources by those with expensive desires:

> It is not by itself an objection to the use of primary goods that it does not accommodate those with expensive tastes. One must argue in addition that it is

unreasonable, if not unjust, to hold people responsible for their preferences and to require them to make out as best they can. But to argue this seems to presuppose that citizens' preferences are beyond their control as propensities or cravings which simply happen. Citizens seem to be regarded as passive carriers of desires. The use of primary goods, however, relies on a capacity to assume responsibility for our ends. This capacity is part of the moral power to form, to revise, and rationally to pursue a conception of the good. . . . In any particular situation, then, those with less expensive tastes have presumably adjusted their likes and dislikes over the course of their lives to the income and wealth they could reasonably expect; and it is regarded as unfair that they now should have less in order to spare others from the consequences of their lack of foresight or self-discipline.[3]

Since individuals are responsible for forming "their aims and ambitions in the light of what they can reasonably expect," they recognize that "the weight of their claims is not given by the strength or intensity of their wants and desires."[4] Those people who have developed expensive tastes in disregard of what they can reasonably expect have no claim to be subsidized by others, no matter how strongly felt those desires are.[5]

So the two fundamental components of liberal justice—respect for liberty and fairness in the distribution of material resources—both preclude consequential neutrality. However ambiguous his terminology is, Rawls has to be interpreted as endorsing justificatory neutrality.[6] As Rawls puts it, government is neutral between different conceptions of the good, "not in the sense that there is an agreed public measure of intrinsic value or satisfaction with respect to which all these conceptions come out equal, but in the sense that they are not evaluated at all from a social standpoint."[7] The state does not justify its actions by reference to some public ranking of the intrinsic value of different ways of life, for there is no public ranking to refer to. This kind of neutrality is consistent with the legitimate nonneutral consequences of cultural competition and individual responsibility. Indeed, and I'll return to this point, one might think that good ways of life are most likely to establish their greater worth, and individuals are most likely to accept responsibility for the costs of their choices, when the state is constrained by justificatory neutrality—that is, when individuals cannot "use the coercive apparatus of the state to win for themselves a greater liberty or larger distributive share on the grounds that their activities are of more intrinsic value."[8]

Neutrality and Possessive Individualism

I now want to consider three versions of the claim that liberal neutrality, as envisioned by Rawls, is excessively individualistic. The first version, advanced separately by Schwartz and Nagel shortly after the publication of *A Theory of Justice*, focuses on the content of people's aims and ambitions. Rawls claims that a state which gives each individual the largest possible share of resources and liberties to pursue their disparate ends, consistent with the claim of others to an equal share, lives up to the requirements of justificatory neutrality. But, according to Schwartz and Nagel, this presupposes a kind of possessive individualist theory of human motivation. It suggests that what people want in life is to maximize their share of social resources (rather than promote the good of others), and indeed to maximize their material good (rather than promote their spiritual or emotional well-being). Such a theory of motivation may suit the self-seeking and materialistic culture of contemporary capitalist cultures, but it penalizes those who value other ends. "Consider a socialist somewhat in the lines of the early Marx. This individual believes that a good life must rest on self-realization through labor . . . and that a person is morally harmed by the possession of more than a certain minimal amount of wealth."[9] Such a socialist will claim "that his good is furthered by just enough wealth so that he is decently fed, housed, and clothed" and that

> he would be harmed by living in a society based on a preference for a greater rather than a lesser amount of wealth. He could say that living in such a society he would devote valuable time to thinking about material wealth and trying to decide whether or not to avoid the temptation of attempting to acquire more possessions. . . . In addition, the socialist could claim that a system based on a preference for a greater amount of wealth would be against his interest since it would prevent him from forming strong ties of affection with other human beings. He could claim that, in such a system, people would tend to be more interested in wealth than in other people.[10]

Now this might seem at first glance to be attacking the idea of consequential neutrality, since Schwartz emphasizes that not all ways of life will fare equally well in a Rawlsian society. But the objection is not simply that communal ways of life will fare less well. After all, they might fare badly, not because primary goods are less useful for communal ways of life, but simply because most people choose not to use them for that purpose. Rather, the claim is that primary goods (beyond a certain point) are only useful for individualistic ends, and so Rawls's demand that society aim to increase the share of primary goods available to individuals reflects a decision that individualistic ways of life should be promoted at the expense of nonindividualistic ways of life, a decision which violates justificatory neutrality. The problem is not simply that communal ways of life do less well but, rather, that the reason they do less well is that Rawls's account of primary goods is arbitrarily and unfairly biased against them, since that account is based on (nonneutral) assumptions about people's individualistic aims.[11]

But this critique misinterprets Rawls's justification for the importance of primary goods.[12] Rawls does not assume anything like a possessive individualist theory of motivation. On the contrary, one of the things that people can do, and indeed are expected to do, with their resources and liberties is to join or create meaningful associations and attachments, including spiritual and emotional ones. Schwartz claims that material resources (above a certain minimum) are not useful in the pursuit of nonmaterialistic ends, and so Rawls's primary goods scheme is biased against the socialist who sees the good life as self-realization through labor and views material wealth as positively harmful. But Schwartz's discussion here is far too quick. The socialist needs resources in order to pursue a life of self-realizing labor—she needs access to land or other raw materials and to the technology which enables work to be creative and variable rather than merely onerous and repetitive. Someone who only has enough wealth to be decently clothed has no way to ensure that her labor is self-realizing, since the conditions under which she works will be determined by the exigencies of nature or by the aims of those who own the land and tools. Even if she wishes to live in harmony with nature and use only simple tools and techniques (perhaps the socialist is converted to deep ecology), she must still have control over resources. The desire to keep an ecological habitat in its natural condition requires restrictions on the way other people use not only the immediate habitat but also the surrounding land, air, and water. These nonindividualistic and nonmaterialistic ways of life require that substantial amounts of social resources be set aside for their purposes. It is entirely wrong to suppose that the less materialistic someone is, the less of an interest she has in Rawls's primary goods.[13]

Indeed, it is difficult to imagine a variable way of life which is genuinely harmed by, or even indifferent to, increases in the availability of material resources. One would not need resources if there was nothing in one's life which could go better or worse, nothing which would count as success or failure in the pursuit of one's goals. But so long as there are things that matter in one's life, things that are worth defending and promoting, then there will be threats to the promotion of those values. Resources help one to exercise some control over the social and natural environment, and hence control the direction and consequences of those environments for the pursuit of one's values.

There may be some ways of life which are not aided by increased amounts of Rawls's primary goods. Rawls cites the case of religious lifestyles which include a vow of personal poverty, although that too may be a little quick. Monks committed to personal asceticism often belong to monastic orders that have large land holdings, revenues from which help pay for the land, buildings, and maintenance of their community and which are used in promoting their good works. Moreover, the vow of poverty is often understood as a renunciation of their legitimate entitlements under a theory of fairness, not, as Schwartz and Nagel require, a renunciation of things which they think should not be part of a legitimate theory of fairness. In any event, such examples do not show that access to primary goods harms these ways of life, or favors individualistic and materialistic ways of life.[14]

Rawls's emphasis on what individuals are entitled to may seem misplaced for people who deploy their resources in group relations and activities. But a theory of individual entitlement is required, even for communally oriented people, because it teaches each person what is available for the pursuit of their attachments. As Dworkin says, "We are free to make decisions [about our attachments] with respect to the resources that are properly assigned to us in the first instance, though not, of course, to dispose in this way of resources that have been assigned, or rather are properly assignable, to others. Equality enters our plans by teaching us what is available to us, to deploy in accordance with our attachments and other concerns."[15] Rawls invokes a standard of individual entitlement, not because of an individualistic theory of motivation, but because of his principle of individual responsibility. If people are to be legitimately held responsible for any expensive aims and attachments they may have, then there must be a standard of individual entitlement in the light of which they can adjust those aims.

This requirement of justice holds just as much for communally oriented people as for materialistic people. Communally oriented socialists can have expensive desires. The Marxian socialist wants a piece of land on which to labor cooperatively so as to "humanize" the natural world.[16] But the naturalist wants the same land left unhumanized, and the monk wants it for sacred purposes, to build a community that will honor God. Each of these aims has costs for other people, who must forgo their aims with respect to that land. It is naive to expect that the desired land will automatically be available for one's preferred purposes, and it is selfish to demand that it be automatically available. The test of what is properly available for the pursuit of these ends is given by the difference principle. The naturalist may want more resources set aside than is allotted him under the difference principle, but he is responsible for adjusting his claims to the rightful claims of others, and to demand excess resources for his naturalist aims would be just as unfair as it would be for a materialistic person to demand excess resources in order to purchase consumer goods. The nonindividualistic content of their aims does not excuse socialists or naturalists from taking into account the legitimate claims of others.

Schwartz and Nagel might accept that we should take into account the cost of our choices for other people but claim that the problem with Rawls's theory is that the costs are assessed in a biased way, since a Rawlsian society produces people whose basic preference is for more wealth. Costs would be assessed differently in a society that is designed to produce socialist individuals: the socialist's desire for land would not be as costly, since fewer people would have conflicting desires.

But while it is true that Rawls's theory makes the costs of a particular choice dependent on the extent to which other people's aims coincide or conflict, that does not show that the primary goods scheme is biased against communal ways of life. For the extent to which other people share one's ends will depend on the judgments the others freely make when considering the various ways of life available to them. If socialists are unable to convince others of the worth of that way of life, then it will be difficult to acquire the resources necessary to start up a socialist community. On the other hand, if materialists are unable to convince people of the value of a high income and a consumer life-style, then they will have difficulty attracting people to choose income over leisure, or monotonous but productive labor over enjoyable but less productive labor. These are indeed problems which materialists have faced when promoting consumerism in various cultures, and Marx predicted that they will reoccur when people can acquire a decent standard of living in a shortened workday. Rawlsian neutrality does not prejudge the relative value of self-realizing labor and consumer goods, and the relative difficulty of pursuing these different ways of life is determined by the choices the members of a given society freely make at a given moment. Schwartz and Nagel do not explain how socialists are disadvantaged by this arrangement, or why their choices should be subsidized regardless of how costly they are for others, and regardless of how attractive the members of a society find that way of life. As Rawls says, communal ends that cannot flourish under this arrangement should not "be upheld by the coercive apparatus of the state. If socially collective communitarian aims could survive in no other way, why should we regret their demise, and consider the original position unfair and biased against them?"[17]

Schwartz and Nagel note that socialists are disadvantaged by Rawlsian neutrality in contrast to a society which is designed to produce as many socialists as possible. But every way of life would do better in a society designed to ensure that no one had conflicting preferences. That does not establish a legitimate grievance, since no one has the right that other people be socialized so as to best fit one's own way of life (other people are not resources to be distributed or molded so as to promote one's ends). Fairness for the adherents of different ways of life requires that people be guaranteed a fair share of resources to pursue their way of life, and the freedom to seek out new adherents. It does not require that each way of life be guaranteed a certain number of adherents, and indeed fairness precludes treating people as resources to be distributed or molded so that each way of life fares equally well. The question is whether socialists are disadvantaged by Rawls's scheme with respect to the things which they have a legitimate claim to—that is, resources and liberties, but not other people's preferences—and Schwartz and Nagel do not establish this.[18]

One respect in which communally oriented people may be disadvantaged is that they must coordinate the deployment of resources distributed to individuals, and this coordination involves costs and effort that individualistic people avoid. Communally oriented people would prefer that resources be distributed directly to groups and then allow individualistic people to withdraw their resources from the group (this would involve costs for individualistic people that communally oriented people avoid). This problem would be solved if there were mechanisms for communally oriented people to receive benefits communally and for individualistic people to receive benefits individually. And this is indeed what Rawls endorses. He proposes that one branch of the state be organized so as to facilitate such coordination.[19] Rawls would not object if various marital and cultural groups pay taxes, and receive benefits, collectively, where the members have so agreed.

It is true that any collective provision of benefits requires the ongoing consent of individuals. But this requirement reflects Rawls's commitment to autonomy, not any commitment to individualistic aims. According to the "ideal of the person" underlying Rawls's theory, individuals "do not regard themselves as inevitably bound to, or identical with, the pursuit of any particular complex of fundamental interests that they may have at any given moment."[20] People are capable not simply of pursuing their given ends, but also of reflecting on the value of those ends, considering alternatives, and revising even their most deeply held beliefs about what is worthwhile in life:

As free persons, citizens recognize one another as having the moral power to have a conception of the good. This means that they do not view themselves as inevitably tied to the pursuit of the particular conception of the good and its final ends which they espouse at any given time. Instead, as citizens, they are regarded as, in general, capable of revising and changing this conception on reasonable and rational grounds. Thus it is held to be permissible for citizens to stand apart from conceptions of the good and to survey and assess their various final ends.[21]

According to Rawls, this ability for autonomous choice is one of our two fundamental moral powers, and respect for autonomy requires that individuals retain the right to opt out of any particular communal practice (and corresponding communal provision of benefits). Hence Rawls's two principles of justice are designed to ensure that individuals can "stand apart" from their current ends—the liberties and resources distributed by Rawls's two principles do not preempt or penalize the attempt by individuals to form and revise their conceptions of the good, or to acquire the information needed to make those judgments rationally and intelligently. Since individuals can come to question their ends, they must have access to resources which are flexible, which can be translated into the goods and services appropriate for other ways of life, including, of course, other communal ways of life.[22]

Rawls's commitment to the importance of primary goods, therefore, is not evidence of possessive individualism, but rather of two distinct ideas: (a) our way of life should reflect our autonomous choice, and so the resources available to us must be flexible; and (b) we are responsible for the costs of our choices, and hence there must be some standard which teaches us what is available to us to use in accordance with our attachments. Neither of these is primarily concerned with the content of people's ends. Rather they concern the relationship between the individual and her ends—and individual's ends are not fixed or imposed by others but, rather, are the objects of her autonomous and responsible choice.

Neutrality and Atomistic Individualism

The second and third versions of the claim that neutrality is excessively individualistic accept Rawls's emphasis on the capacity for autonomous choice. But autonomous choices are only possible in certain contexts, and these two objections claim that liberal neutrality is incapable of ensuring the existence and flourishing of that context. While both objections attribute this failure of neutrality to a certain kind of atomistic individualism, they locate the failure in different places—the second objection centers on the need for a shared cultural structure that provides individuals with meaningful options, and the third centers on the need for shared forums in which to evaluate these options.

Neutrality and a Pluralist Culture

The second objection claims that liberal neutrality is incapable of guaranteeing the existence of a pluralistic culture which provides people with the range of options necessary for meaningful individual choice. Autonomy requires pluralism, but "any collective attempt by a liberal state to protect pluralism would itself be in breach of liberal principles of justice. The state is not entitled to interfere in the movement of the cultural market place except, of course, to ensure that each individual has a just share of available necessary means to exercise his or her moral powers. The welfare or demise of particular conceptions of the good and, therefore, the welfare or demise of social unions of a particular character is not the business of the state."[23] The state is not allowed to protect pluralism, yet if the cultural marketplace proceeds on its own it will eventually undermine the cultural structure which supports pluralism. Neutrality may ensure that government does not denigrate a way of life that some individuals think is worthy of support, but, "whatever else can be said about this argument one point is decisive. Supporting valuable ways of life is a social rather than an individual matter . . . perfectionist ideals require public action for their viability. Anti-perfectionism in practice would lead not merely to a political stand-off from support for valuable conceptions of the good. It would undermine the chances of survival of many cherished aspects of our culture."[24] The problem, then, is not that liberal neutrality fails to achieve its aim of genuine neutrality (as the possessive individualism objection claimed) but, rather, that neutrality undermines the very conditions in which it is a worthwhile aim.

Liberal neutrality is therefore self-defeating. There seem to be two possible ways out of this dilemma. One is to deny that the value of autonomous choice depends on a viable and flourishing culture. This is the "atomist" route which accepts "the utterly facile moral psychology of traditional empiricism,"[25] according to which an individual's capacity for meaningful choice is self-sufficient outside of society and culture. This route is inadequate, since our dependence on the cultural structure for worthwhile ways of life is undeniable, and few if any liberals have ever been "concerned purely with individual choices . . . to the neglect of the matrix in which such choices can be open or closed, rich or meagre."[26]

The second response is to accept that meaningful autonomous choice requires a viable culture but insist that good ways of life will sustain themselves in the cultural marketplace without state assistance.[27] But this too is an inadequate response. In conditions of freedom, people are able to assess and recognize the worth of good ways of life and will support them. But the interests people have in a good way of life, and the forms of support they will voluntarily provide, do not necessarily involve sustaining its existence for future generations. My interest in a valuable social practice may be best promoted by depleting the resources which the practice requires to survive beyond my lifetime. Even if the cultural marketplace can be relied on to ensure that existing people can identify valuable ways of life, there is no reason to assume that it can be relied on to ensure that future people have a valuable range of options.

So let us grant Raz's argument that state support may be needed to ensure the survival of an adequate range of options for those who have not yet formed their aims in life. Why does that require rejecting neutrality? Consider two possible cultural policies. In the first case, the government ensures an adequate range of options by providing tax credits to individuals who make culture-supporting contributions in accordance with their personal perfectionist ideals. The state acts to ensure that there is an adequate range of options, but the evaluation of these options occurs in civil society, outside the coercive apparatus of the state.[28] In the second case, the evaluation of different conceptions of the good becomes a political question, and the government intervenes, not simply to ensure an adequate range of options, but to promote particular options. Now Raz's argument simply does not address this choice. What is "decisive" in Raz's argument is that one or the other of these policies must be implemented, but he has not given a decisive reason, or any reason at all, to prefer one policy over the other.

A perfectionist state might hope to improve the quality of people's options by encouraging the replacement of less valuable options by more valuable ones. But it is worth repeating that liberal neutrality also hopes to improve the range of options, and the cultural marketplace is valued because it helps good ways of life displace bad. Each side aims to secure and improve the range of options from which individuals make their autonomous choices. What they disagree on is where perfectionist values and arguments should be invoked. Are good ways of life more likely to establish their greater worth when they are evaluated in the cultural marketplace of civil society, or when the preferability of different ways of life is made a matter of political advocacy and state action? Hence the dispute should perhaps be seen as a choice, not between perfectionism and neutrality, but between social perfectionism and state perfectionism—for the flip side of state neutrality is support for the role of perfectionist ideals and arguments in civil society.[29]

Neutrality and Collective Deliberations

The third and final objection accepts that liberal neutrality recognizes the necessity of having a secure cultural structure. But it claims that a different sort of atomistic individualism is found in the liberal account of how cultural options should be evaluated. The liberal preference for the cultural marketplace over the state as the appropriate arena for evaluating different life-styles stems from an individualistic belief that judgments about the good should be made by isolated individuals, whose autonomy is ensured by protecting them from social pressures. Liberals think that autonomy is promoted when judgments about the good are taken out of the political realm. But in reality individual judgments require the sharing of experiences and the give and take of collective deliberations. Individual judgments about the good always depend on, and flow from, the collective evaluation of shared practices. They become a matter of purely subjective and arbitrary whim if they are cut off from collective deliberations:

> Self-fulfillment and even the working out of personal identity and a sense of orientation in the world depend upon a communal enterprise. This shared process is the civic life, and its root is involvement with others: other generations, other sorts of persons whose differences are significant because they contribute to the whole upon which our particular sense of self depends. Thus mutual

interdependency is the foundational notion of citizenship . . . outside a linguistic community of shared practices, there would be biological *homo sapiens* as logical abstraction, but there could not be human beings. This is the meaning of the Greek and medieval dictum that the political community is ontologically *prior* to the individual. The polis is, literally, that which makes man, as human being, possible.[30]

Or, as Crowley puts it, state perfectionism is "an affirmation of the notion that men living in a community of shared experiences and language is the only context in which the individual and society can discover and test their values through the essentially political activities of discussion, criticism, example, and emulation. It is through the existence of organised public spaces, in which men offer and test ideas against one another . . . that men come to understand a part of who they are."[31] The state should be the proper arena in which to formulate and pursue our visions of the good, because the good for individuals requires collective interaction and inquiry— it cannot be pursued or even known, presocially.

But this misconstrues the sense in which Rawls claims that the evaluation of ways of life should not be a public concern. Liberal neutrality does not restrict the scope of perfectionist ideals in the collective activities of individuals and groups. Perfectionist ideals, although excluded from a liberal state, "have an important place in human affairs," and, hence, an important place in a liberal society.[32] Collective activity and shared experiences concerning the good are at the heart of the "free internal life of the various communities of interests in which persons and groups seek to achieve, in modes of social union consistent with equal liberty, the ends and excellences to which they are drawn."[33] Rawls's argument for the priority of liberty is grounded in the importance of this "free social union with others."[34] He simply denies that "the coercive apparatus of the state" is an appropriate forum for those deliberations and experiences: "While justice as fairness allows that in a well-ordered society the values of excellence are recognized, the human perfections are to be pursued within the limits of the principle of free association. . . . [Persons] do not use the coercive apparatus of the state to win for themselves a greater liberty or larger distributive shares on the grounds that their activities are of more intrinsic value."[35]

Unfortunately, civic republicans, who make this objection most frequently, rarely distinguish between collective activities and political activities. It is of course true that participation in shared linguistic and cultural practices is what enables individuals to make intelligent decisions about the good life. But why should such participation be organized in and through the state, rather than through the free association of individuals? It is true that we should "create opportunities for men to give voice to what they have discovered about themselves and the world and to persuade others of its worth."[36] But a liberal society does create opportunities for people to express and develop these social aspects of individual deliberation. After all, freedom of assembly, association, and speech are fundamental *liberal* rights. The opportunities for collective inquiry simply occur within and between groups and associations below the level of the state—friends and family, in the first instance, but also churches, cultural associations, professional groups and trade unions, universities, and the mass media. These are some of the "organized public spaces of appearance" and "communication communities" of a liberal society.[37] Liberals do not deny that "the public display of character and judgment and the exchange of experience and insight" are needed to make intelligent judgments about the good, or to show others that I "hold [my] notion of the good responsibly."[38] Indeed, these claims fit comfortably in many liberal discussions of the value of free speech and association.[39] What the liberal denies is that I should have to give such an account of myself *to the state*.

A similar failure to confront the distinctive role of the state weakens radical critiques of liberalism, like that of Habermas. Habermas, in his earlier writings at least, wants the evaluation of different ways of life to be a political question, but unlike communitarians and civic republicans, he does not hope or expect that this political deliberation will serve to promote people's embeddedness in existing practices.[40] Indeed, he thinks that political deliberation is required precisely because in its absence people will tend to accept existing practices as givens and thereby perpetuate the false needs and false consciousness which accompany those historical practices.[41] Only when existing ways of life are "the objects of discursive will-formation," can people's understanding of the good be free of deception. Rawls's view of distributive justice does not demand the scrutiny of these practices and, hence, does not recognize the emancipatory interest people have in escaping false needs and ideological distortions.

But why should the evaluation of people's conceptions of the good be tied to their claims on resources, and hence to the state apparatus? Communities smaller than the entire political society, groups and associations of various sizes, might be more appropriate forums for those forms of discursive will formation which involve evaluating the good and interpreting one's genuine needs. While Habermas rejects the communitarian tendency to uncritically endorse existing social practices as the basis for political deliberations about the good, he shares their tendency to assume that anything which is not politically deliberated is thereby left to an individual will incapable of rational judgment.

So the liberal commitment to state neutrality does not manifest abstract individualism either in regard to the importance of a shared cultural context for meaningful individual options, or in regard to the importance of the sharing of experiences and arguments for meaningful individual evaluation of those options. Liberal neutrality does not deny these shared social requirements of individual autonomy but, rather, provides an interpretation of them.

Evaluating the Neutrality Debate

I have argued that liberal neutrality is not excessively individualistic, either in terms of the way it conceives the content of people's ends, or in the way that people evaluate and pursue those ends. Of course neutrality may be indefensible for other reasons. Neutrality requires a certain faith in the operation of nonstate forums and processes for individual judgment and cultural development, and a distrust of the operation of state forums and processes for evaluating the good. Nothing I have said so far shows that this optimism and distrust are warranted. Indeed, just as critics of neutrality have failed to defend their faith in political forums and procedures, so liberals have failed to defend their faith in nonstate forums and procedures. The crucial claims have not been adequately defended by either side.

In fact, it is hard to avoid the conclusion that each side in the neutrality debate has failed to learn the important lesson taught by the other side. Despite centuries of liberal insistence on the importance of the distinction between society and the state, communitarians still seem to assume that whatever is properly social must become the province of the political. They have not confronted the liberal worry that the all-embracing authority and coercive means which characterize the state make it a particularly inappropriate forum for the sort of genuinely shared deliberation and commitment that they desire. Despite centuries of communitarian insistence on the historically fragile and contingent nature of our culture, and the need to consider the conditions under which a free culture can arise and sustain itself, liberals still tend to take the existence of a tolerant and diverse culture for granted, as something which naturally arises and sustains itself, the ongoing existence of which is therefore simply assumed in a theory of justice. Hegel was right to insist that a culture of freedom is a historical achievement, and liberals need to explain why the cultural marketplace does not threaten that achievement either by failing to connect people in a strong enough way to their communal practices (as communitarians fear), or conversely, by failing to detach people in a strong enough way from the expectations of existing practices and ideologies (as Habermas fears). A culture of freedom requires a mix of both exposure and connection to existing practices, and also distance and dissent from them. Liberal neutrality may provide that mix, but that is not obviously true, and it may be true only in some times and places. So both sides need to give us a more comprehensive comparison of the opportunities and dangers present in state and nonstate forums and procedures for evaluating the good.

While both sides have something to learn from the other, that is not to say that the truth is somewhere in between the two. I cannot provide here the sort of systematic comparison of the empirical operation of state and nonstate forums and procedures that is required for a proper defense of neutrality, but I want to suggest a few reasons why state perfectionism would have undesirable consequences for our society. I will assume, for the moment, that the public ranking of the value of different ways of life which a perfectionist state appeals to would be arrived at through the collective political deliberation of citizens, rather than through the secret or unilateral decisions of political elites.

What are the consequences of having a collectively determined ranking of the value of different conceptions of the good? One consequence is that more is at stake when people publicly formulate and defend their conception of the good. If people do not advance persuasive arguments for their conception of the good, then a perfectionist state may take action which will make their way of life harder to maintain.

In a liberal society with a neutral state, on the other hand, people who cannot persuade others of the value of their way of life will lose out in the competition with other conceptions of the good being advanced in the cultural marketplace, but they will not face adverse state action.

Why is that an undesirable consequence? In principle, it is not undesirable—it may simply intensify the patterns of cultural development, since the pros and cons of different ways of life might be revealed more quickly under the threat of state action than would occur in the cultural marketplace, where people are sometimes reluctant to confront opposing values and arguments. However, I believe that state perfectionism would in fact serve to distort the free evaluation of ways of life, to rigidify the dominant ways of life, whatever their intrinsic merits, and to unfairly exclude the values and aspirations of marginalized and disadvantaged groups within the community.

First, state perfectionism raises the prospect of a dictatorship of the articulate and would unavoidably penalize those individuals who are inarticulate. But being articulate, in our society, is not simply an individual variable. There are many culturally disadvantaged groups whose beliefs and aspirations are not understood by the majority. Recent immigrants are an obvious example whose disadvantage is partly unavoidable. But there are also groups which have been deliberately excluded from the mainstream of American society, and whose cultural disadvantage reflects prejudice and insensitivity. The dominant cultural practices of our community were defined by one section of the population—that is, the male members of the upper classes of the white race—and were defined so as to exclude and denigrate the values of subordinate groups. Members of these excluded groups—women, blacks, Hispanics—have been unable to get recognition for their values from the cultural mainstream and have developed (or retained) subcultures for the expression of these values, subcultures whose norms, by necessity, are incommensurable with those of the mainstream. It is unfair to ask them to defend the value of their way of life by reference to cultural standards and norms that were defined by and for others. Even where these historical factors are absent, the majority is likely to use state perfectionism to block valuable social change that threatens their preferred cultural practices. This cultural conservatism need not be malicious—the majority may simply not see the value of cultural change, partly due to incomprehension, partly from fear of change.

State perfectionism would also affect the kinds of arguments given. Minority groups whose values conflict with those of the majority often put a high value on the integrity of their practices and aim at gaining adherents from within the majority slowly, one by one. But where there is state perfectionism, the minority must immediately aim at persuading the majority, and so they will describe their practices in such a way as to be most palatable to the majority, even if that misdescribes the real meaning and value of the practice, which often arose precisely in opposition to dominant practices. There would be an inevitable tendency for minorities to describe and debate conceptions of the good in terms of dominant values, which then reinforces the cultural conservatism of the dominant group itself.

In these and other ways, the threats and inducements of coercive power would

distort rather than improve the process of individual judgment and cultural development. Some of these problems also arise in the cultural marketplace (i.e., penalizing
the inarticulate, social prejudice). Insensitivity and prejudice will be problems no
matter which model we choose, since both models reward those groups who can
make their way of life attractive to the mainstream. But state perfectionism intensifies
these problems, since it dictates to minority groups when and how they will interact
with majority norms, and it dictates a time and place— political deliberation over
state policy—in which minorities are most vulnerable. State neutrality, on the other
hand, gives culturally disadvantaged groups a greater ability to choose the time and
place in which they will confront majority sensitivities and to choose an audience
with whom they are most comfortable. There will always be an imbalance in the
interaction between culturally dominant and subordinate groups. State neutrality
ensures that the culturally subordinate group has as many options as possible
concerning that interaction, and that the costs of that imbalance for the subordinate
groups are minimized. State perfectionism, I think, does just the opposite.

Some of these problems could be avoided if the public ranking of ways of life was
determined by political elites, insulated from popular debate and prejudice. Indeed,
an enlightened and insulated political elite could use state perfectionist policies to
promote the aims and values of culturally disadvantaged groups. Just as the Supreme
Court is supposed to be more able to protect the rights of disadvantaged groups
because of its insulation from political pressures, so an insulated political elite may
be able to give a fairer hearing to minority values than they get in the cultural
marketplace. But this raises troubling questions about accountability and the danger
of abuse (after all, if majority groups are insensitive to minority aspirations, why
won't they elect leaders who are similarly insensitive?). And, in any event, why
shouldn't the aim of the political elite be to counteract the biases of the cultural
marketplace, which affect the public evaluation of all minority values, rather than
deciding for themselves which minority values are worth promoting? Using state
power to counteract biases against minority values may be legitimate, not because of
a general principle of perfectionism, but because of a general principle of redressing
biases against disadvantaged groups.

These are some of the reasons why liberals distrust state perfectionism for our
society.[42] Communitarians are right to insist that we examine the history and
structure of a particular culture, but it is remarkable how little communitarians
themselves undertake such an examination of our culture. They wish to use the ends
and practices of our cultural tradition as the basis for a politics of the common good,
but they do not mention that these practices were historically defined by a small
segment of the population, nor do they discuss how the exclusionary history would
affect the politicization of debates about the value of different ways of life. If we look
at the history of our society, surely liberal neutrality has the great advantage of its
potential inclusiveness, its denial that marginalized and subordinate groups must fit
into the historical practices, the "way of life," which have been defined by the
dominant groups. Forcing subordinate groups to defend their ways of life, under
threat or promise of coercive power, is inherently exclusive. Communitarians simply
ignore this danger and the cultural history which makes it so difficult to avoid.[43]

While liberalism need not be committed to neutrality in all times and places, the relationship between the culture and the state in our society makes neutrality particularly appropriate for us. However, certain features of that relationship also make neutrality particularly difficult to implement. I have discussed different ways a neutral state might protect and promote its culture. But if we look at actual states and actual cultures, we will quickly notice that most liberal democracies contain more than one cultural community. Most countries contain many cultures, like the French, English, and aboriginal cultures in Canada. When we say that the cultural context can be enriched or diminished, whose culture are we discussing? Whose language should be used in the schools and courts and media? If immigration policy should give consideration to the consequences of immigration on the cultural structure, as most liberals have agreed, then shouldn't we accept demands by Francophones in Quebec, or the Inuit in Northern Canada, to have some control over immigration into their cultural communities? What does liberal neutrality require when the state contains more than one culture?

The dominant view among contemporary liberals, to which Rawls apparently subscribes, is that liberalism requires the "absence, even prohibition, of any legal or governmental recognition of racial, religious, language or [cultural] groups as corporate entities with a standing in the legal or governmental process, and a prohibition of the use of ethnic criteria of any type for discriminatory purposes, or conversely for special or favored treatment."[44] But this view, which achieved its current prominence during the American struggle against racial segregation, has only limited applicability. Once we recognize the importance of the cultural structure and accept that there is a positive duty of the state to protect the cultural conditions which allow for autonomous choice, then cultural membership does have political salience. Respect for the autonomy of the members of minority cultures requires respect for their cultural structure, and that in turn may require special linguistic, educational, and even political rights for minority cultures. Indeed, there are a number of circumstances in which liberal theories of equality should recognize the special status of minority cultures (as prewar liberal theories often did).[45] The attempt to answer questions about the rights of cultural communities with the formula of color-blind laws applying to persons of all races and cultures is hopelessly inadequate once we look at the diversity of cultural membership which exists in contemporary liberal democracies.[46] However, the alternatives have rarely been considered in contemporary liberal writings, which are dominated (often unconsciously) by the model of the nation-state.[47]

Conclusion

The real issue concerning neutrality is not individualism: nothing in Rawls's insistence on state neutrality is inconsistent with recognizing the importance of the social world to the development, deliberation, and pursuit of individuals' values. It is commonly alleged that liberals fail to recognize that people are naturally social or communal beings. Liberals supposedly think that society rests on an artificial social contract, and that a coercive state apparatus is needed to keep naturally asocial people together in society. But there is a sense in which the opposite is true—liberals believe that people naturally form and join social relations and forums in which they come to understand and pursue the good. The state is not needed to provide that communal context and is likely to distort the normal processes of collective deliberations and cultural development. It is communitarians who seem to think that individuals will drift into anomic and detached isolation without the state actively bringing them together to collectively evaluate and pursue the good.[48]

The question is not whether individuals' values and autonomy need to be situated in social relations but whether the relevant relations are necessarily or desirably political ones. This should be the real issue in debates over neutrality, and settling that issue requires a closer examination of the relationship between society, culture, and the state than either defenders or critics have so far provided.

Notes

1. Joseph Raz, *The Morality of Freedom* (Oxford: Oxford University Press, 1986), p. 117.

2. J. S. Mill, *On Liberty,* ed. David Spitz (New York: Norton, 1975), p. 54.

3. John Rawls, "Social Unity and Primary Goods," in *Utilitarianism and Beyond,* ed. Amartya Sen and Bernard Williams (Cambridge: Cambridge University Press, 1982), pp. 168–69; see also Rawls, "Fairness to Goodness," *Philosophical Review* 84 (1975): 553.

4. John Rawls, "Kantian Constructivism in Moral Theory: The Dewey Lectures 1980," *Journal of Philosophy* 77 (1980): 545.

5. This principle of responsibility is also central to Dworkin's equality of resources scheme: the cost to others of the resources we claim should "figure in each person's sense of what is rightly his and in each person's judgment of what life he should lead, given that command of justice" (Ronald Dworkin, "What Is Equality? Part 2," *Philosophy and Public Affairs* 10 [1981]: 289). Indeed, Dworkin's scheme does a better job than Rawls's difference principle of distinguishing the costs that people are responsible for from the costs that are an unchosen part of people's circumstances. Some people argue that an accurate assessment of individual responsibility requires going beyond primary goods or equality of resources to "equal opportunity for welfare" (Richard Arneson, "Equality and Equal Opportunity for Welfare," *Philosophical Studies* 55 [1989]: 79–95, or "equal access to advantage" (G. A. Cohen, "On the Currency of Egalitarian Justice," *Ethics,* in this issue). While these critiques of Rawls's account of primary goods are important, they are not moves away from justificatory neutrality.

6. Although I cannot argue the point here, I believe that the other major statements of liberal neutrality must similarly be interpreted as endorsing justificatory neutrality—e.g., Bruce Ackerman, *Social Justice in the Liberal State* (New Haven, Conn.: Yale University Press, 1980), pp. 11, 61; Charles Larmore, *Patterns of Moral Complexity* (Cambridge: Cambridge University Press, 1987), chap. 3, esp. pp. 44–47; Ronald Dworkin, "Liberalism," in *Public and Private Morality,* ed. Stuart Hampshire (Cambridge: Cambridge University Press, 1978), p. 127, and *A Matter of Principle* (London: Harvard University Press, 1985), p. 222; Robert Nozick, *Anarchy, State and Utopia* (New York: Basic, 1974), pp. 272–73 (for an extended exegetical discussion of these passages, see David Knott, *Liberalism and the Justice of Neutral Political Concern* [D. Phil. thesis, Oxford University, 1989], chap. 2). Hence, I will be using "liberal neutrality" and "justificatory neutrality" interchangeably. It is quite possible that 'neutrality' is not the best word to describe the policy at issue. Rawls himself has avoided the term until recently because of its multiple and often misleading meanings—e.g., neutrality in its everyday usage usually implies neutral con-

sequences (John Rawls, "The Priority of Right and Ideas of the Good," *Philosophy and Public Affairs* 17 [1988]: 260, 265; cf. Raz, chap. 5). He has instead used the term "priority of the right over the good." But that too has multiple and misleading meanings, since it is used by Rawls to describe both the affirming of neutrality over perfectionism, and the affirming of deontology over teleology. These issues need to be kept distinct, and neither, viewed on its own, is usefully called a matter of the "priority of the right"; see my "Rawls on Teleology and Deontology," *Philosophy and Public Affairs* 17 (1988): 173–190, for a critique of Rawls's usage of "priority of the right." Given the absence of any obviously superior alternative, I will continue to use the term "neutrality."

7. Rawls, "Social Unity," p. 172; cf. Rawls, *A Theory of Justice* (London: Oxford University Press, 1971), p. 94.

8. Rawls, *Theory of Justice,* p. 329.

9. Adina Schwartz, "Moral Neutrality and Primary Goods," *Ethics* 83 (1973): 302.

10. Ibid., p. 304; cf. Jurgen Habermas, *Communication and the Evolution of Society,* trans. Thomas McCarthy (Boston: Beacon, 1979), pp. 198–99.

11. Thomas Nagel, "Rawls on Justice," *Philosophical Review* 82 (1973): 228–29.

12. Both Schwartz and Nagel use the issue of individualistic conceptions of the good to make broader claims about Rawls's theoretical project. According to Schwartz, this issue is one example of the way in which Rawls invokes more than "minimalist" assumptions about reason and morality; according to Nagel, this issue is one example of the way in which Rawls exaggerates the relationship between impartiality and choice under ignorance. Both of these broader claims could be true even if, as I will argue, the particular example they cite is misconceived.

13. Schwartz's claim that material resources are harmful depends, I think, on confusing equality of resources with equality of income. People should be free to decide how and when their labor, or the fruits of their labor, will be sold in the economic marketplace, and many valuable ways of life will seek partial or total exclusion from it. People will not sacrifice all their leisure, or accept the degradation of their work conditions, in return for additional income, and some people put leisure and quality of work well above income in their scale of priorities. But this emphasis on values other than income, far from conflicting with a desire for resources, requires access to resources. We all want to do things, or produce things, which are not marketable, but these activities require resources which other people desire for conflicting purposes. The socialist prefers developing her personal skills, and the monk prefers celebrating God, to selling goods and services in the market. But the socialist and monk require land and other resources to pursue their nonmaterialist ends. One way to legitimately acquire those resources is to spend part of one's time acquiring income through the provision of goods and services others desire. But the more one desires to pursue nonmarketable activities, and to avoid income-producing activities, then the more dependent one is on acquiring resources through one's claim to a fair division of society's wealth. The groups which are least interested in earning income for a materialistic life-style are precisely the groups which are most dependent on their fair share of society's wealth.

14. Rawls, *Theory of Justice,* pp. 142–43.

15. Ronald Dworkin, "In Defense of Equality," *Social Philosophy and Policy* 1 (1983): 31.

16. Karl Marx, *Economic and Philosophical Manuscripts* (London: Lawrence & Wishart, 1977), pp. 306–9.

17. Rawls, "Fairness to Goodness," p. 551. Rawls has recently retracted the claim that there is no reason to regret the loss of life-styles which cannot sustain themselves in a free society. As he rightly says, these ways of life may well have had considerable value. An aristocratic life-style may have value, even if would-be aristocrats cannot find people in a free society who are willing to be their subordinates. But while the loss of aristocratic life-styles may be a cause for legitimate regret, it is not a cause for legitimate grievance, for it is not the product of arbitrary biases

(Rawls, "Priority of Right," pp. 266–67). See also Dworkin's explanation of the fairness of liberal neutrality in "What is Equality? Part 3: The Place of Liberty," *Iowa Law Review* 73 (1987): 1–54, where he notes that neutrality "allows each person's social requirements—the social setting he claims he needs in order successfully to pursue his chosen way of life—to be tested by asking how far these requirements can be satisfied within an egalitarian structure that measures their cost to others" (p. 31).

18. Rawls, "Priority of Right," pp. 265–66.

19. Rawls, *Theory of Justice,* pp. 282–84. This passage refers only to the exchange branch of government, but the same reasoning seems equally applicable to distribution (p. 280).

20. John Rawls, "Reply to Alexander and Musgrave," *Quarterly Journal of Economics* 88 (1974): 641.

21. Rawls, "Kantian Constructivism," p. 544.

22. This feature of Rawls's theory is discussed in Allen Buchanan, "Revisability and Rational Choice," *Canadian Journal of Philosophy* 5 (1975): 395–408; and Dworkin, "In Defense of Equality," pp. 24–30. Rawls's view of the self as able to stand apart from its ends has been vigorously criticized by communitarians—e.g., Alasdair MacIntyre, *After Virtue: A Study in Moral Theory* (London: Duckworth, 1981), chap. 15; Michael Sandel, *Liberalism and the Limits of Justice* (Cambridge: Cambridge University Press, 1982), pp. 150–165. They argue that this view of the self as "unencumbered" by social attachments is at odds with our "deepest self-understandings." I believe the communitarians are simply wrong here (see my "Liberalism and Communitarianism," *Canadian Journal of Philosophy* 18 [1988]: 181–203), but Rawls himself wishes to remain agnostic on the question of whether our self-understandings are or are not bound to any particular complex of ends. He now argues that people can accept his account of the self for the purposes of determining our public rights and responsibilities, without necessarily accepting it as an accurate portrayal of our deepest self-understandings (John Rawls, "Justice as Fairness: Political not Metaphysical," *Philosophy and Public Affairs* 14 [1985]: 240–44; cf. "Kantian Constructivism," p. 545). I raise some questions about the possibility and/or desirability of this agnosticism in *Liberalism, Community, and Culture* (Oxford: Oxford University Press, 1989), pp. 58–61.

23. Wesley Cragg, "Two Concepts of Community," *Dialogue* 25 (1986): 47.

24. Raz, *Morality of Freedom,* p. 162.

25. Charles Taylor, *Philosophy and the Human Sciences: Philosophical Papers* (Cambridge: Cambridge University Press, 1985), vol 2, p. 197.

26. Ibid, p. 207. See e.g., Rawls, *Theory of Justice,* pp. 563–64; Dworkin, *A Matter of Principle,* pp. 220–24.

27. Rawls, *Theory of Justice,* pp. 331–32; Jeremy Waldron, "Autonomy and Perfectionism in Raz's *Morality of Freedom,*" *University of Southern California Law Review* 62 (1989), in press; Robert Nozick, "Commentary on 'Art as a Public Good,'" *Art and the Law* 9 (1985): 162–64.

28. This is endorsed by Dworkin in *A Matter of Principle,* chap. 11. This use of tax credits would only be fair if the distribution of resources in society was in fact just. Indeed, it might not be fair even if the difference principle was honored, since it gives disproportionate power in shaping cultural development to those who are endowed with (undeserved) natural talents, as they are likely to have more disposable income. I assume there are ways to ensure that this operates fairly while still leaving the evaluation of cultural options outside the political sphere. For a discussion of the problem of fairness in influence over culture, in the context of the neutrality/perfectionist debate, see Amy Gutmann, *Democratic Education* (Princeton, N.J.: Princeton University Press, 1987), chap. 9, esp. pp. 263–64.

29. Failure to recognize this undermines Beiner's argument against liberal neutrality, which he concludes by saying: "Even if the state is or tries to be neutral (which likely proves impossible), in any case the wider social order in which the individual is nourished *is not.* Liberal 'neutralism' is therefore a mirage. It is hard to see why the *state* is constrained to be neutral (whatever that might mean) if social life as a whole is and must be, however, much denied by liberals, strongly

partial towards a particular way of life" (Ronald Beiner, "What's Wrong with Liberalism?" in *Law and Community,* ed. Leslie Green and Alan Hutchinson [Toronto: Carswell, in press]). This is entirely off target. The best reason for state neutrality is precisely that social life is nonneutral, that people can and do make discriminations among competing ways of life in their social life, affirming some and rejecting others, without using the state apparatus. If individuals are unable to make these judgments in social life, then state perfectionism might be the appropriate way to enable people to discriminate among different conceptions of the good (although it is unclear how moving from the cultural marketplace to the state would remove the disability). So the argument for state neutrality presupposes, rather than denies, social nonneutrality.

30. William Sullivan, *Reconstructing Public Philosophy* (Berkeley: University of California Press, 1982), pp. 158, 173.

31. Brian Lee Crowley, *The Self, the Individual, and the Community: Liberalism in the Political Thought of F. A. Hayek and Sidney and Beatrice Webb* (Oxford: Oxford University Press, 1987), p. 282; see also Beiner, *Political Judgment* (London: Methuen, 1983), p. 152.

32. Rawls, *Theory of Justice,* p. 543.

33. Ibid.

34. Ibid.

35. Ibid., pp. 328–29.

36. Crowley, p. 295.

37. Ibid., pp. 7, 239.

38. Ibid., p. 287.

39. See, e.g., Thomas Scanlon, "Freedom of Expression and Categories of Expression," in *Pornography and Censorship,* ed. David Coop and Susan Wendell (Buffalo, N.Y.: Prometheus, 1983), pp. 141–47; Loren Lomasky, *Persons, Rights, and the Moral Community* (Oxford: Oxford University Press, 1987), p. 111.

40. Habermas seems to endorse this position when he says that the need for a "discursive desolidification of the (largely externally controlled or traditionally fixed) interpretation of our needs" is the heart of his disagreement with Rawls (Habermas, *Communication and the Evolution of Society,* pp. 198–99). However, he now rejects the idea of politically evaluating people's conceptions of the good (Jürgen Habermas, "Questions and Counterquestions," in *Habermas and Modernity,* ed. Richard Bernstein [Cambridge, Mass.: MIT Press, 1985], pp. 214–16). For discussion of the (apparent) shift, see Seyla Benhabib, *Critique, Norm, and Utopia* (New York: Columbia University Press, 1986), chap. 8; and Nanette Funk, "Habermas and the Social Goods," *Social Text* 18 (1988): 29–31.

41. Habermas, *Communication and the Evolution of Society,* pp. 198–99; Benhabib, pp. 312–14.

42. There are other reasons for opposing state perfectionism. I have been discussing the difficulty of finding acceptable procedures for formulating a public ranking of different ways of life. There are also difficulties about how the state should go about promoting its preferred ways of life, once those are identified. Even if the state can be relied on to come up with an accurate ranking and can get people to pursue the right ways of life, it may not be able to get people to pursue them *for the right reasons.* Someone who acts in a certain way in order to avoid state punishment, or to gain state subsidies, is not guided by an understanding of the genuine value of the activity (Waldron; Lomasky, pp. 253–54). This criticism is important and precludes various coercive and manipulative forms of perfectionism, but it does not preclude short-term state intervention designed to introduce people to valuable ways of life. One way to get people to pursue something for the right reasons is to get them to pursue it for the wrong reasons and hope they will then see its true value. This is not inherently unacceptable, but it occurs often enough in the cultural marketplace. Hence a comprehensive defense of neutrality may need to focus on a prior stage of state perfectionism—i.e., the problems involved in formulating a public ranking of conceptions of the good.

43. On the exclusionary tendencies of communitarianism, see Amy Gutmann, "Communitarian Critics of Liberalism," *Philosophy and Public Affairs* 14 (1985): 318–22; Don Herzog, "Some Questions for Republicans," *Political Theory* 14 (1986): 481–90; H. Hirsch, "The Threnody of Liberalism: Constitutional Liberty and the Renewal of Community," *Political Theory* 14 (1986): 435–38; Nancy Rosenblum, *Another Liberalism: Romanticism and the Reconstruction of Liberal Thought* (Cambridge, Mass.: Harvard University Press, 1987), pp. 178–81.

44. Milton Gordon, "Toward a General Theory of Racial and Ethnic Group Relations," in *Ethnicity: Theory and Experience,* ed. Nathan Glazer and Daniel Moynihan (Cambridge, Mass.: Harvard University Press, 1975), p. 105.

45. Minority rights were a common feature of prewar liberalism, both in theory (e.g., L. T. Hobhouse, *Social Evolution and Political Theory* [New York: Columbia University Press, 1928], pp. 146–47) and practice (e.g., the League of Nations). I attempt to provide a liberal theory of the rights of minority cultures in "Liberalism, Individualism, and Minority Rights," in *Law and Community,* ed. Leslie Green and Alan Hutchinson (Toronto: Carswell, 1989), and *Liberalism, Community, and Culture,* chaps 7–10.

46. Even in a genuine "nation-state," there are questions about how to deal with immigrants from other cultures. Liberals have historically disagreed over the extent to which respect for the autonomy of existing members of the polity requires restrictions on immigration which might damage the cultural structure. They have also disagreed over the extent to which respect for the autonomy of immigrants requires encouraging or compelling their assimilation to the cultural structure of the new country. Again, the requirements of liberal neutrality are not at all obvious.

47. The assumption that the political community is culturally homogeneous is clear in a number of passages in Rawls and Dworkin—e.g., John Rawls, "The Basic Structure as Subject," in *Values and Morals,* ed. Alvin Goldman and Jaegwon Kim (Dordrecht: Reidel, 1978), p. 55, and "On the Idea of Free Public Reason" (1988, photocopy), p. 8; Dworkin, *A Matter of Principle,* pp. 230–33. While revising that assumption would affect the conclusions they go on to draw about the distribution of rights and responsibilities, Rawls and Dworkin never discuss what changes would be required in culturally plural countries. Indeed, they do not seem to recognize that any changes would be required. For a criticism of Rawls's inattention to cultural pluralism, see Vernon Van Dyke, "Justice as Fairness: For Groups?" *American Political Science Review* 69 (1975): 607–14.

48. For example, Crowley says that politics makes possible "a context within which our own self-understandings *may* be articulated and compared with others" (p. 290; my emphasis). But it would be more accurate to say, as he indeed goes on to say, that "politics both *makes* us test dialogically the adequacy of our present self-awareness and makes us aware of other dimensions articulated by other people" (p. 290; my emphasis). Since Crowley never discusses this shift, it seems that he believes that individuals are only able to deliberate collectively when they are made to do so. A similar belief may explain why Sullivan thinks that state perfectionism is needed to ensure that no one is "cut off" from collective deliberations (Sullivan, p. 158). Since people in a liberal society are only cut off from the associations and forums of civil society if they cut themselves off, state perfectionism is needed only if one is assuming that uncoerced people will choose not to participate in collective deliberations. Liberals make the opposite assumption that uncoerced individuals will tend to form and join collective associations, and participate in collective deliberations (the suggestion that nonpolitical activity is inherently solitary is also present in Sandel's claim that under communitarian politics "we can know a good in common that we cannot know alone" [Sandel, p. 183]).

PART VI

Feminist Justice

21

The Subjection of Women

JOHN STUART MILL

The object of this Essay is to explain as clearly as I am able, the grounds of an opinion which I have held from the very earliest period when I had formed any opinions at all on social or political matters, and which, instead of being weakened or modified, has been constantly growing stronger by the progress of reflection and the experience of life: That the principle which regulates the existing social relations between the two sexes—the legal subordination of one sex to the other—is wrong in itself, and now one of the chief hindrances to human improvement; and that it ought to be replaced by a principle of perfect equality, admitting no power or privilege on the one side, nor disability on the other.

The very words necessary to express the task I have undertaken, show how arduous it is. But it would be a mistake to suppose that the difficulty of the case must lie in the insufficiency or obscurity of the grounds of reason on which my conviction rests. The difficulty is that which exists in all cases in which there is a mass of feeling to be contended against. So long as an opinion is strongly rooted in the feelings, it gains rather than loses in stability by having a preponderating weight of argument against it. For if it were accepted as a result of argument, the refutation of the argument might shake the solidity of the conviction; but when it rests solely on feeling, the worse it flares in argumentative contest, the more persuaded its adherents are that their feeling must have some deeper ground, which the arguments do not reach; and while the feeling remains, it is always throwing up fresh intrenchments of argument to repair any breach made in the old. And there are so

From *The Subjection of Women,* Chap. 1. First published in 1869.

many causes tending to make the feelings connected with this subject the most intense and most deeply-rooted of all those which gather round and protect old institutions and customs, that we need not wonder to find them as yet less undermined and loosened than any of the rest by the progress of the great modern spiritual and social transition; nor suppose that the barbarisms to which men cling longest must be less barbarisms than those which they earlier shake off. . . .

In the first place, the opinion in favour of the present system, which entirely subordinates the weaker sex to the stronger, rests upon theory only; for there never has been trial made of any other; so that experience, in the sense in which it is vulgarly opposed to theory, cannot be pretended to have pronounced any verdict. And in the second place, the adoption of this system of inequality never was the result of deliberation, or forethought, or any social ideas, or any notion whatever of what conducted to the benefit of humanity or the good order of society. It arose simply from the fact that from the very earliest twilight of human society, every woman (owing to the value attached to her by men, combined with her inferiority in muscular strength) was found in a state of bondage to some man. Laws and systems of polity always begin by recognising the relations they find already existing between individuals. They convert what was a mere physical fact into a legal right, give it the sanction of society, and principally aim at the substitution of public and organized means of asserting and protecting these rights, instead of the irregular and lawless conflict of physical strength. Those who had already been compelled to obedience became in this manner legally bound to it. Slavery, from being a mere affair of force between the master and the slave, became regularized and a matter of compact among the masters, who, binding themselves to one another for common protection, guaranteed by their collective strength the private possessions of each, including his slaves. In early times, the great majority of the male sex were slaves, as well as the whole of the female. And many ages elapsed, some of them ages of high cultivation, before any thinker was bold enough to question the rightfulness and the absolute social necessity, either of the one slavery or of the other. . . .

If people are mostly so little aware how completely, during the greater part of the duration of our species, the law of force was the avowed rule of general conduct— any other being only a special and exceptional consequence of peculiar ties—and from how very recent a date it is that the affairs of society in general have been even pretended to be regulated according to any moral law, as little do people remember or consider how institutions and customs, which never had any ground but the law of force, last on into ages and states of general opinion which never would have permitted their first establishment. Less than forty years ago, Englishmen might still by law hold human beings in bondage as saleable property; within the present century they might kidnap them and carry them off, and work them literally to death. This absolutely extreme case of the law of force, condemned by those who can tolerate almost every other form of arbitrary power, and which, of all others, presents features the most revolting to the feelings of all who look at it from an impartial position, was the law of civilized and Christian England within the memory of persons now living: and in one half of Anglo-Saxon America three or four years ago, not only did slavery exist, but the slave trade, and the breeding of slaves expressly for it, was a general practice between slave states. Yet not only was there a greater strength of sentiment against it, but, in England at least, a less amount either of feeling or of interest in favour of it, than of any other of the customary abuses of force: for its motive was the love of gain, unmixed and undisguised; and those who profited by it were a very small numerical fraction of the country, while the natural feeling of all who were not personally interested in it, was unmitigated abhorrence. So extreme an instance makes it almost superfluous to refer to any other; but consider the long duration of absolute monarchy. In England at present it is the almost universal conviction that military despotism is a case of the law of force, having no other origin or justification. Yet in all the great nations of Europe except England it either still exists, or has only just ceased to exist, and has even now a strong party favourable to it in all ranks of the people, especially among persons of station and consequence. Such is the power of an established system, even when far from universal, when not only in almost every period of history there have been great and well-known examples of the contrary system, but these have almost invariably been afforded by the most illustrious and most prosperous communities. In this case, too, the possessor of the undue power, the person directly interested in it, is only one person, while those who are subject to it and suffer from it are literally all the rest. The yoke is naturally and necessarily humiliating to all persons, except the one who is on the throne, together with, at most, the one who expects to succeed to it. How different are these cases from that of the power of men over women! I am not now prejudging the question of its justifiableness. I am showing how vastly more permanent it could not but be, even if not justifiable, than these other dominations which have nevertheless lasted down to our own time. Whatever gratification of pride there is in the possession of power, and whatever personal interest in its exercise, is in this case not confined to a limited class, but common to the whole male sex. Instead of being, to most of its supporters, a thing desirable chiefly in the abstract, or, like the political ends usually contended for by factions, of little private importance to any but the leaders, it comes home to the person and hearth of every male head of a family, and of every one who looks forward to being so. The clodhopper exercises, or is to exercise, his share of the power equally with the highest nobleman. And the case is that in which the desire of power is the strongest: for every one who desires power, desires it most over those who are nearest to him, with whom his life is passed, with whom he has most concerns in common, and in whom any independence of his authority is oftenest likely to interfere with his individual preferences. If, in the other cases specified, power manifestly grounded only on force, and having so much less to support them, are so slowly and with so much difficulty got rid of, much more must it be so with this, even if it rests on no better foundation than those. We must consider, too, that the possessors of the power have facilities in this case, greater than in any other, to prevent any uprising against it. Every one of the subjects lives under the very eye, and almost, it may be said, in the hands, of one of the masters—in closer intimacy with him than with any of her fellow-subjects—with no means of combining against him, no power of even locally overmastering him, and, on the other hand, with the strongest motives for seeking his favour and avoiding to give him offence. In struggles for political emancipation, everybody knows how often its champions are bought off by bribes, or daunted by terrors. In the case of women, each individual of the subject-class is in a chronic state of bribery and intimidation combined. In setting up the standard of resistance, a large number of the leaders, and still more of the followers, must make an almost complete sacrifice of the pleasures or the alleviations of their own individual lot. If ever any system of privilege and enforced subjection had its yoke tightly riveted on the necks of those who are kept down by it, this has. . . .

All causes, social and natural, combine to make it unlikely that women should be collectively rebellious to the power of men. They are so far in a position different from all other subject classes, that their masters require something more from them than actual service. Men do not want solely the obedience of women, they want their sentiments. All men, except the most brutish, desire to have, in the woman most nearly connected with them, not a forced slave but a willing one, not a slave merely, but a favourite. They have therefore put everything in practice to enslave their minds. The masters of all other slaves rely, for maintaining obedience, on fear; either fear of themselves, or religious fears. The masters of women wanted more than simple obedience, and they turned the whole force of education to effect their purpose. All women are brought up from the very earliest years in the belief that their ideal of character is the very opposite to that of men; not self-will, and government by self-control, but submission, and yielding to the control of others. All the moralities tell them that it is the duty of women, and all the current sentimentalities that it is their nature, to live for others; to make complete abnegation of themselves, and to have no life but in their affections. And by their affections are meant the only ones they are allowed to have—those to the men with whom they are connected, or to the children who constitute an additional and indefeasible tie between them and a man. When we put together three things—first, the natural attraction between opposite sexes; secondly, the wife's entire dependence on the husband, every privilege or pleasure she has being either his gift, or depending entirely on his will; and lastly, that the principal object of human pursuit, consideration, and all objects of social ambition, can in general be sought or obtained by her only through him, it would be a miracle if the object of being attractive to men had not become the polar star of feminine education and formation of character. And, this great means of influence over the minds of women having been acquired, an instinct of selfishness made men avail themselves of it to the utmost as a means of holding women in subjection, by representing to them meekness, submissiveness, and resignation of all individual will into the hands of a man, as an essential part of sexual attractiveness. Can it be doubted that any of the other yokes which mankind have succeeded in breaking, would have subsisted till now if the same means had existed, and had been as sedulously used, to bow down their minds to it? If it had been made the object of the life of every young plebeian to find personal favour in the eyes of some patrician, of every young serf with some seigneur; if domestication with him, and a share of his personal affections, had been held out as the prize which they all should look out for, the most gifted and aspiring being able to reckon on the most desirable prizes; and if, when this prize had been obtained, they had been shut out by a wall of brass from all interests not centering in him, all feelings and desires but those which he shared or inculcated; would not serfs and seigneurs, plebeians and patricians, have been as broadly distinguished at this day as men and women are? and would not all but a thinker here and there, have believed the distinction to be a fundamental and unalterable fact in human nature?

The preceding considerations are amply sufficient to show that custom, however universal it may be, affords in this case no presumption, and ought not to create any prejudice, in favour of the arrangements which place women in social and political subjection to men. But I may go farther, and maintain that the course of history, and the tendencies of progressive human society, afford not only no presumption in favour of this system of inequality of rights, but a strong one against it; and that, so far as the whole course of human improvement up to this time, the whole stream of modern tendencies, warrants any inference on the subject, it is, that this relic of the past is discordant with the future, and must necessarily disappear.

For, what is the peculiar character of the modern world—the difference which chiefly distinguishes modern institutions, modern social ideas, modern life itself, from those of times long past? It is, that human beings are no longer born to their place in life, and chained down by an inexorable bond to the place they are born to, but are free to employ their faculties, and such favourable chances as offer, to achieve the lot which may appear to them most desirable. Human society of old was constituted on a very different principle. All were born to a fixed social position, and were mostly kept in it by law, or interdicted from any means by which they could emerge from it. As some men are born white and others black, so some were born slaves and others freemen and citizens; some were born patricians, others plebeians; some were born feudal nobles, others commoners and *roturiers*. A slave or serf could never make himself free, nor, except by the will of his master, become so. In most European countries it was not till towards the close of the middle ages, and as a consequence of the growth of regal power, that commoners could be ennobled. Even among nobles, the eldest son was born the exclusive heir to the paternal possessions, and a long time elapsed before it was fully established that the father could disinherit him. Among the industrious classes, only those who were born members of a guild, or were admitted into it by its members, could lawfully practise their calling within its local limits; and nobody could practise any calling deemed important, in any but the legal manner—by processes authoritatively prescribed. Manufacturers have stood in the pillory for presuming to carry on their business by new and improved methods. In modern Europe, and most in those parts of it which have participated most largely in all other modern improvements, diametrically opposite doctrines now prevail. Law and governnent do not undertake to prescribe by whom any social or industrial operation shall or shall not be conducted, or what modes of conducting them shall be lawful. These things are left to the unfettered choice of individuals. Even the laws which required that workmen should serve an apprenticeship, have in this country been repealed: there being ample assurance that in all cases in which an apprenticeship is necessary, its necessity will suffice to enforce it. The old theory was, that the least possible should be left to the choice of the individual agent; that all he had to do should, as far as practicable, be laid down for him by superior wisdom. Left to himself he was sure to go wrong. The modern conviction, the fruit of a thousand years of experience is, that things in which the individual is the person directly interested, never go right but as they are left to his own discretion; and that any regulation of them by authority, except to protect the rights of others, is sure to be mischievous. This conclusion, slowly arrived at, and not adopted until almost every possible application of the contrary theory had been made with disastrous result, now (in the industrial department) prevails universally in the most advanced countries, almost universally in all that have pretensions to any sort of advancement. It is not that all processes are supposed to be equally good, or all persons to be equally qualified for everything; but that freedom of individual choice is now known to be the only thing which procures the adoption of the best processes, and throws each operation into the hands of those who are best qualified for it. Nobody thinks it necessary to make a law that only a strong-armed man shall be a blacksmith. Freedom and competition suffice to make blacksmiths strong-armed men, because the weak-armed can earn more by engaging in occupations for which they are more fit. In consonance with this doctrine, it is felt to be an overstepping of the proper bounds of authority to fix beforehand, on some general presumption, that certain persons are not fit to do certain things. It is now thoroughly known and admitted that if some such presumptions exist, no such presumption is infallible. Even if it be well grounded in a majority of cases, which it is very likely not to be, there will be a minority of exceptional cases in which it does not hold; and in those it is both an injustice to the individuals, and a detriment to society, to place barriers in the way of their using their faculties for their own benefit and for that of others. In the cases, on the other hand, in which the unfitness is real, the ordinary motives of human conduct will on the whole suffice to prevent the incompetent person from making, or from persisting in, the attempt.

If this general principle of social and economical science is not true; if individuals, with such help as they can derive from the opinion of those who know them, are not better judges than the law and the government, of their own capacities and vocation; the world cannot too soon abandon this principle, and return to the old system of regulations and disabilities. But if the principle is true, we ought to act as if we believed it, and not to ordain that to be born a girl instead of a boy, and more than to be born black instead of white, or a commoner instead of a nobleman, shall decide the person's position through all life—shall interdict people from all the more elevated social positions, and from all, except a few, respectable occupations. Even were we to admit the utmost that is ever pretended as to the superior fitness of men for all the functions now reserved to them, the same argument applies which forbids a legal qualification for members of Parliament. If only once in a dozen years the conditions of eligibility exclude a fit person, there is a real loss, while the exclusion of thousands of unfit persons is no gain; for if the constitution of the electoral body disposes them to choose unfit persons, there are always plenty of such persons to choose from. In all things of any difficulty and importance, those who can do them well are fewer than the need, even with the most unrestricted latitude of choice; and any limitation of the field of selection deprives society of some chances of being served by the competent, without ever saving it from the incompetent.

At present, in the more improved countries, the disabilities of women are the only case, save one, in which laws and institutions take persons at their birth, and ordain that they shall never in all their lives be allowed to compete for certain things. . . .

The social subordination of women thus stands out an isolated fact in modern social institutions; a solitary breach of what has become their fundamental law; a single relic of an old world of thought and practice exploded in everything else, but retained in the one thing of most universal interest. . . .

The least that can be demanded is, that the question should not be considered as prejudged by existing fact and existing opinion, but open to discussion on its merits, as a question of justice and expediency; the decision on this, as on any of the other social arrangements of mankind, depending on what an enlightened estimate of tendencies and consequences may show to be most advantageous to humanity in general, without distinction of sex. And the discussion must be a real discussion, descending to foundations, and not resting satisfied with vague and general assertions. It will not do, for instance, to assert in general terms, that the experience of mankind has pronounced in favour of the existing system. Experience cannot possibly have decided between two courses, so long as there has only been experience of one. If it be said that the doctrine of the equality of the sexes rests only on theory, it must be remembered that the contrary doctrine also has only theory to rest upon. All that is proved in its favour by direct experience, is that mankind have been able to exist under it, and to attain the degree of improvement and prosperity which we now see; but whether that prosperity has been attained sooner, or is now greater, than it would have been under the other system, experience does not say. On the other hand, experience does say, that every step in improvement has been so invariably accompanied by a step made in raising the social position of women, that historians and philosophers have been led to adopt their elevation or debasement as on the whole the surest test and most correct measure of the civilization of a people or an age. Through all the progressive period of human history, the condition of women has been approaching nearer to equality with men. This does not of itself prove that the assimilation must go on to complete equality; but it assuredly affords some presumption that such is the case.

Neither does it avail anything to say that the *nature* of the two sexes adapts them to their present functions and position, and renders these appropriate to them. Standing on the ground of common sense and the constitution of the human mind, I deny that any one knows, or can know, the nature of the two sexes, as long as they have only been seen in their present relation to one another. If men had ever been found in society without women, or women without men, or if there had been a society of men and women in which the women were not under the control of the men, something might have been positively known about the mental and moral differences which may be inherent in the nature of each. What is now called the nature of women is an eminently artificial thing—the result of forced repression in some directions, unnatural stimulation in others. It may be asserted without scruple, that no other class of dependents have had their character so entirely distorted from its natural proportions by their relation with their masters; for, if conquered and slave races have been, in some respects, more forcibly repressed, whatever in them has not been crushed down by an iron heel has generally been let alone, and if left with any liberty of development, it has developed itself according to its own laws; but in the case of women, a hot-house and stove cultivation has always been carried on of some of the capabilities of their nature, for the benefit and pleasure of their masters. . . .

Hence, in regard to that most difficult question, what are the natural differences between the two sexes—a subject on which it is impossible in the present state of society to obtain complete and correct knowledge—while almost everybody dogmatizes upon it, almost all neglect and make light of the only means by which any partial insight can be obtained into it. This is, an analytic study of the most important department of psychology, the laws of the influence of circumstances on character. For, however great and apparently ineradicable the moral and intellectual differences between men and women might be, the evidence of their being natural differences could only be negative. Those only could be inferred to be natural which could not possibly be artificial—the residuum, after deducting every characteristic of either sex which can admit of being explained from education or external circumstances. The profoundest knowledge of the laws of the formation of character is indispensable to entitle any one to affirm even that there is any difference, much more what the difference is, between the two sexes considered as moral and rational beings; and since no one, as yet, has the knowledge, (for there is hardly any subject which, in proportion to its importance, has been so little studied), no one is thus far entitled to any positive opinion on the subject. Conjectures are all that can at present be made; conjectures more or less probable, according as more or less authorized by such knowledge as we yet have of the laws of psychology, as applied to the formation of character.

Even the preliminary knowledge, what the differences between the sexes now are, apart from all questions as to how they are made what they are, is still in the crudest and most incomplete state. . . .

One thing we may be certain of—that what is contrary to women's nature to do, they never will be made to do by simply giving their nature free play. The anxiety of mankind to interfere in behalf of nature, for fear lest nature should not succeed in effecting its purpose, is an altogether unnecessary solicitude. What women by nature cannot do, it is quite superfluous to forbid them from doing. What they can do, but not so well as the men who are their competitors, competition suffices to exclude them from, since nobody asks for protective duties and bounties in favour of women; it is only asked that the present bounties and protective duties in favour of men should be recalled. If women have a greater natural inclination for some things than for others, there is no need of laws or social inculcation to make the majority of them do the former in preference to the latter. Whatever women's services are most wanted for, the free play of competition will hold out the strongest inducements to them to undertake. And, as the words imply, they are most wanted for the things for which they are most fit; by the apportionment of which to them, the collective faculties of the two sexes can be applied on the whole with the greatest sum of valuable result.

The general opinion of men is supposed to be, that the natural vocation of a woman is that of a wife and mother. I say, is supposed to be, because, judging from acts—from the whole of the present constitution of society—one might infer that their opinion was the direct contrary. They might be supposed to think that the alleged natural vocation of women was of all things the most repugnant to their nature; insomuch that if they are free to do anything else—if any other means of living, or occupation of their time and faculties, is open, which has any chance of appearing desirable to them—there will not be enough of them who will be willing to accept the condition said to be natural to them. If this is the real opinion of men in general, it would be well that it should be spoken out. I should like to hear somebody openly enunciating the doctrine (it is already implied in much that is written on the subject)—"It is necessary to society that women should marry and produce children. They will not do so unless they are compelled. Therefore it is necessary to compel them." The merits of the case would then be clearly defined. It would be exactly that of the slaveholders of South Carolina and Louisiana. "It is necessary that cotton and sugar should be grown. White men cannot produce them. Negroes will not, for any wages which we choose to give. *Ergo* they must be compelled." An illustration still closer to the point is that of impressment. Sailors must absolutely be had to defend the country. It often happens that they will not voluntarily enlist. Therefore there must be the power of forcing them. How often has this logic been used! and, but for one flaw in it, without doubt it would have been successful up to this day. But it is open to the retort—First pay the sailors the honest value of their labour. When you have made it as well worth their while to serve you, as to work for other employers, you will have no more difficulty than others have in obtaining their services. To this there is no logical answer except "I will not": and as people are now not only ashamed, but are not desirous, to rob the labourer of his hire, impressment is no longer advocated. Those who attempt to force women into marriage by closing all other doors against them, lay themselves open to a similar retort. If they mean what they say, their opinion must evidently be, that men do not render the married condition so desirable to women, as to induce them to accept it for its own recommendations. It is not a sign of one's thinking the boon one offers very attractive, when one allows only Hobson's choice, "that or none." And here, I believe, is the clue to the feelings of those men, who have a real antipathy to the equal freedom of women. I believe they are afraid, not lest women should be unwilling to marry, for I do not think that any one in reality has that apprehension; but lest they should insist that marriage should be on equal conditions; lest all women of spirit and capacity should prefer doing almost anything else, not in their own eyes degrading, rather than marry, when marrying is giving themselves a master, and a master too of all their earthly possessions. And truly, if this consequence were necessarily incident to marriage, I think that the apprehension would be very well founded. I agree in thinking it probable that few women, capable of anything else, would, unless under an irresistible *entrainement,* rendering them for the time insensible to anything but itself, choose such a lot, when any other means were open to them of filling a conventionally honourable place in life: and if men are determined that the law of marriage shall be a law of despotism, they are quite right, in point of mere policy, in leaving to women only Hobson's choice. But, in that case, all that has been done in the modern world to relax the chain on the minds of women, has been a mistake. They never should have been allowed to receive a literary education. Women who read, much more women who write, are, in the existing constitution of things, a contradiction and a disturbing element: and it was wrong to bring women up with any acquirements but those of an odalisque, or of a domestic servant.

22

Justice and Gender

SUSAN OKIN

We as a society pride ourselves on our democratic values. We don't believe people should be constrained by innate differences from being able to achieve desired positions of influence to improve their well-being; equality of opportunity is our professed aim. The Preamble to our Constitution stresses the importance of justice, as well as the general welfare and the blessings of liberty. The Pledge of Allegiance asserts that our republic preserves "liberty and justice for all."

Yet substantial inequalities between the sexes still exist in our society. In economic terms, full-time working women (after some very recent improvement) earn on average 71 percent of the earnings of full-time working men. One-half of poor and three-fifths of chronically poor households with dependent children are maintained by a single female parent. The poverty rate for elderly women is nearly twice that for elderly men.[1] On the political front, two out of a hundred U.S. senators are women, one out of nine justices seems to be considered sufficient female representation on the Supreme Court, and the number of men chosen in each congressional election far exceeds the number of women elected in the entire history of the country. Underlying and intertwined with all these inequalities is the unequal distribution of the unpaid labor of the family.

An equal sharing between the sexes of family responsibilities, especially child care, is "the great revolution that has not happened."[2] Women, including mothers of young children, are, of course, working outside the household far more than their mothers did. And the small proportion of women who reach high-level positions in politics, business, and the professions command a vastly disproportionate amount of space in the media, compared with the millions of women who work at low-paying, dead-end jobs, the millions who do part-time work with its lack of benefits, and the millions of others who stay home performing for no pay what is frequently not even acknowledged as work. Certainly, the fact that women are doing more paid work does not imply that they are more equal. It is often said that we are living in a postfeminist era. This claim, due in part to the distorted emphasis on women who have "made it," is false, no matter which of its meanings is intended. It is certainly not true that feminism has been vanquished, and equally untrue that it is no longer needed because its aims have been fulfilled. Until there is justice within the family, women will not be able to gain equality in politics, at work, or in any other sphere.

. . . The typical current practices of family life, structured to a large extent by gender, are not just. Both the expectation and the experience of the division of labor by sex make women vulnerable. As I shall show, a cycle of power relations and decisions pervades both family and workplace, each reinforcing the inequalities between the sexes that already exist within the other. Not only women, but children of both sexes, too, are often made vulnerable by gender-structured marriage. One-quarter of children in the United States now live in families with only one parent—in almost 90 percent of cases, the mother. Contrary to common perceptions—in which the stituation of never-married mothers looms largest—65 percent of single-parent families are a result of marital separation or divorce.[3] Recent research in a number of states has shown that, in the average case, the standard of living of divorced women and the children who live with them plummets after divorce, whereas the economic situation of divorced men tends to be better than when they were married.

A central source of injustice for women these days is that the law, most noticeably in the event of divorce, treats more or less as equals those whom custom, workplace discrimination, and the still conventional division of labor within the family have made very unequal. Central to this socially created inequality are two commonly made but inconsistent presumptions: that women are primarily responsible for the rearing of children; and that serious and committed members of the work force (regardless of class) do not have primary responsibility, or even shared responsibility, for the rearing of children. The old assumption of the workplace, still implicit, is that workers have wives at home. It is built not only into the structure and expectations of the workplace but into other crucial social institutions, such as schools, which make no attempt to take account, in their scheduled hours or vacations, of the fact that parents are likely to hold jobs.

Now, of course, many wage workers do not have wives at home, Often, they *are* wives and mothers, or single, separated, or divorced mothers of small children. But neither the family nor the workplace has taken much account of this fact. Employed wives still do by far the greatest proportion of unpaid family work, such as child care and housework. Women are far more likely to take time out of the workplace or to work part-time because of family responsibilities than are their husbands or male partners. And they are much more likely to move because of their husbands' employment needs or opportunities than their own. All these tendencies, which are due to a number of factors, including the sex segregation and discrimination of the workplace itself, tend to be cyclical in their effects: wives advance more slowly than their husbands at work and thus gain less seniority, and the discrepancy between their wages increases over time. Then, because both the power structure of the family and what is regarded as consensual "rational" family decision-making reflect the fact that the husband usually earns more, it will become even less likely as time goes on that the unpaid work of the family will be shared between the spouses. Thus the cycle of inequality is perpetuated. Often hidden from view within a marriage, it is in the increasingly likely event of marital breakdown that the socially constructed inequality of married women is at its most visible.

This is what I mean when I say that gender-structured marriage *makes* women vulnerable. These are not matters of natural necessity, as some people would believe. Surely nothing in our natures dictates that men should not be equal participants in the rearing of their children. Nothing in the nature of work makes it impossible to adjust it to the fact that people are parents as well as workers. That these things have not happened is part of the historically, socially constructed differentiation between the sexes that feminists have come to call *gender*. We live in a society that has over the years regarded the innate characteristic of sex as one of the clearest legitimizers of different rights and restrictions, both formal and informal. While the legal sanctions that uphold male dominance have begun to be eroded in the past century, and more rapidly in the last twenty years, the heavy weight of tradition, combined with the effects of socialization, still works powerfully to reinforce sex roles that are commonly regarded as of unequal prestige and worth. The sexual division of labor has not only been a fundamental part of the marriage contract, but so deeply influences us in our formative years that feminists of both sexes who try to reject it can find themselves struggling against it with varying degrees of ambivalence. Based on this linchpin, "gender"—by which I mean *the deeply entrenched institutionalization of sexual difference*—still permeates our society.

The Construction
of Gender

Due to feminism and feminist theory, gender is coming to be recognized as a social factor of major importance. Indeed, the new meaning of the word reflects the fact that so much of what has traditionally been thought of as sexual difference is now considered by many to be largely socially produced.[4] Feminist scholars from many disciplines and with radically different points of view have contributed to the enterprise of making gender fully visible and comprehensible. At one end of the spectrum are those whose explanations of the subordination of women focus primarily on biological difference as causal in the construction of gender,[5] and at the other end are those who argue that biological difference may not even lie at the core of the social construction that is gender;[6] the views of the vast majority of feminists fall between these extremes. The rejection of biological determinism and the corresponding emphasis on gender as a social construction characterize most current feminist scholarship. Of particular relevance is work in psychology, where scholars have investigated the importance of female primary parenting in the formation of our gendered identities,[7] and in history and anthropology,[8] where emphasis has been placed on the historical and cultural variability of gender. Some feminists have been criticized for developing theories of gender that do not take sufficient account of differences *among* women, especially race, class, religion, and ethnicity.[9] While such critiques should always inform our research and improve our arguments, it would be a mistake to allow them to detract our attention from gender itself as a factor of significance. Many injustices are experienced by women *as women,* whatever the differences among them and whatever other injustices they also suffer from. The past and present gendered nature of the family, and the ideology that surrounds it, affects virtually all women, whether or not they live or ever lived in traditional families. Recognizing this is not to deny or de-emphasize the fact that gender may affect different subgroups of women to a different extent and in different ways.

The potential significance of feminist discoveries and conclusions about gender for issues of social justice cannot be overemphasized. They undermine centuries of argument that started with the notion that not only the distinct differentiation of women and men but the domination of women by men, being natural, was therefore inevitable and not even to be considered in discussions of justice. As I shall make clear in later chapters, despite the fact that such notions cannot stand up to rational scrutiny, they not only still survive but flourish in influential places.

During the same two decades in which feminists have been intensely thinking, researching, analyzing, disagreeing about, and rethinking the subject of gender, our political and legal institutions have been increasingly faced with issues concerning the injustices of gender and their effects. These issues are being decided within a fundamentally patriarchal system, founded in a tradition in which "individuals" were assumed to be male heads of households. Not surprisingly, the system has demonstrated a limited capacity for determining what is just, in many cases involving gender. Sex discrimination, sexual harassment, abortion, pregnancy in the workplace, parental leave, child care, and surrogate mothering have all become major and well-publicized issues of public policy, engaging both courts and legislatures. Issues of family justice, in particular—from child custody and terms of divorce to physical and sexual abuse of wives and children—have become increasingly visible and pressing, and are commanding increasing attention from the police and court systems. There is clearly a major "justice crisis" in contemporary society arising from issues of gender.

Theories of Justice and the Neglect of Gender

During these same two decades, there has been a great resurgence of theories of social justice. Political theory, which had been sparse for a period before the late 1960s except as an important branch of intellectual history, has become a flourishing field, with social justice as its central concern. Yet, remarkably, major contemporary theorists of justice have almost without exception ignored the situation I have just described. They have displayed little interest in or knowledge of the findings of feminism. They have largely bypassed the fact that the society to which their theories are supposed to pertain is heavily and deeply affected by gender, and faces difficult issues of justice stemming from its gendered past and present assumptions. Since theories of justice are centrally concerned with whether, how, and why persons should be treated differently from one another, this neglect seems inexplicable. These theories are *about* which initial or acquired characteristics or positions in society legitimize differential treatment of persons by social institutions, laws, and customs. They are *about* how and whether and to what extent beginnings should affect outcomes. The division of humanity into two sexes seems to provide an obvious subject for such inquiries. But, as we shall see, this does not strike most contemporary theorists of justice, and their theories suffer in both coherence and relevance because of it. This book is about this remarkable case of neglect. It is also an attempt to rectify it, to point the way toward a more fully humanist theory of justice by confronting the question, "How just is gender?"

Why is it that when we turn to contemporary theories of justice, we do not find illuminating and positive contributions to this question? How can theories of justice that are ostensibly about people in general neglect women, gender, and all the inequalities between the sexes? One reason is that most theorists *assume,* though they do not discuss, the traditional, gender-structured family. Another is that they often employ gender-neutral language in a false, hollow way. Let us examine these two points.

The Hidden Gender-Structured Family

In the past, political theorists often used to distinguish clearly between "private" domestic life and the "public" life of politics and the marketplace, claiming explicitly that the two spheres operated in accordance with different principles. They separated out the family from what they deemed the subject matter of politics, and they made closely related, explicit claims about the nature of women and the appropriateness of excluding them from civil and political life. Men, the subjects of the theories, were able to make the transition back and forth from domestic to public life with ease, largely because of the functions performed by women in the family.[10] When we turn to contemporary theories of justice, superficial appearances can easily lead to the impression that they are inclusive of women. In fact, they continue the same "separate spheres" tradition, by ignoring the family, its division of labor, and the related economic dependency and restricted opportunities of most women. The judgment that the family is "nonpolitical" is implicit in the fact that it is simply not discussed in most works of political theory today. In one way or another, as will become clear in the chapters that follow, almost all current theorists continue to assume that the "individual" who is the basic subject of their theories is the male head of a fairly traditional household. Thus the application of principles of justice to relations between the sexes, or within the household, is frequently, though tacitly, ruled out from the start. In the most influential of all twentieth-century theories of justice, that of John Rawls, family life is not only assumed, but is assumed to be just—and yet the prevalent gendered division of labor within the family is neglected, along with the associated distribution of power, responsibility, and privilege. . . .

Moreover, this stance is typical of contemporary theories of justice. They persist, despite the wealth of feminist challenges to their assumptions, in their refusal even to discuss the family and its gender structure, much less to recognize the family as a political institution of primary importance. Recent theories that pay even less attention to issues of family justice than Rawls's include Bruce Ackerman's *Social Justice in the Liberal State,* Ronald Dworkin's *Taking Rights Seriously,* William Galston's *Justice and the Human Good,* Alasdair MacIntyre's *After Virtue* and *Whose Justice? Whose Rationality?,* Robert Nozick's *Anarchy, State, and Utopia,* and Roberto Unger's *Knowledge and Politics* and *The Critical Legal Studies Movement.*[11] Philip Green's *Retrieving Democracy* is a welcome exception.[12] Michael Walzer's *Spheres of Justice,* too, is exceptional in this regard, but . . . the conclusion that can be inferred from his discussion of the family—that its gender structure is unjust—does not sit at all easily with his emphasis on the shared understandings of a culture as the foundation of justice.[13] For gender is one aspect of social life about which clearly, in the United States in the latter part of the twentieth century, there are no shared understandings.

What is the basis of my claim that the family, while neglected, is *assumed* by theorists of justice? One obvious indication is that they take mature, independent human beings as the subjects of their theories without any mention of how they got to be that way. We know, of course, that human beings develop and mature only as a result of a great deal of attention and hard work, by far the greater part of it done by women. But when theorists of justice talk about "work," they mean paid work performed in the marketplace. They must be assuming that women, in the gender-structured family, continue to do their unpaid work of nurturing and socializing the young and providing a haven of intimate relations—otherwise there would be no moral subjects for them to theorize about. But these activities apparently take place outside the scope of their theories. Typically, the family itself is not examined in the light of whatever standard of justice the theorist arrives at.[14]

The continued neglect of the family by theorists of justice flies in the face of a great deal of persuasive feminist argument . . . Scholars have clearly revealed the interconnections between the gender structure inside and outside the family and the extent to which the personal is political. They have shown that the assignment of primary parenting to women is crucial, both in forming the gendered identities of men and women and in influencing their respective choices and opportunities in life. Yet, so far, the simultaneous assumption and neglect of the family has allowed the impact of these arguments to go unnoticed in major theories of justice.

False Gender Neutrality

Many academics in recent years have become aware of the objectionable nature of using the supposedly generic male forms of nouns and pronouns. As feminist scholars have demonstrated, these words have most often *not* been used, throughout history and the history of philosophy in particular, with the intent to include women. *Man, mankind,* and *he* are going out of style as universal representations, though they have by no means disappeared. But the gender-neutral alternatives that most contemporary theorists employ are often even more misleading than the blatantly sexist use of male terms of reference. For they serve to disguise the real and continuing failure of theorists to confront the fact that the human race consists of persons of two sexes. They are by this means able to ignore the fact that there are *some* socially relevant physical differences between women and men, and the even more important fact that the sexes have had very different histories, very different assigned social roles and "natures," and very different degrees of access to power and opportunity in all human societies up to and including the present.

False gender neutrality is not a new phenomenon. Aristotle, for example, used *anthropos*—"human being"—in discussions of "the human good" that turn out not only to exclude women but to depend on their subordination. Kant even wrote of "all rational beings as such" in making arguments that he did not mean to apply to women. But it was more readily apparent that such arguments or conceptions of the good were not about all of us, but only about male heads of families. For their authors usually gave at some point an explanation, no matter how inadequate, of why what they were saying did not apply to women and of the different characteristics and virtues, rights, and responsibilities they thought women ought to have. Nevertheless, their theories have often been read as though they pertain (or can easily be applied) to all of us. Feminist interpretations of the last fifteen years or so have revealed the falsity of this "add women and stir" method of reading the history of political thought.[15]

The falseness of the gender-neutral language of contemporary political theorists is less readily apparent. Most, though not all, contemporary moral and political philosophers use "men and women," "he or she," "persons," or the increasingly ubiquitous "self." Sometimes they even get their computers to distribute masculine and feminine terms of reference randomly.[16] Since they do not explicitly exclude or differentiate women, as most theorists in the past did, we may be tempted to read their theories as inclusive of all of us. But we cannot. Their merely terminological responses to feminist challenges, in spite of giving a superficial impression of tolerance and inclusiveness, often strain credulity and sometimes result in nonsense. They do this in two ways: by ignoring the irreducible biological differences between the sexes, and/or by ignoring their different assigned social roles and consequent power differentials, and the ideologies that have supported them. Thus gender-neutral terms frequently obscure the fact that so much of the real experience of "persons," so long as they live in gender-structured societies, *does* in fact depend on what sex they are.

False gender neutrality is by no means confined to the realm of theory. Its harmful effects can be seen in public policies that have directly affected large numbers of women adversely. It was used, for example, in the Supreme Court's 1976 decision that the exclusion of pregnancy-related disabilities from employers' disability insurance plans was "not a gender-based discrimination at all." In a now infamous phrase of its majority opinion, the Court explained that such plans did not discriminate against women because the distinction drawn by such plans was between pregnant women and "non-pregnant *persons*."[17]

Examples of false gender neutrality in contemporary political theory will appear throughout this book; I will illustrate the concept here by citing just two examples. Ackerman's *Social Justice in the Liberal State* is a book containing scrupulously gender-neutral language. He breaks with this neutrality only, it seems, to *defy* existing sex roles; he refers to the "Commander," who plays the lead role in the theory, as "she." However, the argument of the book does not address the existing inequality or role differentiation between the sexes, though it has the potential for doing so.* The full impact of Ackerman's gender-neutral language without attention to gender is revealed in his section on abortion: a two-page discussion written, with the exception of a single "she," in the completely gender-neutral language of fetuses and their "parents."[18] The impression given is that there is no relevant respect in which the relationship of the two parents to the fetus differs. Now it is, of course, possible to imagine (and in the view of many feminists, would be desirable to achieve) a society in which differences in the relation of women and men to fetuses would be so slight as to reasonably play only a minor role in the discussion of abortion. But this would have to be a society without gender—one in which sexual difference carried no social significance, the sexes were equal in power and interdependence, and "mothering" and "fathering" a child meant the same thing, so that parenting and earning responsibilities were equally shared. We certainly do not live in such a society. Neither is there any discussion of one in Ackerman's theory, in which the division of labor between the sexes is not considered a matter of social (in)justice. In such a context, a "gender-neutral" discussion of abortion is almost as misleading as the Supreme Court's "gender-neutral" discussion of pregnancy.

A second illustration of false gender neutrality comes from Derek Phillips's *Toward a Just Social Order.* Largely because of the extent of his concern—rare among theorists of justice—with how we are to *achieve and maintain* a just social order, Phillips pays an unusual amount of attention to the family. He writes about the family as the locus for the development of a sense of justice and self-esteem, of an appreciation of the meaning of reciprocity, of the ability to exercise unforced choice, and of an awareness of alternative ways of life.[19] The problem with this otherwise admirable discussion is that, apart from a couple of brief exceptions, the family itself is presented in gender-neutral terms that bear little resemblance to actual, gender-structured life.[20]† It is because of "parental affection," "parental nurturance," and "child rearing" that children in Phillips's families become the autonomous moral agents that his just society requires its citizens to be. The child's development of a

---

*Ackerman's argument about how we arrive at social justice is in most essentials similar to Rawls's. . . . I think such methods can be useful in challenging gender and achieving a humanist theory of justice.

†He points out the shortcomings of the "earlier ethic of sacrifice," especially for women. He also welcomes the recent lessening of women's dependence on their husbands, but at the same time blames it for tending to weaken family stability. The falseness of Phillips's gender neutrality in discussing parenting is clearly confirmed later in the book (chaps. 8 and 9), where paid work is "men's" and it is "fathers" who bequeath wealth or poverty on their children.

sense of identity is very much dependent upon being raised by "parental figures who themselves have coherent and well-integrated personal identities," and we are told that such a coherent identity is "ideally one built around commitments to work and love." This all sounds very plausible. But it does not take into account of the multiple inequalities of gender. In gender-structured societies—in which the child rearers are women, "parental nurturance" is largely mothering, and those who do what society regards as "meaningful work" are assumed *not* be be primary parents— women in even the best of circumstances face considerable conflicts between love (a fulfilling family life) and "meaningful work." Women in less fortunate circumstances face even greater conflicts between love (even basic care of their children) and any kind of paid work at all.

It follows from Phillips's own premises that these conflicts are very likely to affect the strength and coherence in women of that sense of identity and self-esteem, coming from love and meaningful work, that he regards as essential for being an autonomous moral agent. In turn, if they are mothers, it is also likely to affect their daughters' and sons' developing senses of their identity. Gender is clearly a major obstacle to the attainment of a social order remotely comparable to the just one Phillips aspires to—but his false gender-neutral language allows him to ignore this fact. Although he is clearly aware of how distant in some other respects his vision of a just social order is from contemporary societies,[21] his use of falsely gender-neutral language leaves him quite unaware of the distance between the type of family that might be able to socialize just citizens and typical families today.

The combined effect of the omission of the family and the falsely gender-neutral language in recent political thought is that most theorists are continuing to ignore the highly political issue of gender. The language they use makes little difference to what they actually do, which is to write about men and about only those women who manage, in spite of the gendered structures and practices of the society in which they live, to adopt patterns of life that have been developed to suit the needs of men. The fact that human beings are born as helpless infants—not as the purportedly autonomous actors who populate political theories—is obscured by the implicit assumption of gendered families, operating outside the range of the theories. To a large extent, contemporary theories of justice, like those of the past, are about men with wives at home.

Gender as an Issue of Justice

For three major reasons, this state of affairs is unacceptable. The first is the obvious point that women must be fully included in any satisfactory theory of justice. The second is that equality of opportunity, not only for women but for children of both sexes, is seriously undermined by the current gender injustices of our society. And the third reason is that, as has already been suggested, the family—currently the linchpin of the gender structure—must be just if we are to have a just society, since it is within the family that we first come to have that sense of ourselves and our relations with others that is at the root of moral development.

Counting Women In

When we turn to the great tradition of Western political thought with questions about the justice of the treatment of the sexes in mind, it is to little avail. Bold feminists like Mary Astell, Mary Wollstonecraft, William Thompson, Harriet Taylor, and George Bernard Shaw have occasionally challenged the tradition, often using its own premises and arguments to overturn its explicit or implicit justification of the inequality of women. But John Stuart Mill is a rare exception to the rule that those who hold central positions in the tradition almost never question the justice of the subordination of women.[22] This phenomenon is undoubtedly due in part to the fact that Aristotle, whose theory of justice has been so influential, relegated women to a sphere of "household justice"—populated by persons who are not fundamentally equal to the free men who participate in political justice, but inferiors whose natural function is to serve those who are more fully human. The liberal tradition, despite its supposed foundation of individual rights and human equality, is more Aristotelian in this respect than is generally acknowledged.[23] In one way or another, almost all liberal theorists have assumed that the "individual" who is the basic subject of the theories is the male head of a patriarchal household.[24] Thus they have not usually considered applying the principles of justice to women or to relations between the sexes.

When we turn to contemporary theories of justice, however, we expect to find more illuminating and positive contributions to the subject of gender and justice. As the omission of the family and the falseness of their gender-neutral language suggest, however, mainstream contemporary theories of justice do not address the subject any better than those of the past. Theories of justice that apply to only half of us simply won't do; the inclusiveness falsely implied by the current use of gender-neutral terms must become real. Theories of justice must apply to all of us, and to all of human life, instead of *assuming* silently that half of us take care of whole areas of life that are considered outside the scope of social justice. In a just society, the structure and practices of families must afford women the same opportunities as men to develop their capacities, to participate in political power, to influence social choices, and to be economically as well as physically secure.

Unfortunately, much feminist intellectual energy in the 1980s has gone into the claim that "justice" and "rights" are masculinist ways of thinking about morality that feminists should eschew or radically revise, advocating a morality of care.[25] The emphasis is misplaced, I think, for several reasons. First, what is by now a vast literature on the subject shows that the evidence for differences in women's and men's ways of thinking about moral issues is not (at least yet) very clear; neither is the evidence about the source of whatever differences there might be.[26] It may well turn out that any differences can be readily explained in terms of roles, including female primary parenting, that are socially determined and therefore alterable. There is certainly no evidence—nor could there be, in such a gender-structured society—for concluding that women are somehow naturally more inclined toward contextuality and away from universalism in their moral thinking, a false concept that unfortunately reinforces the old stereotypes that justify separate spheres. The capacity of reactionary forces to capitalize on the "different moralities" strain in feminism is particularly evident in Pope John Paul II's recent Apostolic Letter, "On the Dignity of Women," in which he refers to women's special capacity to care for others in arguing for confining them to motherhood or celibacy.[27]

Second, . . . I think the distinction between an ethic of justice and an ethic of care has been overdrawn. The best theorizing about justice, I argue, has integral to it the notions of care and empathy, of thinking of the interests and well-being of others who may be very different from ourselves. It is, therefore, misleading to draw a dichotomy as though they were two contrasting ethics. The best theorizing about justice is not some abstract "view from nowhere," but results from the carefully attentive consideration of *everyone's* point of view. This means, of course, that the best theorizing about justice is not good enough if it does not, or cannot readily be adapted to, include women and their points of view as fully as men and their points of view.

Gender and Equality of Opportunity

The family is a crucial determinant of our opportunities in life, of what we "become." It has frequently been acknowledged by those concerned with real equality of opportunity that the family presents a problem.[28] But though they have discerned a serious problem, these theorists have underestimated it because they have seen only half of it. They have seen that the disparity among families in terms of the physical and emotional environment, motivation, and material advantages they can give their children has a tremendous effect upon children's opportunities in life. We are not born as isolated, equal individuals in our society, but into family situations: some in the social middle, some poor and homeless, and some superaffluent; some to a single or soon-to-be-separated parent, some to parents whose marriage is fraught with conflict, some to parents who will stay together in love and happiness. Any claims that equal opportunity exists are therefore completely unfounded. Decades of neglect of the poor, especially of poor black and Hispanic households, accentuated by the policies of the Reagan years, have brought us farther from the principles of equal opportunity. To come close to them would require, for example, a high and uniform standard of public education and the provision of equal social services—including health care, employment training, job opportunities, drug rehabilitation, and decent housing—for all who need them. In addition to redistributive taxation, only massive reallocations of resources from the military to social services could make these things possible.

But even if all these disparities were somehow eliminated, we would still not attain equal opportunity for all. This is because what has not been recognized as an equal opportunity problem, except in feminist literature and circles, is the disparity *within* the family, the fact that its gender structure is itself a major obstacle to equality of opportunity. This is very important in itself, since one of the factors with most influence on our opportunities in life is the social significance attributed to our sex. The opportunities of girls and women are centrally affected by the structure and practices of family life, particularly by the fact that women are almost invariably primary parents. What nonfeminists who see in the family an obstacle to equal opportunity have *not* seen is that the extent to which a family is gender-structured can make the sex we belong to a relatively insignificant aspect of our identity and our life prospects or an all-pervading one. This is because so much of the social construction of gender takes place in the family, and particularly in the institution of female parenting.

Moreover, especially in recent years, with the increased rates of single motherhood, separation, and divorce, the inequalities between the sexes have *compounded* the first part of the problem. The disparity among families has grown largely because of the impoverishment of many women and children after separation or divorce. The division of labor in the typical family leaves most women far less capable than men of supporting themselves, and this disparity is accentuated by the fact that children of separated or divorced parents usually live with their mothers. The inadequacy—and frequent nonpayment—of child support has become recognized as a major social problem. Thus the inequalities of gender are now directly harming many children of both sexes as well as women themselves. Enhancing equal opportunity for women, important as it is in itself, is also a crucial way of improving the opportunities of many of the most disadvantaged children.

As there is a connection among the parts of this problem, so is there a connection among some of the solutions: much of what needs to be done to end the inequalities of gender, and to work in the direction of ending gender itself, will also help to equalize opportunity from one family to another. Subsidized, high-quality day care is obviously one such thing; another is the adaptation of the workplace to the needs of parents. . . .

The Family as a School of Justice

One of the things that theorists who have argued that families need not or cannot be just, or who have simply neglected them, have failed to explain is how, within a formative social environment that is *not* founded upon principles of justice, children can learn to develop that sense of justice they will require as citizens of a just society. Rather than being one among many co-equal institutions of a just society, a just family is its essential foundation.

It may seem uncontroversial, even obvious, that families must be just because of the vast influence they have on the moral development of children. But this is clearly not the case. I shall argue that unless the first and most formative example of adult interaction usually experienced by children is one of justice and reciprocity, rather than one of domination and manipulation or of unequal altruism and one-sided self-sacrifice, and unless they themselves are treated with concern and respect, they are likely to be considerably hindered in becoming people who are guided by principles of justice. Moreover, I claim, the sharing of roles by men and women, rather than the division of roles between them, would have a further positive impact because the experience of *being* a physical and psychological nurturer—whether of a child or of another adult—would increase that capacity to identify with and fully comprehend the viewpoints of others that is important to a sense of justice. In a society that minimized gender this would be more likely to be the experience of all of us.

Almost every person in our society starts life in a family of some sort or other. Fewer of these families now fit the usual, though by no means universal, standard of previous generations, that is, wage-working father, homemaking mother, and children. More families these days are headed by a single parent; lesbian and gay parenting is no longer so rare; many children have two wage-working parents, and receive at least some of their early care outside the home. While its forms are varied, the family in which a child is raised, especially in the earliest years, is clearly a crucial place for early moral development and for the formation of our basic attitudes to others. It is, potentially, a place where we can *learn to be just*. It is especially important for the development of a sense of justice that grows from sharing the experiences of others and becoming aware of the points of view of others who are different in some respects from ourselves, but with whom we clearly have some interests in common.

The importance of the family for the moral development of individuals was far more often recognized by political theorists of the past than it is by those of the present. Hegel, Rousseau, Tocqueville, Mill, and Dewey are obvious examples that come to mind. Rousseau, for example, shocked by Plato's proposal to abolish the family, says that it is

> as though there were no need for a natural base on which to form conventional ties; as though the love of one's nearest were not the principle of the love one owes the state; as though it were not by means of the small fatherland which is the family that the heart attaches itself to the large one.[29]

Defenders of both autocratic and democratic regimes have recognized the political importance of different family forms for the formation of citizens. On the one hand, the nineteenth-century monarchist Louis de Bonald argued against the divorce reforms of the French Revolution, which he claimed had weakened the patriarchal family, on the grounds that "in order to keep the state out of the hands of the people, it is necessary to keep the family out of the hands of women and children."[30] Taking this same line of thought in the opposite direction, the U.S. Supreme Court decided in 1879 in *Reynolds v. Nebraska* that familial patriarchy fostered despotism and was therefore intolerable. Denying Mormon men the freedom to practice polygamy, the Court asserted that it was an offense "subversive of good order" that "leads to the patriarchal principle, . . . [and] when applied to large communities, fetters the people in stationary despotism, while that principle cannot long exist in connection with monogamy."[31]

However, while de Bonald was consistent in his adherence to an hierarchical family structure as necessary for an undemocratic political system, the Supreme

Court was by no means consistent in promoting an egalitarian family as an essential underpinning for political democracy. For in other decisions of the same period—such as *Bradwell v. Illinois,* the famous 1872 case that upheld the exclusion of women from the practice of law—the Court rejected women's claims to legal equality, in the name of a thoroughly patriarchal, though monogamous, family that was held to require the dependence of women and their exclusion from civil and political life.[32] While bigamy was considered patriarchal, and as such a threat to republican, democratic government, the refusal to allow a married woman to employ her talents and to make use of her qualifications to earn an independent living was not considered patriarchal. It was so far from being a threat to the civil order, in fact, that it was deemed necessary for it, and as such was ordained by both God and nature. Clearly in both *Reynolds* and *Bradwell,* "state authorities enforced family forms preferred by those in power and justified as necessary to stability and order."[33] The Court noticed the despotic potential of polygamy, but was blind to the despotic potential of patriarchal monogamy. This was perfectly acceptable to them as a training ground for citizens.

Most theorists of the past who stressed the importance of the family and its practices for the wider world of moral and political life by no means insisted on congruence between the structures or practices of the family and those of the outside world. Though concerned with moral development, they bifurcated public from private life to such an extent that they had no trouble reconciling inegalitarian, sometimes admittedly unjust, relations founded upon sentiment within the family with a more just, even egalitarian, social structure outside the family. Rousseau, Hegel, Tocqueville—all thought the family was centrally important for the develop-ment of morality in citizens, but all defended the hierarchy of the marital structure while spurning such a degree of hierarchy in institutions and practices outside the household. Preferring instead to rely on love, altruism, and generosity as the basis for family relations, none of these theorists argued for *just* family structures as necessary for socializing children into citizenship in a just society.

The position that justice within the family is irrelevant to the development of just citizens was not plausible even when only men were citizens. John Stuart Mill, in *The Subjection of Women,* takes an impassioned stand against it. He argues that the inequality of women within the family is deeply subversive of justice in general in the wider social world, because it subverts the moral potential of men. Mill's first answer to the question, "For whose good are all these changes in women's rights to be undertaken?" is: "the advantage of having the most universal and pervading of all human relations regulated by justice instead of injustice." Making marriage a relationship of equals, he argues, would tranform this central part of daily life from "a school of despotism" into "a school of moral cultivation."[34] He goes on to discuss, in the strongest of terms, the noxious effect of growing up in a family not regulated by justice. Consider, he says, "the self-worship, the unjust self-preference," nourished in a boy growing up in a household in which "by the mere fact of being born a male he is by right the superior of all and every one of an entire half of the human race." Mill concludes that the example set by perpetuating a marital structure "con-tradictory to the first principles of social justice" must have such "a perverting influence" that it is hard even to imagine the good effects of changing it. All other attempts to educate people to respect and practice justice, Mill claims, will be superficial "as long as the citadel of the enemy is not attacked." Mill felt as much hope for what the family might be as he felt despair at what it was not. "The family, justly constituted, would be the real school of the virtues of freedom," primary among which was "justice, . . . grounded as before on equal, but now also on sympathetic association."[35] Mill both saw clearly and had the courage to address what so many other political philosophers either could not see, or saw and turned away from.

Despite the strength and fervor of his advocacy of women's rights, however, Mill's idea of a just family structure falls far short of that of many feminists even of his own time, including his wife, Harriet Taylor. In spite of the fact that Mill recognized both the empowering effect of earnings on one's position in the family and the limiting effect of domestic responsibility on women's opportunities, he balked at questioning the traditional division of labor between the sexes. For him, a woman's choice of marriage was parallel to a man's choice of a profession: unless and until she had fulfilled her obligations to her husband and children, she should not undertake anything else. But clearly, however equal the legal rights of husbands and wives, this position largely undermines Mill's own insistence upon the importance of marital equality for a just society. His acceptance of the traditional division of labor, without making any provision for wives who were thereby made economically dependent upon their husbands, largely undermines his insistence upon family justice as the necessary foundation for social justice.

Thus even those political theorists of the past who have perceived the family as an important school of moral development have rarely acknowledged the need for congruence between the family and the wider social order, which suggests that families themselves need to be just. Even when they have, as with Mill, they have been unwilling to push hard on the traditional division of labor within the family in the name of justice or equality.

Contemporary theorists of justice, with few exceptions, have paid little or no attention to the question of moral development—of how we are to *become* just. Most of them seem to think, to adapt slightly Hobbes's notable phrase, that just men spring like mushrooms from the earth.[36] Not surprisingly, then, it is far less often acknowledged in recent than in past theories that the family is important for moral development, and especially for instilling a sense of justice. As I have already noted, many theorists pay no attention at all to either the family or gender. In the rare case that the issue of justice within the family is given any sustained attention, the family is not viewed as a potential school of social justice.[37] In the rare case that a theorist pays any sustained attention to the development of a sense of justice or morality, little if any attention is likely to be paid to the family.[38] Even in the rare event that theorists pay considerable attention to the family *as* the first major locus of moral socialization, they do not refer to the fact that families are almost all still thoroughly gender-structured institutions.[39]

Among major contemporary theorists of justice, John Rawls alone treats the family seriously as the earliest school of moral development. He argues that a just, well-ordered society will be stable only if its members continue to develop a sense of justice. And he argues that families play a fundamental role in the stages by which this sense of justice is acquired. From the parents' love for their child, which comes to be reciprocated, comes the child's "sense of his own value and the desire to become the sort of person that they are."[40] The family, too, is the first of that series of "associations" in which we participate, from which we acquire the capacity, crucial for a sense of justice, to see things from the perspectives of others. . . . This capacity—the capacity for empathy—is essential for maintaining a sense of justice of the Rawlsian kind. For the perspective that is necessary for maintaining a sense of justice is not that of the egoistic or disembodied self, or of the dominant few who overdetermine "our" traditions or "shared understandings," or (to use Nagel's term) of "the view from nowhere," but rather the perspective of every person in the society for whom the principles of justice are being arrived at. . . . The problem with Rawls's rare and interesting discussion of moral development is that it rests on the un-explained *assumption* that family institutions are just. If gendered family institutions are *not* just, but are, rather, a relic of caste or feudal societies in which responsibilities, roles, and resources are distributed, not in accordance with the principles of justice he arrives at or with any other commonly respected values, but in accordance with innate differences that are imbued with enormous social significance, then Rawls's theory of moral development would seem to be built on uncertain ground. This problem is exacerbated by suggestions in some of Rawls's most recent work that families are "private institutions," to which it is not appropriate to apply standards of justice. But if families are to help form just individuals and citizens, surely they must be *just families*.

In a just society, the structure and practices of families must give women the same opportunities as men to develop their capacities, to participate in political power and influence social choices, and to be economically secure. But in addition to this, families must be just because of the vast influence that they have on the moral development of children. The family is the primary institution of formative moral development. And the structure and practices of the family must parallel those of the larger society if the sense of justice is to be fostered and maintained. While many theorists of justice, both past and present, appear to have denied the importance of at least one of these factors, my own view is that both are absolutely crucial. A society that is committed to equal respect for all of its members, and to justice in social distributions of benefits and responsibilities, can neither neglect the family nor accept family structures and practices that violate these norms, as do current gender-based structures and practices. It is essential that children who are to develop into adults with a strong sense of justice and commitment to just institutions spend their earliest and most formative years in an environment in which they are loved and nurtured, *and* in which principles of justice are abided by and respected. What is a child of either sex to learn about fairness in the average household with two full-time working parents, where the mother does, at the very least, twice as much family work as the father? What is a child to learn about the value of nurturing and domestic work in a home with a traditional division of labor in which the father either subtly or not so subtly uses the fact that he is the wage earner to "pull rank" on or to abuse his wife? What is a child to learn about responsibility for others in a family in which, after many years of arranging her life around the needs of her husband and children, a woman is faced with having to provide for herself and her children but is totally ill-equipped for the task by the life she agreed to lead, has led, and expected to go on leading?

Notes

1. U.S. Department of Labor, *Employment and Earnings: July 1987* (Washington, D.C.: Government Printing Office, 1987); Ruth Sidel, *Women and Children Last: The Plight of Poor Women in Affluent America* (New York: Viking, 1986), pp. xvi, 158. See also David T. Ellwood, *Poor Support: Poverty in the American Family* (New York: Basic Books, 1988), pp. 84–85, on the chronicity of poverty in single-parent households.

2. Shirley Williams, in Williams and Elizabeth Holtzman, "Women in the Political World: Observations," *Daedalus* 116, no. 4 (Fall 1987): 30.

3. Twenty-three percent of single parents have never been married and 12 percent are widowed. (U.S. Bureau of the Census, Current Population Reports, *Household and Family Characteristics: March 1987* [Washington, D.C.: Government Printing Office, 1987], p. 79). In 1987, 6.8 percent of children under eighteen were living with a never-married parent. ("Study Shows Growing Gap Between Rich and Poor," *New York Times,* March 23, 1989, p. A24). The proportions for the total population are very different from those for black families, of whom in 1984 half of those with adult members under thirty-five years of age were maintained by single, female parents, three-quarters of whom were never married. (Frank Levy, *Dollars and Dreams: The Changing American Income Distribution* [New York: Russell Sage, 1987], p. 156).

4. As Joan Scott has pointed out, *gender* was until recently used only as a grammatical term. See "Gender: A Useful Category of Historical Analysis," in Joan Wallach Scott, *Gender and the Politics of History* (New York: Columbia University Press, 1988), p. 28, citing Fowler's *Dictionary of Modern English Usage.*

5. Among Anglo-American feminists see, for example, Mary Daly, *Gyn/Ecology: The Metaethics of Radical Feminism* (Boston: Beacon Press, 1978); Susan Griffin, *Woman and Nature: The Roaring Inside Her* (New York: Harper & Row, 1978). For a good, succinct discussion of radical feminist biological determinism, see Alison Jaggar, *Feminist Politics and Human Nature* (Totowa, N.J.: Rowman and Allanheld, 1983).

6. See, for example, Sylvia Yanagisako and Jane Collier, "The Mode of Reproduction in Anthropology," in *Theoretical Perspectives on Sexual Difference,* ed. Deborah Rhode (New Haven: Yale University Press, in press).

7. Nancy Chodorow, *The Reproduction of Mothering: Psychoanalysis and the Sociology of Gender* (Berkeley: University of California Press, 1978); Dorothy Dinnerstein, *The Mermaid and the Minotaur: Sexual Arrangements and Human Malaise* (New York: Harper & Row, 1976). For further discussion of this issue and further references to the literature, see chapter 6, note 58, and accompanying text.

8. Linda Nicholson, *Gender and History* (New York: Columbia University Press, 1986); Michelle Z. Rosaldo, "The Use and Abuse of Anthropology," *Signs* 5, no. 3 (1980); Joan Wallach Scott, *Gender and the Politics of History* (New York: Columbia University Press, 1986).

9. For such critiques, see Bell Hooks, *Ain't I a Woman: Black Women and Feminism* (Boston: South End Press, 1981), and *Feminist Theory: From Margin to Center* (Boston: South End Press, 1984); Elizabeth V. Spelman, *Inessential Woman: Problems of Exclusion in Feminist Thought* (Boston: Beacon Press, 1989).

10. There is now an abundant literature on the subject of women, their exclusion from nondomestic

life, and the reasons given to justify it, in Western political theory. See, for example, Lorenne J. Clark and Lynda Lange, eds., *The Sexism of Social and Political Thought* (Toronto: University of Toronto Press, 1979); Jean Bethke Elshtain, *Public Man, Private Woman: Women in Social and Political Thought* (Princeton: Princeton University Press, 1981); Genevieve Lloyd, *The Man of Reason: "Male" and "Female" in Western Philosophy* (Minneapolis: University of Minnesota Press, 1984); Mary O'Brien, *The Politics of Reproduction* (London: Routledge & Kegan Paul, 1981); Susan Moller Okin, *Women in Western Political Thought* (Princeton: Princeton University Press, 1979); Carole Pateman, "Feminist Critiques of the Public/Private Dichotomy," in *Public and Private in Social Life*, ed. S. Benn and G. Gaus (London: Croom Helm, 1983); Carole Pateman and Elizabeth Gross, eds., *Feminist Challenges: Social and Political Theory* (Boston: Northeastern University Press, 1987); Carole Pateman, *The Sexual Contract* (Stanford: Stanford University Press, 1988); Carole Pateman and Mary L. Shanley, eds., *Feminist Critiques of Political Theory* (Oxford: Polity Press, in press).

11. Bruce Ackerman, *Social Justice in the Liberal State* (New Haven: Yale University Press, 1980); Ronald Dworkin, *Taking Rights Seriously* (Cambridge: Harvard University Press, 1977); William Galston, *Justice and the Human Good* (Chicago: University of Chicago Press, 1980); Alasdair MacIntyre, *After Virtue* (Notre Dame: University of Notre Dame Press, 1981), and *Whose Justice? Which Rationality?* (Notre Dame: University of Notre Dame Press, 1988); Robert Nozick, *Anarchy, State, and Utopia* (New York: Basic Books, 1974); Roberto Unger, *Knowledge and Politics* (New York: The Free Press, 1975), and *The Critical Legal Studies Movement* (Cambridge: Harvard University Press, 1986).

12. Philip Green, in *Retrieving Democracy: In Search of Civic Equality* (Totowa, N.J.: Rowman and Allanheld, 1985), argues that the social equality that is prerequisite to real democracy is incompatible with the current division of labor between the sexes. See pp. 96–108.

13. Michael Walzer, *Spheres of Justice* (New York: Basic Books, 1983).

14. This is commented on and questioned by Francis Schrag, "Justice and the Family," *Inquiry* 19 (1976): 200, and Walzer, *Spheres of Justice*, chap. 9.

15. See note 10 of this chapter. The phrase is Dale Spender's.

16. See, for example, David Gauthier, *Morals by Agreement* (Oxford: Oxford University Press, 1986), passim and p. vi. Fortunately, Gauthier's computer was able to control its zeal for randomization enough to avoid referring to Plato and Rawls as "she" and Queen Gertrude and Mary Gibson as "he."

17. *General Electric v. Gilbert,* 429 U.S. 125 (1976), 135–36; second phrase quoted from *Geduldig v. Aiello,* 417 U.S. 484 (1974), 496–97, emphasis added.

18. Ackerman, *Social Justice,* pp. 127–28. He takes gender neutrality to the point of suggesting a hypothetical case in which "a couple simply *enjoy* abortions so much that they conceive embryos simply to kill them a few months later."

19. Derek L. Phillips, *Toward a Just Social Order* (Princeton: Princeton University Press, 1986), esp. pp. 187–96.

20. Ibid., pp. 224–26.

21. Ibid., esp. chap. 9.

22. I have analyzed some of the ways in which theorists in the tradition avoided considering the justice of gender in "Are Our Theories of Justice Gender-Neutral?" in *The Moral Foundations of Civil Rights,* ed. Robert Fullinwider and Claudia Mills (Totowa, N.J.: Rowman and Littlefield, 1986).

23. See Judith Hicks Stiehm, "The Unit of Political Analysis: Our Aristotelian Hangover," in *Discovering Reality: Feminist Perspectives on Epistemology, Metaphysics, Methodology, and Philosophy of Science,* ed. Sandra Harding and Merrill B. Hintikka (Dordrecht, Holland: Reidel, 1983).

24. See Carole Pateman and Theresa Brennan, " 'Mere Auxiliaries to the Commonwealth': Women and the Origins of Liberalism," *Political Studies* 27, no. 2 (June 1979); also Susan Moller Okin, "Women and the Making of the Sentimental Family," *Philosophy and Public Affairs* 11, no. 1 (Winter 1982). This issue is treated at much greater length in Pateman, *The Sexual Contract.*

25. This claim, originating in the moral development literature, has significantly influenced recent feminist moral and political theory. Two central books are Carol Gilligan, *In a Different Voice* (Cambridge: Harvard University Press, 1982); and Nel Noddings, *Caring: A Feminine Approach to Ethics and Moral Education* (Berkeley: University of California Press, 1984). For the influence of Gilligan's work on feminist theory, see, for example, Seyla Benhabib, "The Generalized and the Concrete Other: The Kohlberg-Gilligan Controversy and Feminist Theory," in *Feminism as Critique*, ed. Benhabib and Drucilla Cornell (Minneapolis: University of Minnesota Press, 1987); Lawrence Blum, "Gilligan and Kohlberg: Implications for Moral Theory," *Ethics* 98, no. 3 (1988); and Eva Kittay and Diana Meyers, eds., *Women and Moral Theory* (Totowa, N.J.:Rowman and Allenheld, 1986). For a valuable alternative approach to the issues, and an excellent selective list of references to what has now become a vast literature, see Owen Flanagan and Kathryn Jackson, "Justice, Care and Gender: The Kohlberg-Gilligan Debate Revisited," *Ethics* 97, no. 3 (1987).

26. See, for example, John M. Broughton, "Women's Rationality and Men's Virtues: A Critique of Gender Dualism in Gilligan's Theory of Moral Development," *Social Research* 50, no. 3 (1983); Owen Flanagan, *Varieties of Moral Personality: Ethics and Psychological Realism* (Cambridge: Harvard University Press, forthcoming), ch. 8; Catherine G. Greeno and Eleanor E. Maccoby, "How Different Is the 'Different Voice'?" and Gilligan's reply, *Signs* 11, no. 2 (1986); Debra Nails, "Social-Scientific Sexism: Gilligan's Mismeasure of Man," *Social Research* 50, no. 3 (1983); Joan Tronto, " 'Women's Morality': Beyond Gender Difference to a Theory of Care," *Signs* 12, no. 4 (1987); Lawrence J. Walker, "Sex Differences in the Development of Moral Reasoning: A Critical Review," *Child Development* 55 (1984).

27. See extracts from the Apostolic Letter in *New York Times,* October 1, 1988, pp. A1 and 6. On the reinforcement of the old stereotypes in general, see Susan Moller Okin, "Thinking Like a Woman," in Rhode, ed., *Theoretical Perspectives.*

28. See esp. James Fishkin, *Justice, Equal Opportunity and the Family* (New Haven: Yale University Press, 1983); Phillips, *Just Social Order,* esp. pp. 346–49; Rawls, *Theory,* pp. 74, 300–301, 511–12.

29. Jean-Jacques Rousseau, *Emile: or On Education,* trans. Allan Bloom (New York: Basic Books, 1979), p. 363.

30. Louis de Bonald, in *Archives Parlementaires,* 2e série (Paris, 1869), vol. 15, p. 612; cited and translated by Roderick Phillips, "Women and Family Breakdown in Eighteenth-Century France: Rouen 1780–1800," *Social History* 2, (1976): 217.

31. *Reynolds v. Nebraska,* 98 U.S. 145 (1879), 164, 166.

32. *Bradwell v. Illinois,* 83 U.S. 130 (1872).

33. Martha Minow, "We, the Family: Constitutional Rights and American Families," *The American Journal of History* 74, no. 3 (1987): 969, discussing *Reynolds* and other nineteenth-century cases.

34. John Stuart Mill, *The Subjection of Women* (1869), in *Collected Works,* ed. J. M. Robson (Toronto: University of Toronto Press, 1984), vol. 21, pp. 324, 293–95. At the time Mill wrote, women had no political rights and coverture deprived married women of most legal rights, too. He challenges all this in his essay.

35. Mill, *Subjection of Women,* pp. 324–25, 294–95.

36. Hobbes writes of "men . . . as if but even now sprung out of the earth . . . like mushrooms." "Philosophical Rudiments Concerning Government and Society," in *The English Works of Thomas Hobbes,* ed. Sir William Molesworth (London: John Bohn, 1966), vol. 2, p. 109.

37. For example, Walzer, *Spheres of Justice,* chap. 9, "Kinship and Love."

38. See Alan Gewirth, *Reason and Morality* (Chicago: University of Chicago Press, 1978). He discusses moral development from time to time, but places families within the broad category of "voluntary associations" and does not discuss gender roles within them.

39. This is the case with both Rawls's *A Theory of Justice* (Cambridge: Harvard University Press, 1971), . . . and Phillips's sociologically oriented *Toward a Just Social Order,* as discussed above.

40. Rawls, *Theory,* p. 465.

23

Socialist Feminism
and Human Nature

ALISON M. JAGGAR

. . . Like radical feminism, socialist feminism is a daughter of the contemporary women's liberation movement. It is a slightly younger daughter, born in the 1970s and, like most younger daughters, impressed by its elder sister, while wanting at the same time to avoid her mistakes. The central project of socialist feminism is the development of a politial theory and practice that will synthesize the best insights of radical feminism and of the Marxist tradition and that simultaneously will escape the problems associated with each. So far, socialist feminism has made only limited progress toward this goal: "It is a commitment to the *development* of an analysis and political practice, rather than to one which already exists."[1] In spite of the programmatic nature of its achievement so far, I believe that socialist feminism constitutes a distinctive approach to political life, one that offers the most convincing promise of constructing an adequate theory and practice for women's liberation.

Any attempt to define socialist feminism faces the same problems as attempts to define liberal feminism, radical feminism or Marxism. Feminist theorists and activists do not always wear labels and, even if they do, they are not always agreed on who should wear which label. Moreover, there are differences even between those wearing the same label and, in addition, dialogue between feminists of different tendencies has led to modifications in all their views. Most Marxists, for instance, now take the oppression of women much more seriously than they did prior to the emergence of the women's liberation movement, while radical feminists are paying

Abridged from *Feminist Politics and Human Nature* (1983), pp. 123–132. Reprinted by permission of the author.

increasing attention to class, ethnic and national differences between women. As a result, the line between socialist feminism and other feminist theories is increasingly blurred, at least on the surface. For all these reasons, it is inevitable that my account of socialist feminism, like my account of the other feminist theories, will be stipulative as well as reportive. As in defining the other theories, I shall identify socialist feminism primarily by reference to its distinctive, underlying conception of human nature.

The easiest way to provide a preliminary outline of socialist feminism is in terms of its similarities and contrasts with the other feminist theories, especially with Marxism and radical feminism to which it is most closely linked. In a very general sense, all feminists address the same problem: what constitutes the oppression of women and how can that oppression be ended?. Both liberal feminists and traditional Marxists believe that this question can be answered in terms of the categories and principles that were formulated originally to deal with other problems. For them, the oppression of women is just one among a number of essentially similar types of problems. Socialist feminism shares with radical feminism the belief that older established political theories are incapable, in principle, of giving an adequate account of women's oppression and that, in order to do so, it is necessary to develop new political and economic categories.

Like radical feminists, socialist feminists believe that these new categories must reconceptualize not only the so-called public sphere, but also the hitherto private sphere of human life. They must give us a way of understanding sexuality, childbearing, childrearing and personal maintenance in political and economic terms. Unlike many American radical feminists, however, socialist feminists attempt to conceptualize these activities in a deliberately historical, rather than a universal and sometimes biologistic, way. A defining feature of socialist feminism is that it attempts to interpret the historical materialist method of traditional Marxism so that it applies to the issues made visible by radical feminists. To revise Juliet Mitchell's comment, it uses a feminist version of the Marxist method to provide feminist answers to feminist questions.[2]

Ever since its inception in the mid-1960s, the women's liberation movement has been split by a chronic dispute over the relation between feminism and Marxism. This dispute has taken a number of forms, but one of the most common ways of interpreting it has been in terms of political priorities. The political analysis of traditional Marxism has led to the position that the struggle for feminism should be subordinated to the class struggle, whereas a radical feminist analysis has implied that the struggle for women's liberation should take priority over the struggle for all other forms of liberation. Socialist feminism rejects this dilemma. Not only does it refuse to compromise socialism for the sake of feminism or feminism for the sake of socialism; it argues that either of these compromises ultimately would be self-defeating. On the socialist feminist analysis, capitalism, male dominance, racism and imperialism are intertwined so inextricably that they are inseparable; consequently the abolition of any of these systems of domination requires the end of all of them. Socialist feminists claim that a full understanding of the capitalist system requires a recognition of the way in which it is structured by male dominance and, conversely, that a full understanding of contemporary male dominance requires a recognition of the way it is organized by the capitalist division of labor. Socialist feminists believe that an adequate account of "capitalist patriarchy" requires the use of the historical materialist method developed originally by Marx and Engels. They argue, however, that the conceptual tools of Marxism are blunt and biased until they are ground into precision on the sharp edge of feminist consciousness.

One question that arises from this preliminary characterization is whether socialist feminism is or is not a variety of Marxism. Obviously, the answer to this question depends both on one's understanding of socialist feminism and on one's interpretation of Marxism. Political motivations are also involved. Some Marxists do not want the honorific title of Marxism to be granted to what they see as heresy,[3] others want to appropriate for Marxism at least those aspects of socialist feminism that they perceive as correct. Similarly, some socialist feminists want to define themselves as Marxists in opposition to other types of socialists; others see no reason to give Marx credit for a theory and a practice that reveals a social reality ignored and obscured by traditional Marxism. My own view is that socialist feminism is unmistakably Marxist, at least insofar as it utilizes the method of historical materialism. I shall argue that socialist feminism is in fact the most consistent application of Marxist method and therefore the most "orthodox" form of Marxism. . . .

The Socialist Feminist Conception of Human Nature

Socialist feminism is committed to the basic Marxist conception of human nature as created historically through the dialectical interrelation between human biology, human society and the physical environment. This interrelation is mediated by human labor or praxis. The specific form of praxis dominant within a given society creates the distinctive physical and psychological human types characteristic of that society.

Traditional political theory has given theoretical recognition only to a very limited number of human types. It is true that liberals acknowledge individual human variation; indeed, this acknowledgment is a necessary part of their arguments for a firm limitation on the extent of state power. As we have seen, Locke and Mill explain the reasons for at least some of this variation in terms of the social opportunities available to different classes, and liberal feminists explain psychological differences between the sexes in terms of sex-role socialization. Ultimately, however, liberals view the differences between people as relatively superficial, and they assume that underlying these superficial differences is a certain fixed human nature which is modified but not fundamentally created by social circumstances. Marxists, by contrast, view human nature as necessarily constituted in society: they believe that specific historical conditions create distinctive human types. Within contemporary capitalism, they give theoretical recognition to two such types, the capitalist and the proletariat. However, the traditional Marxist conception of human nature is flawed by its failure to recognize explicitly that all human beings in contemporary society belong not only to a specific class; they also have a specific sex and they are at a specific stage in the life cycle from infancy to death. In addition, although this point was not emphasized earlier because it is not a specifically feminist point, all humans in modern industrial society have specific racial, ethnic and national backgrounds. Contemporary society thus consists of groups of individuals, defined simultaneously by age, sex, class, nationality and by racial and ethnic origin, and these groups differ markedly from each other, both physically and psychologically. Liberal political theory has tended to ignore or minimize all these differences. Marxist political theory has tended to recognize only differences of class. The political theory of radical feminism has tended to recognize only differences of age and sex, to understand these in universal terms, and often to view them as determined biologically. By contrast, socialist feminism recognizes all these differences as constituent parts of contemporary human nature and seeks a way of understanding them that is not only materialist but also historical. In particular, it has insisted on the need for a more adequate theoretical understanding of the differences between women and men. Given that its methodological commitment is basically Marxist, it seeks this understanding through an examination of what it calls the sexual division of labor.[4] In other words, it focuses on the different types of praxis undertaken by women and men in order to develop a fully historical materialist account of the social construction of sex and gender.

The differences between women and men are both physical and psychological. Socialist feminist have begun to look at both these aspects of human nature. Some theorists, for instance, have studied variations in menstruation and menopause and have discovered that often these variations are socially determined.[5] Marian Lowe has begun to investigate the ways in which society influences women's sporting achievements, as well as their menstrual patterns.[6] Iris Young has explored some of the socially determined ways in which men and women move differently from each other and experience space, objects, and even their own bodies differently.[7] She has observed that women in sexist society are "physically handicapped." Interesting work has also been done on women's body language.[8] In undertaking these sorts of investigations, socialist feminists focus on the dialectical relationship between sex and society as it emerges through activity organized by gender norms. The methodological approach of socialist feminists makes it obvious that they have abandoned an ahistorical conception of human biology. Instead, they view human biology as being, in part, socially constructed. Biology is "gendered" as well as sexed.

In spite of their interest in the physical differences between women and men, contemporary feminists have been far more concerned with psychological differences, and socialist feminist theory has reflected that priority. Its main focus has been on the social construction not of masculine and feminine physical types, but rather of masculine and feminine character types. Among the many socialist feminist theorists who have worked on this project are Juliet Mitchell, Jane Flax, Gayle Rubin, Nancy Chodorow and, perhaps, Dorothy Dinnerstein.[9] All these theorists have been impressed by how early in life masculine and feminine character structures are established and by the relative rigidity of these structures, once established. To explain the mechanism by which psychological masculinity and feminity are imposed on infants and young children, all utilize some version of psychoanalysis. This is because they view psychoanalytic theory as providing the most plausible and systematic account of how the individual psyche is structured by gender. But unlike Freud, the father of psychoanalysis, socialist feminist theorists do not view psychological masculinity and femininity as the child's inevitable response to a fixed and universal biological endowment. Instead, they view the acquisition of gendered character types as the result of specific social practices, particularly procreative practices, that are not determined by biology and that in principle, therefore, are alterable. They want to debiologize Freud and to reinterpret him in historical materialist terms. As Gayle Rubin puts it: "Psychoanalysis provides a description of the mechanisms by which the sexes are divided and deformed, of how bisexual, androgynous infants are transformed into boys and girls." . . .[10]

The distinctive aspect of the socialist feminist approach to human psychology is the way in which it synthesizes insights drawn from a variety of sources. Socialist feminism claims all of the following: that our "inner" lives, as well as our bodies and behavior, are structured by gender; that this gender-structuring is not innate but is socially imposed; that the specific characteristics that are imposed are related systematically to the historically prevailing system of organizing social production; that the gender-structuring of our "inner" lives occurs when we are very young and is reinforced throughout our lives in a variety of different spheres; and that these relatively rigid masculine and feminine character structures are a very important element in maintaining male dominance. Given this conception of human psychology, one of the major theoretical tasks that socialist feminism sets itself is to provide a historical materialist account of the relationship between our "inner" lives and our social praxis. It seeks to connect masculine and feminine psychology with the sexual division of labor. . . .

It is generally accepted, by non-feminists and feminists alike, that the most obvious manifestation of the sexual division of labor, in contemporary society if not in all societies, is marked by the division between the so-called public and private spheres of human life. The line between these two spheres has varied historically: in the political theory of ancient Greece, for instance, "the economy" fell within the private sphere, whereas in contemporary political theory, both liberal and Marxist, "the economy" is considered—in different ways—to be part of the public realm. Wherever the distinction has existed, the private realm has always included sexuality and procreation, has always been viewed as more "natural" and therefore less "human" than the public realm, and has always been viewed as the realm of women[11] Although women have always done many kinds of work, they have been defined primarily by their sexual and procreative labor; throughout history, women have been defined as "sex objects" and as mothers.

Partly because of this definition of women's work and partly because of their conviction that an individual's gender identity is established very early in life, much socialist feminist theory has focused on the area of sexuality and procreation. Yet the theory has been committed to conceptualizing this area in terms that are historical, rather than biological, and specific, rather than universal. Socialist feminism has accepted the radical feminist insight that sexual activity, childbearing, and childrearing are social practices that embody power relations and are therefore appropriate subjects for political analysis. Because of its rejection of biological determinism, however, socialist feminism denies the radical feminist assumption that these practices are fundamentally invariant. On the contrary, socialist feminists have stressed historical variation both in the practices and in the categories by which they are understood. Zillah Eisenstein writes:

> None of the processes in which a woman engages can be understood separate from the relations of the society which she embodies and which are reflected in the ideology of society. For instance, the act of giving birth to a child is only termed an act of motherhood if it reflects the relations of marriage and the family. Otherwise the very same act can be termed adultery and the child is "illegitimate" or a "bastard." The term "mother" may have a significantly different meaning when different relations are involved—as in "unwed mother." It depends on what relations are embodied in the act.[12]

In the same spirit, Ann Foreman writes that "fatherhood is a social invention . . . located in a series of functions rather than in biology."[13] Rayna Rapp writes that even "being a child is a highly variable social relation."[14] Using the same historical approach, Ann Ferguson has argued that the emergence of lesbianism, as a distinct sexual identity, is a recent rather than a universal phenomenon insofar as it presupposes an urban society with the possibility of economic independence for women.[15] More generally, "It was only with the development of capitalist societies that 'sexuality' and 'the economy' became separable from other spheres of society and could be counter-posed to one another as realities of different sorts."[16]

Other authors have claimed that there is no transhistorical definition of marriage in terms of which the marital institutions of different cultures can be compared usefully.[17] Even within a single society, divisions of class mean that the working-class family unit is defined very differently from the upper-class family unit, and that it performs very different social functions.[18] One author denies that the family is a "bounded universe" and suggests that "we should extend to the study of 'family' [a] thoroughgoing agnosticism."[19] In general, socialist feminist theory has viewed human nature as constructed in part through the historically specific ways in which people have organized their sexual, childbearing and childrearing activities. The organization of these activities both affects and is affected by class and ethnic differences, but it is seen as particularly important in creating the masculine and feminine physiques and character structures that are considered appropriate in a given society.

The beginnings of this conception of human nature are already evident, to some extent, in the work of Marx and Engels. Engels' famous definition of the materialist conception of history in his introduction to *The Origin of the Family, Private Property and the State* states clearly:

The social organization under which the people of a particular historical epoch and a particular country live is determined by both kinds of production: by the state of development of labor on the one hand and of the family on the other.[20]

Moreover, Marx and Engels warn explicitly against conceptualizing procreation in an ahistorical way. In *The German Ideology,* they mock an ahistorical approach to "the concept of the family,"[21] and Engels' own work in *Origin* is designed precisely to demonstrate historical change in the social rules governing the eligibility of an individual's sexual partners. However, Marx and Engels view changes in the social organization of procreation as ultimately determined themselves by changes in the so-called mode of production, at least in postprimitive societies. Consequently, they see procreation as being now only of secondary importance in shaping human nature and society. One reason for this view may be that Marx and Engels still retain certain assumptions about the "natural," presumably biological, determination of much procreative activity. Thus, they do not give a symmetrical treatment to the human needs for food, shelter, and clothing, on the one hand, and to sexual, childbearing and childrearing needs, on the other. They view the former as changing historically, giving rise to new possibilities of social organization, but they regard human procreative needs as more "natural" and less open to historical transformation. Socialist feminists, by contrast, emphasize the social determination of sexual, childbearing and childrearing needs. They understand that these needs have developed historically in dialectical relation with changing procreative practices. Consequently, they are prepared to subject sexual and procreative practices to sustained political analysis and to reflect systematically on how changes in these practices could transform human nature.

Although socialist feminist theory stresses the importance of the so-called private sphere of procreation in constructing the historically appropriate types of masculinity and femininity, it does not ignore the so-called public sphere. It recognizes that women have always worked outside procreation, providing goods and services not only for their families but for the larger society as well. Socialist feminism claims that the conception of women as primarily sexual beings and/or as mothers is an ideological mystification that obscures the facts, for instance, that more than half the world's farmers are women,[22] and that, in the United States, women now make up almost half the paid labor force. Indeed, the Department of Labor projects that women will constitute 51.4 percent of the U.S. paid labor force by 1990.[23]

For socialist feminism, women, just as much as men, are beings whose labor transforms the non-human world. Socialist feminists view the slogan "A women's place is everywhere" as more than a call for change: for them, it is already a partial description of existing reality.

Only a partial description, however. Although socialist feminism recognizes the extent of women's productive work, it recognizes also that this work has rarely, if ever, been the same as men's. Even in contemporary market society, socialist feminism recognizes that the paid labor force is almost completely segregated by sex; at every level, there are "women's specialties." Within the contemporary labor force, moreover, women's work is invariably less prestigious, lower paid, and defined as being less skilled than men's, even when it involves such socially valuable and complex skills as dealing with children or sick people. Socialist feminism sees, therefore, that the sexual division of labor is not just a division *between* procreation and "production": it is also a division *within* procreation and *within* "production." Consequently, socialist feminism does not view contemporary masculinity and femininity as constructed entirely through the social organization of procreation; these constructs are elaborated and reinforced in nonprocreative labor as well. . . .

We can now summarize the socialist feminist view of human nature in general and of women's nature in particular. Unlike liberalism and some aspects of traditional Marxism, socialist feminism does not view humans as "abstract, genderless" (and ageless and colorless) individuals,[24] with women essentially indistinguishable from men. Neither does it view women as irreducibly different from men, the same yesterday, today and forever. Instead, it views women as constituted essentially by the social relations they inhabit. "(T)he social relations of society define the particular activity a woman engages in at a given moment. Outside these relations, 'woman' becomes an abstraction."[25]

Gayle Rubin paraphrases Marx thus:

> What is a domesticated woman? A female of the species. The one explanation is as good as the other. A woman is a woman. She only becomes a domestic, a wife, a chattel, a playboy bunny, a prostitute, or a human dictaphone in certain relations. Torn from these relationships, she is no more the helpmate of a man than gold in itself is money.[26]

To change these relationships is to change women's and so human nature.

Since history is never static, continuing changes in human nature are inevitable. As Marx himself remarked, "All history is nothing but a continuous transformation of human nature."[27] Socialist feminists want women to participate fully in taking conscious social control of these changes. They deny that there is anything especially natural about women's relationships with each other, with children or with men. Instead, they seek to reconstitute those relationships in such a way as to liberate the full power of women's (and human) creative potential.

No contemporary feminist would deny this goal, stated in the abstract. Just as at one time everyone was against sin, so now everyone is in favor of liberating human potential. Just as people used to disagree over how to identify sin, however, so now there is disagreement over what are human potentialities, which ones should be developed and how this development should be undertaken. Every conception of human nature implies an answer to these questions, and socialist feminism has its own distinctive answer. Unlike liberalism, the socialist feminist ideal of human fulfilment is not individual autonomy; for reasons that will be explained more fully later, socialist feminism views the ideal of autonomy as characteristically masculine as well as characteristically capitalist. The socialist feminist conception of human fulfillment is closer to the Marxist ideal of the full development of human potentialities through free productive labor, but socialist feminism construes productive labor more broadly than does traditional Marxism. Consequently, the socialist feminist ideal of human well-being and fulfilment includes the full development of human potentialities for free sexual expression, for freely bearing children and for freely rearing them.

To many Marxists, the theory of alienation expresses Marx's conception of human nature in capitalist society. As the theory is traditionaly interpreted, alienation characterizes primarily workers' relation to wage labor; however, Marx saw that the way workers experience wage labor also affects the way they experience the rest of their lives. Because their wage labor is coerced, their activity outside wage labor seems free by contrast.

> We arrive at the result that man (the worker) feels himself to be freely active only in his animal functions—eating, drinking and procreating, or at most also in his dwelling and in personal adornment—while in his human functions he is reduced to an animal. The animal becomes human and the human becomes animal.[28]

To socialist feminists, this conception of alienation is clearly male-biased. Men may feel free when eating, drinking, and procreating, but women do not. As the popular saying has it, "A woman's work is never done." An Englishman's home may be his castle, but it is his wife's prison. Women are compelled to do housework, to bear and raise children and to define themselves sexually in terms of men's wishes. The pressures on women to do this work are almost overwhelming:

> When I say that women are subject to a form of compulsive labor, I mean that they may only resist with great difficulty, and that the majority succumb. The same may be said of non-owners when it comes to wage work. In both cases, it is not compulsive in the sense that one is driven to it with whips and chains (though that happens, too!), but in the sense that no real alternative is generally available to women, and that everything in society conspires to ensure that women do this work. While a nonowner may attempt small independent production, or simply refuse to work and live off begging or state welfare, that is not proof of his freedom. The same is true of women. While a woman may with great difficulty resist doing reproductive work, that is no proof that she is "free" not to do it.[29]

One way in which socialist feminists are attempting to conceptualize contemporary women's lack of freedom is by extending the traditional Marxist theory of alienation. . . . Iris Young's reflections on "the struggle for our bodies," cited earlier in this chapter, suggest that women suffer a special form of alienation from their bodies. Similarly, Sandra Bartky claims that women are alienated in cultural production, as mothers and sexual beings. She believes that feminine narcissism is the paradigm of a specifically feminine form of sexual alienation.[30] Ann Foreman argues that femininity as such is an alienated condition: "While alienation reduces the man to an instrument of labour within industry, it reduces the woman to an instrument for his sexual pleasure within the family."[31] One may define the goal of socialist feminism as being to overcome all forms of alienation but especially those that are specific to women.

If it is difficult to envision what nonalienated industry would be like, it seems almost impossible to foresee the form of nonalienated sexuality or parenthood. Because of the ideological dogma that these are determined biologically, it is even harder to envision alternatives to prevailing sexual and procreative practices than it is to the capitalist mode of production. Alternative ways of organizing procreation tend to be viewed as science fiction; indeed, they are considered more often in fiction than in political theory. A number of socialist feminists are experimenting with alternatives in procreation, but the extent and validity of those experiments is limited, of course, by their context in a society that is emphatically neither socialist nor feminist.

The one solid basis of agreement among socialist feminists is that to overcome women's alienation, the sexual division of labor must be eliminated in every area of life. Just as sexual segregation in nonprocreative work must be eliminated, so men must participate fully in childrearing and, so far as possible, in childbearing.[32] Normative heterosexuality must be replaced by a situation in which the sex of one's lovers is a matter of social indifference, so that the dualist categories of heterosexual, homosexual and bisexual may be abandoned. Some authors describe the ideal as androgyny,[33] but even this term is implicitly dualistic. If it is retained for the present, we must remember that the ultimate transformation of human nature at which socialist feminists aim goes beyond the liberal conception of psychological androgyny to a possible transformation of "physical" human capacities, some of which, until now, have been seen as biologically limited to one sex. This transformation might even include the capacities for insemination, for lactation and for gestation so that, for instance, one woman could inseminate another, so that men and nonparturitive women could lactate and so that fertilized ova could be transplanted into women's or even into men's bodies. These developments may seem farfetched, but in fact they are already on the technological horizon;[34] however, what is needed much more immediately than technological development is a substantial reduction in the social domination of women by men. Only such a reduction can ensure that these or alternative technological possibilities are used to increase women's control over their bodies and thus over their lives, rather than being used as an additional means for women's subjugation. Gayle Rubin writes: "We are not only oppressed *as* women, we are oppressed by having to *be* women or men as the case may be."[35] The goal of socialist feminism is to abolish the social relations that constitute humans not only as workers and capitalists but also as women and men. Whereas one version of radical feminism takes the human ideal to be a woman, the ideal of socialist feminism is that women (and men) will disappear as socially constituted categories.

Notes

1. Margaret Page, "Socialist Feminism—a political alternative?, *m/f* 2 (1978):41.

2. Juliet Mitchell, a pioneering author whose work broke the ground for socialist feminism but whose basic orientation is ultimately Marxist, writes, "We should ask the feminist questions, but try to come up with Marxist answers." *Women's Estate* (New York: Pantheon Books, 1971), p. 99.

3. Pun intended. There is in fact an exciting journal named *Heresies: A Feminist Publication on Art & Politics*.

4. A clear statement of this methodological approach is given by Iris Young, "Socialist Feminism and the Limits of Dual Systems Theory," *Socialist Review* 50–51, pp. 169–88. Cf. also Iris Young, "Beyond the Unhappy Marriage: A Critique of the Dual Systems Theory," in Lydia Sargent, ed., *Women and Revolution* (Boston: South End Press, 1981), pp. 43–69. Young in fact uses the term "gender division of labor," but I prefer to follow Nancy Harstock in using the more familiar "sexual division of labor." Harstock justifies her use of the latter term in part because of her belief that the division of labor between women and men is not yet entirely a social affair (women and not men still bear children), in part because she wishes to keep a firm hold of "the bodily aspect of existence." Nancy Harstock, "The Feminist Standpoint: Developing the Ground for a Specifically Feminist Historical Materialism," in Sandra Harding and Merrill Hintikka, eds., *Discovering Reality: Feminist Perspectives on Epistemology, Metaphysics, Methodology and the Philosophy of Science* (Dordrecht: Reidel Publishing Co., 1983).

5. Janice Delaney, Mary Jane Lupton, and Emily Toth, *The Curse: A Cultural History of Menstruation* (New York: E. P. Dutton, 1976).

6. Marian Lowe, "The Biology of Exploitation and the Exploitation of Biology," paper read to the National Women's Studies Association Second National Conference, Indiana University, Bloomington, May 16–20, 1980.

7. Iris Marion Young, "Is There a Woman's World?—Some Reflections on the Struggle for our Bodies," proceedings of *The Second Sex—Thirty Years Later: A Commemorative Conference on Feminist Theory* (New York: The New York Institute for the Humanities, 1979). See also Young's "Throwing Like a Girl: A Phenomenology of Feminine Body Comportment, Motility and Sexuality," *Human Studies 3* (1980):137–56.

8. For example, see Nancy M. Henley, *Body Politics: Sex, Power and Non-Verbal Communication* (Englewood Cliffs, N.J.: Prentice-Hall, 1977).

9. Juliet Mitchell, *Psychoanalysis and Feminism* (New York: Vintage Books, 1975); Gayle Rubin, "The Traffic in Women: Notes on the 'Political Economy' of Sex," in Rayna R. Reiter, ed., *Toward an Anthropology of Women* (New York: Monthly Review Press, 1975), pp. 157–210; Nancy Chodorow, *Mothering: Psychoanalysis and the Sociology of Gender* (Berkeley and Los Angeles: University of California Press, 1978); Dorothy Dinnerstein, *The Mermaid and the Minotaur: Sexual Arrangements and Human Malaise* (New York: Harper & Row, 1977). Dinnerstein's work is idiosyncratic and consequently difficult to categorize. Many of her assumptions, however, are identical with the assumptions of the other theorists mentioned here.

10. Rubin, "Traffic," p. 185.

11. . . . Other theorists who have examined the distinction include Jean Bethke Elshtain, "Moral Woman and Immoral Man: A Consideration of the Public-Private Split and its Political Ramifications," *Politics and Society*, 1974; Jean Bethke Elshtain, *Public Man, Private Woman: Women in Social and Political Thought* (Princeton: Princeton University Press, 1981); and Linda Nicholson, *Feminism as Political Philosophy* (in progress). Cf. also M. Z. Rosaldo, "The Use and Abuse of Anthropology: Reflections on Feminism and Cross-Cultural Understanding," *Signs: Journal of Women in Culture & Society* 5, no. 3 (1980): esp. pp. 396–401.

12. Zillah Eisenstein, "Some Notes on the Relations of Capitalist Patriarchy," in Zillah Eisenstein, ed., *Capitalist Patriarchy and the Case for Socialist Feminism* (New York: Monthly Review Press, 1979), p. 47.

13. Ann Foreman, *Femininity as Alienation: Women and the Family in Marxism and Psychoanalysis* (London: Pluto Press, 1977), pp. 20 and 21.

14. Rayna Rapp, "Examining Family History," *Feminist Studies* 5, no 1 (Spring 1979):177.

15. Ann Ferguson, "Patriarchy, Sexual Identity and the Sexual Revolution," paper read at University of Cincinnati's Seventeenth Annual Philosophy Colloquium on "Philosophical Issues in Feminist Theory," November 13–16, 1980. This paper was later published in *Signs: Journal of Women in Culture and Society* 7, no. 1 (1981):158–72.

16. Robert A. Padgug, "Sexual Matters: On Conceptualising Sexuality in History," *Radical History Review* 20 (Spring/Summer 1979):16.

17. Kathleen Gough, "The Nayars and the Definition of Marriage," in P. B. Hammond, ed., *Cultural and Social Anthropology* (London, New York: Collier-Macmillan, 1964).

18. Rayna Rapp, "Family & Class in Contemporary America: Notes Toward an Understanding of Ideology," *Science and Society* 52, no. 3 (Fall 1978).

19. Ellen Ross, "Rethinking 'the Family'," *Radical History Review* 20 (Spring/Summer 1979):83.

20. Frederick Engels, *The Origin of the Family, Private Property and the State* (New York: International Publishers, 1972), pp. 71–72.

21. Karl Marx and Frederick Engels, *The German Ideology* (New York: International Publishers, 1970), p. 49.

22. *Isis Bulletin, 11,* Geneva, Switzerland.

23. U.S. Bureau of the Census, *A Statistical Portrait of Women in the U.S.* (Washington, D. C.: Department of Commerce, Bureau of the Census, 1977); Current Population Reports, Special Studies Series, P-23, no. 58, pp. 28, 30, 31.

24. Rubin, "Traffic," p. 171.

25. Eisenstein, "Capitalist Patriarchy," p. 47.

26. Rubin, "Traffic," p. 158.

27. Karl Marx, *The Poverty of Philosophy* (New York: International Publishers, 1963), p. 147

28. Karl Marx, *Early Writings,* translated and edited by T. B. Bottomore (New York: McGraw-Hill, 1963), p. 125.

29. Lynda Lange, "Reproduction in Democratic Theory," in W. Shea and J. King-Farlow, eds., *Contemporary Issues in Political Philosophy,* vol. 2 (New York: Science History Publications, 1976), pp. 140–41.

30. Sandra L. Bartky, "Narcissism, Femininity and Alienation," *Social Theory and Practice* 8, no., 2 (Summer 1982):127–43.

31. Ann Foreman, *Femininity as Alienation,* p. 151.

32. Some feminists are beginning to speculate on whether advanced technology will ultimately make it possible for men to be equally involved with women in bearing children. Two authors who consider this question are Shulamith Firestone, *The Dialectic of Sex: The Case for Feminist Revolution* (New York: W. W. Morrow, 1970), and Marge Piercy, *Woman on the Edge of Time* (New York: Fawcett Books, 1977).

33. Ann Ferguson, "Androgyny as an Ideal for Human Development," in Mary Vetterling-Braggin, Frederick A. Elliston, and Jane English, eds., *Feminism and Philosophy* (Totowa, N.J.: Littlefield, Adams, 1977).

34. Barbara Katz Rothman, "How Science is Redefining Parenthood," *Ms,* August 1982, pp. 154–58.

35. Rubin, "Traffic," p. 204.

24

Feminist Justice and the Family

JAMES P. STERBA

Comtemporary feminists almost by definition seek to put an end to male domination and to secure women's liberation. To achieve these goals, many feminists support the political ideal of androgyny.[1] According to these feminists, all assignments of rights and duties are ultimately to be justified in terms of the ideal of androgyny.[2] Since a conception of justice is usually thought to provide the ultimate grounds for the assignment of rights and duties in a society, I shall refer to this ideal of androgyny as "feminist justice."

The Ideal of Androgyny

But how is this ideal of androgyny to be interpreted? In a well-known article, Joyce Trebilcot distinguishes two forms of androgyny.[3] The first form postulates the same ideal for everyone. According to this form of androgyny, the ideal person "combines characteristics usually attributed to men with characteristics usually attributed to women." Thus, we should expect both nurturance and mastery, openness and objectivity, compassion and competitiveness from each and every person who has the capacities for these traits.

By contrast, the second form of androgyny does not advocate the same ideal for everyone but rather a variety of options from "pure" femininity to "pure" masculinity. As Trebilcot points out, this form of androgyny shares with the first the view that

From *Perspectives on the Family* (1990), edited by Robert Moffat, Joseph Gick, and Michael Bayles. Reprinted by permission.

biological sex should not be the basis for determining the appropriateness of gender characterization. It differs in that it holds that "all alternatives with respect to gender should be equally available to and equally approved for everyone, regardless of sex."

It would be a mistake, however, to sharply distinguish between these two forms of androgyny. Properly understood, they are simply two different facets of a single ideal. For, as Mary Ann Warren has argued, the second form of androgyny is appropriate *only* "with respect to feminine and masculine traits which are largely matters of personal style and preference and which have little direct moral significance."[4] However, when we consider so-called feminine and masculine *virtues,* it is the first form of androgyny that is required because, then, other things being equal, the same virtues are appropriate for everyone.

We can even formulate the ideal of androgyny more abstractly so that it is no longer specified in terms of so-called feminine and masculine traits. We can, for example, specify the ideal as requiring no more than that the traits that are truly desirable in society be equally available to both women and men, or in the case of virtues, equally inculcated in both women and men.

There is a problem, of course, in determining which traits of character are virtues and which traits are largely matters of personal style and preference. To make this determination, Trebilcot has suggested that we seek to bring about the second form of androgyny, where people have the option of acquiring the full range of so-called feminine and masculine traits.[5] But surely when we already have good grounds for thinking that certain traits are virtues, such as courage and compassion, fairness and openness, there is no reason to adopt such a laissez-faire approach to moral education. Although, as Trebilcot rightly points out, proscribing certain options will involve a loss of freedom, nevertheless, we should be able to determine at least with respect to some character traits when a gain in virtue is worth the loss of freedom. It may even be the case that the loss of freedom suffered by an individual now will be compensated for by a gain of freedom to that same individual in the future once the relevant virtue or virtues have been acquired.

So understood, the class of virtues will turn out to be those desirable traits that can be justifiably inculcated in both women and men. Admittedly, this is a restrictive use of the term virtue. In normal usage, "virtue" is almost synonymous with "desirable trait."[6] But there is good reason to focus on those desirable traits that can be justifiably inculcated in both women and men, and, for present purposes, I will refer to this class of desirable traits as virtues.

Unfortunately, many of the challenges to the ideal of androgyny fail to appreciate how the ideal can be interpreted to combine a required set of virtues with equal choice from among other desirable traits. For example, some challenges interpret the ideal as attempting to achieve "a proper balance of moderation" among opposing feminine and masculine traits and then question whether traits like feminine gullibility or masculine brutality could ever be combined with opposing gender traits to achieve such a balance.[7] Other challenges interpret the ideal as permitting unrestricted choice of personal traits and then regard the possibility of Total Women and Hells Angels androgynes as a *reductio ad absurdum* of the ideal.[8] But once it is recognized that the ideal of androgyny can not only be interpreted to require of everyone a set of virtues (which need not be a mean between opposing extreme traits), but can also be interpreted to limit everyone's choice to desirable traits, then such challenges to the ideal clearly lose their force.

Actually the main challenge raised by feminists to the ideal of androgyny is that the ideal is self-defeating in that it seeks to eliminate sexual stereotyping of human beings at the same time that it is formulated in terms of the very same stereotypical concepts it seeks to eliminate.[9] Or as Warren has put it, "Is it not at least mildly paradoxical to urge people to cultivate both 'feminine' and "masculine' virtues, while at the same time holding that virtues ought not to be sexually stereotyped?"

But in response to this challenge, it can be argued that to build a better society we must begin where we are now, and where we are now people still speak of feminine and masculine character traits. Consequently, if we want to easily refer to such traits and to formulate an ideal with respect to how they should be distributed in society it is plausible to refer to them in the way that people presently refer to them, that is, as feminine or masculine traits.

Alternatively, to avoid misunderstanding altogether, the ideal could be formulated in the more abstract way I suggested earlier so that it no longer specifically refers to so-called feminine or masculine traits. So formulated, the ideal requires that the traits that are truly desirable in society be equally available to both women and men. So formulated the ideal would, in effect, require that men and women have in the fullest sense an equal right of self-development. The ideal would require this because an equal right to self-development can only be effectively guaranteed by equally inculcating the same virtues in both women and men and by making other desirable traits equally available to both women and men.

So characterized the ideal of androgyny represents neither a revolt against so-called feminine virtues and traits nor their exaltation over so-called masculine virtues and traits.[10] Accordingly, the ideal of androgyny does not view women's liberation as *simply* the freeing of women from the confines of traditional roles thus making it possible for them to develop in ways heretofore reserved for men. Nor does the ideal view women's liberation as *simply* the revaluation and glorification of so-called feminine activities like housekeeping or mothering or so-called feminine modes of thinking as reflected in an ethic of caring. The first perspective ignores or devalues genuine virtues and desirable traits traditionally associated with women while the second ignores or devalues genuine virtues and desirable traits traditionally associated with men. By contrast, the ideal of androgyny seeks a broader-based ideal for both women and men that combines virtues and desirable traits traditionally associated with women with virtues and desirable traits traditionally associated with men. Nevertheless, the ideal of androgyny will clearly reject any so-called virtues or desirable traits traditionally associated with women or men that have been supportive of discrimination or oppression against women or men.

Defenses of Androgyny

Now there are various contemporary defenses of the ideal of androgyny. Some feminists have attempted to derive the ideal from a Welfare Liberal Conception of

Justice. Others have attempted to derive the ideal from a Socialist Conception of Justice. Let us briefly consider each of these defenses in turn.

In attempting to derive the ideal of androgyny from a Welfare Liberal Conception of Justice, feminists have tended to focus on the right to equal opportunity which is a central requirement of a Welfare Liberal Conception of Justice.[11] Of course, equal opportunity could be interpreted minimally as providing people only with the same legal rights of access to all advantaged positions in society for which they are qualified. But this is not the interpretation given the right by welfare liberals. In a Welfare Liberal Conception of Justice, equal opportunity is interpreted to require in addition the same prospects for success for all those who are relevantly similar, where relevant similarity involves more than simply present qualifications. For example, Rawls claims that persons in his original position would favor a right to "fair equality of opportunity," which means that persons who have the same natural assets and the same willingness to use them would have the necessary resources to achieve similar life prospects.[12] The point feminists have been making is simply that failure to achieve the ideal of androgyny translates into a failure to guarantee equal opportunity to both women and men. The present evidence for this failure to provide equal opportunity is the discrimination that exists against women in education, employment and personal relations. Discrimination in education begins early in a child's formal educational experience as teachers and school books support different and less desirable roles for girls than for boys.[13] Discrimination in employment has been well documented.[14] Women continue to earn only a fraction of what men earn for the same or comparable jobs and although women make up almost half of the paid labor force in the U.S., 70% of them are concentrated in just 20 different job categories, only 5 more than in 1905.[15] Finally, discrimination in personal relations is the most entrenched of all forms of discrimination against women.[16] It primarily manifests itself in traditional family structures in which the woman is responsible for domestic work and childcare and the man's task is "to protect against the outside world and to show how to meet this world successfully."[17] In none of these areas, therefore, do women have the same prospects for success as compared with men with similar natural talents and similar desires to succeed.

Now the support for the ideal of androgyny provided by a Socialist Conception of Justice appears to be much more direct than that provided by a Welfare Liberal Conception of Justice.[18] This is because the Socialist Conception of Justice and the ideal of androgyny can be interpreted as requiring the very same equal right of self-development. What a Socialist Conception of Justice purports to add to this interpretation of the ideal of androgyny is an understanding of how the ideal is best to be realized in contemporary capitalist societies. For according to advocates of this defense of androgyny, the ideal is best achieved by socializing the means of production and satisfying people's nonbasic as well as their basic needs. Thus, the general idea behind this approach to realizing the ideal of androgyny is that a cure for capitalist exploitation will also be a cure for women's oppression.

Yet despite attempts to identify the feminist ideal of androgyny with a right to equal opportunity endorsed by a Welfare Liberal Conception of Justice or an equal right of self-development endorsed by a Socialist Conception of Justice, the ideal still transcends both of these rights by requiring not only that desirable traits be equally available to both women and men but also that the same virtues be equally inculcated in both women and men. Of course, part of the rationale for inculcating the same virtues in both women and men is to support such rights. And if support for such rights is to be fairly allocated, the virtues needed to support such rights must be equally inculcated in both women and men. Nevertheless, to hold that the virtues required to support a right to equal opportunity or an equal right to self-development must be equally inculcated in both women and men is different from claiming, as the ideal of androgyny does, that human virtues, sans phrase, should be equally inculcated in both women and men. Thus, the ideal of androgyny clearly requires an inculcation of virtues beyond what is necessary to support a right to equal opportunity or an equal right to self-development. What additional virtues are required by the ideal obviously depends upon what other rights should be recognized. In this regard, the ideal of androgyny is somewhat open-ended. Feminists who endorse the ideal would simply have to go along with the best arguments for additional rights and corresponding virtues. In particular, I would claim that they would have to support a right to welfare that is necessary for meeting the basic needs of all legitimate claimants given the strong case that can be made for such a right from welfare liberal, socialist and even libertarian perspectives.[19]

Now, in order to provide all legitimate claimants with the resources necessary for meeting their basic needs, there obviously has to be a limit on the resources that will be available for each individual's self-development, and this limit will definitely have an effect upon the implementation of the ideal of androgyny. Of course, some feminists would want to pursue various possible technological transformations of human biology in order to implement their ideal. For example, they would like to make it possible for women to inseminate other women and for men to lactate and even to bring fertilized ova to term. But bringing about such possibilities would be very costly indeed.[20] Consequently, since the means selected for meeting basic needs must be provided to all legitimate claimants including distant peoples and future generations, it is unlikely that such costly means could ever be morally justified. Rather it seems preferable radically to equalize the opportunities that are conventionally provided to women and men and wait for such changes to ultimately have their effect on human biology as well. Of course, if any "technological fixes" for achieving androgyny should prove to be cost efficient as a means for meeting people's basic needs, then obviously there would be every reason to utilize them.

Unfortunately, the commitment of a Feminist Conception of Justice to a right of equal opportunity raises still another problem for the view. For some philosophers have contended that equal opportunity is ultimately an incoherent goal. As Lloyd Thomas has put the charge, "We have a problem for those who advocate competitive equality of opportunity: the prizes won in the competitions of the first generation will tend to defeat the requirements of equality of opportunity for the next."[21] The only way to avoid this result, Thomas claims, "is by not permitting persons to be dependent for their self-development on others at all," which obviously is a completely unacceptable solution.

But this is a problem, as Thomas points out, that exists for competitive opportunities. They are opportunities for which, even when each person does her best, there are considerably more losers than winners. With respect to such opportunities, the winners may well be able to place themselves and their children in an advantageous position with respect to subsequent competitions. But under a Welfare Liberal Conception of Justice, and presumably a Feminist Conception of Justice as well, most of the opportunities people have are not competitive opportunities at all, but rather noncompetitive opportunities to acquire the resources necessary for meeting their basic needs. These are opportunities with respect to which virtually everyone who does her best can be a winner. Of course, some people who do not do their best may fail to satisfy their basic needs, and this failure may have negative consequences for their children's prospects. But under a Welfare Liberal Conception of Justice, and presumably a Feminist Conception of Justice as well, every effort is required to insure that each generation has the same opportunities to meet their basic needs, and as long as most of the opportunities that are available are of the noncompetitive sort, this goal should not be that difficult to achieve.

Now it might be objected that if all that will be accomplished under the proposed system of equal opportunity is, for the most part, the satisfaction of people's basic needs, then that would not bring about the revolutionary change in the relationship between women and men that feminists are demanding. For don't most women in technologically advanced societies already have their basic needs satisfied, despite the fact that they are not yet fully liberated?

In response, it should be emphasized that the concern of defenders of the ideal of androgyny is not just with women in technologically advanced societies. The ideal of androgyny is also applicable to women in Third World and developing societies, and in such societies it is clear that the basic needs of many women are not being met. Furthermore, it is just not the case that all the basic needs of most women in technologically advanced societes are being met. Most obviously, their basic needs for self-development are still not being met. This is because they are being denied an equal right to education, training, jobs and a variety of social roles for which they have the native capabilities. In effect, women in technologically advanced societies are still being treated as second-class persons, no matter how well-fed, well-clothed, well-housed they happen to be. This is why there must be a radical restructuring of social institutions even in technologically advanced societies if women's basic needs for self-development are to be met.

Androgyny and the Family

Now the primary locus for the radical restructuring required by the ideal of androgyny is the family. Here two fundamental changes are needed. First, all children irrespective of their sex must be given the same type of upbringing consistent with their native capabilities. Second, mothers and fathers must also have the same opportunities for education and employment consistent with their native capabilities.

Surprisingly, however, some welfare liberals have viewed the existence of the family as imposing an acceptable limit on the right to equal opportunity. Rawls, for example, claims the principle of fair opportunity can be only imperfectly carried out, at least as long as the institution of the family exists. The extent to which natural capacities develop and reach fruition is affected by all kinds of social conditions and class attitudes. Even the willingness to make an effort, to try, and so to be deserving in the ordinary sense is itself dependent upon happy family and social circumstances. It is impossible in practice to secure equal chances of achievement and culture for those similarly endowed, and therefore we may want to adopt a principle which recognizes this fact and also mitigates the arbitrary effects of the natural lottery itself.[22]

Thus, according to Rawls, since different families will provide different opportunities for their children, the only way to fully achieve "fair equality of opportunity" would require us to go too far and abolish or radically modify traditional family structures.

Yet others have argued that the full attainment of equal opportunity requires that we go even further and equalize people's native as well as their social assets.[23] For only when everyone's natural and social assets have been equalized would everyone have exactly the same chance as everyone else to attain the desirable social positions in society. Of course, feminists have no difficulty recognizing that there are moral limits to the pursuit of equal opportunity. Accordingly, feminists could grant that other than the possibility of special cases, such as sharing a surplus organ like a second kidney, it would be too much to ask people to sacrifice their native assets to achieve equal opportunity.

Rawls, however, proposes to limit the pursuit of equal opportunity still further by accepting the inequalities generated by families in any given sector of society, provided that there is still equal opportunity between the sectors or that the existing inequality of opportunity can be justified in terms of its benefit to those in the least-advantaged position.[24] Nevertheless, what Rawls is concerned with here is simply the inequality of opportunity that exists between individuals owing to the fact that they come from different families. He fails to consider the inequality of opportunity that exists in traditional family structures, especially between adult members, in virtue of the different roles expected of women and men. When viewed from the original position, it seems clear that this latter inequality of opportunity is sufficient to require a radical modification of traditional family structures, even if the former inequality, for the reasons Rawls suggests, does not require any such modifications.

Yet at least in the United States this need radically to modify traditional family structures to guarantee equal opportunity confronts a serious problem. Given that a significant proportion of the available jobs are at least 9 to 5, families with pre-school children require day care facilities if their adult members are to pursue their careers. Unfortunately, for many families such facilities are simply unavailable. In New York City, for example, more than 144,000 children under the age of six are competing for 46,000 full-time slots in day care centers. In Seattle, there is licensed day care space for 8,800 of the 23,000 children who need it. In Miami, two children, 3 and 4 years old, were left unattended at home while their mother worked. They climbed into a clothes dryer while the timer was on, closed the door and burned to death.[25]

Moreover, even the available day care facilities are frequently inadequate either because their staffs are poorly trained or because the child/adult ratio in such facilities is too high. At best, such facilities provide little more than custodial care; at worst, they actually retard the development of those under their care. What this suggests is that at least under present conditions if pre-school children are to be adequately cared for, frequently, one of the adult members of the family will have to remain at home to provide that care. But since most jobs are at least 9 to 5, this will require that the adult members who stay at home temporarily give up pursuing a career. However, such sacrifice appears to conflict with the equal opportunity requirement of Feminist Justice.

Now families might try to meet this equal opportunity requirement by having one parent give up pursuing a career for a certain period of time and the other give up pursuing a career for a subsequent (equal) period of time. But there are problems here too. Some careers are difficult to interrupt for any significant period of time, while others never adequately reward latecomers. In addition, given the high rate of divorce and the inadequacies of most legally mandated child support, those who first sacrifice their careers may find themselves later faced with the impossible task of beginning or reviving their careers while continuing to be the primary caretaker of their children.[26] Furthermore, there is considerable evidence that children will benefit more from equal rearing from both parents.[27] So the option of having just one parent doing the child-rearing for any length of time is, other things being equal, not optimal.

It would seem, therefore, that to truly share child-rearing within the family what is needed is flexible (typically part-time) work schedules that also allow both parents to be together with their children for a significant period every day. Now some flexible job schedules have already been tried by various corporations.[28] But if equal opportunity is to be a reality in our society, the option of flexible job schedules must be guaranteed to all those with pre-school children. Of course, to require employers to guarantee flexible job schedules to all those with pre–school children would place a significant restriction upon the rights of employers, and it may appear to move the practical requirements of Feminist Justice closer to those of Socialist Justice. But if the case for flexible job schedules is grounded on a right to equal opportunity then at least defenders of Welfare Liberal Justice will have no reason to object. This is clearly one place where Feminist Justice with its focus on equal opportunity within the family tends to drive Welfare Liberal Justice and Socialist Justice closer together in their practical requirements.

Recently, however, Christina Hoff Sommers has criticized feminist philosophers for being "against the family."[29] Sommer's main objection is that feminist philosophers have criticized traditional family structures without adequately justifying what they would put in its place. In this paper, I have tried to avoid any criticism of this sort by first articulating a defensible version of the feminist ideal of androgyny which can draw upon support from both Welfare Liberal and Socialist Conceptions of Justice and then by showing what demands this ideal would impose upon family structures. Since Sommers and other critics of the feminist ideal of androgyny also support a strong requirement of equal opportunity, it is difficult to see how they can consistently do so while denying the radical implications of that requirement (and the ideal of androgyny that underlies it) for traditional family structures.[30]

Notes

1. Someone might object that if feminist justice is worth considering, why not racial justice? In principle I have no objection to a separate consideration of racial justice although the main issues that are relevant to such a discussion have standardly been taken up in discussions of the other conceptions of justice. By contrast, feminist justice raises new issues that have usually been ignored in discussions of the other conceptions of justice (e.g., equal opportunity within the family), and for that reason, I think, this conception of justice deserves separate consideration.

2. See, for example, Ann Ferguson, "Androgyny as an Ideal for Human Development," in *Feminism and Philosophy,* ed. Mary Vetterling-Braggin and others (Totowa, N.J.: Rowman and Littlefield, 1977), pp. 45–69; Mary Ann Warren, "Is Androgyny the Answer to Sexual Stereotyping?", in *"Femininity," "Masculinity," and "Androgyny,"* ed. Mary Vetterling-Braggin (Totowa, N.J.: Rowman and Littlefield, 1982), pp. 170; A. G. Kaplan and J. Bean, eds., *Beyond Sex-Role Stereotypes: Reading Toward a Psychology of Androgyny* (Totowa, N.J.: Rowman and Littlefield, 1976); Andrea Dworkin, *Women Hating* (New York: Free Press, 1974), Part IV.

3. Joyce Trebilcot, "Two Forms of Androgynism," reprinted in *Feminism and Philosophy,* ed. Vetterling-Braggin et al., pp. 70–78.

4. Warren, "Is Androgyny the Answer," pp. 178–79.

5. Trebilcot, "Two Forms," pp. 74–77.

6. On this point, see Edmund Pincoffs, *Quandaries and Virtues* (Lawrence: University of Kansas Press, 1986), chap. 5.

7. See, for example, Kathryn Pauly Morgan, "Androgyny: A Conceptual Critique," *Social Theory and Practice* 8 (1982): 256–57.

8. See, for example, Mary Daly, *Gyn-Ecology: The Meta-Ethics of Radical Feminism* (Boston: Beacon Press, 1978), p. xi.

9. Margrit Eichler, *The Double Standard* (New York: St. Martin's Press, 1980), pp. 69–71; Elizabeth Lane Beardsley, "On Curing Conceptual Confusion," in *"Femininity," "Masculinity," and "Androgyny,"* ed. Vetterling-Braggin, pp. 197–202; Mary Daly, "The Qualitative Leap Beyond Patriarchal Religion," *Quest* 1 (1975): 20–40; Janice Raymond, "The Illusion of Androgyny," *Quest* 2 (1975): 57–66.

10. For a valuable discussion and critique of these two viewpoints, see Iris Young, "Humanism, Gynocentrism and Feminist Politics," *Women's Studies International Forum* 8, 3 (1985): 173–83.

11. See, for example, Virginia Held, *Rights and Goods* (New York: Free Press, 1984), especially chap. 11; and Gloria Steinem "What It Would Be Like if Women Win," *Time,* 31 August 1979, pp. 22–23; Mary Jeanne Larrabee, "Feminism and Parental Roles: Possibilities for Changes," *Journal of Social Philosophy* 14 (1983): 18. See also National Organization for Women (NOW) Bill of Rights, and United States Commission on Civil Rights, *Statement on the Equal Rights Amendment* (1978).

12. John Rawls, *A Theory of Justice* (Cambridge: Harvard University Press, 1971), p. 73.

13. See, for example, Elizabeth Allgeier and Naomi McCormick, eds. *Changing Boundaries* (Palo Alto, Calif.: Mayfield Publishing Co., 1983), Part I.

14. See, for example, *Toward Economic Justice for Women,* prepared by Women's Economic Agenda Working Group (Institute for Policy Studies, Washington, D.C., 1985); Jo Freeman, ed., *Women: A Feminist Perspective* (Palo Alto, Calif.: Mayfield Publishing Co. 1984), Part 4; *The Women's Movement: Agenda for the '80s,* an Editorial Research Report (Washington, D.C.: Congressional Quarterly Inc., 1981).

15. Alison M. Jagger and Paula Rothenberg, *Feminist Frameworks,* 2nd ed. (New York: McGraw-Hill, 1984), p. 216.

16. See, for example, Joyce Trebilcot, *Mothering* (Totowa, N.J.: Rowman & Allanheld, 1984); Irene Diamond, *Families, Politics and Public Policy* (New York: Longman Inc.,, 1983).

17. Bruno Bettelheim, "Fathers Shouldn't Try to Be Mothers," *Parents Magazine,* October 1956, pp. 40 and 126–29.

18. See, for example, Ann Ferguson, "Androgyny as an Ideal for Human Development," in *Feminism and Philosophy,* ed. Vetterling-Braggin et al.; and Evelyn Reed, "Women: Caste, Class or Oppressed Sex?", in *Mortality in Practice,* ed. James P. Sterba (Belmont, Calif.: Wadsworth Publishing Co., 1983), pp. 222–28.

19. See James P. Sterba, *How to Make People Just* (Totowa, N.J.: Rowman & Allanheld, 1988), especially chaps. 7–9.

20. See Barbara Katz Rothman, "How Science Is Redefining Parenthood." *Ms.,* August 1982, pp. 154–58.

21. D. A. Lloyd Thomas, "Competitive Equality of Opportunity," *Mind* (1977): 398.

22. Rawls, *Theory of Justice,* p. 74.

23. See Bernard Williams, "The Idea of Equality," in *Philosophy, Politics and Society,* 2nd series, ed. Peter Laslett and W. G. Runciman (Oxford: Oxford University Press, 1969), pp. 110–31. For a literary treatment, see Kurt Vonnegut, Jr., "Harrison Bergeron," in *Welcome to the Monkey House* (New York: Dell, 1968), pp. 7–13.

24. Rawls, *Theory of Justice,* pp. 300–01.

25. *New York Times,* 25 November 1987.

26. See Lenore Weitzman, *The Divorce Revolution: The Unexpected Social and Economic Consequences for Women and Children in America* (New York: Free Press, 1985).

27. Dorothy Dinnerstein, *The Mermaid and the Minotaur* (New York: 1977); Nancy Chodorow, *Mothering: Psychoanalysis and the Sociology of Gender* (Berkeley: 1978); Vivian Gornick, "Here's News: Fathers Matter as Much as Mothers," *Village Voice,* 13 October 1975.

28. *New York Times,* 27 November 1987.

29. Christina Hoff Sommers, "Philosophers Against the Family," in *Person to Person,* ed. Hugh LaFollette and George Graham (Philadelphia: Temple University Press, 1988).

30. In "The Equal Obligation of Mothers and Fathers," in *Having Children,* ed. Onora O'Neill and William Ruddick (New York: Oxford University Press, 1979), pp. 227–40, Virginia Held approaches the problem of what should be the relationship of parents to child-rearing by first assuming that both parents have an equal obligation to contribute to the rearing of their children and then seeking to determine what equal obligation requires. She determines that parents have an obligation to exert an equal effort in contributing what their children need. As far as I can tell, Held's results about what parents owe their children complement my results about what parents ought to having coming to them in rearing their children, namely, day care facilities and/or flexible job schedules sufficient to maintain equal opportunity.

25

The Unpersuaded

JANET RADCLIFFE RICHARDS

1. The Chasm

The final problem is one which is not really within feminism itself, but is still most important for feminists. It is that for all the strength of the feminist case, feminism is still an unpopular movement.

It is probably also true to say that the problem is one which most feminists do not take seriously enough. It is, after all, only to be expected that feminism will be widely opposed. Whenever there is a movement which is striving for justice, there are inevitably people whose privileges it plans to take away, and it can hardly expect their support. And although many of the present opponents of feminism are people who in fact would *gain* from its success—nearly all women, and all men who find their traditional role uncongenial—it is part of most feminists' theory that such people have been thoroughly brainwashed, and therefore cannot be expected to support feminism any more than can the people whose real interests are in suppressing it. Feminism is bound by its very nature to be unpopular, its supporters seem to think, and therefore there is not much to be done about the matter.

Of course, there certainly are people whose hostility to feminism must stem from vested interests, and no doubt (however difficult it is to explain the idea of conditioning) there must be many others who are far too deeply immured in their habits to be capable of understanding other possibilities, no matter how well presented, or how much in their interest. Nevertheless, the idea that all the opponents of feminism must come into one or other of these categories is far too comfortable. Feminists must at least *allow* for the possibility that there are in existence people who, in spite of a vested interest in opposing feminism, would support the cause if they thought it

From *The Skeptical Feminist,* pp. 266–291. Reprinted by permission of the author.

was for the general good, but do not think it is. There may be others who (we think) would have everything to gain from feminism's success, and who are perfectly capable of understanding the issues, but are still opposed to the movement. It is at least possible (and I should think very likely) that there are large numbers of these people, and that they are on the other side because feminists have not presented their case in such a way as to attract them. And if they do exist, their conversion is obviously of political importance.

However, even though it is very easy to say that feminists should take care to present their case more attractively, the fact of the matter is that feminism, by its very nature, is a thing which is extremely difficult to get across. The phenomenon of sexual injustice, of taking it for granted that different kinds of treatment are suitable for men and women as such, is so pervasive, so deeply entrenched and so generally taken for granted that to recognize it for what it is is to have a view of the world which is radically different from that of most people. The feminist sees what is generally invisible, finds significance in what is unremarkable, and questions what is presupposed by other enquiries. And since to the uninitiated this is bound to appear no different from imagining the non-existent, making a fuss about nothing, and gratuitously instigating disturbances in the foundations of society, perhaps it is not surprising that there is still not very much public sympathy with feminism. Without a feminist view of things even the best-founded of feminist pronouncements may appear nonsensical.

The ordinary policeman, for instance, harassing prostitutes with a zeal beyond the call of duty, would be genuinely staggered if anyone suggested to him that his attitudes reflected what is probably the most extreme surviving remnant of women's total subjugation to men: the heavy sanctions against all sexual freedom which were designed to reinforce all the other institutions by which women's sexuality and reproduction was kept firmly under male control. To him it almost certainly seems that it is *respect* for women which leads to his loathing of prostitutes. The ordinary housewife, who thinks as a matter of course that her highest duty lies in devotion to her husband and family, no matter what good she could do by spending less time on them and more on other things, would be quite baffled to hear a feminist say that the morality she was accepting was itself a male device to make women accessories to their enforced servitude to men. If a feminist appeared distressed on hearing a woman of high ability talking with satisfaction of a life spent as her husband's ancillary, most people would think it the height of absurdity. In general, if feminists make their ideas and feelings about such things publicly known, without being able to persuade people to follow sympathetically the line of argument which leads to such apparently preposterous conclusions, of course the people who hear them will be hostile to feminism.

If this hostility is to cease, then, people must presumably be persuaded to look seriously at the whole subject. However, how to achieve this presents considerable problems. There are going to be no miraculous conversions, and relatively few even of the women are going to undergo the traumatic experiences which set some off along the feminist path: finding out the realities of trying to get an abortion, getting into the clutches of a violent husband, or encountering blatant discrimination at work. The experiences which everyone has, and which ought to convert everyone to feminism, are themselves not recognizable as significant by anyone who has not already worked through the whole subject. It seems, therefore, that if people are to be persuaded, the persuading must be done by feminists. But here we seem to encounter a vicious circle, because if feminists are seen as the makers of bizarre and exaggerated pronouncements, stirrers up of trouble and strewers of anarchy, they are bound themselves to be objects of suspicion, and in a weak position when it comes to persuading people to take their arguments seriously.

There is no easy way out of this apparent impasse, but there is one thing which feminists certainly can do to set things going in the right direction. That is to deal immediately with the problems which arise *on their own side* of the chasm created by feminism's inherent radicalism. One of the difficulties about a feminist view of things is that once you are deep into it it is not only a radical transformer of everything, but also extremely compelling, and apt to make you forget what things looked like from the other side. This may be why feminists are generally inclined to attribute all opposition to moral and intellectual shortcomings in their opponents. The feminist who can see the oppression of women in the trivia of everyday life, in much the same way as the religious believer can see the hand of God in what is to the atheist the unremarkable course of nature, may also incline to the common religious view that since the truth is manifest the fallen state of the heathen can be imputed only to Sin, or, in this case, vested interests and conditioning.

However, the feminist way of looking at things is not at all manifest, and feminists must do their opponents the justice of recognizing this. Once we have done it we may be more inclined to try to understand what it is which makes many people of good will resist the movement, and from that work out ways of making them more sympathetic.

The matter is no doubt very complicated, but there do seem to be three particularly striking things which often put people off feminism, and which are worth looking at in some detail. The first is the idea that there is no reasonable feminist case at all. The second is the feeling that the whole thing is very much exaggerated. And the third, which is probably by far the most important (and in whose overcoming we might easily overcome the other two) is that people just do not like what they see of either feminists or their politics; that the image of the movement is very *unattractive*. These three subjects will be discussed in turn.

2. The Feminist Case

First there is the matter of the people who cannot see that there is a case for feminism at all; who do not think that women are badly treated by society.

It is, by the way, . . . very important to separate the question of whether anything is wrong with the situation of women from questions about whether there is any justification for particular ideas of ways to put matters right. Most people, including most feminists, take what conspicuous feminists say about political policy and social theory as integral to the whole cause. However, the question of whether anything is wrong is clearly separable from that of what to do about it if it is, and since it must (as a matter of logic) be easier to persuade someone of the first than of both, even feminists who are passionately committed to their political views should not object to taking the subjects one at a time, and stressing to the uninitiated that there *are* two sets of questions. We must, therefore, start by making sure people understand that when we claim that there is a very strong general case for feminism, we are not (at least yet) saying that men and women are exactly the same, or that they ought to be exactly the same, or that the family ought to be abolished, or that children ought to be left in crèches [day nurseries], or that sex roles are pernicious. Feminists are claiming in the first instance only that women are systematically badly treated by society, and that something ought to be done about it.

Transparent as the case for feminism may seem to all those who are involved in it, however, it is undoubtedly the case that to the average well-educated, well intentioned man (in company, for that matter, with a great many women) it is not in the least clear. What is there to justify the feminist assertion that all men oppress all women, or that this or that is a male plot against the female, or that men are interested in women only as sex objects? He has never plotted with other men against women in his life. He certainly does regard them as sex objects, since (although his interest in sex is not to be denied, and he sees no reason why it should be) he is as interested in other aspects of women as he is in those same things in men. And as he looks round the women of his acquaintance he seeks in vain for the slightest sign of oppression. They are healthy, prosperous, capable of independence, frequently assertive, denied no educational opportunity, allowed to rise to the heights of success in public and professional life, and if they stay at home and have children that is because they choose to. That choice, furthermore, is one which men have not.

It is true, of course, that the arguer along these lines probably sees nothing of the grossly exploited outworker slaving every hour of the day for a few shillings, or the office cleaner who looks after her children all day and then works half the night as well in a never ending struggle to make ends meet, and it is more or less certain that he has never even heard of some of the horrors to which women are systematically subjected in other parts of the world. These are all things we can bring to his attention. But even if we do, he is likely to be unperturbed. That, he will say, shows only that *some* women are oppressed. It does not show that all are, or that there is any general case for feminism. He may even go on to say that these things, bad as they are, have nothing to do with the oppression of *women* in particular. Many working-class men are also exploited, and all kinds of barbarities go on in foreign parts which are just as bad for the men who get caught up in them as for the women. Oppression is everywhere, and takes many forms. He may perhaps concede that there are one or two aspects of women's lot which could do with general improvement, but they are all, he thinks, rather insignificant. To say that women in general are oppressed is just a silly exaggeration.

It cannot be denied that feminists often exaggerate, or that a mind attuned to oppression will often start seeing it where it is not. However, the exaggeration is nothing like as bad as it looks. Feminism has a better case than at first appears, and to meet the opposition that case has to be made clearly and systematically. Let us consider how such a case might be made out. And for simplicity let us cast it in the classical form of a series of *Replies to Objections,* with the objector (whom we will go on assuming, for no very special reason, to be male) obligingly, if improbably, arranging his objections in such an order as to allow the replies to them to come out as a systematic exposition of a feminist case.

Objection 1

Feminists (says the objector) claim that women are badly treated by society; that women are at a systematic disadvantage to men. But it is absurd to say that women in general are badly treated. Everywhere you look you see women flourishing. Of course some women are badly off, but then so are a lot of men. Why should we do anything to advance the cause of women in general, when so many men are much worse off than many women? That would be quite unfair to men.

Reply

It is misleading (says the feminist) to say that feminism is a movement whose aim is to advance the cause of women. That suggests that all it wants to do is give advantages to one group at the expense of another. But feminism is not concerned with *a group of people* it wants to make better off, but with a *type of injustice* it wants to eliminate: the injustice which women suffer as a result of being female. And when we say that women are systematically at a disadvantage to men we are not claiming anything so absurd as that all women live lives of abject misery in the power of men; only that being female usually makes you worse off than a man would have been under the same circumstances. Being at an arbitrary disadvantage through being female is equally unjust whether it means that you have to work all hours of the day and night for a pittance while your husband works a normal day and expects a cooked meal in the evening, or whether it means that you can't quite make it to being Lady Chief Justice because the job is unfairly given to a man. The type of injustice is the same in both cases, even though the second woman is probably much better off than the husband of the first. It is this *kind* of injustice to which feminists are opposed.

Objection 2

(In which the testosterone contingent, and others of similar persuasions, make their appearance.) It may be that a woman has to work twice as hard as a man to get to the top of any profession, and that in any situation a woman is likely to be worse off than a corresponding man. That, however, is only because men are more dominant than women, and generally superior. Anyway, even if women were intrinsically equal to men, they would still be handicapped by having children. Women's inequality is a natural phenomenon. If we arranged things so that as many women as men succeeded in life it would be rather like trying to arrange the Olympic Games so that people in wheelchairs had as good a chance of succeeding as the best athletes.

It could be done; we could make men and women equally successful at everything, but only at the cost of artificially holding men back and pushing women forward, and a general lowering of standards from which everyone would suffer. Women should accept their natural limitations.

Reply

Our complaint is not *simply* that women do not succeed as often as men, or that they have to work twice as hard to do as well. Perhaps women are not as competent at many things as men are; perhaps they are held back by hormones and a tendency to hysteria or whatever (though we think it most unlikely); certainly children have always got in the way of women's doing other things, and still do (though that seems rather a reason for trying to arrange things so that women can care for children and still make their full contribution to society than for giving up women's case in despair). However, our complaint has nothing to do with the natural problems from which women suffer. It is that things are made systematically harder for women than for *men in the same position and with identical abilities.* Women are discriminated against. And, incidentally, the very fact that men have for so long made it difficult or impossible for women to do certain kinds of work and reach certain elevated positions shows that really they do *not* believe in women's natural incompetence. If women had been by nature unable to do all these things, there would have been no need for special devices to keep them out.

Objection 3

But men don't make it harder for women to succeed. Employers are always doing what they can to advance women; husbands put up with amazing inconvenience to help their wives' careers. The complaint is quite unfounded.

Reply

We have certainly no wish to deny that such good and generous men exist, though we feel entitled to be sceptical about whether there are all that many of them. But our main reply is John Stuart Mill's:[1]

> Whether the institution to be defended is slavery, political absolutism, or the absolutism of the head of a family, we are always expected to judge of it from its best instances. . . . Who doubts that there may be great goodness, and great happiness, and great affection, under the absolute government of a good man? Meanwhile, laws and institutions require to be adapted, not to good men, but to bad.

Good men will, of course, treat women properly under any circumstnces, but as long as social institutions give men an advantage over women, which bad men can use if they want to, feminists have cause for complaint. We should not be at the mercy of men. It is the social institutions of which we complain primarily, rather than about the behaviour of individual men, much as that may sometimes leave to be desired. (This is, incidentally, a thing some feminists seem inclined to forget. Some seem to be led into implausible exaggeration of men's behaviour by a feeling that the feminist case rests more heavily on arguments that men *individually* treat women badly than it does. Whatever individual men do, we have legitimate cause for complaint in the fact that social institutions distinguish men from women as such, quite irrespective of their other abilities and characteristics, and make everything harder for women.)

Objection 4

But whatever may have been true about social institutions in the past, there are none now which distinguish between men and women. Women can do anything now, and so for that matter can men. There is nothing to stop women from being prime ministers or judges, if that is what they want to be, or, for that matter, men from being nurses or househusbands. If they do not do these things, it is not because there are any *institutions* stopping them.

Reply

In complaining about institutions we are not referring only to highly formalized things such as laws, systems of social security, sex-selection policies for education and professions, and the like. Even in those cases, of course, there is still much blatant discrimination left. But we are meaning to include among institutions far less formal ones than these, and take into acount such things as deeply entrenched conventions and habits; there are still countless ways in which the two sexes are differentiated. Different things are still commonly thought proper for men and women as such. In order to get public approval, there are many contexts in which the sexes have to behave differently.

Objection 5

Even if we allow this rather stretched use of the word "institution," the feminist point is still not made, because those discriminatory institutions do not stop anyone doing anything. Women can do anything they want now (family if they want, career if they want) and have, therefore, nothing to complain about.

Reply

We are not claiming that social institutions generally make things *impossible* for one sex which are possible for the other. The statement "women can do anything now" is misleading. The real question we have to consider is not whether women *can do* certain things, but how difficult it is for them. If social institutions of any degree of formality or informality make it harder for one sex than for the other, there is institutional discrimination. If a woman has to work harder than a man of equal ability to advance as far, or if she has to sacrifice more (a family, public approval and so on) to do it, there is institutional discrimination. The same, of course, is true if a man cannot stay at home and look after children without braving slightly sneering comments from the neighbours. You would have to be amazingly adept in the skills of stout denial to deny that many things are made harder for one sex than for the other.

Objection 6

Even if it is true that the social environment systematically differentiates between women and men, that is still not enough to prove that women are the ones who come off worse. The two sexes probably do as well as each other out of any differences there are. It is hard to say. Perhaps men do worse. Women actually have far more choice than men in many ways: they can either make themselves independent or stay at home protected by a man, as they please. The second option is virtually closed to most men, and anyway they could not take it without being exposed to public contempt. Whatever advantages men have, women have others.

Reply

Of course we agree that there are some drawbacks to the male role and some advantages to the female one, at least for some men and some women. Nevertheless, you cannot seriously maintain that the two are equal, or that men's is worse. If you consider the past there is no doubt at all that the whole structure of society was designed to *keep women entirely in the power of men*. Of course things are now much changed, but we have still by no means escaped our past. Our modern customs and ways of thinking are not completely emancipated from it. This shows most clearly in the matter of status (and status is power, even though not absolute power). Taking the lead, one of the strongest status indicators of all, nearly always falls by convention to men. The man gives orders, drives the car, makes the advances in courtship. In couples where these roles are reversed there is a tendency for social disapproval or mockery; the man is henpecked, the woman wears the trousers. In courtship, a woman who does what men are expected to do is forward, or desperate, or a slut. The present institutions bring about nothing like equality in difference, and since they give most power to men it must be said that, in spite of the odd drawback, men have the advantage.

Objection 7

All that has been shown is that the male role carries with it more power and status, but why do you say that is an advantage? To the extent that men's power is actual it just brings the weight of responsibility, which women have not. In fact very often what happens is that men are so aware of their responsibilities that they lean over backwards, and allow selfish women to trample all over them. To the extent, on the other hand, that men's higher status is nothing more than a social expectation that men should not be outdistanced or led by women, it is a nuisance to have to live up to it, especially now that women are not held down in the way they used to be. In fact the male role has nothing to recommend it at all, and it is time we had Men's Liberation.

Reply

By all means start your Men's Lib; we quite agree that being male is not all a bed of roses. However, don't make the mistake of thinking that your movement would be in opposition to ours, because the drawbacks you have mentioned are not arguments *against* feminism, but *for* it. Get rid of the differential social expectations of which feminists complain, and men can, if they want, have all the advantages women have. Status, responsibility and dependence will be determined by the natures and in-clinations of individuals, not by sex. Men who think the male role a heavy burden should be rushing to embrace feminism. Since, however, we seem in no danger of being submerged in seas of recruits, and since the average complainer about male responsibility would not change places with his wife or secretary for anything, we are entitled to suspect that the male role is not as burdensome as some men would have us think, and that men on the whole are inclined to keep their privileges while complaining about them.

Of course, neither objections nor replies end here, but enough has been said to show the line a general defence of feminism might take. Presumably some feminists would want to argue in a different kind of way. However, all should be prepared to make some such defence of their position, to persuade the well-intentioned critic that what they have to say is worth looking into.

3. The Primary Struggle

It is, of course, by no means certain that the opposition will accept all this, because proof is not the same as persuasion and the power of stout denial is infinite, but let us optimistically presume that everything so far has been conceded. We can now go on to another objection that is very commonly levelled at feminists: that they *exaggerate* everything so much that it is impossible to be as sympathetic to their case as it would be if more moderate claims were made. Feminists may have some sort of case, but it is a relatively trivial one and far too much fuss is made about it.

The accusation of triviality takes two forms, one particular and one general. The particular one is about feminists' making too much of small details: the supposedly neutral use of 'he' in the language; the fact that children's books tend to depict women in aprons; women's being expected to cater for the office party, and so on. In all such cases there is no substitute for detailed argument to show that the level of fuss is not unreasonable; an argument usually taking two stages, the first to prove that the phenomenon in question really is sexist, and the second to show that it has significantly bad consequences for women. Often such arguments can be produced. In other cases feminists may have to change their minds about the seriousness of the matter in hand.

However, there is clearly no scope for general argument on such subjects here, so we should move on to consider the common accusation of the triviality of feminism as a whole. *"How,"* we are asked, *"can you talk about the comparatively insignificant oppression of women, when set beside the issues of racism and imperialism?"*[2]

Robin Morgan, who quotes this attack in the introduction to *Sisterhood is Powerful,* follows it immediately with a determined feminist defence.

> This is a male-supremacist question. Not only because of its arrogance, but because of its ignorance. First it dares to weigh and compute human suffering. . . . Second, the question fails to even minimally grasp the profoundly radical analysis beginning to emerge from revolutionary feminism: that capitalism, imperialism, and racism are *symptoms* of male supremacy—sexism.

She also adds that half of the oppressed people of the world are women, and that we have to fight "for these sisters to *survive*" before there is any chance of being able to talk to them as oppressed women, and concludes, "More and more, I begin to think of a worldwide Women's Revolution as the only hope for life on this planet."

In sentiments of this sort she is joined by countless other feminists. For instance, there is the Redstockings Manifesto once again:[3] "Male supremacy is the oldest, most basic form of domination. All other forms of exploitation and oppression (racism, capitalism, imperialism etc.) are extensions of male supremacy." There is also Shulamith Firestone, who says that radical feminism "sees feminist issues not only as women's first priority, but as central to any larger revolutionary analysis."[4] She quotes as well an earlier feminist, Angelina Grimke:[5] "The slave may be freed and woman be where she is, but women cannot be freed and the slave remain where he is." And there is Elizabeth Gould Davis, who thinks that "restoring women to their age-old leadership in government while men confine themselves to their gadgetry and games . . . may constitute the last hope for mankind."[6] For all of these writers the main contention against the sceptical anti-feminist is the same: *feminism is the primary struggle.* This is the contention we now have to assess.

We had better start by distinguishing two issues which might arise under the primary struggle heading. There seems little doubt that most of the feminists who make the claim think that *as a matter of fact* if women's wrongs were put right everything else would go right too, and that justifies their giving first priority to women's issues. Mixed in with this, however, there seem to be hints of a different idea, that feminism is *morally* the most important issue, and sexual oppression the worst type of oppression. That question had better be discussed first.

The question is obviously an important one. In spite of Robin Morgan's strictures on the arrogance of 'daring' to assess degrees of suffering, it is surely morally outrageous that anyone should *fail* to do so. Some forms of suffering and oppression are infinitely worse than others, and (other things being equal) we should obviously concentrate on the worst sorts first. Is women's oppression the worst kind of oppression?

It is often said, apparently in defense of some such position as this, that women are the poorest of the poor and the most oppressed of the oppressed, and that wherever there is a badly treated man, there is a woman attached to him who suffers even more. Perhaps that is true; it seems quite likely. However, if it is intended as an argument for the moral primacy of feminism it seems to rest on some confusion between feminism as a movement *to improve the position of women* (to benefit a particular group of people) and as a movement to *eliminate sex-based injustice,* and it works in neither case. If the worst off people in the world are women that is an excellent reason for attending to their sufferings as the highest priority, but no reason at all for generally advancing women. If, on the other hand, feminism is, as we are taking it to be, an attack on sex-based injustice, the fact that the worst off people in the world are women is no defence at all of the priority of feminism, because their position might be much worse in virtue of the kind of suffering they endured *in common with their men* than in virtue of what they were subjected to because of their sex. Their being the worst off people does not make the primary issues feminist ones. . . .

To argue that sexism was morally the most important issue it would be necessary to show that if all sex-based injustices were immediately eliminated, that in itself, irrespective of any additional benefits which might follow from it, would immediately remove all the worst problems of the world. Could that possibly be true? It seems unlikely. Certainly some of the things which women suffer as women are appalling, but they seem no worse than other kinds of institutionalized slavery which still exist, or brutal dictatorships (of left or right), or the exploitation of abjectly poor countries by rich ones. The elimination of any of these kinds of injustice might bring about a greater good than righting the wrongs of women. However, even if that is not true, even if the worst injustices suffered by women are the worst there are, it does not follow that feminism *as a whole* should be of the highest moral priority. Feminist issues are not, as some feminists seem to suggest, an all-or-nothing matter. Some of the injustices suffered by women as women are much worse than others, and even if it were our first moral duty to eliminate the worst of them, nothing would follow about the others. Certainly in the West, where women may suffer injustice but their treatment is not *atrocious,* feminist issues could not possibly be said to have the highest priority. There seems little doubt, for instance, that we should eliminate a worse evil than sexism if we could instantly get rid of all child-deprivation. More controversially, I think that the same is true of people's appalling treatment of animals, which is a particularly serious matter because human chauvinism is such a respectable position to hold that most people do not even *pretend* to care about it. There seems little doubt that in the West, and probably in the world in general, sexism in any form is not the most important moral issue.

Perhaps, however, no feminist would claim that it was, once the argument was cast in that form. Let us, therefore, consider what is undoubtedly at the centre of the primary struggle argument: the idea that if feminist issues could be settled, that would as a matter of fact put the world to rights, and it is that which justifies giving the highest priority to feminism.

This is a matter which it is important to establish properly, if we are to act on it. If feminist issues are not of the greatest *moral* urgency, we need *very good practical* arguments to persuade us to put them first. It is no good saying as a defence of the position that people who do not see things this way have "failed to grasp" the radical analysis of the new feminism. They may have grasped it perfectly well but disagree with it nevertheless, and although assertion is common in this area, argument tends to be rather thin.

Usually the idea that if women's problems were put right all other injustices would disappear seems to be based on historical theories about women's oppression being the earliest form of oppression; the first enslavement of people by other people, out of which all other forms of oppression rose. However, there are two problems about this. The first is that the historical theory is itself a *highly* controversial one, which some feminists seem to want to accept on very little better evidence than its fitting the prevailing ideology. (One feminist in a university discussion group was asked what her evidence was for saying that women were the first slaves, and said she didn't know, but there must be some.)[7] But even more important than that, even if we could prove that women were the first slaves, and even if we could prove in addition the very different proposition that there was a causal connection between women's enslavement and subsequent sorts of oppression, it still would not follow that putting things right for women would put everything else right. There would be no reason whatever to presume that there was *still* a causal connection between women's position and other kinds of injustice. The others show every sign of being firmly enough established to go on existing in their own right. You might as well try to argue that if you repatriated all the French people in this country we should all start speaking Anglo-Saxon again.

Another recurrent idea seems to be that in a society of sexual justice, women, who are naturally better fitted to be rulers than men, would take over all government while men occupied themselves with harmless amusements, and we should all be better off as a result of that.[8] However, although I am as ready as the next feminist to think that we might do a great deal better if all important matters were left in the hands of women, if arguments of that sort are to be used in defence of giving high priority to feminist issues we need harder evidence to support them than our own flattering intuitions. Such evidence is conspicuously lacking. Even if we could prove that matriarchies did once exist, for instance, and even if we could show that they had been ideal societies, that would not be enough to show that women would be the best rulers now that everything was so radically different.

It seems, therefore, that any claim that feminism ought to be regarded as everyone's first priority fails for lack of evidence, and that at least until more is forthcoming that claim ought to be dropped. That does not, however, concede total victory to the opposition. Even if feminism is not the most important issue there is, that does not provide the slightest reason for saying that it should be ignored until after The Revolution, or whatever other great cause is said to take priority. We are not limited to doing one thing at a time, and anyway the most serious issues are very often the ones which, for one reason or another, we are not in a position to do very much about. If feminist problems are to hand, we do better to tackle them immediately than sit still and fret about not knowing how to put the world economic system to rights. No *man* is entitled to use *his* dedication to some great cause as an excuse for not doing all he can to deal with injustice to women whenever it comes his way, which, it may be added, is most of the time.

Feminists, in other words, do not need the primary struggle argument to attack any man who agrees that it is unfair that women should wash his socks, but thinks that the unfairness is so insignificant that we had better not bother to do anything about it until we have finished abolishing capitalism. You can work to abolish capitalism, if that is what you want to do, while sharing sock-washing and speech-making fairly between men and women. That sort of line is the best one for feminists who want to say that the fight against sex-based injustice must be fought immediately. There is no need to fall into implausible exaggeration, which only weakens the case.

4. Attractiveness

Finally, we come to the aspect of feminism which probably produces the strongest resistance of all to feminism: the fact that most people think of the movement as an inherently *unattractive* one. They dislike what they see of both feminists and feminist policies, and the result is not only a disinclination to join with feminists, but even a resistance to listening to what they have to say.

This is a very serious matter for the feminist who wants to win converts, because most people's sympathies are far more dictated by their feelings than by anything else, and if those feelings are against feminism it is unlikely that any amount of argument will be effective. This is not even quite so unreasonable as it may appear. The importance of attractiveness is not just a psychological one, because there are all kinds of situations in which reason is simply incapable of determining which political line is the best to take. No matter how carefully we research into the social sciences and use the results as the basis of social planning, the extent of our ignorance and the enormous numbers of variables involved mean that we can never even approach certainty that our policies will have the effects we hope for. This means that very often the most *rational* thing to do is join forces with sensible, reasonable, attractive people, who look as though they are heading for a kind of world which would be worth living in. Even if people were more rational than they are, therefore, attractiveness would still be important, and feminists could not afford to be unconcerned about the unattractive image of feminism.

It is no accident that feminism is so generally disliked, since like other movements of its kind it contains a high potential for unattractiveness in its very nature. However, once the problem is taken seriously it should at least be possible to see where the difficulties lie, and so take the first step towards eliminating them. I want to concentrate, in conclusion, on three particular problems which feminism seems to have in this area.

The first of these is that the movement suffers from a natural hazard of all reforming movements, of being identified in the public eye with their conspicuous extremes. This is pretty well inevitable, since a woman who is not a conspicuous feminist is not likely to be thought of as a feminist at all by most people, but it is unfortunate that there is nothing which earns conspicuousness so quickly as doing or saying things that people dislike or disapprove of. The result is that the feminists who are most strident, bitter and generally *unprepossessing,* (and such feminists certainly do exist) are taken to be typical of all, even though they are certainly not. Furthermore, this trouble is compounded by the fact that many other women, whose general opinions should certainly count as feminist, are reluctant to associate themselves with such unattractiveness, and fall into prefacing their feminist opinions with "I'm not a feminist, but . . .". It all strengthens the general conviction that no attractive woman is a feminist.

No doubt part of the solution to this problem is to try to persuade these other feminists to agree that that is what they are. However, a more fundamental way of looking at the problem is to move a step further back, and ask why it is that *individual* feminists are so often unattractive (at least to the outsider). The image of the movement comes from the individuals in it; if large numbers of them are unattractive, the movement as a whole is bound to be so too, and it seems that the nature of feminism raises problems about attractiveness for individual feminists quite as much as it does for the movement as a whole. Those are the most important ones to try to resolve.

The first of these is particularly tricky to deal with. It is the inherent difficulty of being attractive while rebelling against a situation which is rigged from the start to your disadvantage. As Germaine Greer said, "Because they have the upper hand, men usually conduct themselves with more grace than women do upon the battleground."[9] Grace is attractive, and men can carry on smoothly in their positions of advantage, using patronizing tones of voice with women or taking their services for granted often without even realizing it, admired by all, while looking with disdain at the women who do summon up the moral courage to challenge the status quo, and who become, in the unequal struggle, strident, nagging, troublesome, humourless, bitter, and generally disliked. It is most unfair, but it is a fact. It is also one which few people understand. Most people tend to think in a vague sort of way that feminists ought to be much *nicer* about their campaign if they are going to go in for it at all, without there being much comprehension of how very difficult it is to do anything about the status quo from within its conventions. Society tends to take an unreasonably dim view of makers of fusses and upsetters of apple carts. Feminists who do get trapped into ungracious behaviour can, with a great deal of justice, argue that the women who manage to remain "nice" are nearly always giving in, and putting up with what ought to be resisted. This is quite true. Many strong, feminist women allow themselves to slip into collaboration with the opposition rather than appear in so unpleasant a light.

This is a serious matter, and not only because of public relations. For women themselves there is nothing so wearing and draining as fighting an endless battle of nagging and backbiting, whose main result is to make them seem as unpleasant to themselves as they do to everyone else, however well they may understand the situation they are in. I suspect that finding a way to escape this trap may be one of the most important issues for present day feminism. Perhaps part of the solution, at least as a temporary measure, may just be to keep off that particular battleground altogether, by keeping out of the way of men who are likely to push women into such a position, and at all costs avoiding getting into their power as wives, mistresses or employees. Meanwhile, in the long term, feminists should probably be going in for an intensive study of social psychology, with a view to applying their discoveries to situations such as these. It must be possible, if we are determined enough and take the question seriously, to find techniques of one-up-womanship; ways of taking the opposition by surprise, and emerging triumphant from the tricky corners without any sacrifice of grace or humour. That, however, is a different subject, and yet another which is far beyond the scope of this book.

The final attractiveness problem inherent to feminism, on the other hand, is something which it is appropriate to discuss, or at least speculate about, here. This problem is that it is extremely difficult to be a feminist of any sort, even a relatively inconspicuous one, without doing and recommending things which people will certainly dislike and disapprove of. Feminism is in its nature radical, bound to pursue policies which are at the very least unfamiliar, and since people's wishes have been formed in a background of tradition, feminism cannot help opposing many of those wishes.

This is indeed what happens, and most people see the feminist movement as opposed to the very substance of their dreams. The traditional ideas of romance, which depend on keeping men and women in their relative positions of power and dependence, still preoccupy at least nine-tenths of the population. Most women still dream about beauty, dress, weddings, dashing lovers, domesticity and babies; most men still aspire to success with beautiful women, relationships in which they are dominant, and a home where their slippers are warmed and their wishes given priority over everything else. There may not be much hope, for most people, of fulfilling these wishes in their entirety, but if feminists seem (as they do) to want to eliminate nearly all of these things—beauty, sex conventions, families and all—for most people that simply means the removal of everything in life which is worth living for. Feminists are bound not to be liked if their feelings and aspirations seem so totally alien to those of most people.

Furthermore, feminists may well feel that this particular problem of attractiveness is one they can do nothing at all about. It is absolutely essential to take a radical approach to feminism, because if the old troubles are not removed by their roots they will only go on sprouting to plague us for ever. If feminists alter their policies just to make themselves more attractive to the unconverted they might as well give up the struggle altogether; and therefore, it seems, unpopularity must just be accepted as a fact of revolutionary life.

To a large extent there is no doubt that it must. There is no point whatever in modifying radical policies in an attempt to please the public, even those parts of it which are not so self-interested or so deeply conservative that they will automatically resist substantial change of any kind. However, what might nevertheless be possible is for feminists to make themselves and their policies more attractive without any sacrifice of radicalism at all. It is necessary to enter an extended speculation at this point, but I suspect that feminists may be putting off more people than they need, and (which is why the subject is an appropriate one to go into here) that their doing so may stem from a particular kind of confusion.

The first part of the speculation is that the deepest root of many people's opposition to feminism may not be simply self-interest or conservatism, and not even their failing to understand that it is necessary to sacrifice some things they value in order to achieve others which are more important. It may rather be their thinking of feminists as people whose ideas about what kind of things are enjoyable or worth having are radically different from their own. If this is true, it would certainly account for a good deal of resistance to the movement. However badly you may think you are treated under the present system, there is not the slightest point in supporting a movement which offers you fair shares but appears to offer them in a kind of world it would be a misery to live in, devoid of all the things which made life worth living. It would be better to go on having unfair shares in the world as it was. And you could be the most passionate devotee of justice in the world, and still not think there was much to be said for joining forces with a group of people whose commitment to justice seemed to consist in planning to deal out scrupulously fair shares of what nobody wanted.

I suppose many feminists might well say that they really had different kinds of preference from people in general, and would put this down to their having abandoned all the likes and dislikes which had been inculcated by a corrupt patriarchal society. However, to continue the speculation, I suspect that feminist preferences may often seem radically different from other people's, and indeed may even become radically different, as a result of the blurring of an important distinction. It is one which has already been referred to in the section on feminist dress: the difference between something which must be got rid of because it is bad in itself, and something which must go because, in spite of being inherently good or harmless, it is getting in the way of more important things.

There are certainly bound to be a great many things which people in general find attractive and desirable, but which feminists must insist on getting rid of. However, there is a world of psychological difference between being told by a revolutionary movement that some of the things you value must *unfortunately* go because the cost of keeping them is too high, and having it implied that these things have no redeeming features whatever, are valued at all only because people have been conditioned into approving of them by a society which has nothing to recommend it, and must be got rid of at first opportunity quite irrespective of any further harm they might cause. The first kind of revolutionary looks like a fundamentally congenial kind of person who is trying to be realistic about possibilities; the second looks like an incomprehensible alien from another world. And if feminists are not fully alive to the distinction between what is bad in itself and what is bad in its consequences, and slip into thinking of everything as *simply* good or bad—to be recommended or not recommended—it is not surprising if they often appear, quite unnecessarily, in the second light.

As Simone de Beauvoir said, "One can appreciate the beauty of flowers, the charm of women, and appreciate them at their true value; if these treasures cost blood or misery they must be sacrificed."[10] There is no need for feminists to say or think that there is nothing good about many of the things other people value; only that they cost more than they are worth. The sacrifice can be recognized as a sacrifice without any risk to feminist policies, or any attenuation of feminist energies in pursuit of them. We can, for instance, accept that the killing of an unborn child is an intrinsically bad thing, but still be totally committed to the campaign for abortion on demand because we think other things are more important than saving foetal life. We can agree that life will in some sense be poorer for women's spending less effort on beauty than they used to, while still insisting that they should be using their energies on more important things than their appearance. Slightly differently, we can accept that there is something very attractive indeed about the traditional ideal of the family, with the cheerful wife making a haven of home for her husband and children, but still resist it to the last as a general ideal, because most women cannot fit themselves into the picture without far too great a sacrifice of their inclinations and abilities. There is absolutely no need for any feminist to imply (as some seem to) that unborn children do not matter in the least, that beauty is totally worthless, or the ideal of the family pernicious from beginning to end.

It may well be the appearance of their having such uncongenial feelings, rather than the policies themselves, which make feminists seem so alien to many people. If this is so, it means that feminists could take the first step towards making the movement less unattractive to outsiders simply by showing themselves more aware of the good *aspects* of the traditional view of things, at the same time as insisting that many must go because they cannot be kept without injustice to women. However, to continue the speculation, a more careful distinction between what is bad in itself and what is bad only in its consequences might have even further reaching results. Feminist policies might actually be *made* more attractive to other people (and, for that matter, to many feminists themselves) without any sacrifice of feminist principle. Once feminists allow themselves to admit that some of the things they want to abandon may not be *intrinsically* bad, they may be able to devise ways of keeping some of them after all.

Various examples of this have already been suggested. We can keep some beauty of dress, once it has been accepted that it is not the beauty which is objectionable but the disproportionate fuss and inconvenience which have traditionally gone with it, and which can be attacked independently. We may find we can keep some cultural sex differences, once it is realized that it is only the ones which are degrading to women which are actually harmful. And though perhaps at present we have no better idea than crèches as the solution to the problem of the working mother, if we accept that crèches are not ideal, rather than feeling obliged to argue that mothers want to be with their children only because they have been conditioned into it, there may come a time when we can think of something better. With a more careful separation of the elements and aspects of good and bad, both in what feminists want to achieve and in what they are trying to replace, radical feminist policies could be far less austere than they are at present. Much of the present unattractiveness is quite unnecessary.

And this is an excellent point on which to end, not only because it is important in itself, but also because this *unnecessary* unattractiveness of feminism brings the argument back to where it started, at the very beginning of the book, with feminism's tendency to undermine its own intentions through leaping too hastily to conclusions.

This can be seen by reference to the ideal of radicalism. Feminists are anxious that their policies should be radical, because they are afraid that if they attack only the symptoms of the traditional oppression of women, leaving its roots untouched, the trouble will keep on reviving, perhaps in new and unfamiliar forms. That, as far as it goes, must be right. The difficulty, however, comes in deciding what policies really *are* radical: which ones will *really* eliminate all traces of the traditional oppression. If too hasty judgments are made, policies may be formulated which look radical to the superficial glance, but which really perpetuate the trouble because they are too simple a reaction against the past. The consequences will then be exactly what was feared in the first place: feminist policies will be insufficiently radical to prevent the evils of the past from appearing in a new form. And, to continue the speculation of the previous paragraphs, it does seem likely that some feminists' failure to distinguish carefully enough between the good and bad *aspects* of the patriarchal traditions which are obviously bad *overall,* and in particular to be too quick to see everything about entrenched tradition as dangerous to women, may have exactly that effect.

Consider how some radical feminist thinking seems to go. (If this is a caricature, it is a recognizable one.) Feminists recognize that many things about tradition are oppressive to women: families, the association of women with children, sex roles, femininity, beauty demands and innumerable others. Even the very existence of the sex distinction itself is seen by some feminists as oppressive. Therefore, the radical impulse seems to be, *get rid of all these things entirely.* And it is easy to see the point. If families are eliminated, families will no longer oppress women; if we end women's special connection with children, children will no longer come between women and whatever else they want to do; if people can be persuaded by some means to stop caring about beauty, beauty demands will stop diverting women's attention from matters of much greater moment. And if we find that by the progress of medical science we can end the sex distinction altogether, then it will follow as the night the day that we shall be able to stop sex distinctions from causing any trouble whatsoever.

However, tautologously true as all that may be, if such policies are supposed to be *radical* in taking away all traces of women's domination by men, undoing the evil of the past by pulling it up by the roots, they fail completely. This is because they do leave a residue of evil, much of which is probably unnecessary, and which can also be traced to the direct influence of the past.

The potential for harm of such sweeping policies must be obvious. Although the total removal of the situation which allows the existence of some evil would certainly eliminate the evil *in that particular form,* it might easily cause new and different troubles. People no longer encumbered by families might find themselves instead discontented and rootless; mothers freed from the demands of their children might find a new frustration as large as the new freedom; women whose faces had been their fortunes might find themselves left without any fortune at all; and the loss of pleasure in sexual difference might seem to everyone a very high price to pay even for the total elimination of all possibility of sexism. It is true that some such drawbacks might be inevitable, losses to be accepted for the sake of greater gains. Howver, it is equally true that many might not be, and perhaps might well be avoided altogether by a less direct rejection of the past. And if unnecessary problems did arise through feminists' feeling impelled to reject the whole of some patriarchal structure or attitude, problems which could have been avoided altogether if the reaction had been less direct, it would mean that tradition *was* still allowed to cause trouble, in however unexpected a form.

Radical feminism cannot go in for a simple rejection of everything which happens to have male fingerprints on it, because to do that is to accept part of the legacy of patriarchy, by conceding that the traditional packages must be left intact, to be accepted or rejected as wholes. It is to *accept* that if certain things exist at all, they must take the form they have always taken: one oppressive to women. But that is not in the least radical. What is necessary is to insist on *splitting up the packages,* looking at the good and bad aspects of tradition and keeping what is good wherever we can. That is the radical thing to do, even though it may produce policies which look reformist to the casual glance.

Unless feminists do this, they once again fall into the trap of setting out on a path which leads away from the goal they themselves want to achieve. The radical impulse to rout patriarchy turns unnoticed into a perverse device for perpetuating its influence. Whenever, in their determination to escape the evils of the past, feminist react too hastily and discard too much, and in doing so make their plans for a feminist future less good for everyone than need have been the case, they are allowing the shadow of the past to stay and dim the future. Patriarchal man has a kind of success, since even though he may not see much to please him in what is to be brought about, he can at least take a grim satisfaction in seeing the effects of his social arrangements linger on to the detriment of women. But matters may be even worse. If by the same haste feminists make their policies look so bleak and un-attractive that even women themselves prefer the present state of masculist injustice to the drab and severe alternative which feminists seem to be offering, patriarchy's triumph is complete. Feminism concedes a major victory with scarcely a struggle, and by its own policies contrives its own defeat.

If all this is right, and a too-hasty reaction against the legacy of the past is indeed alienating many of feminism's natural supporters, it constitutes the final argument against the largest group of people who claim to have little time for reason and argument in political matters: the ones whose perpetual refrain is that reason is useless because *people are not rational,* and will never be persuaded by reason out of their prejudice or self-interest. Of course this group must be right in its basic claim. Few people, even among the most committed supporters of rationality, would want to argue that the suffragettes would have done better to have maintained a sweet reasonableness than they did by chaining themselves to railings or leaping under horses. However, this undoubted fact gives no ground whatever to the anti-rationalist argument, because the first political purpose of care in reasoning, in feminism as in any other movement, is *not* the conversion of outsiders by rational persuasion. It is making sure that feminists themselves do not inadvertently set out on courses which will undermine their own intentions, by formulating policies which actually work against their own goal of eliminating injustice or by embarking on political strategies which will turn out to have played into the hands of the enemy.

If reason is bound to be generally ineffective as a means of confounding the politics of the opposition, then certainly the main practical tools of feminists must be non-rational persuasion and hard political manoeuvring. However, the last thing which follows from this is that reason is not worth bothering about. What follows is that the greatest possible care must be taken not to make the uphill grind even worse than it need be, through the careless presentation of a feminist image and feminist policies which drive the movement's natural supporters back into the traditional camp. If a more careful formulation of radical feminist policies will lead not only to a better plan for the future, but also to a kind of radical feminism which is attractive and understandable to the people who are at present its opponents, then no feminists—least of all the ones who feel that reason has no place in political achievement—can afford to be careless in argument. The very impossibility of reaching most of the unpersuaded by the force of reason becomes the final demonstration of the indispensability of care in argument amongst feminists themselves.

Notes

1. Mill, 'The Subjection of Women', in *The Feminist Papers,* ed. Rossi, p. 209.
2. Morgan, *Sisterhood Is Powerful,* p. xxxix.
3. Ibid., p. 599.
4. Firestone, *The Dialectic of Sex,* p. 42.
5. Ibid., p. 119.
6. Gould Davis, *The First Sex,* p. 336.
7. I am grateful to Peter Alexander for this story, and for other valuable accounts of feminism in practice.
8. See, e.g., Gould Davis, *The First Sex,* p. 336.
9. Greer, *The Female Eunuch,* p. 283.
10. Beauvoir, *The Second Sex,* p. 462.

Suggestions for Further Reading

Anthologies

Garner, Richard T., and Andrew Oldenquist. *Society and the Individual: Readings in Political and Social Philosophy.* Belmont, Calif.: Wadsworth, 1990.
Solomon, Robert, and Mark Murphy. *What Is Justice?* New York: Oxford University Press, 1990.
Stewart, Robert. *Readings in Social and Political Philosophy.* New York: Oxford University Press, 1986.

Basic Concepts

Plato. *The Republic.* Trans. Francis Cornford. New York: Oxford University Press, 1945.
Pieper, Joseph. *Justice.* London: Faber and Faber, 1957.

Libertarian Justice

Hayek, F. A. *The Constitution of Liberty.* Chicago: University of Chicago Press, 1960.
Hospers, John. *Libertarianism.* Los Angeles: Nash, 1971.
Machan, Tibor. *Individuals and Their Rights.* La Salle, Ill.: Open Court, 1989.
Narveson, Jan. *The Libertarian Idea.* Philadelphia: Temple University Press, 1989.
Nozick, Robert. *Anarchy, State and Utopia.* New York: Basic Books, 1974.
Rasmussen, Douglas, and Douglas Den Uyl. *Liberty and Nature.* La Salle, Ill.: Open Court, 1990.

Socialist Justice

Engels, Friedrich. "Socialism: Utopian and Scientific." In Arthur Mendel, ed., *Essential Works of Marxism,* pp. 45–82. New York: Bantam Books, 1961.
Cauthen, Kenneth. *The Passion for Equality.* Totowa, N.J.: Rowman and Littlefield, 1987.

Fisk, Milton. *Ethics and Society: A Marxist Interpretation of Value.* New York: New York University Press, 1980.

Harrington, Michael. *Socialism Past and Future.* New York: Arcade, 1989.

Macpherson, C. B. *The Life and Times of Liberal Democracy.* New York: Oxford University Press, 1977.

Peffer, R. G. *Marxism, Morality, and Social Justice.* Princeton, N.J.: Princton University Press, 1990.

Welfare Liberal Justice: The Social Contract Perspective

Rousseau, Jean-Jacques. *The Social Contract and Discourse on the Origin of Inequality.* Ed. Lester Crocker. New York: Washington Square Press, 1967. (*The Social Contract* originally published 1762; *Discourse on the Origin of Inequality* originally published 1754.)

Ackerman, Bruce A. *Social Justice in the Liberal State.* New Haven, Conn.: Yale University Press, 1980.

Rawls, John. *A Theory of Justice.* Cambridge, Mass.: Harvard University Press, 1971.

Sterba, James P. *How to Make People Just.* Totowa, N.J.: Rowman and Littlefield, 1988.

Welfare Liberal Justice: The Utilitarian Perspective

Sidgwick, Henry. *The Methods of Ethics.* New York: Dover, 1966.

Narveson, Jan. *Morality and Utility.* Baltimore: Johns Hopkins Press, 1967.

Singer, Peter. *Practical Ethics.* Cambridge, England: Cambridge University Press, 1979.

Smart, J. J. C., and Bernard Williams. *Utilitarianism For and Against.* Cambridge, England: Cambridge University Press, 1973.

Communitarian Justice

Hegel, G. W. F. *Philosophy of Right.* Trans. T. M. Knox. New York: Oxford University Press, 1962. (Originally published 1821.)

Finnis, John. *Natural Law and Natural Rights.* Oxford: Clarendon Press, 1980.

MacIntyre, Alasdair. *After Virtue.* Notre Dame, Ind.: University of Notre Dame Press, 1981.

Oldenquist, Andrew. *The Nonsuicidal Society.* Bloomington, Ind.: Indiana University Press, 1986.

Sandel, Michael. *Liberalism and the Limits of Justice.* Cambridge, England: Cambridge University Press, 1982.

Walzer, Michael. *The Spheres of Justice.* New York: Basic Books, 1983.

Feminist Justice

Wollstonecraft, Mary. *A Vindication of the Rights of Woman.* New York: Norton, 1967. (Originally published 1792.)

Eisenstein, Zillah. *Feminism and Sexual Equality*. New York: Monthly Review Press, 1984.

Frye, Marilyn. *The Politics of Reality*. New York: Crossing Press, 1983.

Jaggar, Alison M. *Feminist Politics and Human Nature*. Totowa, N.J.: Rowman and Allanheld, 1983.

Kourany, Janet, James Sterba, and Rosemarie Tong. *Feminist Philosophies*. Englewood Cliffs, N.J.: Prentice-Hall, 1991.

MacKinnon, Catharine. *Toward a Feminist Theory of the State*. Cambridge, Mass.: Harvard University Press, 1989.

Tong, Rosemarie. *Feminist Thought*. Boulder, Colo.: Westview Press, 1989.